Hryhorij Savyč Skovoroda
An Anthology of Critical Articles

Hryhorij Savyč Skovoroda

An Anthology of Critical Articles

Edited by
Richard H. Marshall, Jr.
and
Thomas E. Bird

 Canadian Institute of Ukrainian Studies Press
Edmonton   1994   Toronto

Canadian Institute of Ukrainian Studies Press
University of Alberta   University of Toronto
Edmonton, Alberta   Toronto, Ontario
T6G 2E8 CANADA   M5S 1A1 CANADA

Copyright © 1994 Canadian Institute of Ukrainian Studies
ISBN 0-895571-03-0

George Y. Shevelov's "Prolegomena to Studies of Skovoroda's Language and Style" first appeared in his *In and Around Kiev*, (Heidelberg: Karl Winter Universitätsverlag, 1991). It appears in this volume with the consent of the Karl Winter Universitätsverlag.

Canadian Cataloguing in Publication Data

Main entry under title:

Hryhorij Savyč Skovoroda

Includes bibliographical references and index.
ISBN 1-895571-03-0

1. Skovoroda, Hryhoriĭ Savych, 1722-1794.
I. Marshall, Richard H., 1932-   II. Bird, Thomas E.
III. Canadian Institute of Ukrainian Studies.

B4218.S474H8 1994   197   C94-931922-8

All rights reserved.

No part of this publication may be reproduced, stored in a retrieval system or transmitted in any form or by any means, electronic, mechanical, photocopying, recording or otherwise without the prior permission of the copyright owner.

Printed in Canada

Dedication

The present volume of essays about the life and work of Hryhorij Skovoroda is dedicated to Dmytro Čyževs'kyj, one of the foremost Slavists of our time and a pioneer in the study of Skovoroda, as a token of admiration and regard for a great scholar and in recognition of the signal contribution that he made to Slavic studies at universities on two continents.

Studia Slavica ab amicis discipulisque oblata

Dmytro Čyževs'kyj
(1894-1977)

Table of Contents

Foreword
Marc Raeff xi

An Introduction to the Life and Thought of H.S. Skovoroda
Dmytro Čyževs'kyj 1

Part One: Skovoroda and Society

1. Skovoroda and Society
   Stephen P. Scherer 63
2. H.S. Skovoroda as Teacher: The Image as Model
   J.L. Black 75

Part Two: Skovoroda and Literature

1. Prolegomena to Studies of Skovoroda's Language and Style
   George Y. Shevelov 93
2. The Poetry of Skovoroda
   Karen L. Black 133
3. From Strength to Strength: Observations on Hryhorij Skovoroda and Vasyl' Barka
   Bohdan Rubchak 159
4. Gogol' and H.S. Skovoroda: The Problem of the "External Man"
   Mikhail Weiskopf 187
5. Andrej Belyj and Hryhorij Skovoroda
   Aleksandr Lavrov 203
6. Textological Notes on Skovoroda's *Alphabet*
   Bohdan Struminski 215

Part Three: The Philosophy and Theology of Skovoroda

1. Skovoroda's Metaphysics
   George L. Kline 223

2. Skovoroda's Moral Philosophy
   Taras Zakydalsky 239
3. An Introduction to the Theological Thought of Hryhorij Skovoroda
   Petro B.T. Bilaniuk 251
4. A Note on the Character, Orthodoxy, and Significance of Skovoroda's Thought
   Stephen P. Scherer 275

Part Four:
   A Bibliography of Skovorodiana
   Richard Hantula 285

Index 311

Foreword

Marc Raeff

All societies and cultures, like the proverbial stream of Heraclitus, are in constant flux: they change and take new directions. Creative personalities who swim with the prevailing current find recognition and may also have an impact on their contemporaries. Those, however, who either cling to a rock in the middle of the stream or who rush ahead of the current to the next river bend are rejected as belonging to the past or are misunderstood for speaking from a perspective that has not yet been experienced. Most of the time this kind of creative figure is fated to live in relative obscurity, known only to a few, and finds recognition only later under vastly changed circumstances. Even when "rediscovered," his contribution may be far different from what he had intended. Such was precisely the fate of the Ukrainian philosopher and writer Hryhorij Skovoroda, the subject of the papers collected in this volume.

In his lifetime, which spanned most of the eighteenth century, a profound transformation took place both in his native Ukraine and in the Russian Empire of which it was part. To my mind, it largely explains Skovoroda's relative isolation and lack of recognition in his own lifetime and his "rediscovery" by subsequent generations, both in Ukraine and in Russia. In summarizing the double transformation to set the symposium papers in their historical context, I cannot do full justice to its complexity, and some generalizations will be unavoidable.

Let us first cast a glance at the development of Russian culture in the eighteenth century. Peter I, the first emperor, opened a "window onto Europe" by forcing the pace of Muscovy's Europeanization and "modernization." However one assesses the character and results of Peter's policies, it cannot be denied that he brought about a radical reorientation in the ways of life and thinking of the

Russian elites. Within the span of barely two generations, the Russian cultural, but also social and political, elites had internalized the cultural interests and values of their Western and Central European counterparts.

The beginnings of an active effort at Europeanizing Muscovy may be traced back to the second half of the seventeenth century under the influence of the Mohyla Academy in Kyiv and the foreign colony of Moscow. Naturally, at first, the focus was on religious culture; Central and West European secular culture held little place in Muscovite life. Peter I, on the other hand, no longer had any religious concerns: his aim was to secularize the ways and thinking of his elites by introducing them to contemporary European philosophical and scientific culture. But because he still had to make use of graduates from the Kyiv Academy and turned primarily to North European (mainly German and Protestant) instructors and models, the "baroque" metaphysical and spiritual components of European culture—e.g., Leibniz, Pietism, and the "Rosicrucian Enlightenment"— remained a significant influence throughout the eighteenth century.

In order to associate themselves with the European elites, the Russians established as their first priority the adoption of the secular culture—material and intellectual—of the "West." Throughout the eighteenth century, from the reign of Peter I to that of Paul I, the Russian imperial elites strove to assimilate and creatively apply intellectual and artistic values and models provided by Versailles and Paris and their imitators in the Germanies. The secularizing process was reinforced by the changes Peter I introduced in the administration and function of the church. As is well known, Peter replaced the patriarch with an appointed collegiate body, the Holy Synod, which was totally dependent on the state whose interests it had to support and promote.

Along with secularism, the Petrine Europeanization also introduced the Russian elites to the notions of the dignity and respect owed the individual. This in turn imposed on the individual the obligation to develop his mental and spiritual potential to the utmost, so as to be worthy of such respect. In the early stages of Europeanization this obligation entailed acquiring a secular outlook, intellectual skills, and scientific (technical) and humanistic knowledge; inevitably, however, it was also to imply the enhancement of the whole person, especially his spiritual—moral and religious—life and values. Not surprisingly, therefore, the moral and religious development of the individual became the next priority. Toward the end of the reign of Catherine II, determined efforts were made to fulfill this aspiration by lay and clerical personalities, as well as by such organizations as Masonic lodges and societies dedicated to publishing useful translations, promoting education and philanthropy. The fruits of these efforts, however, were not to be gathered until the following century.

It should be noted that the process of secularization leading to a revival of spiritual concerns explains the ongoing, albeit "underground," interest in seventeenth-century German metaphysics and mysticism. As the reader of the symposium papers (especially those of Čyževs'kyj, Kline, Bilaniuk, and Shevelov's analysis of Skovoroda's language) will readily observe, Skovoroda's ideas and values illustrate the role of German mystical spiritualism and metaphysics on the one hand and the yearnings for an individualized religious life on the other. Both elements were to play a significant role in Russia's nineteenth-century intellectual history. Skovoroda's relative obscurity and isolation from the mainstream of imperial Russian intellectual and cultural developments in the eighteenth century are thus readily explained by the fact that his creative life coincided with the early stages of Russia's assimilation of European secular Enlightenment.

If the cultural and intellectual conditions of the eighteenth-century Russian Empire were unpropitious for the reception of Skovoroda's writings, the sociocultural situation of his native Ukraine was hardly more favourable. Kyiv and Left-Bank Ukraine had come under the protectorate of Muscovy in 1654, and subsequently they were fully incorporated into the Russian Empire. This is not the place to describe and analyze this process, many aspects of which are still both inadequately investigated and controversial. I shall mention only two significant consequences it had for the cultural life of Ukraine. I have alluded to the role played by graduates of the Kyiv Academy in the early stages of the Europeanization of Muscovy. It resulted in a massive (by eighteenth-century standards) "brain drain" of educated Ukrainians, who took up service (and frequently also residence) in the St. Petersburg establishment. Not only was the Russian church dominated by Ukrainian and Ukrainian-educated hierarchs, but throughout the eighteenth century Ukrainians played a leading part in the development of Russian secular literature, education, the arts and sciences.[1] No doubt, this "brain drain" contributed to the impoverishment of Ukrainian cultural life and, indirectly, to the decline of the Ukrainian language as a medium of intellectual discourse and communication. In fact, we may speak of a russification of Ukrainian high culture. Skovoroda's own peculiar amalgam of several linguistic elements (as suggested by Professor Shevelov's article), in which the emerging modern literary Russian was a significant component, illustrates this process, but also explains the limited circulation and popularity of his writings in his native Ukraine, as well as in Russia proper.

In addition, some social circumstances prevailing in eighteenth-century Ukraine affected Skovoroda's literary predicament. As a result of the vastly increased power of the Russian Empire, its establishment—court and government—could not only impose its goals and institutions on newly incorporated territories, but also provided the attraction of careers and material rewards for members of local non-Russian political and social elites. Not unexpectedly,

---

1. Cf. David Saunders, *The Ukrainian Impact on Russian Culture, 1750-1850* (Edmonton: Canadian Institute of Ukrainian Studies, 1985).

therefore, representatives of the Cossacks *staršyna* and rich landowners, as well as the middle and poorer Ukrainian nobles, sought admission into the ranks of the dominant Russian service nobility. Since the Table of Ranks instituted by Peter I had opened access to the ruling elite of the empire on the basis of education and achievement, and since the imperial civil and military institutions were in need of competent personnel, Ukrainians who had a better education than the Russians were welcomed and easily attained leading positions. Associating themselves with St. Petersburg, these Ukrainians also became largely russified and abandoned their native literary and cultural traditions. Economically they also had more to gain by becoming assimilated to the Russian nobility, for this gave them firmer control over the peasantry, which was virtually enserfed by the legislation of Catherine II. The reorganization of provincial government in 1775 provided for the participation of local elites in local administration, thus further contributing to the Ukrainian nobility's involvement in the imperial establishment. Lastly, the Charter to the Nobility (1785), which required the official sanction of membership in the imperial nobility, put the final seal on the russification of the Ukrainian elite.

At the same time, the need to document their claim to noble status led the Ukrainian elite to rediscover the history of their native land. As the rediscovery of the religious-spiritual heritage had resulted from an assimilation of the rational secular Enlightenment, so did the wish for incorporation into the imperial establishment give rise to a new form of historical and cultural Ukrainian identity. This process found an institutional framework thanks to the establishment in the early nineteenth century of such educational and cultural centres as the university at Xarkiv and the Bezborod'ko lycée in Nižen. A new Ukrainian national consciousness was about to emerge and lead to the rise of modern Ukrainian literature and national aspirations.[2]

Modern national consciousness, however, grew on the soil of Romanticism and its worship of the Folk—the people—which in Slavic lands in fact meant the peasantry. Its literary programme involved "going back" to the people's traditions and spoken language. Little wonder that in this context Skovoroda was of interest to the extent that he personified and illustrated the life of the Ukrainian people of his time. This aspect of Skovoroda involved only a fraction of his literary output, and bore no relation to his philosophic ideas and spiritual seekings. On the other hand, in Russia proper, his religious and spiritual concerns were to find a receptive soil in the religious and metaphysical renaissance of the Silver Age at the end of the nineteenth century. His "rediscovery" by Vladimir Solov'ev,

---

2. I have dealt with some of these developments in greater detail in "Ukraine and Imperial Russia: Intellectual and Political Encounters from the Seventeenth to the Nineteenth Century" in *Ukraine and Russia in Their Historical Encounter*, ed. Peter J. Potichnyj, Marc Raeff, Jaroslaw Pelenski and Gleb N. Žekulin (Edmonton: CIUS Press, 1992).

Andrej Belyj, and the Symbolists bears witness to this.

The two "rediscoveries" eventually converged to bring about heightened interest in all aspects of Skovoroda's intellectual and literary legacy. At first this took place slowly in the 1920s and 1930s, but it has come to fruition recently in a series of monographs and critical editions of his works. The symposium whose papers are published in the present volume offers a scholarly summation of the pivotal role played by the lonely wandering sage of eighteenth-century Ukraine in the cultural and intellectual history of Eastern Slavdom.

An Introduction to the Life and Thought of H.S. Skovoroda

Dmytro Čyževs'kyj

The Man and His Fate

1. *The Life of Skovoroda*

The figure of Skovoroda stands at the end of the baroque period in the history of Ukrainian letters. Although he himself was part of the culture of the Ukrainian baroque, his period represented a transition to a new form of culture. He was therefore seen by many of his contemporaries as an "archaic," even decadent, representative of the past. He stood in the shadow of a growing giant—the rationalism of the Enlightenment. For Skovoroda, however, this new spirit was without a soul, a monstrosity, the child of the devil, Goliath, the Beast of the Apocalypse! Thus he could not and would not become part of his times. It is no wonder, then, that few of his contemporaries were interested in him. Although Skovoroda managed during his lifetime to assemble a small circle around himself, for which he had neither the intention nor the will to create any external cohesion, it could not assert itself after his death against that "monster," the spirit of the Enlightenment, and disappeared beneath the waves of those tempestuous times. And with this, Skovoroda himself fell into obscurity. We may also add that Skovoroda lived in Ukraine, and tenaciously held fast to his native soil. It was precisely during the period of his influence, however, that Ukraine was demoted from its position as a Russian vassal state to a simple imperial province. In the course of the eighteenth century, St. Petersburg attracted all the vital forces of the empire. Thus there developed in the provinces an intellectual vacuum that could not be filled even by the creation of local cultural centres (Xarkiv University). The currents of the intellectual movement unleashed by Skovoroda were swallowed up by the bleak spiritual wasteland of this increasingly provincialized nation.

Skovoroda also alienated himself from succeeding generations by the fact that, in language and literary style, his work conforms closely to the tradition of the Kyiv baroque, a tradition that became wholly foreign to the later period. By the eighteenth century, the Great Russian literary language had already detached itself from its Old Church Slavonic base. It was precisely on this foundation that Skovoroda, like his Kyivan predecessors, built. The new Ukrainian literary language arose in the years following Skovoroda's death, also on a entirely new foundation: the Ukrainian vernacular. On a purely linguistic level, then, Skovoroda's work became as foreign to the Ukrainian world as it did to the Great Russian. Thus Skovoroda sank into oblivion together with all the glorious poetry of the Ukrainian baroque.

Only those Romantic ("pre-Romantic") motifs that are so strong in Skovoroda, as in all baroque mystics, found a certain degree of approval in the Ukrainian (less in the Great Russian) literary world during the nineteenth century. For the Ukrainian Romantics, however, Skovoroda was primarily a representative of "Ukrainian folk wisdom," a glorious flower of the disappearing folk life. Russian and Ukrainian sectarians of various persuasions had a somewhat more profound understanding of Skovoroda. He supplied the sectarians primarily with material for the construction of their own religious systems; they remained indifferent to him as a figure and to his actual intentions.

It remains for us, then, to discover Skovoroda, that figure wrapped within a century of legends, and to sift out the sagas, false interpretations, and pseudoscholarly attempts to impute to Skovoroda now one, now another world-view.

We know Skovoroda mainly as an intellectual figure. As a person he had become a legend within a few years after his death. If we wish to determine a few more dates concerning his temporal life, it is merely in order to enter into his intellectual world, which alone preoccupies us in this book.

Although many dates from Skovoroda's life are known to us, his inner development will most likely remain a secret. In his writings we encounter a fully developed personality. His letters, his poems, his fables—nothing points to the way in which he arrived at his world-view. Thus, for example, the beautiful poems, in which one would hope to see a reflection of his inner conflicts, are, first of all, not dated (it cannot even be ruled out that many of them might have been produced as early as his student years in Kyiv as a practical application of the writing courses that he, like every student in Kyiv, had to attend), and secondly, the baroque style in which they are written prevents us from evaluating as the expression of his personal life that which is merely the traditional mode of poetic production. There is no justification for reading Skovoroda's personal life into these poems. His correspondence as well is scarcely informative, as it belongs to the later period of his life and is written throughout in a tone that represents its author as a fully developed individual, firm in his convictions. In addition, these letters are for the most part addressed to a student at the Xarkiv

Collegium, concerning whom he, as a professor at the Collegium, allowed himself to be governed by certain "pedagogical" considerations.

We are thus directed to a single source—the biography of Skovoroda from the pen of the very student who was the recipient of the letters mentioned above, and whom, after many years, Skovoroda visited shortly before his death. During this visit, Skovoroda recounted much of his life (the author of this biography, Myxajlo Kovalins'kyj, also knew much from his own experience), thus himself providing an important source for the biography. Kovalins'kyj recorded Skovoroda's biography shortly after the latter's death, when the memory of what had been related was still fresh and living. It was an extremely successful biography, and, in any event, one of the most beautiful pieces of prose of the Russian literature of that period. But this beauty, which at first captivates the reader of Kovalins'kyj's work, is precisely what makes it questionable. And when one considers that Kovalins'kyj was a Freemason; that he was steeped in mystical literature (in Skovoroda's biography he cites, among other things, a discussion with him concerning St. Martin, referring to the Swiss mystic Dutoit, to Philo, Tacitus, Xenophon, etc.); that he was otherwise well-read; and, most importantly, that during his trips abroad he had ample opportunity to read a large amount of Western literature, the doubts become serious questions. It may therefore be presumed that Kovalins'kyj was influenced in his writing by mystical literature. The external dates must in any event be generally correct. Many of them can be verified or supplemented by other sources. Thus what is left to us is merely a skeleton of a Skovoroda biography, which cannot augment the impressions we gain from his writings or endow them with vital content.

Other reminiscences of Skovoroda are without exception written by persons who knew him no better during his lifetime, and who from the outset intended their works to be readable, perhaps even amusing portraits of this "crank." When attempts were made thirty years later to collect materials about Skovoroda (including extant folk tales), all that was left was a Skovoroda legend. When one of these witnesses clearly contradicts one of Kovalins'kyj's assertions, we have no basis for believing one side or the other, for Kovalins'kyj's assertions can never be regarded as absolutely correct or complete.

Thus, in a biography of Skovoroda, one must limit oneself to a small number of known facts.

Skovoroda was born to a Cossack family in the town of Čornuxy in the province of Poltava on 22 November 1722. References to Skovoroda's family discovered by historians indicate that they belonged to a poorer class of Cossacks, but one that was nevertheless a free and economically independent part of the Ukrainian population. There were also quite rich Cossacks in Čornuxy, one of whom, an uncle of Skovoroda, held a post at the court of St. Petersburg. One of Skovoroda's brothers studied in the mid-1700s at the gymnasium in Breslau, probably with the help of a patron. The province of Poltava—Skovoroda's homeland—is an area that has produced many eminent Ukrainians: to name just a few, the famous writer Nikolai Gogol'; Pamfil Jurkevyč, the Moscow philosopher and teacher of important Russian thinkers (for example, Vladimir Solov'ev), and other important Ukrainian writers, historians, etc. The question of whether blood, historical relationships, or geography influenced this cannot be decided here. Ukraine (above all, the Poltava landscape) was repeatedly praised in Russian, Ukrainian, and Polish literature of the eighteenth and nineteenth centuries as a beautiful and idyllic country, a land of song and sumptuous natural beauty. In Skovoroda's writings as well, memories of this fair landscape live on. He once wrote of the picturesque area surrounding Xarkiv: "The land is embellished with forests, hills, springs, and gardens. I was born in just such a place." In the eighteenth century, Ukraine stood at a high point in its cultural and economic life. We have a list of village schools (mostly attached to churches) in eighteenth-century Ukraine. In the district of Čornuxy alone there were eleven village schools, of which at least one was located in the village itself. Čornuxy, incidentally, was a larger village in which there were four fairs annually, attended by merchants from Kyiv itself. Skovoroda most likely attended one of the village schools, where he learned to read and write and sang in the church choir. As early as 1738-9 he was studying at the Kyiv Academy, the only Ukrainian institution of higher learning at the time. In spite of its theological orientation, the academy educated middle-class and noble children as well, and on occasion was even sought out by foreigners. Based on the Jesuit schools, the Kyiv Academy nonetheless was able to give its instructors—apart from those in the theological faculties—greater freedom in the choice of intellectual direction, a freedom that was important in philosophy. In the first half of the eighteenth century, Cartesians and Wolffians as well as Aristotelians could exercise influence here as philosophy instructors.

At that time Russia was ruled by Elizabeth (1740-60), daughter of Peter I. At the beginning of the forties Ukrainian influence at court was strong. The empress loved the art of singing above all. Court music (including Western music) flourished, and Ukrainian choirs played an important role. Skovoroda, who had a good voice and was musically inclined, was summoned from the academy in 1742—perhaps through the intercession of his aforementioned uncle, Poltavcev—and assigned to a court choir. Two or three years later he returned to the academy, where he studied for six more years. To the period of his last years of study belongs a manuscript that he transcribed with other students at the academy: a copy of a seventeenth-century work by the German-Ukrainian scholar, Adam von Zernikow, entitled "De processione Spiritus Sancti"; in the pages of this transcript is the signature "Gregorius Skovoroda." We may suppose that at this time Skovoroda acquired his excellent Latin (the language of instruction at the academy); learned Greek, which he later taught at Xarkiv; and German, of which, according to reliable witness, he had a good command. On the other hand, it has recently been proved that his knowledge of Hebrew never advanced above the beginner's level. Among the academy's professors in Skovoroda's time one must single out Heorhij Konys'kyj and Myxail Kozačyns'kyj. Under Konys'kyj, a brilliant lecturer and poet, Skovoroda most likely studied philosophical subjects—logic, ethics, physics, metaphysics; he could only have got to know Kozačyns'kyj, a student of German universities (Leipzig), outside the course of his studies. In his works Skovoroda also mentions other Ukrainian theologians of the time, such as Teofan Prokopovyč and Varlaam Laščevs'kyj, and quotes their poetry (including excerpts from their religious dramas). One gets the impression that Skovoroda always remembered the academy and his years of study there with gratitude. He fitted well into the intellectual circle of the Kyiv Academy with its Latin learning, its spiritual baroque poetry, its polemical writings, and its aesthetic tastes. It was on this foundation that his further development continued.

Skovoroda did not complete his studies. Usually only those students who wished to choose a spiritual vocation graduated. For secular students, who accounted for half the enrollment at the time, the final examination was unimportant, since it did not provide them with any special privileges in the outside world. Skovoroda left during the final course in theology. He did not, however, return home. His father had died in the interim; his brother had been in St. Petersburg almost since Skovoroda's admission to the academy, so that apparently only his mother remained at home. As Kovalins'kyj reports, "Skovoroda wanted to see foreign lands." He availed himself of the first opportunity to do this, accepting the position of a cleric (probably a church lector) with a Russian mission in Hungary (Tokay), which administered the Russian imperial vineyards there. He remained there about two years. According to Kovalins'kyj, he also visited Vienna, Budapest, Pressburg, and other neighbouring areas, "where he wanted above all to meet persons famous for their knowledge and scholarship." He used his command of German and Latin to this end, "in order to gain the acquaintance and friendship of scholars and thereby acquire knowledge that he could not obtain at home." Later unreliable reports speak of Skovoroda's travels or journeys on foot through all of Germany and even Italy, of study in Halle, and so forth. Skovoroda's teacher at that time is said to have been Christian Wolff (died 1754), who was certainly no longer active in Halle, and who, as an outspoken representative of the Enlightenment, could scarcely have had any significance for the development of Skovoroda's world-view.

These travels are undoubtedly legendary. Kovalins'kyj himself had travelled a great deal in Europe, and could therefore easily have determined where Skovoroda had been and reported these details, if only Skovoroda had actually made such trips. By the "surrounding area" of Budapest, Vienna, and Pressburg, only the immediate area is to be understood. Skovoroda probably also visited the then university city of Trnava, where he could also have made the acquaintance of

Slavic professors. This, the sole Hungarian university at the time, moved from Trnava to Budapest in 1777. Kovalins'kyj could easily have forgotten the name Trnava (Lat. Tyrnavia). Skovoroda could have visited Breslau, where his brother was perhaps still studying. Breslau, however, can hardly be considered to be in the "surrounding area" of Budapest, Vienna, and Pressburg. Some thought Munich to be in the "surrounding area" of Vienna. There is no point in pursuing Skovoroda's alleged foreign travels unless one believes that he came to know and was influenced by intellectual movements that had never found their way to Kyiv. No one, however, has ever been able to point to an instance in Skovoroda's works in which his foreign travels could clearly be demonstrated to have played a role in his intellectual development. I was the first to show (as early as 1929) that Skovoroda's world-view touched that of the Western mystics at many points. If, however, he was able to read the works of the Church Fathers and the ancient philosophers in the academy library in Kyiv as easily as in Vienna, Munich, or Halle, he could have become acquainted with the works of the German mystics of the modern era in Kyiv as well. The works of the church mystics were available in the Ukrainian libraries of the period that are known to us, and in the latter part of the century a compatriot of Skovoroda's of similar intellectual bent, S. Hamalija, also a student of the academy, translated some of the works of Böhme into Russian. Skovoroda's foreign travels have been used to explain his alleged leanings toward rationalist philosophy and the learning of the Enlightenment. But this was rather a forced interpretation, and one should not forget that the universities of Vienna and Trnava (and perhaps this is even truer of Munich, which had no university at the time) had nothing in common with Enlightenment attitudes. In Vienna and elsewhere Skovoroda would undoubtedly have first visited the theologians. These would have been Catholic theologians even less conciliatory toward modern science than the Kyiv theologians, who had the quasi-Protestant theology of Prokopovyč behind them. It is not out of the question, however, that during his travels a few mystical works happened to fall into Skovoroda's hands, or that he met some person or other abroad who made him aware of these works. In a passage that has gone unnoticed until now, Skovoroda stated in 1773 that he had been reading the Bible for *thirty years* (since about 1743). Does this mean that a student at a church school and then at a religious academy actually only began to read the Bible in his twentieth year? Do not these words more likely imply that Skovoroda experienced a religious change of heart at that time or, more precisely, that during the period coinciding with his foreign travels he discovered how to "correctly read the Bible," i.e., to interpret it mystically, to extract the hidden mystical meaning? This indication of a change in Skovoroda's life is the only evidence that allows us to justify assertions concerning his foreign travels. Skovoroda's partiality toward the Germans may also be due to the experience of these travels. When he later spoke of "his dear Germans," he must have been referring either to a literary sympathy for the Germans or to acquaintances he made on his travels. Thus, whatever we have to say concerning Skovoroda's foreign travels is simply based on suppositions.

After two and a half years, Skovoroda was home again. Discussions with friends and acquaintances, among whom were priests and princes of the church, further strengthened the good reputation that he had enjoyed since his student years as a learned and talented person. Soon afterwards he was appointed instructor of poetry at the seminary in Perejaslav, Ukraine. He espoused wholly unconventional ideas concerning versification (from analyzing Skovoroda's poetic style, it may be assumed that he sought innovations in rhyme: he regarded masculine and feminine rhymes as equal, and wished to introduce "imperfect rhymes." There is no support for the hypothesis that he had appropriated the ideas of the Great Russian verse theoretician, Lomonosov.) Accordingly, he came into conflict with the bishop who exercised authority over the institution. Skovoroda did not want to renounce his ideas and made fun of the bishop, who wished to be not only a bearer of ecclesiastical values, but also a legislator of poetic art. After responding with a sharp letter—"alia res sceptrum, alia plectrum"—Skovoroda lost his position. Since he had no means of support, his situation became unbearable. This seems to have been the first time in Skovoroda's life that he had to endure severe problems—he himself later said it was then that he learned how to bear suffering. He then became tutor in the home of a wealthy landowning family of the area, but lost this position a few months later. At the end of 1754 or the beginning of 1755 he travelled to Moscow with his friend Volodymyr Kaligraf, who had just been appointed professor of theology at the Moscow Academy. Although attempts were made to win him for the academy, he soon returned to Perejaslav, where the landowning family for which he had been house tutor requested him back. Skovoroda stayed with them a full four years. Aside from his duties as a teacher, he also found time to write; a few of the poems from his "Garden of Divine Songs" belong to this period. Concerning Skovoroda's life at this time, Kovalins'kyj reports, though in rather general terms: "Isolation leads to thinking. Skovoroda dedicated himself to philosophy, to the search for truth. When he was free from his duties, he would often go into the fields, forests, and groves to think. The dawn was his walking companion, and the forests partook in his joy." Skovoroda turned over in his mind various possibilities about his course in life. After careful consideration, however, he had to reject them all. "He made no choice, but rather resolved in his heart to distinguish his life by moderation, contentedness, purity, humility, industry, patience, good nature, by simple habits, by sincerity, and to renounce all vain striving, all cares for increase in property, all efforts toward superfluous things."

The turning point in Skovoroda's spiritual life occurred following a dream that Kovalins'kyj relates—so he claims—in Skovoroda's own words: "At midnight on 24 November 1758, I dreamt I was observing different sorts of human life in various places. In one place there were imperial palaces, costumes, music, and dance. Lovers were singing, gazing upon themselves in mirrors, running from one room to another, taking off their masks, lying upon sumptuous beds, and so forth. From there a force led me to the simple people, among whom the same things were going on, but in different manner and means. The people went through the streets with glasses in their hands, noisy, rejoicing, staggering, as simple people do; here too were affairs of the heart pursued in similar fashion. Here men stood in one row and women in another in order to see which were comely, which were similar, and which could be partners. From there I went to the hostels, where I heard about horses, carriages, hay, business deals, quarrels, etc. Finally, the secret force led me to a large and glorious temple in which, on the day of the Descent of the Holy Spirit, I read the mass with the deacon. As the deacon and I bowed before the altar, I experienced the sweetest joy, which I cannot describe. But here too human depravity showed its face. Avarice went around with a moneybag, and did not venture far from one of the priests. Even to the holy altar there penetrated the odour of meat being consumed in chambers close to the temple, to which many doors in the choir led. I saw terrible things there. Since there was not enough meat and poultry for everyone, they killed a man dressed in black with bare knees and shabby sandals, held him in the fire and roasted his calf, cut off the meat with its melting fat, bit it off and devoured it. They did this as if worshipping by means of this [sacrificial] rite. Unable to bear the stench and the hideous scene any longer, I left. This dream invigorated as much as it shocked me." In its theme this dream bears a remarkably strong resemblance to "journeys around the world" such as "Peregrinus" by Johann Valentin Andreä or "The Labyrinth of the World" by Comenius, so one might very well believe that this passage had a literary source. On the other hand, we can hardly believe that a loyal and devoted youth, as Kovalins'kyj was, could ascribe to his master his own literary invention. This dream, which unquestionably brings together different facets of Skovoroda's inner life, could easily have led to his final decision to turn away from all worldly paths toward a "spiritual" renunciation of the "world" in general. Just as, for Comenius, the stoning of the wise Solomon and his companions showed that the world had rejected their "pansophical" ideal, thereby demonstrating the hopelessness of life within the labyrinth of this world, so for Skovoroda the spectacle of "God's servant" slaughtered and cannibalized demonstrated the incompatibility of his life's ideals with those of the world. This poor servant of God is in some sense Skovoroda's double. For Skovoroda monasticism—inner monasticism, to be sure, not the external form of cloistered life—is one form, and perhaps the most important, of the imitation of Christ: "Christ was a monk," we read somewhat later in one of Skovoroda's letters. This vision is thus a presentiment of the Christ condemned to burn at the stake in Dostoevskij's "Great Inquisitor" or an echo of such themes in spiritual mysticism, as in the "Paradoxa" 15-17 of Sebastian Franck:

"God is the devil of the world, Christ the world's Antichrist... God is the antithesis and opponent of the world." The world manifests itself as the "world of the devil" in that it mutinies against its God. If this dream actually came to Skovoroda unexpectedly, then it was an illumination, a lightning bolt striking his innermost self, burning much in him to ashes. With this, Skovoroda's fate was sealed; his relationship to the world and his way through it determined. From then on Skovoroda had nothing more to do with "the world of the devil," nothing more to seek in it.

For the time being, however, he continued his pedagogical activities. The instruction of his private students had most likely ended by 1759. He was then summoned by Bishop Mytkevyč to become professor of poetics at the Xarkiv Collegium. Skovoroda accepted the position. But after a year his old friend Jakubovyč, an abbot close to the bishop, attempted to persuade him to become a monk. Skovoroda sharply rejected this proposal and with this took leave of the school. He went on to live for an extended period in seclusion with one of his new-found friends. It is here that Kovalins'kyj begins to speak for the first time of "friends" and "acquaintances" of Skovoroda as if they were, to some extent, a community. Skovoroda now devoted himself to spiritual exercises and the task of writing. He did not, however, withdraw from society, as he was to do in later life. Discovering during a visit to Xarkiv that the nephew of one of his friends, and his future biographer, Myxajlo Kovalins'kyj, of whom he had grown fond, was studying at the Collegium, he returned to the city to teach Greek in one of the preliminary classes. He remained there from 1762 to 1764. This marks the period of his friendship with the young Kovalins'kyj, to whom he revealed his opinions and whom he continually helped, tutoring him privately in Greek and often writing letters to him. In 1764 Skovoroda accompanied him to Kyiv, where Kovalins'kyj heard a discussion with the monks in which an attempt was again made to convince Skovoroda to become a monk. Skovoroda again decisively rejected the proposal, since for him the monastic life—under some circumstances, at least—was only an attempt by the world to "capture" a man "in its net by means of the sacred [religion]." After two months Skovoroda returned to Xarkiv, but the faculty did not accept him back. He had become such a famous personality in Xarkiv, however, that the new governor wanted him to accept a teaching post. We possess documents showing that the governor, Ščerbinin, almost forced Skovoroda to teach a course in ethics at the "school for the children of the nobility" in 1768. This course has survived in synoptic form, and in it Skovoroda's entire mystical world-view, as we know it from his later writings, can already be perceived in germinal form. The new bishop—Mytkevyč had died in the interim—was dissatisfied with this new mode of instruction. Having been taken to task, Skovoroda answered that his lectures had to differ from the usual ones, since the nobility was different from the clergy. "All were struck dumb by this response," reports Kovalins'kyj. Nevertheless, the bishop's displeasure may have been the reason for Skovoroda's relinquishing this position a year later (1769). Thus began the last period of Skovoroda's life.

"Skovoroda went into deep isolation," writes Kovalins'kyj. He moved to a lonely bee-keeper's house in the middle of a dense forest near Xarkiv. It was here that he wrote his first dialogues. For the next quarter-century he led a life of continuous wandering, finding lodging with various friends from the circle of landowners he knew. For the most part, however, he lived—at least during the summer—outdoors or in monasteries, mainly in the idyllically situated monasteries surrounding Xarkiv, where he had numerous friends and school comrades. He by no means avoided Xarkiv. He also visited Kyiv again in 1770. He often travelled on foot, making journeys in later years that lasted months, as, for example, to Taganrog on the Sea of Azov, or to visit his friend Kovalins'kyj in Orel province. He worked on his writings in solitude, copying them down himself in his calligraphic script and sending them to all his friends. He also wrote letters, but these contain scant personal material, as they were dedicated—like his writings—to the propagation of his ideas. An extended Skovoroda community formed—a community not in the sense of an organization such as the Freemasons, who arrived in Russia and Ukraine at that time—but rather an "invisible community" of Skovoroda's friends and admirers. It is perhaps no accident that Skovoroda referred to himself as a *starčyk* and was so described by others. The word is reminiscent of the Russian *starec*. Paisij Velyčkovs'kyj, who restored the *starcy* in Russia, was, coincidentally, a compatriot of Skovoroda, a pupil at the Kyiv Academy, and was born and died in the same years as Skovoroda. To his closest friends, Skovoroda played the same role of "spiritual father" as the *starcy* did for their disciples. At that time, Skovoroda became famous in the literal sense of the word—people wanted to see and hear him, even those who did not in the least share his world-view. Perhaps for this reason alone, his flight from society took on exaggerated, anecdotal, and unusual forms. He wished to hide himself. Certainly it was only later that the "Skovoroda legend" became embellished with many anecdotes to this effect. In any event, Skovoroda went the way of the inner life, a path upon which none of his friends could follow. In this sense he was truly "alone."

Skovoroda's withdrawal from the world could be described in terms of Christian mysticism as a "purification" and "catharsis." He experienced the ecstatic state of illumination and unification with the Divinity, a description of which has been left to us by Kovalins'kyj, and of which we will later speak. Skovoroda's life during this time was "internally cloistered," just as he had earlier regarded his way of life as a kind of "monasticism." Kovalins'kyj describes Skovoroda's life during this period in a part of his work that shows obvious signs of strong literary influence. Nevertheless we cite the passage, which in any case is so characteristic of the Skovoroda legend: "The philosophy that Skovoroda took into his heart brought him as great a joy as is possible for an earthly being. He was free from the chains of every compulsion, conceit, care and trouble, and found all his desires fulfilled because they were so limited. He experienced joy that cannot be compared with that of any fortunate man, since he concerned himself with the lessening of his needs rather than with their increase.—When the sun lit the innumerable candles on the emerald-green carpet and with its generous hand offered a feast for his senses, he took this cup of joy, in which were mixed none of life's cares, no ardent sighs, no vain distractions, and savouring this joy with his lofty mind, he said in the total peace of contentment, "Thanks be to the Blessed Lord, who has made easy that which is necessary, and unnecessary that which is difficult!" Whenever he became tired of thinking and sought a change of pace, he visited an old beekeeper who lived in a nearby apiary, taking his favourite dog along for company, and all three would share supper.—The night offered rest from the strain of thought, which imperceptibly exhausted his physical strength; light and restful sleep allowed images of the harmony of nature to rise in his fantasy.— He liked to devote midnight to prayer, which, in the deep stillness of the senses and of nature, he combined with his thoughts about God. He then gathered all his thoughts around him and contemplated with a critical eye the dark dwelling place of his earthly person, calling to the divine element within himself, "Rise up, ye slothful and ever sinking thoughts of my spirit! Arise and ascend to the heights of eternity!" Then a conflict would suddenly arise, and his heart would become a battlefield: the love of self joined forces with the Prince of this World, with secular judgement, with the weakness inherent in human transience, and with all earthly things, and fought to capture him with all the strength of its will in order to seat itself upon the throne of his freedom and become the equal of God Himself. Against this, the thought of God moved him toward the sole eternal, true Good, omnipresent and all-penetrating, and compelled him to arm himself with all the divine weapons in order to be able to stand firm against the attacks of this false thinking. Such a battle! How many feats of heroism! The demons blustered and raged: one had to remain awake, steadfast, and courageous. Heaven and hell battle in a wise heart; could he remain idle, indifferent, accomplishing no heroic deeds, yielding no gain for mankind? Thus he spent the midnight hours in battle against the forces of the dark world. The dawning light covered him with the glow of victory, and celebrating [this victory] in his spirit, he went out into the fields to share his prayer of thanks with all of nature."

In the final year of his life, Skovoroda also paid his last visit to Kovalins'kyj. He arrived at Kovalins'kyj's estate in 1794 and remained there three weeks. Despite Kovalins'kyj's attempts to dissuade him, he returned to Ukraine. He found his last lodging on the estate of his friend Kovalevs'kyj. A different source reports on his last days there: "His final lodging was a small, pleasant room with a view of the garden. To be sure, he was seldom in this room: he was either conversing with the estate owner, a good and pious old man, or walking in the garden or in the fields." It was a beautiful October day. Neighbours had come to visit his host and to hear Skovoroda himself. "At dinner Skovoroda was unusually happy and garrulous; he even joked, told stories about his past, his journeys, about the difficult times in his life." After the meal, he went unnoticed from the room. In the evening, when Kovalevs'kyj went looking for Skovoroda, "he found him under a shady lime tree. The sun was setting, its last rays piercing through the thick canopy. Skovoroda had a spade in his hands and was digging a hole, a long and narrow grave. That evening they waited for him in vain. The next morning he did not come to tea. When the master of the house went to look for him in his room, Skovoroda was already dead." That was on 29 October 1794.

He was buried at the place in the garden where he liked to play the flute early in the morning, by the side of a pond. Twenty years later his remains were removed to a churchyard, where his grave is still located. On his tombstone are the words, "The world wished to capture me, but it did not succeed." These words best sum up the nature of Skovoroda's life.

2. *The Intellectual Environment*

By including in our presentation of Skovoroda's thought so many parallels from the history of Christian mysticism—not least, Western mysticism—we are not trying to demonstrate "borrowings" and "influences." Unquestionably, however, Skovoroda had access to many of the authors cited and was perhaps familiar with them. This will now be discussed in greater detail.

Unfortunately, only Kovalins'kyj makes direct reference to Skovoroda's reading matter. But Skovoroda himself spoke of his small "exquisite library," consisting of "books read by few," which he carried on his journeys. A character in one of Skovoroda's dialogues speaks of his "favourite little book, which I always carry with me." As becomes evident from the dialogue, the book contains mystical teachings. Skovoroda seldom quoted, and of the many thinkers we find "quoted" in his writings, nothing remains (Thales, Pythagoras, Socrates). Skovoroda translated (more correctly: worked on) Cicero and Plutarch. Unfortunately, these translations have never been published. Kovalins'kyj mentions in his list Skovoroda's favourite authors: Plutarch, Philo, Cicero, Horace, Lucian, Clement of Alexandria, Origen, Nilus, Dionysius (the Pseudo-Areopagite), Maximus the Confessor and "the more modern ones corresponding to these." These "ones corresponding" would interest us the most! Only because of the striking paralells in style and thought may we suppose Skovoroda's acquaintance with Valentin Weigel (and the pseudo-Weigelian writings) and Angelus Silesius. Knowing the reading matter of his Ukrainian contemporaries can help us reach further conclusions. We would like at this point to turn to Kyivan scholarship as one of the sources on which to base our assumptions concerning the scope of Skovoroda's reading.

Generally, an "internal relationship" can be shown between Skovoroda and medieval and modern German mysticism. We would like to summarize here the principal facts concerning the relationship of the Ukrainian theology of his time to that elsewhere in the world, above all to mystical theology and philosophy.

For our purposes, it suffices to indicate to the diverse relationships between the old Ukraine and the West. From the sixteenth to the eighteenth century we encounter individual Ukrainians, almost exclusively theologians, who strove to gain the knowledge they required in Western Europe in order to deal with the multifarious religious conflicts then raging—and often entire groups of Ukrainian students in Prague, Cracow, Vilnius, Olmütz, Ingolstadt, Vienna, Leiden, Breslau, Leipzig, Amsterdam, Paris, Oxford, Cambridge, Rome, Padua, Danzig, Königsberg, Halle, Göttingen, Edinburgh, etc. They brought back to their homeland not only training in specific subjects, but also books and manuscripts. At both Ukrainian institutions of higher learning—in Ostrih (1580 until about 1608) and in Kyiv (from 1644), other subjects, primarily philosophy, were pursued in addition to the theological curriculum. However limited the scope of these studies might have been—the focus of both schools was, after all, the education of defenders of Greek Orthodoxy—it nevertheless laid the foundation that made it possible for students to pursue their own readings of philosophical works. The Catholic and Uniate Ukrainians sought to base their theological training on Western sources alone, as did the less numerous Protestants. In any event, there existed in Ukraine Catholic, Uniate and, for a time, even a Protestant theological institution of learning. The numerous Latin manuscripts of theological and philosophical courses that survive bear witness to the nature of education in these schools. We happen to possess reports from the beginnings of the Kyiv Academy concerning the philosophical and theological works used there: two bills for books purchased in Poland by the founder of the academy, Peter Mohyla, have survived. With the passage of time, the number of documents of this and similar type increases: certain books that happened to be mentioned in the polemical writings of the time, correspondence concerning book purchases, and occasional catalogues of greater and lesser private libraries of princes of the church, as well as of learned individuals from other circles. From the period directly preceding Skovoroda there are a number of sources of this kind: numerous notes in the diary of Jakiv Markovyč, a student and friend of Teofan Prokopovyč, who was a professor at the academy and later Peter the Great's collaborator; and the library catalogues of two princes of the church of the Petrine era, Prokopovyč and Stefan Javors'kyj. The latter's library was in existence at Xarkiv when Skovoroda was a professor at the Xarkiv Collegium, and although Skovoroda had already completed his studies, he may have used the library on occasion. Above all, it is Markovyč's diary entries and the catalogues of the libraries owned by Javors'kyj and Prokopovyč that enable us to imagine what the typical selection of books was in Ukraine at that time.

Admittedly, all sources of this type are to be used with caution. First of all, they are incomplete. A fire that destroyed the academy library in the eighteenth century is primarily responsible for this. In addition, Prokopovyč's library, which survived, and was one of the largest of its kind—the catalogue includes 3,192 titles—has only been researched recently, and not in depth. The course manuscripts, which sometimes contain bibliographical references (the names of theological and philosophical writers are at least mentioned), have only been superficially described (we know little of their content), and have been stored to the present day in the National Library in Kyiv and in other Russian and Ukrainian libraries. On the other hand, the mention of this or that writer or the reference to a certain work or a citation could just as well have been taken from a secondary source, or a name might have been known by reputation. All our conclusions are therefore at least partly hypothetical.

What is important for us is that Kyiv's acquaintance with ancient, medieval and modern philosophy, however superficial, was much broader than is usually supposed. We shall limit ourselves to citing names. In order to ensure greater clarity, without bothering particularly about the chronology of our sources (which belong to the period between the sixteenth and eighteenth centuries in any event), we may divide them into a number of groups.

Among the ancient philosophers, Aristotle, above all, is represented by the *Organum, Physics, Metaphysics, Ethics, Politics*, and *Rhetoric*. Skovoroda himself quotes from the *Magna moralia*. We then find mentioned, after Plutarch's *Moralia*, Philo of Alexandria, Cicero, Seneca, Boethius, Julian the Apostate; also Stobaeus, Diogenes Laertius, and the pseudo-Galenic history of philosophy. Plato is seldom cited. There are, however, many Platonic elements in the works of Philo and the Church Fathers, primarily among the Areopagites and in St. Augustine, one of the most beloved authors in old Ukraine. In addition, there are many philosophers who could only have been known through secondary sources, as we possess none of their works or only fragments; thus Pythagoras, Democritus, Socrates, Zeno the Stoic...

As far as the patristic works are concerned, naturally all the important Church Fathers were known. Given the state of current research into the sources, however, it is impossible to determine how broad and thorough this acquaintance was. One can only assert with certainty that the Latin Fathers were the more widely and easily read, and that even the Greek Fathers were read in Latin translations. Augustine, above all, became a greatly favoured author. We learn from Jakiv Markovyč's diary that, decades after his studies at the Kyiv Academy, he continued, at least on occasion, to read Augustine and quote him in his diary, which during this period was otherwise filled with business and social entries.

The preoccupation with the scholastic literature of the Middle Ages is no doubt due to the necessity of coming to terms with Catholic theology. Astoundingly, not only were representatives of the leading schools of Scholasticism well known, but also representatives of mystical schools of thought, as well as disciples of the later Scotus. Again, it cannot be ascertained without more thorough research, which unfortunately has not been undertaken, to what extent this knowledge was based on independent study and to what extent on collections of quotations and compendia (such collections are also recorded in many Ukrainian library catalogues). In any event it may be supposed that foreign study, especially in Catholic schools, facilitated a more thorough understanding of Thomas Aquinas. In addition to Aquinas, we find other names in our sources: Albert the Great, Hugo de St. Victor, Bonaventura, Duns Scotus; Dionysius the Carthusian is also mentioned, and certainly some of the philosophical figures from nearby Cracow University were well known. Also interesting is the assertion that representatives of philosophies such as nominalism were known. A compatriot and contemporary of Skovoroda, Bohomo[d]levs'kyj, professor at the Theological Academy in Moscow, transmitted a knowledge of Raymundus Lullus, delving into the *Ars Magna* in his lectures. Interest in Arabic and Jewish philosophy, from which a number of works had already been translated by the late fifteenth and early sixteenth centuries by the so-called "Judaizers," also found a response at the Kyiv Academy.

The Renaissance evoked various responses in Ukraine, above all, of course, in art. We are concerned here primarily with literature. From the end of the sixteenth century onward, Renaissance writers were more often mentioned in Ukrainian literature. The letters of Petrarch were quoted, one of Boccaccio's novels was translated, and attempts were made at a free version of so voluminous a work as Tasso's *Gerusalemme Liberata*. The influence of the formal quality of Renaissance writing on Ukrainian literature of the time (mediated, to a great extent, through Polish literature) is unmistakable. In theological and religious polemical writings, Renaissance writers were often mentioned and quotations reproduced from their works. The authors cited include Lorenzo Valla, Machiavelli (Mohyla had already purchased his works), Gemistius Pletho, Pico della Mirandola, Zabarella (the Renaissance Aristotelian), Peter Ramus (the anti-Aristotelian), Cardanus, Giordano Bruno, Nicholas of Cusa, Erasmus (whose works were used in Latin classes along with those of classical authors), Agrippa von Nettesheim, Jean Bodin, Francis Bacon and Johannes Kepler, I. L. Vives...

A number of the authors we have just mentioned lived at the zenith of the baroque, steeped in baroque culture. If we recall that the flower of Ukrainian art was baroque art, especially as expressed in architecture, and that Ukrainian literature of the seventeenth and eighteenth centuries was baroque literature, then it is natural that we should place special emphasis on the influence of the baroque.

There developed during the eighteenth century, and thus during Skovoroda's lifetime, a particular interest in modern philosophy, although it cannot be ruled out that this interest was strong in the previous century as well, but left no recognizable traces in the literature. The acquaintance with Suárez is easily understood. In addition to the Catholic neoscholastics (and apparently rather early), Protestant scholasticism became known (Melanchthon, Alstedt, and Protestant theology in general from Luther onwards; of special importance to Ukraine, it seems, were Gerhard, Quinstädt, and Buddeus). Descartes' name is in evidence. The book by the Cartesian Purchotius (Pourchot) was for a while the philosophy textbook at the academy. In the political opinions of Teofan Prokopovyč, the influence of Hobbes and Grotius may be detected. We find a Latin edition of Hobbes in a Ukrainian library. Locke was translated at the Kyiv Academy in 1689. Spinoza (perhaps known only by name) is mentioned in the work "De Atheismo" by Prokopovyč. Comenius was known (including his mystical "pansophical" works). A friend of Skovoroda, the Moscow professor Volodymyr Kaligraf, also a student of the Kyiv Academy, was an admirer of Leibniz. Around the middle of the century, the older textbooks were replaced by those of Baumeister or Winkler, and the Wolffian school also began to gain ground. A firm knowledge of modern mysticism also began in the eighteenth century. In addition to Bernhard, Bonaventura, Tauler (it should not be forgotten that editions of Tauler also included Eckhart's sermons), and the "Imitatio Christi," Jakob Böhme became known. From Skovoroda's writings it would appear that he had most likely read Angelus Silesius and Valentin Weigel. "Weigelians" were mentioned by a compatriot of Skovoroda at the beginning of the eighteenth century, and at least one of Weigel's and one of Silesius' works had been translated into Russian by the end of the eighteenth century. This does not exclude yet further influence by many, especially Protestant, mystics, which has not yet been researched, unfortunately, like many other questions concerning Ukrainian intellectual history of that period.

There was also a handwritten translation of the "Theologia deutsch"; Arnd's "On True Christianity" was known (in a Latin translation, among others; a Ukrainian-Old Church Slavonic translation appeared in Halle in 1735). Translations of Böhme's works existed in Russia (probably also in Ukraine) by the turn of the eighteenth century. We have already mentioned writers such as Nicholas of Cusa and Agrippa von Nettesheim. The modern Catholic mystics were also known; we encounter the works of a number of them in Ukraine: Maximilian Sandaeus, Blosius, the "emblematic mystics." One should not forget how widely distributed mystical literature was in Great Russia in Skovoroda's time; not only the writings of Weigel and Böhme were read, but also those of Böhme's disciples (e.g., Pordage), Angelus Silesius, St. Martin, Oetinger, Ph.M. Hahn, and others.

With these cursory observations, we have drawn the boundaries of Skovoroda's possible acquaintance with intellectual life in the West. His life gave him numerous opportunities to expand these boundaries.

These relationships link Skovoroda at each and every point to Platonism, to the mystical Church Fathers, and to the German mystics. This should come as no surprise, for these traditions were strong enough in Ukraine to impress themselves directly upon the intellectual perception of a mystical writer. That Skovoroda expanded and strengthened these relationships during his foreign travels is thoroughly understandable.

Skovoroda lets it be understood, at least by way of suggestion, that he owes a spiritual debt abroad. We may disregard his legendary travels through all of Germany and Italy, and ignore reports of his studies in Halle and elsewhere. Concerning his theological interests, for example, he could have learned the same at the University of Vienna (perhaps more thoroughly) as in Kyiv. No other special knowledge of eighteenth-century philosophy is to be found in his writings.

The Principles

There are in Skovoroda's works certain external characteristics that one is inclined to regard as purely stylistic features. The predilection for antithesis, the dynamic of thoughts impelled by contradictions, the complex and daring metaphors are all characteristics of the literary style of the baroque. But in Skovoroda these features have much more than a mere stylistic significance. They are not merely the principles of his linguistic mode of expression, but also the foundations of his thought and the postulates of his philosophical and theological system. Perhaps it is precisely in this that Skovoroda's greatness lies: that in his works form and content, external organization and the philosophical material inseparably bind together and fully permeate each other.

In any case, we wish to comprehend from the outset the full importance of these features for the theoretical content of Skovoroda's system.

3. *Coincidentia oppositorum*

One facet of Skovoroda's thought that has given researchers particular difficulty is his fondness for antithesis, the interplay of opposites, contradictory formulations and paradoxical points. Faced with this constantly antithetical style, many despairing researchers have seen in Skovoroda's work impenetrable, incomprehensible chaos.

A compilation of opposing statements from Skovoroda's works in no way shows his thought to be "unsystematic." The contradictions in Skovoroda's statements concerning this or that problem may be explained by the fact that he belongs to those thinkers for whom each and every true essence is by its very nature contradictory.

To understand Skovoroda one must realize that he is a "dialectician." Yes, a "dialectician," admittedly not in the modern sense of the word, but in the traditional sense stemming from ancient philosophy. The "dialectical" method in this original sense entails two basic concepts: first, the "antithesis," the revelation of the opposing elements in every real object; and second, the principle of the "circular" movement of thought, the recognition of the dynamic character of the thought process. These two elements of the dialectical method—and indeed in a form reminiscent of Philo, Proclus, or of many of the Church Fathers—are strongly expressed in Skovoroda and even exaggerated in a paradoxical manner, both in the discussion of particular questions and of the basic principles of his philosophy.

There are three main lines of development leading to Skovoroda's "dialectic": ancient, "heathen" philosophy; the philosophy of the Church Fathers; and medieval and modern Western mysticism. In these three spheres we find different forms of dialectical thought expressed in many ways, from serious philosophical thought about the nature of true being to harmless linguistic word-play.

At the very beginnings of Greek philosophy stands Heraclitus with his antithetical statements: "God is night-day, winter-summer, war-peace, satiety-hunger." Antithetical thought came to full flower primarily in Platonism. For Plato the unification of opposites is an essential element of philosophical method. His system of basic categories is a system of opposites; true essence is characterized by the unification of opposing categories: identity and otherness, rest and motion. The opposites should be acknowledged together and at the same time (ξυναμφότερα). Only this unification of opposites, their "interweaving," their mutuality (μίξις, ξύμμιξις, κοινωνία, μέθεξις), makes the ideal true being possible. This antithetical character is part of the nature of every object. The analysis of pairs of opposites—unity and multiplicity, being and nothingness—is the theme of Plato's most profound work, the *Parmenides*. Interest in the problem of opposition, of antithesis is also apparent in the works of Aristotle: the *Aporetics*, the investigation of the various meanings of words (τὸ ποσαχῶς), the definition of basic concepts—of the soul, of "energy," of the "primus motor," of God, especially the imposing features of the basic laws underlying all world events, all movement—these are considered antithetically throughout. The decisive breakthrough in antithetical thinking came in later Platonism with Philo, Plotinus, and Proclus. In Plotinus, all definitions of basic concepts are antithetical. From the One to matter, there is the internal antithesis of that which is. Philo writes (incidentally, in a work with which Skovoroda could not have been familiar): "The One is that which is composed of opposites, so that when it is divided the opposites are recognizable..." "Likewise, the components of the world are bipartite and in reciprocal opposition: earth is divided between mountain and plain, water into fresh and saline...likewise the atmosphere into winter and summer, and likewise into spring and autumn. And from this Heraclitus compiled his books on nature..." Although we may wish to find one of the sources for Skovoroda's antitheses in ancient philosophy, it is much more likely that Holy Scripture led him to antithetical thinking.

Skovoroda himself once pointed to a Christian parallel to his antinomian style—the writings of St. Paul. Following a comparison of "foolishness" and the "wisdom" hidden in foolishness, he writes, "This is the foolishness that St. Paul mentions in the Epistle to the Corinthians. Paul rejoices in that which drives others to the most bitter despair. Does he not have a heart of diamond?" It turns out that "antithesis" is one of the characteristics of the Pauline literary style. This continues the tradition of ancient Hebrew literature, which was wholly based on antithesis, but takes a different form in Paul in that it is not simply an external quality of his style. The antitheses do not merely remain juxtaposed; they become *unified; they overflow, penetrating each other*. The "One" is contrasted with "multiplicity." One God—many men. One Christ—many Christians. One Adam—many condemned by his sin. "As now from this sin of one man damnation has come to all, so also has vindication come to all through the righteousness of one man." "For as in Adam all die, even so in Christ shall all be made alive." Above all, the Christian faith is paradoxical by its very nature—antithetical because its fundamental dogmas pronounce the unification of opposites. Thus sin became the foundation of grace: "Where sin has become mighty, grace has become mightier." Sin is based on the law: "Where there is no law, there is no transgression." "The law has developed just so that sin would become mighty." For a Christian, life and death are bound in union: "We carry at all times the death of Our Lord Jesus in our bodies, so that in our body the life of the Lord Jesus might become manifest. Therefore in life we are always steeped in death, so that Jesus' life might become manifest in our mortal flesh." "For the corruptible must take on incorruptibility, and the mortal must take on immortality."

"It is sown in dishonour and raised in glory." "It is sown in weakness and raised in power." The mission of Christ is perceived and described as inherently paradoxical: "made of a woman, made under the law, to redeem them that were under the law." "Although He is rich, He became poor for your sake, so that you might become rich through his poverty." The religious experience, the Christian's inner condition, is ultimately contradictory: "God has chosen the foolish things of the world to confound the wise; He has chosen the weak things of the world to confound the things which are mighty; He has chosen the base things of the world, and things which are despised, and things which are not to bring to nought things that are." Thus Christians live "by honour and dishonour; by evil report and good report; as deceivers, and yet true; as unknown, and yet known; as dying, and, behold, we live; as chastened, and not killed; as sorrowful, yet always rejoicing; as poor, yet making many rich; as having nothing, and yet possessing all things."

We are directly reminded of Paul's words when in his writings Skovoroda simply paraphrases him: "It is sown rotten, it is raised fragrant; it is sown hard, it is raised tender; it is sown bitter, it is raised sweet; it is sown base, it is raised godly; it is sown senseless and blind, it is raised all-knowing and keen-eyed." It is worth noting that a similar passage may be found in the "Areopagitica," in which the author speaks of those things that show the unification of opposites and says, "in the mortal there must be immortality; in the incomplete, there must be perfection; in that which moves of itself, there must be the need for external motion; the power of consummation in the weak, eternity in the temporal, incorruptibility in that moved by nature; in ephemeral pleasure, eternal duration, and above all, in everything its opposite..."

Antithesis did not enter German mysticism only through the "Areopagitica." Antithetical formulas can be found in every German mystic, and later the number of these formulas increases, so that in Angelus Silesius, and even in Sebastian Franck, we often have to deal with what are practically mechanically minted coins. The entire world becomes characterized antithetically, as does the mystical experience itself. Thus in Mechtild, the soul:

> In the beautiful light, it is in itself blind,
> in the greatest blindness, it sees most clearly,
> in the greatest clarity, which it has in God,
> it is both alive and dead.
> The longer it is dead, the more joyously it lives...
> the poorer it is, the richer it becomes...
> the more tenderly it rests, the more it labours,
> the more it comprehends, the more it keeps silent.

Among the "classics" of German mysticism, Eckhart, Tauler and Suso, as well as among those spiritually akin to them, antithetical formulas are found in full force—their most important and central ideas are expressed in antithetical form. Thus in Eckhart: "He who possesses the least part of the world possesses the most of it. No one possesses the world as much as he who has renounced it fully." "The highest peak of exaltation is precisely in the deepest abyss of debasement—the depths and the heights are one." "Your ignorance is no shortcoming, but rather your highest perfection, and your suffering is your greatest achievement." And in Tauler "equal" and "unequal" are the same. "One should seek tranquillity in discord, joy in sorrow, counsel in bitterness—simplicity in the complex," "peace in hostility, happiness in suffering." The deeper, the higher; deep and high are the same here; "the deeper, the higher; the less, the more." Suso develops a thought from the contradictory character of the divine Being that we shall discuss later. We find the development of this same idea in theoretical form in Nicholas of Cusa, who applies the "coincidentia oppositorum" as much to the divine Being itself (God is "incomprehensibiliter intelligibile," "innominabiliter nominabile") as to the world ("Deus creatus," "infinitas finita").

In more modern mysticism, as already stated, the antithetical style reaches full bloom. According to S. Franck, "God's law is easy and difficult," "The Word of God is life and death." "Only madness possesses wisdom, and ignorance knows all." "Those who pray the most pray the least." "Human will is free and captive." "The world contradicts itself." "Two discordant predicates/ black and white/ exist in one thing and one subject/ which is of two natures/ as man is mortal and immortal." One may justifiably see many of Franck's antithetical formulas merely as word games. Valentin Weigel teaches merely that in God there is a convergence of contradictions, and statements to the effect that the world may be broken down into opposing pairs of elements ("Light and darkness. Love of God and hatred of the world. Life and Death. Faith and infidelity. Bliss and damnation") appear only occasionally in his works. In the pseudo-Weigelian works, however, we find passages such as the following: "From daily experience in time we know that the *contraria* are important *ad perfectionem rerum*." "No one thing can exist without the other/ and in this time and world the contraria attest to the perfection of things. Time is *alteritas* and eternity is *unitas*. Now, in otherness there are contraries, otherwise world and time would not be world and time/ meanwhile, otherness cannot exist/ without unity, and one must take time and eternity together/ thus it follows that contradictions must exist in the Eternal and Celestial with the temporal corporeal/ though here divided *per rationem*, there united *per mentem*. In time and world we find and have: summer winter, heat cold, arid moist, joy sorrow, pleasure pain, day night, wealth poverty, sweet sour, life death, difficult easy, near far, high low, truth lies, and the like./ If there were heat and summer without cold, or winter and cold/ without summer and heat, the world could not exist." And in conclusion: "this temporal world is maintained by contraries and made up of contraries." Böhme's teaching is very complex, but certainly contains the theory of the *bellum omnium*: "war," "row," "battle," "Things—disputing/ for each wants to go its own way." This is not accidental, but necessary: "There must also be a contrary will: for a clear and peaceful will is as nothing/ and bears nothing..." In Angelus Silesius, again, an enormous number of antithetical formulas appear, almost leaving the impression of an ingenious artistic game: "Death makes life," "God dies and lives in us," "God is the smallest and the largest," "God is darkness and light," "Able inability," "Time is eternity," "A lamb and also a lion," "A giant and also a child," "Humility ascends to the heights," "Gain is loss," etc.

With Böhme and Angelus Silesius we are indeed within the baroque period, and in baroque literature antithesis is one of the fundamentals of literary style. We do not need to cite many examples from spiritual and secular works of the baroque period. A disciple of Böhme, Abraham von Franckenberg, formulated the basic law of the world as follows:

> The greatest grows from the smallest,
> the most comes from the least.
> The highest from the lowest.

> Life from death
> Nature from GOD.
>> And back to God...

In general terms:

> In the wisdom of God, nothing has come into being
> which has not found, at the same time, its opposite.

Or, as a secular poet (Hoffmannswaldau) sings:

> What is the world? A ball of inconstancy
> that unites death, life, building and burning,
> where joy and sorrow almost always lie together,
> and yes and no are in quite a battle.

The "fanatic" Quirinus Kuhlmann, master of antithetical paradox and author of "Heavenly Kisses" and "The Indifferent Psalter" (which he fills with antithetical formulas, some grotesque, others truly profound), sees "the vicissitudes of things human" in the following manner:

> Everything changes, everything loves;
>> everything seems to hate something else:
> Whoever considers this/will understand man's wisdom.

It is primarily the paradox of Christian existence that leads directly to Skovoroda's literary and religious concerns, a paradox that was repeated by the baroque poets and philosophers. While Arnd was listing the eighteen pairs of opposites that characterize the Christian life: "Every Christian has two natures," Gottfried Arnold was singing the antithetical nature of Christian life:

> A Christian—a miracle
> I still live in this world,
> but am already lifted up to heaven.
> I bear a yoke that pleases me.
> I am an angel and can but praise God.
> I am an imperfect child,
> But am worthy to receive
> That in which naught save holiness is found:
> Indeed I have him, but yet must long for him.
> His cross is light, yet is also heavy,
> After being so closely united with him:
> My heart is full, and yet still empty:
> Filled with love, empty of that which I lament...

Both Skovoroda's Swabian contemporary, Oetinger—from whom there stretches a direct line of development to Schelling, Hegel, and Baader—and Johann Michael Hahn are acquainted with these same antithetical mystical motifs, which go back, in part, to Böhme. This is especially true of Oetinger, who speaks of the double root of all being, the duality of basic principles, of the struggle that is "the basis of all things," of the "opposition of things."

And when a modern writer wished to portray the concept of God poetically, he had to turn back to the antithetical formulas of mysticism:

> I am the one and am the both
> I am the maker and am the made
> I am the sword and am the scabbard
> I am the sacrifice, I am the death-blow
> I am the sight and am the seer
> I am the bow, I am the arrow
> I am the altar and the worshipper
> I am the fire and the fuel
> I am the rich man, I am the pauper
> I am the sign, I am the meaning
> I am the shadow, I am the reality
> I am an end and a beginning.

Skovoroda belongs to the spiritual complex just presented, to the unity beyond time and space of the antithetical thinkers. We may limit ourselves here to a few quotations, since our whole book should, among other things, provide proof of this thesis.

For Skovoroda, the problem of knowledge is not to comprehend being *conceptually* in concepts that are clear and "transparent," free of internal contradictions. It is not the goal of true knowledge to "fix" individual moments of being, to establish and "comprehend" abstract elements torn from the momentary totality of being. Rather, he sees it as the task of philosophy to grasp "true being" as such. True being exists, however, in and through opposites and contradictions. Being, of necessity, would lose its vitality and fullness if the contradictions in its nature could be removed. It is a consequence of this basic idea that Skovoroda knows no definitions, but rather descriptions, vague and ambiguous symbolizations of thought. He seeks in reality that which is polarly opposite, contradictory, mutually incompatible, irreconcilable. The "antinomian" style of Skovoroda's works is the most striking feature of the externals of his thinking. It is remarkable that among the numerous readers and researchers of Skovoroda, V. Petrov alone was, just recently, the first to refer to it.

"In this world as a whole there are *two* worlds forming *one* world: the visible and the invisible world, the living and the dead, the whole and the destructible. The one world is dress, the other body; this one shadow, that one tree; this material, that hypostasis, i.e., the base that contains the material clay, as a drawing bears the colours. Thus the world within the world is eternity in temporality, life in death, resurrection in sleep, light in darkness, in lying—truth, in weeping—joy, in despair—hope." Already two types of opposites are indicated, those in nature and those in the life of man. Skovoroda observes these two types in yet greater detail. "In nature you find no day without darkness and light, no year without warmth and cold." "With the night is also present the morning of God's day." Opposites, by unifying, make everything in the world; thus, "nourishment is formed from hunger and satisfaction, fruit from winter and summer, the day from darkness and light, every creature from life and death. Likewise, in human life you find no condition in which bitterness and sweetness are not mixed…" "Sweetness is the recompense for bitterness, and bitterness the mother of sweetness." "Weeping leads to laughter, and laughter hides within it weeping." The worth of human life is also paradoxical and contradictory. "This sullen wisdom, as invisible as it may be from the outside, inwardly is exalted and glorious." "In a dark and mean exterior, like an old garment, truth is concealed, compared to which every treasure is nothing. Into this meanness the divine ladder has descended, so that those who step upon its rungs may be raised to the heights of divine understanding." "Lift the cover, and you will see and be convinced that this madness is the wisest and only conceals itself with foolishness." "Happy is he who has succeeded in finding tenderness in that which is rough, sweetness in that which is bitter, grace in cruelty, nourishment in poison, moderation in frenzy, life in death, glory in disgrace," "the living in the dead, light in the darkness, like a diamond in the dirt, like the woman in the Gospel who found the gold coin in the mustard waste," "tenderness in hardness, nourishment in emptiness." "You see that which is so bitter, but here at the same time is sweetness. If you feel your labour, feel rest along with it. Your night is also the morning of God's day." Finally we find in Skovoroda the statement: "Thus stands the world. One opposite aids the other." Or, as Skovoroda amusingly puts it, "Where there are fewer cranberries and blueberries, there is also less scurvy; where fewer doctors—less sickness, less gold—fewer needs, less industry—less waste, less science—fewer fools, fewer laws—fewer crimes, fewer arms—fewer wars, fewer cooks—fewer ruined tastes, less honour—less fear, less pleasure—less sorrow, less fame—less shame, fewer friends—fewer enemies, less health—less suffering."

Similar quotations from Skovoroda could be presented ad infinitum. His entire system of thought is built upon such oppositions: we limit ourselves to only a few examples here.

If we previously cited a number of parallels from the history of ancient philosophy and German mysticism, it was not to demonstrate their influence on Skovoroda. This would be entirely pointless. We merely wished to indicate the significance of Skovoroda's further development of this kind of thinking. Skovoroda was unquestionably familiar with the Christian tradition, and it is also beyond doubt that many medieval and modern mystical works were known to him. That he adopted their style of thought and writing appears not just in the external quality of his language, and even less in an external borrowing of content: this connection with mystic literature would not have been possible without an internal readiness for it. These internal prerequisites are, on the one hand, the similarity of the religious experiences of Skovoroda with those in German and patristic mysticism and, on the other, the internally conditioned "recognition" of the mystical literary style. Mystical writings are, from the standpoint of the mystic himself, only the externality, the garment or, indeed, the disguise of the hidden internal subject, the incomplete and imperfect, the non-essential, the superficial expression. In no other form of religious or philosophical writing is the expressive nature of language so strongly pronounced as in mysticism. It is for this very reason that the search for external influences in the study of mystical literature must be rejected from the outset. The similarity in means of expression among the mystics is a *symptom* of spiritual commonality, of membership in a spiritual unity beyond time and beyond space. "Parallels" cited in this and subsequent sections should be regarded as such an "investigation of symptoms."

The antithetical thinking of German idealism developed on a new basis. It should suffice to remark that among the representatives of German idealism there may be found innumerable examples of antithetical formulas. Baader's antithetical style reminds one of the German mystics and the Areopagitica: "Behold the text of all metaphysics—internal and external, visible surface and invisible core, an object's appearance and its essence (effect and cause)!"

In conclusion, one point must be made. Skovoroda's antithetical thinking perhaps lacks a theoretical foundation of the type that the Platonists, the author of the Areopagitica, or Jakob Böhme sought to give it. This is why we often have the impression that there is something uncanny about Skovoroda. The antithetical formulas, as spiritual as they may be (to be spiritual is no essential indication of philosophically or religiously profound and genuine thought!), are still just "formulas," tokens of the mystical literary style. And this is not simply because the formulas are too numerous. Angelus Silesius was indeed able to breathe the greatest religious force into his perhaps even more numerous aphorisms. Skovoroda's theses often remain juxtaposed, not penetrating, but rather bypassing each other. Antithesis in his writings is often limited to the simple recognition of two different sides of one and the same object. Instead of the mystery of contradiction, we have banality (as we often find, for example, in the pseudo-Weigelian writings from which we quoted earlier). An opposite is spatially and temporally separated from other things. This means that it either lies outside the spatial scope of another object, precedes it, or follows it. In the world, opposites are in conflict, meaning that they attack each other from without, displacing each other in the course of time. The ultimate purpose of dialectics is to discover the opposites that are *one*, that blend into one another as they can only in their ideality. Skovoroda's dialectic, however, often assumes a dualistic quality. The "coincidentia oppositorum" breaks up and disintegrates, "explodes" or "impedes" itself, as Hegel puts it, lacking a unity prior to the sundering of elements. For this reason, the theory of the movement of being as a process determined by the interaction of opposites is to be understood as the theory of temporal-spatial development. At least there is often (*not always*) the possibility of a temporal-spatial interpretation. At only a few points in philosophy, in his teachings about God and in his ethics, does Skovoroda's thought remain genuinely "dialectical."

4. Circle of Circles

Dialectics cannot limit itself to the assertion that all true being unifies opposing determinations within itself. The very designation of these determinations as opposing suggests that they somehow "relate to each other" and check each other, whether by conflict or mutual tolerance; that they "unite," "reconcile." The forms of conflict as well as the kinds of reconciliation may vary. Indeed, the hostile or peaceful relations of opposites are most often defined as some form of motion. The description of the reciprocal relationships of opposites as a form of "motion" is pervasive in the history of dialectics. Especially widespread is the image of circular motion: since it draws downward that which is above, and lifts up that which is below, uniting beginning and end, changing direction at every moment, circular motion can best represent the image of the eternal dynamic.

Should we wish to look to ancient tradition, we find that the Orphics already employed circular motion as the image of the world's development, of the perpetual motion of all creatures in a "cycle of becoming" or "a cycle of becoming and passing away" [κύκλος τῆς γενέσεως, κύκλος τῶν γενέσεων καὶ φθίσεων]. Cycle of births, cycle of the soul, the golden chain, the wheel [τροχός]—these are the images of the universal law. Is this the law that Heraclitus has in mind when he says that "in circles the beginning and the end are the same"? For him the world's development is perpetual change, a transition, a conversion [μεταπίπτειν] into something different, a return to the starting point. "The death of the soul is to become water, the death of water is to become earth, but from earth comes water, from water—the soul." For the "upward path" and the "downward path" are one and the same. The Pythagorean Alcmaeon saw this cycle as the most important of human problems: "men perish because they cannot unite their end with their beginning."

Plato introduced some new problems. Basing himself on the dynamic character of the spiritual, Plato sees the life of the soul as circular motion. It is in this manner that the individual soul moves—"it circles," but the world-soul also moves. In Plato's cosmology, the image of the circular motion of the soul unites with the natural image of the circular motion of all heavenly bodies. The circle is also a symbol of God, for in Him beginning and end are the same. This imagery of Plato's was, of course, adopted in Platonic psychology and natural philosophy. In Philo, circular motion forms the basis of all processes in the world; the "quintessence," heaven, and the individual soul move in a circle:

"Since God made types immortal, and allowed them to participate in the eternal, he wished nature to move in a circular path." In Plotinus, the circular motion of different spheres of being forms a "divine round dance" around the centre, around the "One": "We do not always look upon the centre, but when we do, then the goal and the peace beckon us, and we no longer are dissonant with it, since we are actually performing a divinely inspired round dance around it. In this dance the spirit beholds the source of life, the source of the intellect, the principle of being, the reason for goodness, the root of the soul."

Finally, with Proclus, Platonic "antitheses" become a universal method. Every thought, indeed every object, "remains in itself" [μονή, ὕπαρξις] "proceeds from itself" [πρόοδος], "returns to itself" [ἐπιστροφή]. "Everything that is born of something remains with it and at the same time proceeds from it." "Everything that proceeds from something returns, having the energy of the circle. It returns to that from which it emanated, thereby binding the beginning with the end." "The end-points of all divine emanations are the same as their own beginnings, since they complete the return to the beginning of the circle, which is without beginning or end."

Christianity's "philosophy of history" is based on a circular schema, or at least the Christian conception of world history may be ordered in such a way. Beginning with the Fall, mankind proceeds through sin, law, damnation, and death on a downward path. Through Christ, this movement undergoes a reversal—man turns back to God. In heretical Gnosticism, the concept of circular motion is openly expressed. It is interesting, in this respect, that the snake is often used as a symbol of circular motion ("Ophites").

The numerous conceptions of circular motion among the Church Fathers are also based upon Platonism. Platonic conceptions, however, coincide with the Christian image of God as the beginning and end of all things (as in Heb. 3:7). When Gregory of Nyssa expressed certain doubts concerning the use of the image of the circle, since it "compares a boundless substance with a circumscribed figure," this image was already widespread. For Clement of Alexandria, the world is the "circle of all powers, in which Christ is alpha and omega." And Origen's fundamental idea of "the return of all things" [ἀποκατάστασις ἀπάντων] bases world history on a circular process. The "Areopagitica," based on Proclus, aided in the spread of this image. "Every good gift and every perfect blessing comes from above, since it descends from the Father of Light. But the advance of the light rays emitted by the Father, which find their way to us as his benevolent gift, as a power formed in the One, leads back again to His divine simplicity. For everything proceeds from Him and to Him, as Holy Scripture says." And just as the essence of the world lies in circular motion, so does the life and perception of man in its fullest perfection—in its unity with God. The ascent of the soul is its "spiral," a spiral movement, while the stage of unity with God is a circular movement. "Thus does divine love demonstrate with special clarity its boundlessness, like an eternal circle, around goodness, from goodness, in goodness, and to goodness, propelling itself in deceptive revolutions, proceeding in constantly identical manner, remaining, returning." From this comes the image of the English "roundelay," the symbolic representation of angels by "wheels," etc. If God is the beginning and the end, He is simultaneously also the centre of the circle formed by all creation: "The wholeness (Godhead) is received by each member of the circle, but not divided, as is the point in the middle of the circle by all its radii." The circle with all its radii converging at the centre is an image of the unity and existence of all things in God.

Medieval and modern mystics acquired the image of circular motion from pseudo-Dionysius. All nature proceeds from God and returns to God in the "De divisione naturae" of John Scotus Erigena. The wheel is one of the favourite images of Hildegard of Bingen. We also encounter this image in Bernhard, Bonaventura, and Thomas Aquinas. In Eckhart, the "loving soul" "must run a circle." We also find this circular motion of the soul in Suso, who left a schematic representation of the entire circular motion of the world from God and back to God. For him, the circle is also an image of God. This image is also to be found in Alanus ab Insulis, and still earlier in "Liber XXIV philosophorum": "Deus est sphaera intelligibilis, cuius centrum ubique, circumfrentia nusquam." [God is the sphere of the intelligible, its centre everywhere, its circumference nowhere.] This is a statement that Skovoroda quotes and introduces with the words, "Remember the dictum of the ancient philosophers..." For Suso, God is the beginning and end of all things: "He is at once within all things and outside all things—God is like a circular wheel whose mid-point is everywhere and circumference nowhere." Nicholas of Cusa speaks of God as the "endless circle," the "unending sphere." The image of such a circle continues throughout the philosophy of the Renaissance, even in Pico and Bruno. In modern mysticism, it naturally appears in a new form. Weigel writes: "et sicut in centro omnes lineae simul et simul sunt unum, item in aeternitate omnia tempora unum tempus..." [just as in the centre all lines are one and the same, so in eternity every time is one time]. Jakob Böhme emphasizes that the "turning," the circular motion, is by no means only a symbol of the highest activity of the spirit, but also a symbol of the unrest and torment of the world separated from God: "Because it does not find rest/ and is thus ever pierced from below/ it becomes like a turning wheel/ that spins in fear and anguish..." "Since there is no rest here/ the turning wheel spins quickly/ like a rapid thought/ for the spur drives it so quickly..." "As he cannot flee/ or climb above himself/ he thus spins like a wheel..." Böhme speaks of a "wheel of nature," but at the same time God is symbolized by a wheel: "Thus the nature of divinity is everywhere, unto the deepest depths/ like a wheel or an eye/ since the beginning always contains the end/..." It is little wonder that this image, so central in Böhme, appears in numerous forms among his successors. Thus Comenius sees the entire world and

God as a system of autokinetic circles and wheels. In his "Centrum Securitatis," he develops a detailed comparison of the world with a circle, dividing the circle into centre, circumference, and radii. Comenius also calls to mind the words of a "philosopher": "Deus est circulus, cujus centrum est ubique, et circumferentia nusquam." He also discusses the wheels of Ezekiel. The circle without beginning or end also appears in different forms in the works of Abraham von Franckenberg. Angelus Silesius employs the same image: to him the soul of man is "a wheel that runs of itself and has no rest." "The centre of love is God, and its circle as well." "God is my centre when I clasp Him within me: my circumference when out of love I flow into Him."

> Eternity is like a circle
> that turns within itself;
> like a snake that with effort
> sits wound upon itself;
> is like a wheel
> that round and round its axle swings,
> and indeed makes no stop at port
> as long as it endures…

Oetinger derives circular motion from his universal principle of the "conflict of all things," supported by appropriate images from Holy Scripture. Skovoroda's younger contemporary, J.M. Hahn, follows Böhme in his abundant use of the concept of the circle.

In Skovoroda as well opposites do not remain in fixed position; they move in reference to each other. Skovoroda does not have in mind a linear motion or a spiral, which is simultaneously progressive and cyclical. For him the motion of opposites, which—as we have seen—fills everything, is much more a movement "within a circle." Skovoroda sees the form of "dialectical movement" in a circle reaching back to its beginning, turning back upon itself.

Since the opposites relate to each other, they constitute a "triad" formed from the opposites themselves and from their reciprocal relationships. The opposites do not disappear in this motion, since the motion itself would thereby be suspended. Since they do continue to exist, they constitute *two* basic principles of the world, alongside which there is a *third*, which is the unification of both.

We have already indicated above that Skovoroda often interpreted the internal antithesis of true being as spatial-temporal. Both antitheses are spatially-temporally separate principles, forces, powers. He occasionally gives a spatial-temporal interpretation to the principle of the unification of opposites, i.e., the principle of movement. "The circle" is a spatial or, above all, a "temporal" circle, signifying a return in the temporal course of world development to "the identical," "the equal," "the original," etc. Circular motion is therefore a universal law of return, of recurrence. The movement always returns to one of the basic principles of the world, to the beginning. The point of departure for Skovoroda's dualistic world-view is thus sharply emphasized: one of the basic principles maintains a certain precedence, a superiority, a priority over the others. This differentiation is indicated by many value-laden terms. The dualism of his world-view becomes a dualism of values, a religiously coloured doctrine of the battle between the "good" and the "evil" principle, of the conflict between "light" and "darkness," etc.

This internal struggle not only divides the world as a whole, but is also the law of life for every individual part of the world.

It is entirely characteristic of Skovoroda's thought that the principle of motion, of the unification of opposites, should be visualized in terms of diverse symbols and images. But this is not simply a product of the character of Skovoroda's thinking. The large number of symbols that he uses for the principle of circular motion is a product of the complexity of this "circling." Skovoroda perhaps feels that the purely dynamic characteristics of "circular motion" threaten to relativize his world-image. He therefore wishes to give a form to this basic principle of his philosophy, a form that would permit a static as well as a dynamic interpretation. The highest principle, that of the overcoming of opposites, therefore becomes in its very essence "antithetical." If the consistency with which Skovoroda maintains his antithetical world-view seems primitive and naive, this world-view remains, nonetheless, magnificent in its unity, as the primitive often is.

Two antithetical principles unite to form a third. "In order that there be no confusion resulting from the two natures forming one nature, thus leading to idolatry, the Creator separated the light of His glory from the darkness of our bodies, truth from the material shadow... So that no strife would arise to disrupt the dyad, now united in a single being, he made the day out of darkness and light, out of morning and evening... God made this day from opposing natures: from the evil and the good, from the ephemeral and the permanent, from hunger and satiety, from weeping and joy, into an indissoluble unity. Both separating and binding, the eternal heavens are fixed between the common and the celestial waters.

Skovoroda uses many forms of expression to illustrate the theory of the unification of opposites.

One of the passages cited above has precisely this meaning: "It is sown rotten, it is raised fragrant; it is sown hard, it is raised tender; it is sown bitter, it is raised sweet; it is sown base, it is raised godly; it is sown senseless and blind, it is raised all-knowing and keen-eyed." Through "resurrection" the opposites in that which is resurrected are united in the "third." And the image of "morning" and "evening" embraces movement in its opposing elements: "Morning and evening... *lead somewhere*." "The beginning...ends as it begins, and begins as it ends; decays as it is born, is born as it decays; healing opposition through opposition, and wisely helping enemies through the inimical."

The unification of opposing principles is also a "return." Everything in the world returns to itself. "The first and last point is the same, and where (movement) began, there does (it) end." The human soul returns "home" to God. So does matter, which again becomes "formless dust." Indeed, so does all creation: "Just as the whole mix of creatures flows from the divine source, thus will it also return to that which is beginning and end, and which should lead us from death to life, from earth to heaven." "Everything returns to its beginningless end as in a ring—and to its beginningless beginning." Skovoroda's eschatology is constructed on the basis of these images.

The symbols with which Skovoroda expresses these thoughts are the following:

1. The first image is a triangle or an angle.—"One is three; I see three, but these are one." "One and two and three are the same." "Trinity in unity and unity in trinity are impossible, unless it is a unity."

2. The second symbol of the unification of opposites is the circle. "Truth is well-rounded, like an eternal bow." "The circle is the original figure, the father of the quadrilateral, the square and countless others…" In the circle, "beginning and end are the same." "In the ring, the first and the last are one and the same, and where it begins, there also does it end." Therefore, "the wheel is an image embracing the unending wheel of God's eternity, and is like the earth, which imitates it." In the circle, "the celestial hides within the earthly, the transient in the eternal."

3. As symbols of the circle (symbols of symbols!) we find all possible round objects. "What is a ring? Circle, wheel, eternity." Then come "chains," "the globe, which is composed of numerous circles—as of wheels." "A bowl is a greater part of a sphere than a plate, and a plate a greater part than a hoop." We encounter the globe in this sense in Proclus and Nicholas of Cusa. "Bread," "coins," "grapes and garden fruit," "crowns," "necklaces," "apples," "the sun"—all these are symbols of the circle. "Is not a millstone also a ring?" Self-mockingly, with true Ukrainian humour, Skovoroda lists all sorts of objects. "Then the third one"—speaking of a certain person—"began to bend these same hoops and scrub. It seems to me that you will soon add to your stock of wheels also sieves, bowls, breads, unleavened bread, every style of pancake, eggs, spoons, and nuts and other things. Add peas and beans and raindrops as well. One finds all of these, I believe, in the Bible. And don't forget the fruit from the gardens of Solomon and Jonah's pumpkin and watermelons!"

4. A further and extremely important symbol for Skovoroda is the snake. "When it hangs in a ring, it is the symbol of eternity." "The snake holding its tail in its jaws causes us to realize that the endless beginning, the beginningless end, ends as it begins and begins as it ends." For the snake "is clever and winds itself into a ring so that one cannot see where it means to go unless one

discovers its head. Thus is eternity everywhere and nowhere, because it is invisible, concealing its hypostasis."

5. A final symbol is the seed, the kernel. This symbol leads to metaphysical problems (see below). "The whole world hides itself, as a beautiful blooming tree hides in its seed, then emanates from it." "When a kernel decays in the field, new greenness comes out of it, and the decay of the old is at the same time the birth of the new; thus, where decay is, there is also renewal."

In more recent times this symbol of the circle enjoyed a renaissance in German Idealism. Not only in Baader, who speaks of the "totality of natural phenomena in their...constantly repeating cycles," but also in Schelling: "that original, essential, and enduring life indeed ascends from the depths to the heights, but upon arriving there directly returns to the beginning in order to ascend again." It is "an eternally, internally revolving life—a kind of circle—an unceasing wheel, a continuous rotary motion. The concept of the beginning, like that of the end, is suspended by this revolution." We find the same in Hegel, for whom individual life, substance, truth and science are all "circles," since each contains within itself its end, its goal and its development, its beginning. "The concept of law is a return to self, making itself the object; thus progress is not undetermined and eternal; rather a goal is there, namely the return to self. Thus there is a certain circularity here; the spirit seeks itself." For the Romantics, circular motion is the essence of the world's development: "For to the wise man, the muddled din of earthly life becomes silent; he perceives the path of the eternal natural law; finitude drops its cloak, and he views in reverent awe the eternal powers interweaving and the wheels spinning in perpetual motion" (Tieck).

In the modern poetical recastings of mystical symbolism by R. M. Rilke, we find the same image:

> I live my life in growing circles,
> which stretch out over everything—
> ----------
> I circle around God, around the ancient tower,
> and circle for thousands of years—
>
> You are a wheel upon which I stand:
> from your many dark axles
> one becomes heavy again and again
> and turns closer to me,
> and my willing works grow
> from recurrence to recurrence...

5. Transience as Allegory

Skovoroda unites with his "dialectics" another element that at first appears to be merely external, but is actually as essential to his world-view as his attempt to describe true being by means of oppositions. It is no accident that we find the same trait in ancient Platonism, in the Church Fathers, and among the medieval and baroque mystics, in other words, in the three spiritual currents with which Skovoroda is associated. We refer to Skovoroda's "symbolism."

The characteristic element in the style of his works is his continual reference to the concrete—to the concrete in life, art, and religious tradition—in order to bring greater clarity to the general. For *us*, admittedly, this does not bring clarity, but is a hindrance to our understanding, since symbols never disclose the image-laden content with complete clarity. The fact that a symbol always *requires* an explanation, an interpretation of that which is symbolized, is, in Skovoroda's opinion, the *advantage* of symbolic knowledge. One penetrates deeper if one does not merely accept the given, but rather contemplates and illuminates it from within oneself. (We shall later discuss Skovoroda's "theory of knowledge" in greater detail.)

Skovoroda's philosophical style is based on a peculiar return from the conceptual form of philosophizing to a living symbolic form, on a turning from the conceptual to the perceptual meanings of words. Skovoroda turns the vocabulary of philosophy to his own purposes, whereby concepts become symbols. As for the pre-Socratics concepts lie embryonically dormant beneath figurative expressions ("water," "fire," "ἄπειρον," "Δίκη," etc.), so in Skovoroda's work concepts are hidden by the profusion of allegories and symbols, as we have already seen in our analysis of his dialectics. Also, as with the pre-Socratics, each of Skovoroda's symbols does not have a definite, "fixed," specific meaning within a sharply delineated area, but rather contains a multiplicity of meanings, some of which are close, while others diverge greatly. Symbolic structures are represented here in full bloom, and have the tendency to swallow up everything conceptual, exact, "dry." Skovoroda is no "Ukrainian Socrates," as he is sometimes groundlessly called, but rather a Ukrainian pre-Socratic who is in possession of all the conceptual equipment of post-Socratic philosophy, and who behaves to some extent like a child let loose in this whole complicated apparatus, this workshop of the mind, playing with it and building from it—instead of conceptual forms—symbolic constructions, which are, of course, not without sense or meaning.

It is not only concepts, however, that possess a symbolic function for Skovoroda. It is also particular facts—above all those that are historical or considered historical—for example, the facts of biblical history, as well as every specific thing, the whole world with all its living beings and inanimate objects, all natural phenomena and products of culture, that are figuratively employed and interpreted.

Skovoroda bases himself on the tradition of the ancient sages. "Truth displayed itself to the sharp eye of the wise man not from afar—as the common mind sees it—but clearly, as in a mirror; and as living men, seeing this living image, they compared it with various transitory forms. No rose, no narcissus, no lily can display such lively colours as the images of invisible divine truth created by these wise men from the shadows of heavenly and earthly images. From these are born hieroglyphics, emblems, symbols, mysteries, parables, fables, allegories, proverbs..." Elsewhere Skovoroda speaks of "miraculous signs, crests, seals." It is not merely the difference between the "wise" and the "common" mind that is important here. Everything in the world is ambiguous in that it has a physical, perceptible side—has "the earth," the "worldly" within it—but simultaneously contains true being, which must be "extracted," "unveiled," expounded. Therefore Skovoroda speaks of "a multitude of images." "The whole world of shadows, down to its last line, from the grapes to the nettles, from the threads to the thongs, maintains its existence through the higher (world)... Every phenomenon is an image, is body, shadow, idol, and nothingness..." "Every thought crawls lowly as a snake upon the earth. But each also has the eye of a dove, which sees the beautiful image of truth above the waves of the flood. All this rubbish breathes with God and with eternity, and the Spirit of God hovers over all this filth and deception." Through "figures" man may penetrate to truth itself. "The truth that appears in these figures seems to travel back and forth above them. These figures, by becoming part of divine reason, seem to leave the earth and, perceiving their beginning, fall back again, as leaves in autumn fall to the original place of their decay." In other words, "symbols" and "figures" are only transient masks of "truth." Figures are "the satchels for gold, and the shells for God's seed. This is the parable and the true ποίησις, i.e., creation: God's gold is placed in corporeal emptiness; perhaps someone will discover it and find in the little basket the fair Jewish child, the man who has come from a place higher than the waters of the sirens..." Therefore Skovoroda calls on his readers: "Leave the physical fairy tales to toothless infants. It is all old wives' tales and fables and emptiness, which does not lead to safe haven. Like the Israelites, quickly hack to pieces all flesh. I am angry with you for remaining by that which is a shell. Destroy it and extract the core of divine power."

Each symbol is based upon three accounts of being: simple being, representational being (being in its representational function), and the hidden being that is represented. In order to decipher, distinguish between these different kinds of being. In place of divided, detached "transitoriness," there enter "new thoughts, eternal thoughts." "You, my son, when you read the book of the visible and evil world, in every case hold up the eye of your heart to the head of the matter, to its source...that is the true theology of Abraham—to see in each thing the spirit abiding within it." The knowledge of symbols is the ascent to God. And just as this single, omnipotent spirit, descending from on high, created the entire darkness of celestial, earthly, subterranean and oceanic forms (stars, animals, gold, pearls), so can He reclaim the living from the dead, plenitude from the wasteland, pleasantness from abomination, illumination from darkness. And God said: let there be light. And there was light."

It is characteristic of symbols that each symbol has a *number of meanings*. In many instances Skovoroda expressly indicates the ambiguity of symbols. "Images" can also be images of images. "The sun is the archetype, i.e., the original and most important image, and the copies and images representing it are innumerable. Such a figure is called an antitype—i.e., a different image replaces the primary one. They all flow, however, back to the sun as to their source."

Skovoroda often gives an explanation of the words "emblem" and "symbol." "The ancient sages had their own special language. They expressed their thoughts through images as well as through words. These images were those of heavenly and earthly creatures. Thus, for example, the sun meant truth; a ring or a snake biting its tail—eternity; the anchor—resolution or will; the dove—the sense of shame; the stork—piety; the grain and its seed—thinking and thought. There were also invented images, for example, the sphinx, sirens, the phoenix, the seven-headed serpent, etc. In Greek, an image that conceals a secret within it is called an emblem, that is, an enclosure, an insertion like a diamond in a ring. When two or three such images were placed together, this was called σύμβολον; in Latin, *conjectura*; we might say: combination, mixture. Such images, secretly representing eternity, were chiselled by the ancients on seals, on rings, on vessels, on plates, on temple walls, and were thus called hieroglyphics, i.e., sacred sculptures, and the expounders received the name hierophants—sanctuary heralds or *mystagogoi*—secret guides." "A symbol is composed of two or three figures that represent transience and eternity." "Such figures, which embody a secret power within themselves, were called by the Greek philosophers ἐμβλήματα, ἱερογλύφικα, emblems, hieroglyphics." "The figures are often called witnesses, guards, and angels."

Skovoroda called this (presumed) "ancient symbolism" "the heathen theology." "The legendary books of the ancient sages—these are the ancient theology. In this manner they depicted the immaterial essence of God through images. And thus the invisible was represented visibly through the images of creatures." "We had not yet heard the name mathematics when our ancestors possessed the finished temple of the Christian school. In this school the whole human race learned of the joy intended for it, and that is the catholic, i.e., related-to-all, science. The heathen temples of idols, divine places, or idolatrous churches are at the same time temples of the teaching and of the school of Christ."

To write a history of symbolism before Skovoroda is a great task, for which perhaps only the barest preparations have been made. Ancient philosophy, patristic writings and medieval and modern mysticism—all were thoroughly symbolic without elucidating the basis of this symbolic way of philosophizing or, indeed, clearly stating that their thinking was symbolic in character. In any event, the concept of the symbol had already been discussed in Platonism. In the various subsequent ramifications of Platonic thought, the theory of symbolism came to be expressed in different ways. In ancient Platonism we find all the theories of symbolism that are to be encountered in medieval and modern philosophy. In any case, the theories developed by Skovoroda are most closely related to those of the patristic tradition and its "philosophy of symbolism," which has appeared recently in Russian religious philosophy. The few statements by Skovoroda that we have cited contain, in baroque terminology, the basic postulates of the theory of symbolism of such Russian philosophers as Florenskij, Bulgakov, Berdjaev, Losskij, and Losev. For Skovoroda, as for contemporary Russian religious philosophy, the symbol is not merely a sign, but rather an object just as worthy and real as that which is "symbolized." The actual character of the object itself may be ascribed to the symbolic object (symbols as angels). And in comparison to scientific, rational thought, "symbolic thought" is not to be debased to a "primitive" level; rather one sees in symbolic (for example, religious) thought a mode of thinking that in many respects is more vital and deals more fully and profoundly with reality than does formal discursive thought.

The realization that symbolic thinking is a specific kind of thinking, having its own function and meaning, has become fairly widespread in more recent times. There has not, however, been much progress toward a new evaluation of the symbolic thought of the past. Here we can only look briefly at some of the elements of symbolic thought in mysticism and take note of a few parallels with Skovoroda.

In dealing with the theory of the exegesis of Holy Scripture in Philo and among the Church Fathers, we come up against a great variety of different ideas. Philo bases all his scriptural interpretations on the concept of symbolism: "After the literal narration, it is proper to render the allegorical sense as well, since in all, or at least in most of the law there is an allegorical sense." In the law, "everything is a visible symbol of the invisible reality and an indication of the unspoken teaching." The Church Fathers based their ideas on those of Philo. As early as Justin we find considerations of symbols. In Tertullian there is a classification of symbols: figures, enigmas, allegories, parables. The idea of such an interpretation found wide-ranging acceptance; the question only remained as to how many and which levels of meaning one should distinguish: the literal, the moral, and the spiritual or mystical—this was certainly the most common division. Origen unites the theory of Scriptural exegesis with his general metaphysical perspective: the "letter" of Scripture is the visible shell, while the sense is the spirit enveloped by it.

In Philo, Scriptural interpretation is bound up with older notions of Egyptian hieroglyphics as secret mystical script. The same thought returns in Plotinus: the Egyptians do not write, but rather create images. In addition, Plutarch (*De Iside et Osiride*), Porphyrius, Iamblichus (*De Aegypt. Myst.*), and Cicero share this view. This idea was adopted by the Church Fathers (Eusebius). Clement of Alexandria gives a detailed exposition, working out a classification of "symbolic script" (not only for Egyptian, but for every possible script as well): "The Egyptians first taught their students that mode of writing called epistle script, then the hieratic, and finally the hieroglyphic. This is further divided into two classes, one expressing itself directly through phonetic signs, while the other is a symbolic script." The symbolic script represents things either directly, by imitation, or through symbolic signs (tropic), or expresses itself purely allegorically through certain riddles (enigmatic). Thus they draw a circle to represent the sun and a crescent-like symbol to represent the moon. These are examples of the direct script. They create symbols by taking certain objects, adapting them, and then applying them to something else, extending them here, transfiguring them there. The following is an example of the enigmatic mode: while representing the stars with the bodies of snakes because of their winding courses, they represent the sun with the image of a scarab, because it forms a ball of cow dung and rolls it in front of itself.

The "Areopagitica" (in agreement with Proclus) gives a detailed justification for the symbolic method. The sacraments and the hierarchy are to be understood spiritually or symbolically. One can only see "the celestial in palpable images, the all-inclusive in colour and fullness, the divine in human analogies, the immaterial in the material, the supernatural in that which is natural." Thus sanctified objects from the world of the senses are likenesses of spiritual objects; they lead us by the hand and provide a path to the latter. The realm of ideas in turn constitutes the point of departure for the understanding of those elements of the hierarchy that fall under the senses. The language of images is the echo [ἀπήχημα] of divine harmony and beauty.

During the Middle Ages symbolism flowered in ecclesiastical and secular art. A theoretical foundation for "symbolism" already existed in Bonaventura's theory of "similitudes" (analogies between individual objects in the world): "All creatures of the visible world lead to God, because they are the shadow, echo and image of that first, powerful, essential, wisest, and foremost Creator; of that eternal light, origin and abundance; of that witnessing, forming, and ordering art." Thus also Hugo de St. Victor: "external things are simultaneously the arteries through which the invisible beauty of God reveals itself and flows to us. For it is impossible to represent the invisible except through the visible, and therefore theology deems it necessary to use visible allusions in the explanation of the invisible." And in German mysticism, aside from the profuse utilization of ancient Christian symbolism, the realization is not wanting that one "must arrive at the invisible through visible objects."

Symbolic art took on new forms in the Renaissance and baroque. Interest in the "theory" of symbolism grew greatly and was expressed in discussions concerning the problem of symbolism, linking up with the ancient and patristic traditions. Thus Ficino, who had to deal with the problem of symbolic writing in connection with Plotinus, as well as in the translation of Iamblichus' writings on the Egyptian mysteries, gives a symbolic interpretation of Plato's symposium: "every word is a symbol"! We find the same in the Renaissance translation of Poimander. And Paracelsus considers: "What do we have of the knowledge of things without the light of nature? This light of nature stretches from the visible to the invisible and is just as wonderful in the invisible as in the visible. And therein I behold the light of nature; thus does the invisible become visible. What the eyes give...that requires my proof...and much proof is necessary in order to make it so that the invisible may be beheld visibly." For Paracelsus, "the temporal is an offspring of heaven, thus through its essence and image we are allowed to embrace its spirit: this is the doctrine of the signs." Erasmus (*Adagia*) uses the same symbol as Skovoroda—"Festina lente." One of the theoreticians of baroque symbolism was Athanasius Kircher, who also associated the Egyptians with the symbolic. His works, *Obeliscus Pamphilius* (Rome, 1650) and *Oedipus Aegyptiacus* (Rome, 1653), present a general theory of symbolism that offers nothing new in terms of content, and is of interest to us only inasmuch as it contains many similarities with the work of Skovoroda. "The nature of the symbol is to lead us to the understanding of an object by means of its perceptible similarity to other objects; its peculiar feature is that it conceals itself beneath the veil of an obscure word." Symbols are divided into insignias, mirrors, crests, riddles, fables, myths, proverbs, and tales, which then further subdivide. The art of the baroque is thoroughly saturated with elements of symbolism, about which more will be said later.

Modern mysticism, in particular, is permeated with elements of symbolism. For Franck, "the external world is the image and likeness of the internal." "The world is merely a transient image." For Weigel the entire visible world is merely a symbol. "One should consider the Complications and Explications. The visible, material heaven and earth is a compressed vapour that has arisen from the invisible fire; thus were all corporeal things concealed in the invisible spirit."

So influential and widely read an author as Johann Arnd established the importance of emblematic thought in the Protestant world: "For just as the Lord God revealed divine secrets through images in the Old and New Testaments, so God planted prophecies in nature through images; for all of nature and all its elements—animal, vegetable, and mineral—are filled with wonderful images, signs, and pictures... And thus these pictures in nature are God's alphabet, through which He profoundly explains nature to all those who understand it and read this wonderful script and alphabet of God, from which more natural wisdom may be gleaned in an hour than from many profound and detailed heathen books." "This is how the Egyptian and Persian philosophers known as magi acquired their glorious, natural, and useful arts, in which this true philosophy is described through images, and such writing is called hieroglyphics...""Since nature reveals itself so powerfully through images, as willed by God, it is not wrong or impious to possess such images; rather, it is profoundly impious and ignorant to disregard or disrespect these."

For Böhme as well, the world is "an allegory of the abyss/ or a mirror of eternity...it consists of "external images." "It is the visible world/ that is a revelation of the inner spiritual world/ from the eternal light/ and from the eternal darkness/ from the spiritual tapestry: And it is a projection of eternity/ through which eternity has made itself visible..." "For/ this world is an allegory of God's being/ and GOD is revealed in the terrestrial allegory..." "If we observe the essence of the visible world/ and observe the essence of its creatures, we find within it the image of the invisible spiritual world/ that is concealed in the visible world/ as is the soul in the body..." "The whole external world with its beings/ is a sign or image of the internal spiritual world."

The pansophical strivings of Comenius were also directed toward the same "journey through the visible toward the invisible." To this complex of ideas belongs all of pansophism, as well as the concept of the "sign," the recognition of the "alphabet," the script that discloses all of nature. The concept of the "language of nature" (to some extent in Böhme) and the mystical interpretation of alchemy are all part of the same set of ideas.

The symbolic world-view enjoyed a new flowering in the Romantic era. The forerunners of the Romantic world-view had already expressed the symbolic idea with unambiguous clarity: thus, for Hamann, all of nature is, "it seems, merely an expression, an allegory...of God," "all of visible nature is nothing more than the hands and face of a clock," "the treasure of human knowledge and happiness exists in images." Herder devotes several pages to this theme. The human race "is dependent upon images, since they give it an expression of things." "Is not nature also a script, a very legible and lofty script of God to man?" All creation is a "hieroglyph," "God's first attempt at writing." According to Baader, "All things spiritual are...[merely] reproduced in the physical... So-called physical, material nature is...a symbol and copy of internal, spiritual nature." "Form, figure, visible image, structure of an object! It is only visible as a living (organic) being. Is it not but the letter, the hieroglyph of its internal being?" "Images are good for the soul. They are its proper nourishment. Eating them, chewing them over affords pleasure, and without this nourishment, there is no health for the soul..." And for Schleiermacher, "the external world with its laws, as with its fleeting phenomena, beams back to us like a mirror, in a thousand tender and sublime allegories, that which is most essential and most exalted in our being." We find similar passages in Görres. Friedrich Schlegel and Arthur Schopenhauer also deal with or allude to symbols. Above all, symbolism appears in the German Romantic poets. Thus Tieck, "What then are fruit and flower, forest, field and sea, man and beast, but the suggestive sign and cipher in which the eternal creative force has written and stored its thoughts?" "They exist because they have meaning." In Novalis, the apprentice von Sais rejoices in "these wonderful piles of objects and figures in the halls, which seem to me as if they were pictures, shells, ornaments grouped around a divinely wondrous image, and this has always remained in my thoughts." This same idea finds its speculative expression in Schelling and, with particular beauty and depth, in Solger and Hegel. Although Skovoroda's thoughts may take a subordinate place in this history of ideas, his importance for Ukrainian intellectual history, for the very reason that he belongs to this development, is central and commanding. Having no connection with the Ukrainian Romantics of the nineteenth century, he nevertheless expounded many ideas that we then find in Kuliš, as well as in P. Jurkevyč, and perhaps even in Potebnja. All of them borrowed these ideas, for the most part, from German Romanticism. This also indicates Skovoroda's "typological" and "characterological" importance in Ukraine's cultural history.

It is simply incomprehensible that those researching Skovoroda have, without exception, *all* overlooked the passages in which a series of images is described in few—though often also in abundant—words. These are the images that express Skovoroda's favourite ethical ideas, but because they are presented in a somewhat haphazard order, they give the impression of constituting a foreign body in Skovoroda's works, of having been extracted from different sources and belonging to some tradition-bound complex. The images themselves are attached to the manuscript of his "Alphabet of the World." It is a great pity for Skovoroda studies that his drawings have never been the subject of scholarly research.

Following a brief discussion of the problem of symbolism (in the manner with which we are already familiar) and a brief reference to the main ideas of Skovoroda's ethics, one of the main characters in the dialogue, Grigorij, invites the entire company into his chamber. The discussion goes on as follows:

"Afanasij: Ha! Where did you get so many new pictures? Look: the entire room is covered with them.

Grigorij:Look for yourselves! That is why I invited you. But do not insult them. They are all dear to me.

Afanasij: What is this foolishness? Everywhere animals, birds, forests, mountains, cattle, floods, fish, reptiles, etc., etc. What a heathen paradise.

Grigorij: Together with St. Peter, I slaughter it all and eat with relish in the name of God: nothing is unclean to me.

Afanasij: O, please do not destroy everything. Show mercy at least to the mountains and the trees. Let us look at the first picture above the door."

There follows, in rather colourful fashion, a description of the symbolic images in which each image corresponds to a proverb. Thus we see a nightingale teaching its children to sing (saying: "Parents are our best teachers"); a stag wounded by an arrow and grazing on grass (a medicinal herb, according to Skovoroda's explanation; saying: "Nature surpasses art"); a sea-shell ("Seek yourself inside yourself"); a narcissus beholding itself in the water ("Know yourself"); moths circling a candle ("My passion destroys me"); then we see Actaeon, Atlas, Phaeton, a blind man carrying a cripple on his shoulder, etc. In another of Skovoroda's works, we again find a description of images: a sheaf of grass ("All flesh is straw"), a snake biting its tail (an image of eternity), an arrow flying toward a star ("He alone can satisfy me"), a plant scattering seeds ("I await the life of the world to come"), a swallow flying over the sea ("In winter I find no rest here"). We come across this same swallow in a third passage, in which a series of images is again described... Images are to be found everywhere in Skovoroda's works; of the main ones that recur frequently, one could easily list a hundred.

One is reminded by all this profusion of colourful "symbols" of various collections of "emblemata et symbola," which were very widespread and popular throughout Europe in the sixteenth, seventeenth and eighteenth centuries. While Skovoroda certainly drew upon various West European collections, he also used a Russian work of this type entitled *Symbola et emblemata selecta*, which was published in 1705 in Amsterdam by order of Peter the Great. This book contains 840 copper engravings, which are on the whole very well executed. The illustrations are in groups of six. An aphoristic text in eight languages (Russian, or more usually Old Church Slavonic, Latin, French, Italian, Spanish, English, Dutch, and German) accompanies the images. The first edition of this book immediately became a great rarity, since—as it is reported—the ship bringing the books to St. Petersburg capsized off the coast of Sweden. Few copies remain. Later, however, three additional editions appeared, though of lesser artistic accomplishment (1743, 1788, 1811). In any event, this work enjoyed great popularity. Many traces of the *Symbola et emblemata* are to be found in Russian and Ukrainian intellectual history (and even in Turgenev, in "The Eagle's Nest" and "A King Lear of the Steppes").

This collection seems to have been known in Ukraine. One of the most interesting representatives of eighteenth-century Ukraine, Jakiv Markovyč—pupil and friend of Teofan Prokopovyč—relates in his diary that he gave a painter a collection of symbols to copy. This could very well have been the collection mentioned above. A Ukrainian bishop in Rostov (province of Jaroslav) in the mid-eighteenth century, Arsenij Macijevyč, ordered gates for the Kremlin (i.e., fortress) and for the church upon which no less than 72 symbols from this collection are represented (no one has yet alluded to the source of these interesting representations). Other collections of this type were also known in Ukraine.

Looking through the Amsterdam collection we again find many of Skovoroda's images. Most importantly, the images are accompanied, almost without exception, by *the same* proverbs... Yet there are many that are particular to

Skovoroda or to the *Symbola et emblemata selecta*, for example, "The small bird, the rooster, conquers the lion." In the *Symbola...* we find the symbol of a crowing rooster and an obviously distressed lion illustrating the saying, "*Tremorem injicio fortissimo*. I cause the strongest to tremble." Curiously, we find in the same collection a nearly identical engraving with the saying, "*Veni, vidi, vici:* I came, I saw, I conquered." According to Skovoroda's explanation, a stag is slain by an eagle when the eagle alights upon the stag's head and beats him in the eyes with his mighty wings, thereby driving him to his death. The *Symbola...* contains this symbol with the saying, "*Instante victoria*: I slay him through his diligence."

A number of other images not in the Amsterdam collection are present in other collections of "Symbola et emblemata." Skovoroda relates in one of his fables: "On the wall of a large room in Xarkiv, I once saw among other wise emblems the following: a turtle-like animal with a long tail, on its shell a large ornamental star: for this reason the Romans called this creature *stellio*, for stella means star. Underneath was written *sub luce lues*, meaning: beneath light is a running sore. Also related to this is the proverb from the Gospels concerning the whited sepulchres." We find a portrayal fitting this description in a collection of political emblems by Saavedra and in a voluminous collection that J. Boschius published in Augsburg in 1702. On occasion Skovoroda mentions the remora, a fish that, despite its small size, could bring a ship to a halt. We encounter a similar story concerning the remora in the "Physiologists," as well as a depiction of it in a very famous collection of emblems by J. Camerarius. This allows us to suppose that Skovoroda was acquainted with other collections in addition to the Amsterdam *Symbola et emblemata*, which is all the more likely as such collections were widely known in Ukraine during the seventeenth and eighteenth centuries.

We have already indicated that the use of symbols in philosophical thought is very ancient. The fragments remaining from the pre-Socratics are filled with images, which on this pre-conceptual level become the bearers of concepts. Later, however, primarily in Platonism, more extensive use is made of images.

In Plato's writings there are a number of images that are also to be found in Skovoroda, for instance, the stork. We may mention Plato's "love of storks." The soul is a seed that after death "soon comes into another body and grows like a seed." We also find a "blind wanderer" in Plato. For him the magnet is the symbol of man filled with divine power. We shall cite other examples later. Two fable-parables from the *Theaetetus* are used by Skovoroda in another sense. For Plato an opinion is like a clay vessel: "by knocking on it, one may discover by the sound whether it is undamaged or cracked." And Skovoroda relates the following fable: "An old woman was buying pots. 'How much does this pretty one cost?' 'One and a half kopecks,' answered the potter. 'And for that ugly one there—half a kopeck, of course?' 'For that one I would not take anything less than two kopecks.' 'Why is that?' 'Here, madam,' said the master, 'one does not choose by appearance. We check whether a pot rings clearly (by knocking on it).'" In Plato, knowledge is compared to bird-catching; this comparison is to be found in Skovoroda as well.

Understandably, a long series of identical images, transformed in various ways, stretches through the entire development of Platonism. Images are especially numerous in Philo, in whose works there is an interesting fusion of Platonic images with biblical ones, some of which are very similar. Later Platonism and patristic philosophy share the same tendency to use symbols. The Middle Ages witnessed a blossoming of symbolic art. Among the common symbols there are a number used by Skovoroda with which we have become acquainted. We need merely indicate the use of the motif of the blind and the lame in ecclesiastical art. The most comprehensive collections of symbols, compiled sometimes as hieroglyphics and sometimes as emblems of a philosophical, theological, iconographical, or other nature, appeared during the Renaissance. Works of this nature—above all pictorial works—made their appearance in all countries, denominations and artistic styles from the sixteenth to the eighteenth century, influencing literature, graphic art, mysticism, philosophy, preaching, and teaching in numerous ways. Many of these collections also contain various images that are to be found in Skovoroda. The list of emblematic collections begins with *Hypnerotomachia Poliphili* (written in 1467, published in 1499). We intend to refer here only to those writings that found their way to Ukraine. These are the collections of Andreas Alciatus, Joachim Camerarius (several editions), O. Vaenus or Veen (*Amorum emblemata*, Antwerp, 1608), Hermann Hugo (*Pia desideria*), Saavedra Faxardo (*Idea Principis Christiano-Politici*), Johannes de Boria, J. Boschius (*Symbolographia*, Augsburg, 1702). Of no less importance are the simple descriptions and compendia of symbols *without* biblical portrayals. Of special note among these collections are the following: H. Lauretus (*Sylva allegroriarum totius sacrae scripturae*, 2 volumes, Venice, 1575), J. Masenius (*Speculum imaginum veritatis occultae, exhibens symbola, emblemata, hieroglyphica, aenigmata*, Cologne, 1664), various works by Athanasius Kircher, Philippus Piccinellus (*Mundus symbolicus*, 1681), Scarlatus Octavius (*Homo et ejus partes...*, 2 volumes, Augsburg, 1695), but above all, the works of Maximilianus Sandaeus, which have a pronounced mystical colouring (*Theologica symbolica*, Mainz, 1626 and other works; Sandaeus' works influenced Angelus Silesius). Many of the works cited also contain theoretical observations concerning symbolism (essential in Sandaeus).

This literature may have directly affected Skovoroda. Emblematic works could also have influenced him, however, through their effect on graphic art, literature, and theology.

There is ample evidence of the influence of emblematic collections on graphic art. We find emblematic elements among many of the important representatives of the art of the modern era: in Dürer (drawings to illustrate the work of Horus Apollo), Leonardo da Vinci, Raphael, Titian, Benvenuto Cellini, Bernini, Jacques Callot (Lux claustri and Vita Beatae Mariae), and, in the nineteenth century, in P.O. Runge. Most of all, the influence of emblems was important in ecclesiastical art: confessional differences in this area were of no importance. The following monuments are cited as examples of symbolic and emblematic elements in German church art: the Hall of Mary on the Frauenberg in Fulda, St. Michael's (Bamberg), the Parring monastery church in Regensburg, Fulda Cathedral, the chapel of St. Agnes in Augsburg Cathedral, the castle chapels at Saalfeld and Eisenberg, the church in Oppurg, St. Marien and St. Wenzel in Naumburg, several village churches in the province of Saxony, St. Fides in Bamberg, the upper vicarage in Bamberg, the main church and the prelate's chapel on the Michelsberg (Bamberg), the Chapel of the Mother of God on the Judengasse in Bamberg, the church at Dormitz near Bamberg, and the Chapel of the Saviour in Schwäbisch Gmünd. The Lorbeer House in Bamberg and Schrottenberg Castle in Reichmannsdorf are examples of secular art. Skovoroda himself attests to his acquaintance with mural painting. He could have seen such paintings in Hungary or Austria as well as in Xarkiv. And there is evidence that mural paintings were also common in Ukraine.

The influence of emblems in literature is also of no small importance. Although their influence on Shakespeare is perhaps questionable, it is certain for Erasmus (*Apophthegmata*), Rabelais, Fischart, and for all of German baroque literature. Harsdörfer often mentions Saavedra; the poems of J.V. Andreä are full of symbolic motifs, and one finds them in M. Opitz, N. Reusner, Rottenhagen, Lohenstein, and Balde, nor can they be ignored in F. Spee; several baroque writers produced emblem books themselves. Above all, symbolism entered the language of the mystical poets, from Daniel Czepko and Angelus Silesius to Gottfried Arnold and Rilke's *Book of Hours*. The influence of symbolism on all the preaching of the baroque should not be underestimated.

The Ukrainian baroque was no exception.

A very interesting and rewarding theme would be to pursue the role of symbolism in the history of philosophy; to establish the origin of symbolism (for instance, the Platonic symbols cited above) in pre-Socratic philosophy and Greek mythology; to research the role of these symbols in the entire development of ancient Platonism and their fusion with Christian symbols, which derived in part from other sources; and then to follow the fate of these symbols through the history of medieval Scholasticism into modern philosophy. A number of attempts have been made to deal with this task, but as yet we possess no exhaustive work. And this in spite of the fact that this symbolism pervades the entire development of philosophy up to the present! For instance, the famous *tabula rasa* appears in some form from Plato and Aristotle, through the Middle Ages, up to Locke and Comenius. This image has also been rendered in emblematics: we find a *tabula rasa* in numerous emblem collections with the caption *Ad omnia* ("Proper to all"; for instance, in Saavedra, Boschius, and the Amsterdam *Symbola et emblemata*). The *tabula rasa* is also mentioned in Grimmelshausen's *Simplicissimus*. Symbols are mentioned very often by Baader; some examples from his diary include: γνῶθι σεαυτόν, *nosce te ipsum, ne te quaesiveris extra*, in which the saying is the symbol of a sea-shell! In his *Philosophy of History*, Hegel views the course of history in terms of symbols—the phoenix, plants and seeds, circle and centre are all symbols familiar to us. Mathematical symbols such as circle, centre, and triangle were used with great frequency in philosophy from Plato and Plotinus up to the Romantic period (Novalis, Baader, Schelling).

The importance of emblematics in mysticism is also not to be underestimated. Indeed, Platonic symbolism and the symbolism of the Song of Solomon—in fact, the symbolism of Holy Scripture as a whole—form the basis of the mystical literature of the early Christian and medieval period. Although the graphic representation of mystical ideas in the Middle Ages is scattered (Hildegard von Bingen, Suso), such representation occurs frequently in the mysticism of the modern period. There are numerous examples of how emblematic representations and mystical ideas influence each other. Among the most important collections of mystical emblems are the works of Daniel Sudermann: *Schöne auserlesene Figuren und hohe Lehren von den begnadeten Liebhabenden Seele...* (Fair Selected Images and Exalted Teachings of the Blessed and Loving Soul...) and *Hohe geistreiche Lehren/ und Erklärungen: Über die führnehmbsten Sprüche deß hohen Lieds Salomonis/ von der Liebhabenden Seele...* (Exalted Spiritual Teachings/ and Explanations: Concerning the Noble Passages of the Exalted Song of Solomon/ of the Loving Soul...) (1623). Both works make extensive use of the teachings of Tauler and Meister Eckhart. Robert Fulda, one of the creators of modern theosophical mysticism, sketched emblematic images (*De Fluctibus*). Although it was only later that Böhme's mysticism inspired the beautiful engravings by Luyken that served as the frontispiece for the edition of 1682 and represented Böhme's visions in such a singular manner, this symbolism underlies much of what Böhme wrote. It is no accident that one of the finest portraits of Böhme is executed in a thoroughly emblematic style. The works of Abraham von Franckenberg and the literature of the Rosicrucians are absolutely inseparable from the mystical symbols and emblematic drawings of which they are mostly comprised.

In Czepko and Angelus Silesius we find a mountain of symbolic material. It is no accident that *Der cherubinische Wandersmann* (The Cherubic Wanderer) is embellished with a symbolic frontispiece. The drawings of Abraham von Franckenberg also display the same interest in the graphic representation of mystical experience. Comenius, in his quest for vivid portrayal, did not, in the final analysis, allow himself to be distracted from these mystical emblematic motifs. Gottfried Arnold produced emblematic illustrations for Arnd's book *Vom wahren Christentum* (On True Christianity), and Arnd's poetry is so full of emblematic motifs that it may truly be termed "emblematic writing": "Here everything becomes allegory; everything attains significance and is elevated in an artistically sublimated sense. The dense profusion of metaphors that burdens the style of these works can mostly be attributed to this emblematic and symbolic mode of writing." Mme. de Guyon composed spiritual songs based on the emblems of Hugo and Vaenus. Oetinger returned to symbolism on a new level, primarily in his *Biblisches und emblematisches Wörterbuch* (Biblical and Emblematic Dictionary), in which he unifies and blends the purely graphic with the philosophical in a unique way. Emblems again appear among the "inspired ones" of the nineteenth century (Gossner). Shortly before the war, an important Russian religious philosopher, Pavel Florenskij, employed mystical emblems (the Amsterdam collection and Vaenus). In Rilke's *Stundenbuch* (Book of Hours), we find a poetical reworking of this same graphic material.

If, as E. Seeberg suggests, one can identify a movement of "emblematic mysticism," then Skovoroda occupies an important place in that movement, as he is one of the most resolute and consistent representatives of the emblematic style in the mystical writing of the modern age.

In Ukraine, Skovoroda was by no means alone as a devotee of the symbolic and the emblematic.

The "Symbola et emblemata" had been a favourite book genre in Ukraine since the seventeenth century. In 1632-3 Peter Mohyla bought a certain *Emblemata*, along with other books. In the library of Epifanij Slavynec'kyj was an *Egyptian Symbolics*. In addition, there were a number of such works in the library of Stefan Javors'kyj (which, incidentally, was in the possession of the Xarkiv Collegium when Skovoroda was a professor there): among others, *Firmamentum Symbolicum* by Sebastian a Matre Dei, *Apelles Symbolicus* by Keten, a Polish emblematic work, collections of fables, *Mystica Mariana* by Sandaeus and, above all, *Pia desideria* by Hugo and *Amoris emblemata* by Vaenus. Camerarius and *Philosophia imaginum* by Menestrerius were in the library of Prokopovyč, who had translated Saavedra into Russian. An anonymous Ukrainian translation of Hugo has survived. The books in Javors'kyj's library, which, as stated, were at Skovoroda's disposal, were probably one of the main sources of symbolism in Ukrainian literature of the seventeenth and eighteenth centuries. The libraries mentioned are interesting inasmuch as they were typical for Ukrainian scholars of the seventeenth century. There is also no lack of independent symbolic works: in the 1780s there appeared a panegyric to Lazar Baranovyč that contains several symbolic plates in the customary style of symbolic and emblematic art. In 1712 a collection of emblematic images appeared under the title *Ethics-Hieropolitics*; it went through several new editions in the course of the eighteenth century. The influence of symbolism was also strong in painting.

Symbolism had no less influence on seventeenth- and eighteenth-century Ukrainian literature and on the preaching of that period. The writers Ioanikij Galjatovs'kyj and Antonij Radyvylovs'kyj and the preacher Stefan Javors'kyj made frequent use of symbolic literature, as was common practice in the West. Skovoroda followed in their footsteps.

A variety of sources confirm the influence of the Amsterdam *Symbola et emblemata* in Ukraine. Although it is open to question whether indeed Markovyč gave this particular collection to a painter in 1724 in order to have a few of the illustrations copied, it is certain that about mid-century, Arsenij Macijevyč of Rostov (province of Jaroslav) commissioned decorations for two large gates based on this book. Skovoroda himself serves as further proof that the *Symbola et emblemata* found readers in Ukraine.

According to a number of researchers, emblematic art also left its stamp on the folk art of Ukraine (for example, in decorations on tiled stoves)... Be that as it may, the *Symbola et emblemata*, which, in all probability, had been recommended to Peter the Great by Ukrainians, enjoyed great popularity in Ukraine.

6. *The Symbolic World*

Skovoroda applied symbolic interpretation to the Bible, with which he had a special relationship. He was a "lover" of the Bible, as he stated in a signature to a letter. He felt himself drawn toward the Bible by a "secret power and magic": "I began to read the Bible around my thirtieth year, and this most beautiful book was my greatest love, for it stilled my years of hunger and thirst with bread and water that is sweeter than honey, and that is the honeycomb of God's truth and righteousness, and I feel toward it a special, natural predisposition. I flee, I flee, and led by my God have escaped all of life's hindrances and all desires of the flesh, in order peacefully to enjoy the embrace of the daughter of God, who surpasses in beauty all the daughters of men. The most useless nuances in it seem important to me: thus a lover always believes. The deeper and more detached from men my isolation became, the happier became my life with this most favoured of all women, and I am satisfied with this fate granted by God. A fair child has been born to me: the perfect and genuine being. I will not die childless."

"The Bible was created by God from the secret sacred images: heaven, moon, sun, stars, evening, morning, clouds, rainbow, paradise, birds, beasts, man, etc.— all images of the summit of heavenly wisdom. All of these are images, and all created things are shadows depicting eternity." "The Bible is the most sacred and wisest organ"; it is "the Word of God and the tongues of fire." "Holy Scripture is like a river or a sea. Often it reveals a depth impenetrable even to the eye of an angel, although on the surface everything seems plain and simple." "The Bible is the new world and God's new humanity, the land of the living, the land and kingdom of love, the sublime Jerusalem."

The Bible is indeed "a small or miniature world." "Is not this world a beautiful temple of the all-knowing God? But there are three worlds. The first is the common or habitable world, in which abides all that has been born; the two others are small and partial worlds. The first is the microcosm, i.e., the small or miniature world—the human being. The second is the symbolic world or the Bible. The Bible is a symbolic world, for in it are assembled the images of heavenly, earthly and subterranean creations, in order that they may become monuments inducing our thought to the understanding of eternal nature, which is concealed beneath transience as is a drawing beneath its colours." For this reason the Bible is often called the "symbolic world" or the "figurative world." The whole world is reflected in the Bible: "like sunshine upon the water and water on the surface of the blue sea, and like the colourful flowers within the artfully woven damask upon the silken field, so at the appropriate time truth opens the fair eye of eternity on the surface of the multitude of creations entwined together in the Bible, which are as innumerable as manna and snowflakes." "Not only the earth together with its fruit and offspring, but all earthly and heavenly figures, which were familiar to the ancients, especially to the Egyptian philosophers—all of these the Israelites consecrated to God."

One should, however, be able to differentiate the external form from the actual content. Skovoroda does not shy away from using the sharpest and most negative expressions for the external form of biblical truth. He dedicated three works of his later period to this problem ("Lot's Wife," "The Serpent of Israel," and "The Flood of the Serpent"). "The Bible is mute to a fool, holy to a holy man. It is the Fall to a good-for-nothing, the Resurrection to a worthy man." "The Bible is man and corpse." "The Bible is a poor and artless pipe when one employs it for corporeal things; it is the prickly thorn-bush, bitter and distasteful water, foolishness—or even, to say it insultingly, filth, dirt, trash, human excrement." In spite of this, it is the greatest musical instrument: "There is nothing greater or more powerful than when one plays it, not for the elements, but for God, not to transience, but to eternity, to the Lord and not to the world." "Our senseless impudence scorns it and does not seek to know it. Creation seems laughable to us; God's rest after his labour, his regret and ire, the formation of Adam from clay, the giving of life's breath, the expulsion from paradise, Lot's drunkenness, Sarah in labour, the Flood, the Tower of Babel, walking upon the sea, the command to sacrifice, the labyrinth of the civil laws, the wandering into any new land, strange wars and victories, the peculiar division of the earth, etc. Is it possible that Enoch and Elijah were taken to heaven? Is it consistent with nature that Joshua made the sun stand still? That the Jordan reversed its course? That iron floated? That there was a virgin who gave birth? That a man could be resurrected? What sort of judge is in the rainbow? What sort of river of fire? What sort of jaws of hell? Believe this, you uncouth antiquity! Our age is enlightened. I do not wonder in the least—they take possession of this inheritance without taste and without teeth; they chew only the simple, bitter crust." "When one reads in the divine book: drunkenness, concubinage, incest, dalliance and the like, one does not stay in these streets of Sodom. For the Bible does not lead to these streets, but rather through them to the high, unsullied lands; it does not lead to this corporeal deception, but rather to the eternal. The Bible has nothing to do with the stomach, with this our sham god, with marriage, with the emperor of the flesh. It is entirely with the sublime God." For the Bible is "Pascha," i.e., "passage, crossing, exit and entrance." "Remove your shoes at home and turn to the divine. For this crossing the Bible is bridge and ladder. There you will find, instead of transience, eternity."

The Bible is pictured as a snake, for the snake has a dual symbolic function. "This seven-headed dragon, the Bible, from which flow waves of bitter waters, has covered the entire globe with superstition. This is nothing other than senseless understanding, but brought into being and defended by God." "The Bible is God and the snake—it is flesh and spirit, nonsense and wisdom, sea and port, flood and ark," it is "the snake, but at the same time God as well. Deceitful, but also truthful. Foolish, and at the same time omniscient. Evil and good at the same time." For the snake "is clever and winds itself into a ring so that one cannot see where it means to go unless one discovers its head. Thus is eternity everywhere and nowhere, because it is invisible, in that it covers its face. As is apparent from its name, the snake has sharp sight. The Greek word δέρκω means "see"; δράκω means "will see"; δρακῶν—"the one seeing beforehand," i.e., the clairvoyant. There is nothing more difficult than for the uncleansed eye to see eternity. When you have thoroughly chewed and tasted these words, "In the beginning was the Word," then understand that the Bible, which has extended its entire figurative Word into a vision of eternity, has itself become God: and God became the Word. Thus I can say without hesitation that the Bible is God and the snake." The snake "spits out the waters of the flood," "spits out nonsense." It "leads the Christian soul into temptation," as for example those who expected the end of the world a thousand years after Christ. "This slanderer will whisper to you that God weeps, becomes angry, sleeps, regrets… Then he relates that men turn into pillars of salt; raise themselves up to the planets; travel in chariots on the bottom of the sea and through the air; that the sun, like a chariot, stops and turns back; that iron floats; that rivers reverse their courses; that city walls fall from trumpet blasts; that mountains skip like lambs; rivers clap their hands; forests and fields rejoice; wolves befriend sheep; oxen graze with lions; children play with snakes; dead bodies are resurrected; stars come from apple trees and groats and quail from the clouds; that wine is made from water; that after drinking it the dumb speak and sing beautifully, etc., etc. Do you not see that the snake crawls over these lies, devours lies, spits out lies? Gaze upon the entire globe and the poor human race. Do you see? Do you see how it is harassed, besieged, inundated with a painful and miserable flood of heresies, conflicts, superstitions, various and disparate faiths? This flood, however, was not sent to us from above, but rather was spat out at us with loathing by those same infernal serpent's jaws, spewed forth in vomit. Now say what this snake deserves for its vomit, its senselessness, for all these injuries and torments, for its ubiquitous laughter; for all this disgrace and horror." "Be merciful and grieve for the innumerable martyrs who sought holiness; those miserable unfortunates who, misled by the lies of this tormentor, gouged out the eyes leading them into temptation, cut off their testicles for the Kingdom of Heaven, or set themselves on fire in great numbers. God captures men with faith, but He also captures them with superstition."

Skovoroda wants to "bring the snake to trial." He comes to the conclusion that the snake must be "raised" from the earth, i.e., that the Bible must be symbolically interpreted. This symbolic interpretation will have the same effect as the bronze snake in the desert, through whose appearance the Jews bitten by snakes were healed.

At one point the Bible is also compared to the sphinx: "What is the Bible? It is the ancient sphinx, the virgin-lion, virgin and lion at the same time. She meets you on your way through the world, where, like a lion, she searches for one whom she can devour."

Skovoroda characterizes the literal interpretation of the Bible as especially injurious and shameful: it leads to superficial disputes, to trivial polemics, superstition, fanaticism, and the formation of sects. "How many pride themselves on their quibbling over Divine Scripture! They puff themselves up with their knowledge of history, geography and mathematics, but always merely through corporeal knowledge." "From such tendencies are born schisms, superstition, and all the other corruption that disturbs the whole of Europe." This renders comprehensible Skovoroda's assertion that the Bible has "brought the Jewish and later also the Christian peoples innumerable and abundant floods of superstition. From this superstition were born oppositions, conflicts, sects, particular and universal enmities, physical and verbal melees, childish fears, etc." "One says to the superstitious person, 'Listen, friend! This cannot happen...this is contrary to nature...something is hidden here...' But he bitterly cries with all his might that Elijah's horse could actually fly, that iron floated, the waters parted, the Jordan reversed its course, that the sun stood still above Joshua, that at the time of Adam snakes possessed human speech... So!...drunk with these dregs, the superstitious man carouses, proclaiming nonsense, as he declares all who differ with him to be enemies and heretics. It is better not to read and not to hear than to read without eyes and hear without ears, and to learn in vain. That is childish sophistry." "The Bible is the deceit and foolishness of God, not because it teaches a lie, but rather because it has laid traces and paths for us in this lie that lead the creeping mind to the heights of truth." "The seed of truth has locked itself within this deceit as in a shell." And "there is no greater malignancy for society than superstition: pamphlets for the hypocrite, a mask for the impostor, a shadow for the loafer, incitement and stimulus for those with a childish mind."

The Bible thus has a dual nature. It is only a *path* to the knowledge of God. "When the path leads out of the valley toward the mountains, its first part lies deep and the last part as high as the mountain to which it leads. Its lowest part takes up those dwelling deeper in the valley, and its higher part ascends to the heights; just for this reason it is called wings, door, end or boundary, haven, sand or coast bordering the sea, and wall. The wall signifies a boundary in that it separates the foreign from that which is ours. And why should this wall made by God not be called a boundary when it is the boundary between the light and the foreign darkness? The wall has a dark side, that which faces the darkness. But the side that faces west is the inner side, and is fully gilded by God's light from on high, so that when he who lives in darkness comes to the door, which outwardly is dark, he sees no beauty and turns back, returning home to darkness. This mediator is also like a bridge linking God and mortals. But if this wondrous bridge conveys mortals into life, then it is worthy to be called resurrection."

In connection with his theory of biblical interpretation, Skovoroda relates a parable that not only expresses his point of view, but is also characteristic of his poetic style: "The Bible is also similar to an ugly cave in which there lived a hermit and where his brother once came to visit him… 'Say, little brother, what keeps you in this dark dwelling?' On hearing these words the hermit pulled away a curtain hanging on the wall. 'Oh, my God!' cried the guest as he beheld a splendour loftier than all human understanding. 'This, brother, is what delights me,' said the recluse. Then the one brother remained to live always with the other." "Imagine a beautiful, fragrant garden upon a mountain that is full of eternal comfort. We would wish that the guests enter! But it is impossible to make one's way inside. Impenetrable thickets, impassable briars, and pathless areas surround this paradise! O sweetest truth of God! When will we penetrate through to you? The ceremonial thornbush does not permit us to pass. We are stuck fast in it. And on the other side of this hardest of walls you, our joy, shine. Who will lead us through the desert?" The Bible "is also like a fish net containing a multitude of globes of precious stone, the worth of which is unknown."

One could say that the preoccupation with the Bible, the analysis of symbolic "images," and the revelation of the content concealed in these images is for Skovoroda an ethical, "gnostic," and religious task. A possible goal in life—perhaps one of the highest possible. "A hermit lived in the deepest isolation. Every day at sunrise he went into a large garden. In the garden there lived a fair

Life and Thought of Skovoroda 55

and gentle bird. The hermit beheld with curiosity the wonderful qualities of this bird, rejoiced, captured him, and thus time went by imperceptibly for him. The bird purposely sat down next to him, encouraging him to try to capture it, and seemed a thousand times to be in his hands, but he could not capture the bird. 'Do not be sad, my friend,' said the bird, 'that you cannot capture me. You will grasp for me your whole life long without catching me, simply as entertainment.' Once the hermit's friend came to see him. After greeting each other, they began a discussion. 'Tell me,' said the guest, 'how do you occupy yourself in this bleak desert? I would have died of boredom here long ago.' 'I have two entertainments,' said the hermit, 'the bird and the beginning. I hunt the bird, but never catch him. I have a thousand and one ornate silken knots. I seek their beginning, but cannot find it.'"

Skovoroda's attitude to the Bible goes back by and large to early Christian exegesis. Any attempt to see the influence of rationalism and the eighteenth-century Enlightenment in his negative attitude toward the formation of sects or in his sharp words against the outward expression of biblical ideas, or indeed to make Skovoroda into a fighter against Christianity, can only be the product of a complete ignorance of the history of Christian theology.

The negative attitude toward the "letter" of Scripture is the same in every symbolic interpretation—inevitably so, since it was believed that one could gain access to the inner hidden meaning only through the complete removal and analysis of the external shell. Philo, who, like other representatives of the "Alexandrine school," was one of the first to apply this exegetical approach to the Bible, and who exercised the most decisive influence upon Christian exegesis, depended here, as elsewhere, perhaps, on Plato. He could find in Plato not merely the boldest explication of Homer, but also a passage that may be interpreted as the direct theoretical foundation for such an exegetical method. I refer to the differentiation between the letter and the internal unity of the language, which is contrasted with the letter. As we have seen, the principle held true for Philo himself that "after the literal narration, it is proper to render the allegorical sense as well, since in all, or at least most of the laws there is an allegorical sense." Sense perception generally is "poor in fools, good in wise men." One has to penetrate it in order to find the true meaning. Philo differentiates three senses of Scripture. Stories and letters are worthless shadows. Philo even explains the creation story allegorically. We find precisely the same interpretation in the Church Fathers. According to Clement of Alexandria, one should not be satisfied with the "corporeal" sense of Scripture, but rather search for the concealed meaning; the literal side of Scripture must be lifted away when it contains something unworthy of God. Letter and meaning have the same relationship to each other as shell and seed. Origen says the same thing. Scripture is obscure. "In each line one finds a key, but not that which belongs to it; the keys are strewn in disorder around the entire house, and is it difficult to locate and choose them." "The literal sense often contains that which is false, unreasonable, contradictory, impossible, useless, and things from which an infinite number of errors have arisen." "What soundly thinking man can accept that there was a first, second, and third day—with morning, evening, and night, when there were neither sun nor moon nor stars nor even a heaven on the first day? Who would be so stupid as to believe that God, like a farmer, planted trees in paradise, among which was also the tree of the knowledge of good and evil; that he went for an afternoon walk in the garden looking for Adam, who had hidden himself under a tree... Can one doubt that all this is to be understood in a mystical sense?" For Gregory of Nyssa the "body of Scripture" is merely a "wall or a garment covering the true meaning." Gregory put up fierce resistance to literal interpretation: "no one can be so stupid" as to interpret Scripture literally. The contemptuous attitude of the "Areopagitica" concerning literalness is understandable without further explanation. If one were to accept Scripture literally, "one would soon believe that the celestial regions were filled with lions, bands of horses, a multitude of birds and other animals and a great variety of other things." Maximus the Confessor also attacks a literal reading of Scripture.

These patristic motifs were sounded again in German mysticism, especially after the Reformation. But even before the Reformation we find isolated remarks tending in this direction. Sharp attacks were directed against the "letter" of Scripture, against "ceremonies," i.e., against the cultic aspects of religion, which revolve precisely around this false literal interpretation of Scripture.

Remarks of this nature by Tauler are modelled on Scripture itself: "for God is a lover of hearts, and that which is external does not concern him, but rather the inner living good will, which carries benevolence within it—not all that which is external, such as fasting, vigils, and other things. Sebastian Franck sounds sharp notes; many passages are quite reminiscent of Skovoroda. The letter is a kind of cipher: "Christ himself says clearly that he speaks allegorically, employing parables (as did Pythagoras with his disciples), so that the secret would remain within the school, hidden by the mantle of the letter." "The letter, therefore, without the light of the Holy Spirit, is like a darkened lantern. Likewise the Old Testament, law, Scripture, and letter. Without the light, the life, the sense, and the interpretation of the Holy Spirit there remains nothing but a killing letter and by no means the Word of God." If one understands Scripture according to the letter, then one would have to "chop off his hands, pluck out his eyes, eat the flesh and drink the blood of Christ." "Because the letter of Scripture is divided and at odds with itself, sects arise. This one taps the dead letter here, that one there. This one understands how it sounds here, that one how it rings there... Now certainly, all sects are from the devil and a fruit of the flesh, bound to time, space, individual, law, and element." "Ceremonies, likewise, are only shadows or images." Godless scripture ("letter") is a "darkened lantern," "a foul cistern." "God's word is a two-edged sword/ he who cannot handle it in the Lord/ cuts himself easily." Franck speaks of a "labyrinth of the letter." Scripture is "peculiar and contentious"; it may be "divided." Franck demonstrates this "division" in the "butchered book" by counterposing quotations that apparently have conflicting meanings. This makes possible the misunderstanding of Scripture. "The Word of God/...is impure to the impure/ and a cause of their becoming evil." Therefore one may say that "the Gospel is a seditious element in the world; the truth a cause for rebellion," "prayer is forbidden to the godless man and is sacrilegious for him." "Scripture is death to the world and a trap; it is life and light to the pious alone"; still further, "God is the devil of the world, Christ the world's Antichrist."

Valentin Weigel, in particular, comes from this tradition. "The Bible was written only as a protection, a reminder, for the faith or spirit of God in us. If you do not have this, if you do not live this, then Scripture is a darkened lantern, indeed a trap, an offense, poison, as we unfortunately experience in all sects, since each and every one cites Scripture, and yet they are unable to agree..." "Scripture is bright and clear, and is the Word of God; Scripture is dark and obscure, indeed poison and death." One should "make judgements based not on the dead letter, but rather on faith in the Spirit, through the inner living judgement in the heart." The devil can "disguise himself as an angel of light and change costume, covering himself with the cloak of Scripture." "The written letter is the shadow of the Word; it is not the Word, but only a reminder of the Word."

> Guess, guess, what is this?
> A white field and black seed,
> Many men traverse it
> and know not what lies therein.

He attacks ceremonies ("The Ceremonial Sand," according to Skovoroda) just as sharply as Franck: "Scholars merely quarrel and dispute over this Scripture about intermediate things/ ceremonies/ and about the washing of hands/ about sacrifice and other things/ that neither make men holy nor damn them/ neither sweet not sour/ do not concern the internal man at all/..." The human church, or the church of ceremony, is painted in the blackest colours: its members are "wolves," "bears and lions," "blind men," "thieves and murderers." "Disputes over the sacraments are in vain"; "Vainly does/ one sect persecute another and accuse it of heresy concerning the sacraments." "Any sect that wages war on another/ persecutes it/ shows only that/ it does not belong to the holy church/ and does not abide in Christ." By propagating false sectarian teachings "you put out your listener's eyes/ deprive him of the hearing and tongues of the inner man." In Weigel we find the teaching, which later became very widespread and whose beginnings go back to Philo and Clement of Alexandria, that God revealed himself in three ways: in the world, the Bible and man himself. This is the origin of Skovoroda's "three worlds." "The Word lies hidden in three places. 1. In the letter of Scripture/ then it is learned from God. 2. It lies hidden in the flesh/ no one knows it/ then it is taken from the Father. 3. It lies in the heart/ no one finds it/ but the believer enlightened by the Holy Spirit."

Böhme is also among those who set themselves against the literal reading of Scripture. He also attacks "ceremonies": "O you world of Antichrist/ what have you done with your ceremonies/ that you have placed them in God's stead: Had you told the sinner of God's wrath and punishment and the Devil's false inclination/ how he must abandon his sins for the will of God and be born, trusting fully in GOD, with true remorse and penitence/ search and ensure/ that all false will,/ desire and covetousness are driven out of his heart/ how well would you have taught!... But the councils are only established so that/ you may be lord/ of silver and gold/ and of men's souls and consciences. Thus you too are Antichrist in your hypocrisy/ you have established ceremonies/ and dissemble in Aaron's image... But it is blasphemy/ that captures the heart/ and leads it into the trap of hypocrisy: it would be better if there were no ceremonies, but rather simple adherence to God's most earnest command/ that He left us in his covenant and testament." "All external ceremonies without an inner foundation/ without the spirit and aid of Christ/ are prostitution before GOD." And similarly, Angelus Silesius:

> Holy Scripture
> Just as the spider sucks poison from the rose/
> so do the evil attain the opposite of 'God's Scripture.

The idea of three worlds in which God reveals himself became widespread after Böhme's time, turning into a common feature of modern German mysticism. As noted above, however, this concept of "three worlds" or "three books" derives from older motifs to be found perhaps in Plotinus, and certainly in the Church Fathers. Among the Byzantine theologians, Maximus the Confessor represented this viewpoint. In more modern times it is to be found in Arnd's "True Christianity," and also to some extent in his "Iconographia." For Arnd, in addition to the Bible, there is also "the inward and the outward book," i.e., "the large and the small world, both of which, if they are illuminated by divine light, are a bright and clear mirror" in which divine secrets may be recognized. The theosophical mysticism of modern times links this with the "astral scripture." Stars are the natural images of letters. For Weigel, as well, "fair creation is a book in which one may read God's eternal goodness; therefore no one may excuse himself and say he knew nothing of God..." Even before Böhme, who adopted this idea, we find the concept of the three worlds. There are three books by the mysterious forgotten mystic, Bartholomaeus Scleus (1596, published only in 1686): God has "very wondrously/ richly and most generously revealed/ described and disclosed his Holy Name/ and his immutable good will to the whole world/ primarily and especially to his chosen ones/ in triple fashion/ way and manner/ in three scriptures and mirrors/ or in three living images or alphabets.... The first one is the MACROCOSM, the second the MESOCOSM, and the third the MICROCOSM. These are the large/ middle and small worlds." "If mortal man cannot grasp/ his Lord God/ or the knowledge of God in a book/ which is in external creation/ then he should turn to the other/ namely the Holy Scripture/ the living Word of God/ if this be for him too obscure/ too dim and too difficult/ then he should turn to the third/ the inwardly concealed world/ which is closest to him/ and thus go into himself/ and learn to know God in himself/ or from himself." This idea is also to be found in the Rosicrucian writings: "The great wondrous book of nature agrees with the Bible"; "nature" and the Bible are equally valued sources of knowledge; the macrocosm corresponds to the microcosm. For Comenius as well there are two paths to wisdom—the world and Holy Scripture. "He wished to explain the world and everything in it and then to assemble a theatre of divine secrets in Scripture." This was unquestionably the main tendency in Comenius' pansophical activities, as well as in his pedagogical ones. Elsewhere he speaks of nature, Scripture, and innate concepts as the three foundations of knowledge given by God. We find the same in Franckenberg. Modern Catholic mysticism voices the same ideas: thus Blosius, "All the world is a book... in it the spiritual and contemplative man recognizes the glory of the Creator." Similar thoughts are expressed by Angelus Silesius:

> Creation is a book: he who reads it wisely/
> to him will God be revealed.

> Many books/ much trouble! He who has read one well
> (I mean Jesus Christ)/ has joy forever.

> —Christ became a living book.
> Man/ if your heart does not become the book of life
> you will never be admitted to God.

> Friend/ it is also enough. If you wish to read more,
> go and become yourself the Scripture and the Being.

Later, for Oetinger, "Scripture mirrors within it the entire development of the world." The views of J.M. Hahn are similar. And we encounter related ideas in Baader and Schelling.

Unquestionably the two streams of mystical interpretation—that of the patristic tradition and that of modern mysticism—flow together in Skovoroda. A number of years after Skovoroda's death, the same occurred in Baader, whose "analogi cal method is reminiscent of Philo, but also of Clement and Origen," and, we might add, also of the modern German mystics. But for Baader as well, Scripture is thoroughly ambiguous, good or bad, dim or bright—"to whom it is given by the Father, he sees everywhere brightly and clearly, where others do not see and deny."

Translated by Walter Petrovitz and Gus Fagan

Original text: Dmitrij Tschižewskij, *Skovoroda: Dichter, Denker, Mystiker* (Munich: Fink, 1974), 9-73.

Part One

Skovoroda and Society

Skovoroda and Society[1]

Stephen P. Scherer

The literature on Hryhorij Savyč Skovoroda (1722-94) is marked by a number of efforts to interpret his life and thought in "class" terms. These interpretations depict him variously as the representative of either an "upper-class or non-class ideology,"[2] a "petty-bourgeois position,"[3] or the "peasants and lower Cossacks."[4] The purposes of this work are: 1) to examine, however briefly, Skovoroda's basic criticisms of society; 2) to discover how his life and thought reflected these critical views; 3) to conclude from this whether one can consider Skovoroda the representative of any particular class and, if not, to determine what his relationship to society was.

When one speaks of Skovoroda's society he means, naturally, Ukrainian society. Skovoroda's attachment to Ukraine was both conscious and profound, as witness his reference to Little Russia as "my mother" and Ukraine as "my aunt."[5] This love for his homeland drew Skovoroda back to Ukraine on a num-

---

1. This article was first published in *Ukrajins'kyj istoryk*, no. 3-4 (1971):12-22.
2. D.I. Bahalij, *Ukrainskij stranstvujuščij filosof G.S. Skovoroda* (Xarkiv, 1922), 38.
3. B.V. Skickij, "Social'naja filosofija G. Skovorody," *Izvestija Gorskogo Pedagogičeskogo Instituta*, VII (Ordžonikidze, 1933), 53.
4. V.E. Evdokimenko and I.A. Tabačnikov, "Filosofskaja i sociologičeskaja mysl' narodov SSSR s konca XVI do poslednej treti XVIII v. Ukraina," Akademija Nauk SSSR, *Istorija filosofii v SSSR*, 5 vols. (Moscow, 1968), I:411.
5. Skovoroda, "Pis'mo do M.I. Kovalinskogo," in H.S. Skovoroda, *Tvory v dvox tomax*, ed. O.I. Bilec'kyj (Kyiv, 1961), II:386. Hereafter cited as *TDT*. Skovoroda not only identified himself with Little Russia and Ukraine, but distinguished between them. He considered Hetman Ukraine, where he was born, as Little Russia, and Slobids'ka Ukraine, where he spent the greater part of his adult

ber of occasions, in 1744 after a two and one-half year stay with the Imperial choir in St. Petersburg, in 1750 after a five-year sojourn in the West, in 1755 after a visit to the monastery of the Holy Trinity and St. Sergius near Moscow, and in 1794, the year of his death, after a final meeting near Orel with his close friend and biographer M.I. Kovalins'kyj.[6] Since Skovoroda lived and worked in Ukraine, with which he consciously and passionately identified himself, it follows that one wishing to understand his relationship to society should consider, at least in general terms, the political, social, and economic developments in Ukraine during the late seventeenth and eighteenth centuries.

With the Xmel'nyc'kyj rebellion of 1648, Poland began to lose its control of Ukraine, which from that time onward fell gradually under the political sway of Russia. The treaties of Perejaslav (1654) and Andrusovo (1667), however controversial, created a situation that Russia exploited to the political disadvantage of Ukraine. Russian political control of Ukraine, which began to develop with the rebellion of 1648, was not completed until the early 1780s, when Catherine II destroyed the last independent Ukrainian political institutions. Skovoroda, therefore, witnessed the final episodes in Russia's abolition of Ukrainian independence, a situation to which he referred adversely, though obliquely, when he wrote that "you profane when you introduce the slave yoke and hard labour into a country of perfect peace and freedom."[7] While this criticism was indirect, Skovoroda made a more candid attack on Russia's ruin of Ukrainian independence in a poem entitled "De Libertate."

> What is freedom? Is it any good?
> Some say it is like unto gold.
> But freedom is not like gold at all,
> For freedom to gold is like wine to gall.
> No matter how one embroiders it,
> My freedom I shall ne'er forfeit.
> Glory forever, o chosen one,
> The father of freedom, heroic Bohdan.[8]

---

life, as Ukraine. For the purposes of this essay the whole region will be referred to simply as Ukraine or left-bank Ukraine. M.I. Kovalinskij, "Žizn' Grigorija Skovorody," *TDT* II:51.

6. Kovalinskij, "Žizn'," *TDT* II:489, 490, 492, 530; Leonid Maxnovec', *Hryhorij Skovoroda: Biohrafija* (Kyiv, 1972), 68-74.

7. Skovoroda, "Knižečka o čtenii svjaščennago pisanija narečenna Žena Lotova," in G. S. Skovoroda, *Sobranie sočinenij*, vol. 5 of *Materialy k istorii i izučeniju russkago sektantstva i staroobrjadčestva*, ed. by V. Bonč-Bruevič (St. Petersburg, 1908-12), 405. Hereafter cited as *Sobranie sočinenij*.

8. Skovoroda, "De Libertate," *TDT* II:80. The reference to "Bohdan" was to Bohdan Xmel'nyc'kyj, who led the 1648 rebellion against Ukraine's Polish overlords. In harking back to Xmel'nyc'kyj, Skovoroda honoured not only the ideal of Ukrainian independence, but also his own Cossack ancestors, who participated in the struggle to achieve it.

Skovoroda's praise of freedom and especially his veneration of Bohdan Xmel'nyc'kyj made this poem an indictment of Russia, whose subjugation of Ukraine was the negation of all that Xmel'nyc'kyj sought and later symbolized.[9]

The remark about the "slave yoke," as well as the poem "De Libertate," with its implied denunciation of those who would sell freedom for their own financial gain, demonstrate that Skovoroda was critical not only of Russia's destruction of Ukrainian independence but also of the social and economic transformations that accompanied this development, the enserfment of the Ukrainian peasantry and the ennoblement of the Cossack officer class. By the late seventeenth century the Cossack officers were becoming the great landowners of Ukraine. In the 1730s, in an effort to ensure themselves the labour necessary to work their estates, they petitioned the Hetman for the abolition of the right of free movement for the peasantry.[10] With the passage of time and the decline of the Hetmanate these requests were addressed to the Russian ruler. Such petitions did not go unheeded, for by decrees of December 1763 and May 1783 Catherine II first restricted the free movement of the Ukrainian peasantry[11] and then abolished it altogether.[12] With these decrees Catherine positioned the last legal planks in the structure of Ukrainian serfdom.

The transformation of the Cossack officer class into members of the Russian nobility accompanied Ukraine's loss of independence and the imposition of serfdom on the Ukrainian peasantry. In fact, all three were interdependent parts of the larger process by which Russia assimilated Ukraine. The creation of this new nobility was completed by Catherine's "Charter to the Nobility" of 1785.[13] Throughout the eighteenth century, therefore, and culminating in the 1780s the Cossack officers, impelled by both the pressure and the encouragement of the Russians, traded Ukrainian independence and the socio-economic position of the Ukrainian peasantry for their own social and economic advantage.[14]

---

9. Skovoroda's negative attitude concerning the consequences of the Russian advance into Ukraine is also witnessed by the following passage: "The hunter does not sleep. Be alert. Carelessness is the mother of misfortune... Indeed, Great Russia considers all of Little Russia as so many grouse. Why be ashamed? The grouse is a stupid bird, but not an evil one." Skovoroda, "Ubogij Žajvoronok: Posvjaščenie," *Sobranie sočinenij,* 479. While this remark was only an aside in the dedication to "Ubogij Žajvoronok," Skovoroda's characterization of the Russo-Ukrainian relationship as one similar to that which obtains between the hunter and the grouse demonstrates how clearly he perceived contemporary events.
10. V.I. Semevskij, *Krest'janskij vopros v Rossii v XVIII i pervoj polovine XIX veka* (St. Petersburg, 1888), I:148.
11. *Polnoe sobranie zakonov Rossijskoj imperii,* Ser. I, XVI, no. 11987.
12. Ibid., XXI, no. 15724.
13. V.A. Mjakotin, *Očerki social'noj istorii Ukrainy v XVII i XVIII vv.* (Prague, 1926), I, pt. 2, 262.
14. Geroid Tanquary Robinson has aptly remarked that this social change "resembles that already observed in the older territories of Muscovy—a compromise between autocrat and aristocrat, at the

If Skovoroda was conscious of his society's lack of freedom, he was even more aware of its low level of spirituality. He incessantly challenged the capacity of the Orthodox church for moral leadership, but particularly in the following veiled attack upon the institutional church:

> The divine law exists eternally, but human tradition [i.e., the institutional church] is neither universal nor eternal. The divine law is the tree of paradise, but human tradition is only its shadow. The law of God is the fruit of life, but tradition is only its leaves. The law of God is God in the human heart, while tradition is the fig leaf that conceals a viper.[15]

Along with this he bitterly criticized what had traditionally been the spiritual centre of Orthodoxy, its monasteries. This attitude was typified by his rejection of an offer to take monastic orders in 1760, a rejection accompanied by the following outburst:

> Do you really wish that I should increase the number of the Pharisees? Eat richly, drink sweetly, dress softly and monasticize! But Skovoroda believes monastic life to consist of a non-acquisitive life, satisfaction with little, abstinence, ...the bridling of self-love in order to fulfill more easily the commandment of love for our neighbour, and the search for divine rather than human glory.[16]

Finally, Skovoroda's indictment of the Orthodox church included his view that its members were, in the main, unreflective and superstitious louts. His concern for the seriousness of this problem led him to contend that, "Nothing is more destructive for society than superstition," and to conclude that, "It was with good reason that Plutarch believed superstition to be more harmful than godlessness."[17]

---

cost, in larger part, of the ploughman." G.T. Robinson, *Rural Russia under the Old Regime* (London, 1932), 24.

15. Skovoroda, "Načal'naja dver' ko xristianskomu dobronraviju," *Sobranieسočinenij*, 71-2. Skovoroda wrote "Načal'naja dver'..." in 1768 and used it as the basis for a series of moral lectures that he gave in 1768-9 in Xarkiv. The anti-church content of these lectures was such that they were delivered under the aegis of the Governor rather than under that of the Bishop. N.I. Petrov, "K biografii ukrainskogo filosofa Grigorija Savviča Skovorody," *Kievskaja starina*, no. 4 (1903):II, 14-16; Vasyl' Kuk, "Do 250-riččja vid narodžennja H. S. Skovorody," *Literaturna Ukraina*, 16 July 1971, 2.

16. Kovalinskij, "Žizn'," *TDT* II:498. See also "Žizn'," 493, and Skovoroda's reference to the "monkish masquerade." Skovoroda, "Beseda narečennaja Dvoe," *Sobranie sočinenij*, 206. Skovoroda's excoriation of monastic life seems especially appropriate when one considers that his own invitation to it on this occasion was marked by counsels concerning the worldly glory and honours that it would provide him. Kovalinskij, "Žizn'," *TDT* II:498.

17. Skovoroda, "Pis'mo k S.I. Tevjašovu," *Sobranie sočinenij*, 362. Skovoroda was fond of a number of classical thinkers and authors, including, besides Plutarch, Pythagoras, Socrates, Plato, Aristotle, Zeno, Epicurus, and Seneca. His admiration for these classical figures evinced his belief

Despite his negative outlook concerning the church, its monasteries and its membership, Skovoroda retained his belief in Orthodoxy's most crucial dogmas, the trinity of God and the divinity of Jesus Christ.[18] Still, his opposition to the church impelled him to seek a more spiritual and ascetic Christianity, one removed from a slavish dependence on both material forms and comforts. In this personal quest for a more spiritual Christianity Skovoroda resembled the "Protestant" sects that developed in Russia and Ukraine during the middle and late eighteenth century, the Doukhobors and the Molokane. Skovoroda and these sectarians knew and admired each other, but in spite of their affinities and mutual affection Skovoroda did not become a sectarian.[19] Two reasons explain his refusal to join with them. First, he rejected the general concept of sectarianism, i.e., the identification of a group of people according to their religious and moral ideals. He indicated this opposition when, in answer to a question about the Martinists,[20] he declared:

> Every sect smells of proprietorship, and where wisdom is property there can be neither the highest aim nor the highest wisdom. I do not know the Martinists, their reasoning or their teachings; if they adopt distinctive rules and ritual so that they may appear wise then I do not want to know them; if they philosophize with simplicity of heart in order to be useful citizens of society, then I esteem them... Love of neighbour has no sects.[21]

Second, Skovoroda disagreed theologically with the Doukhobors and Molokane, since he firmly believed in the Orthodox dogmas of the divine trinity and the divinity of Jesus Christ, and they did not.[22] The result of Skovoroda's disenchantment with the official church therefore was that, while he remained rather Orthodox theologically and did not openly leave the church, he was inclined to

---

in both the efficacy of thought and the universality of truth.

18. Skovoroda, "Dialog. Imja emu: Potop Zmiin," *Sobranie sočinenij*, 511-12; on Skovoroda's theological agreement with Orthodoxy see also: A.S. Lebedev, "G.S. Skovoroda kak bogoslov," *Voprosy filosofii i psixologii*, no. 2 (1895):170-77.

19. There is a marked similarity between Skovoroda's ideas and those advanced by the Ekaterinoslav Doukhobors in their apology of 1791, though it is impossible to prove that Skovoroda directly influenced the writing of this document. P. Miljukov, *Očerki po istorii russkoj kul'tury* (Paris, 1951), II, pt. 1, 124. Along with this it is well known that the Molokane admired some of Skovoroda's works and even used one of his songs in their services. F.V. Livanov, *Raskol'niki i ostrožniki* (St. Petersburg, 1872), II:236-7; F. Kundrinskij, "Filosof bez sistemy," *Kievskaja starina*, no. 3 (1898):436-7.

20. A term sometimes applied to the Russian Masons, many of whom were followers of the French author Claude St. Martin (1743-1803), himself a theosophist and an adherent of Jakob Böhme.

21. Kovalinskij, "Žizn'," *TDT* II: 524.

22. See N.I. Kostomarov, "Vospominanija o Molokanax," *Otečestvennye zapiski*, no. 3 (1869): 60-61; Frederick Conybeare, *Russian Dissenters* (London, 1921), 295; S. Bolshakoff, *Russian Nonconformity* (Philadelphia, 1950), 104.

be somewhat sectarian spiritually.

Skovoroda's praise of freedom, denunciation of the desire for wealth[23] and attack on the Orthodox church demonstrated his negative attitude toward both "official" society and the "official" church. These attitudes, however, were not manifested in heightened political or social activity directed toward the transformation or regeneration of society. For instance, Skovoroda did not propose that the petty bourgeoisie or the peasantry agitate to ameliorate their existence.[24] At the same time he exhibited a rather cavalier opinion on the whole problem of a more equitable distribution of land.[25] Finally, he maintained cordial relations with many individual members of officialdom, the gentry and the clergy, which gives reason to conclude that he did not consider them the enemy *per se*.[26]

Although Skovoroda's negative attitudes toward society and the church did not result in any political or social militancy, they were reflected in both his life and work.[27] This reflection seems to have been threefold: 1) in his life-style; 2) in his vocation; 3) in the content of his thought. Concerning Skovoroda's life-style, a young contemporary wrote that:

> He owned almost nothing, his only possessions being the clothes that he wore. He had no permanent residence... It was his passion to travel from settlement to settlement, from village to village, from farm to farm... The people of the settlements, villages and farms loved him like a member of the family.[28]

This description correctly identified the poverty and incessant travel that characterized Skovoroda's life, but it omitted any mention of the lonely and solitary aspect of his existence. Skovoroda's disciple and biographer, M.I. Kovalins'kyj,

---

23. While Skovoroda's censure of wealth in "De Libertate" appears to have had socio-political grounds, his negative attitude toward the accumulation of money was also based upon moral considerations. Skovoroda, "Razgovor družeskij o duševnom mire," *Sobranie sočinenij*, 220.

24. Concerning Skovoroda's position on the efficacy of a mass movement to effect social change, it is worth noting that nowhere in his work did he even mention the Pugačev uprising (1773-5) or the hajdamaka revolts (1734, 1750, 1768).

25. "If someone who owns land is happy," he argued, "he is not happy because he owns it: Happiness is not attached to landownership." Skovoroda, "Razgovor nazyvaemyj alfavit ili bukvar' mira," *Sobranie sočinenij*, 327.

26. See, for example, Kovalinskij, "Žizn'," *TDT* II:511, 517-20, 530-31; G.P. Danilevskij, "Grigorij Savvič Skovoroda," *Sočinenija G.P. Danilevskago* (St. Petersburg, 1901), XXI:80; N.A. Batalin, "Anekdot o G.S. Skovorode," *Moskvitjanin*, 1849, XXIV, ch. 3, 68.

27. Skovoroda demonstrated his outlook concerning the close relationship between understanding and action in accord with that understanding when he wrote: "It is not difficult to know, but to become habituated. Learning and habit are the same. They reside not in knowledge but in action. Knowledge unaccompanied by action is a torment." Skovoroda, "Basni Xar'kovskija," *TDT* II:113.

28. F.P. Lubjanovskij, "Vospominanija Fedora Petroviča Lubjanovskago," *Russkij arxiv*, 1872, cols. 106-7. See also Gustav Hess de Kalve and Ivan Vernet, "Skovoroda: Ukrainskij filosof," *Ukrainskij vestnik*, no. 4 (1817):111-12.

described this feature of his life when he noted that, "in all the places where he lived, he always chose a solitary corner and lived simply, without any ado."[29] Skovoroda's propensity for solitude was such that he even had to defend himself against charges of misanthropy.[30] His sense of social responsibility led him to oppose any inordinate pursuit of solitude, however, and he wrote concerning this question, "Do you flee from the crowd? In this be moderate, for is not the man who so avoids others that he will not speak with anyone stupid? Such a man is not holy but insane."[31]

Skovoroda's choice of a poverty-stricken, peripatetic, and solitary life, accompanied as it was by his rejection of any regular job, official employment, or ecclesiastical activity, was at least partly attributable to his dissatisfaction with the secular and religious environment that obtained in Ukraine. The adoption of this style of life, then, truly reflected Skovoroda's sense of separation from "official" society, a sense of separation that Alexander Herzen, in characterizing the mid-nineteenth-century Russian intelligentsia, referred to as "a profound sense of alienation from official Russia...and together with this a desire to leave it."[32]

While Skovoroda's life-style was in part the result of his reaction against the society in which he lived, his choice of vocation, namely writing and teaching, witnessed his optimism concerning the potential for improving society.[33] Skovoroda was convinced that nothing was more valuable than a good education, and apropos of this he admonished that anyone who wanted to teach must "study a long time."[34] The study and teaching he counselled did not apply to the material world, but to the discovery of the divinity within man that alone could make man

---

29. Kovalinskij, "Žizn'," *TDT* II:520. It is worth remarking with regard to Skovoroda's life-style that he did not marry, although there is a legend that he fell in love with a beautiful girl in the course of his wanderings and then left her at the altar on their wedding day. Gustav Hess de Kalve and Ivan Vernet, "Skovoroda: Ukrainskij filosof," *Ukrainskij vestnik*, no. 4 (1817):113; I.I. Sreznevskij, "Major, major," *Moskovskij nabljudatel'*, VI (1836):205-38, 435-68, 721-39.

30. Kovalinskij, "Žizn'," *TDT* II:514-15.

31. Skovoroda, "Pis'mo k M.I. Kovalinskomu," *TDT* II:240.

32. Aleksandr Gercen, *Byloe i dumy* (Minsk, 1957), I:240. Although Herzen's description of alienation may properly be applied to Skovoroda, Herzen did not laud Skovoroda's social awareness. He attacked Skovoroda for his exclusive concern with abstruse moral questions and lack of appreciation for real human problems. Aleksandr Gercen, *Sobranie sočinenij v tridcati tomax* (Moscow, 1954-65), II:118, XIX:261.

33. Skovoroda expressed great confidence concerning his own choice of an educational occupation, as witness the following: "Understand that I would be a hundred times happier making clay pans in accord with God's will than writing in opposition to nature. But I feel, until now, that the incorruptible hand of the Eternal supports me in my occupation." Skovoroda, "Razgovor nazyvaemyj alfavit ili bukvar' mira," *Sobranie sočinenij*, 326.

34. Skovoroda, "Blagodarnyj Erodij," *Sobranie sočinenij*, 462; "Razgovor nazyvaemyj alfavit ili bukvar' mira," *Sobranie sočinenij*, 345.

happy. "Is there any empirical study," Skovoroda asked, "that teaches about peace of mind?"[35] He answered resolutely:

> I want no new sciences,
> Only a healthy mind,
> And Christ's understanding
> In which peace I'll find.[36]

The primary aim of Skovoroda's educational activity, therefore, was the creation of the spiritual vision that would provide for individual tranquillity and peace of mind. At the same time he did not neglect the indispensability of this individual spiritual vision for the development of social harmony. He argued, for instance, that the absence of such vision "gave birth to quarrels, arguments, sectarianism, civil and foreign hostilities, and verbal and armed conflicts."[37] Because he believed that individual spiritual regeneration could better social conditions, Skovoroda sought to reach all men with his message about man's divinity. This explains why he engaged in his moral discussions with peasants, landlords, officials, merchants, priests, monks, bishops, and whomever else he encountered in his wanderings through left-bank Ukraine. Finally, in so teaching all men Skovoroda evinced a certain rough egalitarianism, which, though it was based on spiritual rather than on political or social grounds, gave a decidedly democratic cast to his educational activities and further demonstrated his dedication to the spiritual improvement and subsequent social harmony of all men.[38]

Skovoroda's choice of life-style and vocation reflected the influence of his environment, but the content of his teachings did so even more. Throughout an analysis of Skovoroda's thought, one notes his overwhelming emphasis on the existence of the divine in man, nature and the Bible and the necessity of the

---

35. Skovoroda, "Kol'co," *Sobranie sočinenij*, 252.
36. Skovoroda, "Sad božestvennyx pěsnej: Pěsn' 12-ja," *TDT* II:23. In the same vein he wrote: "If a man knows Christ it is unimportant that he knows nothing else; if he does not know Christ it is unimportant that he knows everything else." Skovoroda, "Pis'ma G.S. Skovorody k svjaščenniku Ja. Pravickomu," *Bibliograf*, no. 1 (1894):9. Skovoroda did not mean by this criticism to condemn science thoroughly. "I do not censure science," he wrote, "in fact, I commend its latest achievements." What Skovoroda did censure, however, was the concern with science as something to be studied for its own sake, to the exclusion of any spiritual understanding. Skovoroda, "Razgovor družeskij o duševnom mire," *Sobranie sočinenij*, 225-7.
37. Skovoroda, "Pis'mo k S.I. Tevjašovu," *Sobranie sočinenij*, 362. He gave more concrete examples of these conflicts when he wrote that an incorrect spiritual comprehension "had set Constantinople at odds and disfigured the Parisian streets with fraternal blood...," ibid.
38. Skovoroda best articulated his conception of the spiritual equality of all men in his description of men as so many different-sized vessels filled with the water of divine nourishment. All the vessels, i.e., men—he argued—did not contain the same amount when filled to capacity, but all were equal insofar as they were "equally full." Skovoroda, "Razgovor nazyvaemyj alfavit ili bukvar' mira," *Sobranie sočinenij*, 340-41.

discovery of this divinity for man's happiness. Now one may attribute this emphasis to Skovoroda's educational background[39] or even to his highly developed religious consciousness.[40] But it would be a mistake not to consider his teachings also in light of the political, social and economic turmoil, as well as the spiritual malaise, of Ukraine in the eighteenth century. Skovoroda, faced with the tumult of his time, was impelled to seek something of permanence and stability amid the sea of change. This permanence could not exist, as such, in the physical or apparent world, since this world was so obviously transient and corruptible.[41] But neither could it exist altogether outside the physical world, for this would make the world and man's life in it absurd.[42] Faced with a patent impossibility on the one hand and an evident absurdity on the other, Skovoroda sought and found the immutable and the eternal, the permanence to which he could always cling, in a divinity that was jointly immanent and transcendent. This is not to maintain, of course, that teachings such as his could develop only

---

39. Skovoroda spent the years 1738-42 and 1744-50 at the Kyiv Academy. For indications of the religious nature of the curriculum there see: M. Bulgakov, *Istorija Kievskoj akademii* (Kyiv, 1843), 138-44; B.N. Menšutkin, *Žizneopisanie Mixaila Vasil'eviča Lomonosova* (Moscow and Leningrad, 1947), 24-5; D. Višnevskij, "Obščee napravlenie obrazovanija v Kievskoj akademii v pervoj polovine XVIII stoletija," *Kievskaia starina*, no. 2 (1884):171.
40. See, for instance: Kovalinskij, "Žizn'," *TDT* II:488-9; Skovoroda, "Razgovor družeskij o duševnom mire," *Sobranie sočinenij*, 245; I.M. Snegirev, "Ukrainskij filosof Grigorij Savvič Skovoroda," *Otečestvennye zapiski* XVI, no. 42 (1823):97. An indication of Skovoroda's religious consciousness can be found in his description of a mystical encounter that he experienced in the early 1770s: "Having various thoughts and sensations of soul with reverence and gratitude to God and having arisen early, I went out into the garden to take a walk. The first sensation that I felt with my heart was a certain familiarity, freedom, cheerfulness, and hope with fulfillment. Bringing to this disposition of soul all of my will and desire, I felt within myself an extreme movement that filled me with incomprehensible strength. Momentarily a certain sweet outpouring filled my soul, from which my whole insides burned with fire, and it seemed that a fiery current circulated throughout my surroundings. I began not to walk but to run, for I was carried by some kind of delight, not feeling in myself either hands or feet, but as if I consisted entirely of a fiery substance that was carried into the space of the surroundings. The whole world disappeared before me; a singular feeling of love, tranquillity, and eternity animated my existence. Tears streamed from my eyes, and poured a certain tender harmony into my whole being. I penetrated into myself, and experienced a still more filial assurance than love, and from that hour I consecrated myself in filial service to the divine spirit," Kovalinskij, "Žizn'," *TDT* II:518. As Skovoroda rejoiced in his communion with the divine, so he lamented his experience of its corollary, the "dark night of the soul." "O Father! It is hard to sever my heart from this sticky, elemental filth. Oh, it is hard. I have seen the image of a winged youth. He yearned to fly into the celestial regions, but his foot, attached by a chain to the earth, impeded him. This image is my own." Skovoroda, "Dialog. Imja emu: Potop Zmiin," *Sobranie sočinenij*, 499.
41. This pessimistic view of the apparent world pervades Skovoroda's writing. See, for example, Skovoroda, "Knižečka o čtenii svjaščennago pisanija narečenna Žena Lotova," *Sobranie sočinenij*, 406-8; "Sad božestvennyx pěsnej: Pesn' 2-ja," *TDT* II:9.
42. Skovoroda, "Načal'naja dver' ko xristianskomu dobronraviju," *Sobranie sočinenij*, 63; "Narkiss," *Sobranie sočinenij*, 86.

in a time and a place marked by such rapid transformations and spiritual decay as eighteenth-century Ukraine. It is rather to suggest that the content and emphasis of Skovoroda's thought are more comprehensible when viewed against the backdrop of the society in which he lived and his reaction to it.

Even if one admits the influence of Skovoroda's attitudes toward society on his life and thought, he might find its impact to have been inconsistent or contradictory, particularly as concerned, 1) his rejection of the "official" society and church coupled with his continued efforts to deal with them in his educational efforts, and 2) his revulsion at the world of appearances and resulting preoccupation with the divinity that underlay this world, vis-à-vis his understanding that the awareness of this divinity would ultimately improve human society. The first inconsistency may be dispelled by an appeal to both Skovoroda's personality and his spiritual egalitarianism. However bitterly Skovoroda may have felt about the society and the church, he found it personally difficult not to treat its individual members with consideration. Besides this, his concept of the spiritual equality of men constrained him to view every man as worthy of attention and potentially capable of finding the divinity within himself. The second inconsistency can best be explained in terms of Skovoroda's emphasis on the immanence of God. When Skovoroda rejected the world of appearances and discovered the divinity that sustained it, he concluded that this divinity, though separate from the world, was also immanent in it.[43] Therefore the apparent world, including the individuals who comprised society, possessed a divine spark. More than this, Skovoroda taught that if man came to understand that this divinity was within himself, he would also understand the divine will or law that determined his place in the world. When men acted according to this divine law, and played the role determined for them by God, the strife and contentions that marked a society ignorant of the divine law would cease and harmony would prevail.[44] Skovoroda's preoccupation with the divine, especially with the divine immanence, therefore, led him directly to the belief that individual spiritual regeneration rather than social or ecclesiastical reform would promote social tranquillity.

---

43. Skovoroda articulated this belief in immanent theism in numerous passages. Concerning the relationship between God and man, he enthused that, "God is in human flesh. He exists authentically in our visible flesh, the immaterial in the material, the eternal in the finite, one in all and the whole in each." Skovoroda, "Narkiss," *Sobranie sočinenij*, 101. Regarding the immanence of the divine in nature, he asked, "Isn't He in everything? He is the true tree in the tree, the grass in the grass, the music in the music, the house in the house... He is everything in all." Skovoroda, "Narkiss," *Sobranie sočinenij*, 86.

44. He argued that man's inordinate and therefore "unnatural" desire for honour, wealth and power was the source of "treason, rebellion, conspiracy, theft, the fall of governments, and every unfortunate abyss." Skovoroda, "Razgovor družeskij o duševnom mire," *Sobranie sočinenij*, 220.

Skovoroda's criticism of society, as well as the manner in which this critique was reflected in his life and thought, lead to the conclusion that he did not represent the interests of any single class. His censure of wealth and attack on the church leadership, along with his praise of freedom, poverty-stricken lifestyle and democratic educational efforts seemed to align him with the peasantry and the petty bourgeoisie. On the other hand, his advocacy of a natural order, cordial dealings with officials, gentry and clergy, rejection of any militant action to change the *status quo*, and indifferent attitude on the issue of land distribution marked him as an apologist for the emerging Ukrainian nobility. The irreconcilable contradictions produced by any attempt to depict Skovoroda as the representative of special class interests having become clear, it is necessary to determine his relationship to society in non-class terms.

Skovoroda lived during a harsh and chaotic time in the history of Ukraine, a time marked by Russia's destruction of Ukrainian independence, the enserfment of Ukrainian peasants and Cossacks, and the ennoblement of the Cossack officer class. During this period of rapidly changing political, social and economic relationships, he perceived a deepening spiritual crisis in Russia and Ukraine, a crisis that he interpreted as the logical result of man's inability to predicate his actions on any but material considerations. Because of his own spiritual inclinations, religious education, and revulsion at the contemporary upheaval in society, he concluded that it was just man's loss of spiritual vision that had caused his current social predicament. On the basis of this conclusion he adopted his wandering mode of life and determined to change society by changing man's view of himself. Any class orientation or social militancy on his part would have undermined the achievement of his goal, the creation of a harmonious society based upon man's realization of the existence of the divine law within himself. Skovoroda, then, while remaining detached from society,[45] sought to act effectively within it by reaching every man with the message of his divinity.

---

45. Skovoroda indicated his own profound sense of detachment from society by the epitaph that he chose for himself: "The world chased me, but it did not catch me." Kovalinskij, "Žizn'," *TDT* II:531.

H.S. Skovoroda as Teacher: The Image as Model

J.L. Black

While putting his recollections of the 1830s down on paper, the highly placed Ukrainian bureaucrat in Russian service, F.P. Lubjanovskij, remarked that the peasants of the Xarkiv district still remembered H.S. Skovoroda (1722-94) as a "wise and honest man, who taught us goodness, [and] the fear of God." A few years later, A. Xiždeu also wrote of the continuing popular image of the deceased philosopher as a teacher of all men; and at mid-century, the historian M.I. Kostomarov, whose perspective assigned an organic growth to Ukrainian history and culture, said that Skovoroda's portrait was still displayed in many Ukrainian homes.[1] Indeed, a dynamic part of the cultural legacy left by Skovoroda was his reputation as a great instructor in morality and good sense, and as a confirmed believer in knowledge for its own sake. Yet there is a certain irony about that heritage, for Skovoroda withdrew from formal teaching at precisely the time when Catherine II was placing particular emphasis upon the construction of school systems for her subjects.

From the initial year of her reign in 1762 to the opening in 1786 of Imperial Russia's first public school system, Catherine consulted the works of Europe's best educators and sought personal counsel from the prominent *philosophes* of the day. The chief administrators of her educational policies, Ivan Beckoj (1704-95) and Fedor Jankovič (1741-1814), spent a quarter of a century building

---

1. Kostomarov's comment is cited in E.N. Medinskij, *Istorija russkoj pedagogiki* (Moscow, 1938), 102. "Vospominanija Fedora Petroviča Lubjanovskago," *Russkij arxiv*, no. 1 (1872):98-185, cited here 108; A. Xiždeu, "Grigorij Varsava [sic] Skovoroda," *Teleskop*, pt. XXVI, no. 5 (1835):3-24; no. 8 (1835):151-78; cited here no. 5, 12-15.

for her a programme which, on paper at least, rivalled that of most West European states. And Skovoroda played no role whatsoever in those enterprises.

The purpose of this study is twofold. In the first place, it will attempt to delineate the nature of Skovoroda's opinions about education and the basis for his fame as a teacher. In the second place, it will try to explain the reasons for his divorce from the institutionalized dimension of Imperial Russian education and for the resilience, in spite of that, of his renown as an educator.

Skovoroda was fortunate to be born to parents who saw the value of education, a rare enough phenomenon in the eighteenth century. He was further favoured by being allowed to develop the inclination toward learning that both his first biographer, M.I. Kovalins'kyj (1757-1807), and he himself claim he demonstrated as a boy.[2] At the age of sixteen, Skovoroda persuaded his father to enroll him at the Kyiv Academy, where (except for a two-year sojourn, 1742-44, as a vocalist at Empress Elizabeth's court in St. Petersburg) he took full advantage of an unusually broad syllabus. The predominantly cultural influences at the Academy were derived from its earlier Polish connections. Latin was the school's principal language of instruction and study; the charter granted to it by Moscow in 1694 had made poetics, rhetoric, philosophy and theology the other components of its programme. In 1734, the year Skovoroda entered, elective courses were added in Greek, German and Hebrew. The school had long provided advanced study in music, mainly choral, and Peter I's most able exponent of education, Teofan Prokopovyč, had introduced geometry there in 1707.[3] Perhaps even more important to Skovoroda's education was the fact that disputation, that is, controlled debate between students, was one of the main pedagogical tools of the institution.[4] Much of his later writing was in the form of dialogues in which theses were proposed and debated by fictional protagonists.

---

2. Apparently Skovoroda showed a particular liking for moralizing books and religious services at a very early age. See M.I. Kovalinskij, "Žizn' Grigorija Skovorody" (1794), in *Povne zibrannja tvoriv* (Kyiv, 1973), II:440, and Skovoroda, "Razgovor pjati putnikov o istinnom ščastii v žizni," ibid., I:337-8, 355 (hereafter *PZT*). See also K.E. Benrikov, "G.S. Skovoroda—vydajuščijsja ukrainskij filosof i pedagog (1722-1794)," *Sovetskaja pedagogika*, no. 8 (1951):43-58, cited here, 43, and N.I. Petrov, "Pervyj (malorossijskij) period žizni i naučno-filosofskago razvitija Grigorija Saviča Skovorody," *Trudy Kievskoj duxovnoj akademii*, no. 12 (1902):588-618. A useful summary of his life can be found in S.P. Scherer, "The Life and Thought of Russia's First Lay Theologian, Grigorij Savvič Skovoroda (1722-94)," unpublished Ph.D. dissertation, Ohio State University (1969), 1-46; see also the essays in *Skovoroda, philosophe ukrainien. Colloquium* (18 January 1973) (Paris, 1976), and L.Je. Maxnovec', *Hryhorij Skovoroda: Biohrafija* (Kyiv, 1972).

3. See A. Sydorenko, *The Kievan Academy in the Seventeenth Century* (Ottawa, 1977), 131, and Max J. Okenfuss, "The Jesuit Origins of Petrine Education," in J.G. Garrard, ed., *The Eighteenth Century in Russia* (Oxford, 1973), 110-13, 123. See also Z.I. Xižnjak, *Kievo-Mogiljanskaja akademija* (Kyiv, 1970). On Skovoroda's entry to the Academy in 1734, see Maxnovec' 27-8, where (and passim) the traditional date of 1738 is disproven.

4. Sydorenko, 132.

It is conceivable as well that Skovoroda's leaning toward mysticism and personalized religion was a consequence in part of the fact that the ideas of the Western mystic, Jakob Böhme (1575-1624), were considered important at the Academy. While he was there at least one teacher with whom he had contact, Symon Todors'kyj, was an open admirer of Böhme.[5]

Skovoroda emerged from the school in 1745 as its most outstanding student. He then set out on a three-year tour that brought him into contact with various dimensions of the life of Hungary, Poland, Austria, several German states and, according to some reports, Italy.[6] This was by no means a Grand Tour of the type undertaken by sons of the aristocracy, for he travelled as a musician in the hire of a merchant diplomat, Havrylo Vyšnevs'kyj.[7] These travels enabled Skovoroda to experience the cross-currents of contemporary European intellectual life, which would not have been open to him at the Kyiv Academy. It has been suggested that this experience may not have been of only passing interest, for he later wrote that it was in those very years that he began to accept the Bible as the most valuable source of knowledge.[8] Whether one accepts this hypothesis or not, the fact that the areas visited by Skovoroda were among those in which German Pietism flourished should not be ignored.

Among the characteristics of the Pietists, who had Böhme as one of their predecessors, were a heightened social conscience, religious fundamentalism, practical preaching and, for scholars, Bible study. Under August Hermann Francke the University at Halle disseminated Pietist attitudes and gave impetus to the idea that education was a means for saving souls by instilling ethical and spiritual values in students. There was an overt anti-intellectualism in the Pietist ambition for education. They saw in the rationalism of their era a movement

---

5. See Zdenek V. David, "The Influence of Jacob Boehme on Russian Religious Thought," *Slavic Review* XXI, no. 1 (March 1962):43, 45-8. Petrov sees an important influence on Skovoroda of the humanist ideals of Prokopovyč, Heorhij Konys'kyj, and Samuil Myslavs'kyj, a classmate of Skovoroda's. Together these men brought to the Academy the attitudes of Erasmus, whose writings Skovoroda read with Myslavs'kyj, who later became the Metropolitan of Kiev. See Petrov, 591, 604-13.

6. Maxnovec', 71-2; later (1750-53), but apparently incorrect dates were set by V.F. Èrn, *Grigorij Savvič Skovoroda* (Moscow, 1912), 51, 67-70; and Kovalinskij, 442.

7. Kovalinskij, 440-41; Petrov (592) points out that F.S. Vyšnevs'kyj, by whom Kovalinskij says Skovoroda was employed, died in 1749, and was replaced by his son, Havrylo. Reports contained in Maxnovec' (44-6) show Havrylo Vyšnevs'kyj to have been still alive in 1750. On Vyšnevs'kyj, see A.S. Laškevič, "Rod Višnevskix," *Kievskaja starina*, no. 5 (1887):73-91, and "Pis'ma imperatricy Elizavety Petrovny k general-majoru Višnevskomu," *Russkij arxiv*, no. 2 (1870):273-4.

8. Skovoroda, "Razgovor pjati putnikov," *PZT* I:355. He said that he began to read the Bible at the age of thirty. Joseph T. Fuhrmann, "The First Russian Philosopher's Search for the Kingdom of God," in *Essays on Russian Intellectual History*, ed. L.B. Blair (London, 1971), 36, and Èrn (63-4) both say that Skovoroda was not positively influenced by his travels through Europe.

away from faith in the word of God. In matters of religion they did not concern themselves so much with fine points of doctrine as they did with finding a personal, inner harmony with God. Brotherly love, the dignity of man, and the education of one's heart were the rallying cries of their preaching. Indeed, religion itself was a matter of the heart to Pietists, and they assumed that youngsters could find their way to God if their senses were nurtured carefully. Skovoroda's career after 1766 in many ways came to resemble the ideas expressed by the Pietists.

After returning to his homeland in 1750, Skovoroda spent the subsequent thirteen years teaching in a variety of situations, none of which seems to have satisfied him very much. He lost his first position at a seminary in Perejaslav for attempting to teach poetics by means of a new methodology to which the bishop of Perejaslav objected. Shortly afterwards, in 1755, he was dismissed from another post as tutor to the son of a Ukrainian nobleman named Stepan Tamara. He then spent some time with a friend at the Moscow Academy and was in that city when Russia's first university was opened there. While in Moscow, he was invited to stay at the Holy Trinity Monastery of St. Sergius. Not happy there, Skovoroda returned to Ukraine, where he once again tutored the young Tamara, this time for three years.

In 1759, when Tamara's domestic instruction was deemed sufficient, Skovoroda was offered a post as a teacher of poetics at the collegium in Xarkiv. He left the school in 1760 after declining an invitation to take monastic vows. His refusal had been accompanied by a harsh denunciation of the luxuries and lack of spirituality that had become part of the lives of many of the monks whom he knew.[9] Persuaded to return to Xarkiv by a forgiving Bishop of Belgorod, Skovoroda met the young M.I. Kovalins'kyj there in 1762 and made him his protégé.

Several years later Skovoroda was finally pressured into resigning once again. The immediate bone of contention in 1768-9 was a manual on good behaviour that he prepared for a course of his own. The course was initiated on a request from Catherine II through her leading adviser on education, Ivan Beckoj, with the specific directive that instruction on civil conduct be added to the curriculum of all schools. In spite of such official sanction, Skovoroda's text raised the ire of a new Bishop of Belgorod, who thought that he saw some religious irregular-

---

9. Maxnovec', 157-65; Scherer, 26-8. Soviet writers suggest that the "new methodology" was derived from Lomonosov: see I.Z. Serman, "M.V. Lomonosov, G.S. Skovoroda i bor'ba napravlenij v russkoj i ukrainskoj literaturax XVIII v.," in *Russkaja literatura XVIII veka i slavjanskie literatury* (Moscow and Leningrad, 1963), 72-5. Skovoroda wrote a study guide on poetry for his students two years after the publication of Lomonosov's works, but there is no hard evidence to suggest a connection between them.

ities in it.[10] This incident was only the last in a long series of irritations that turned Skovoroda against rigidly formal pedagogy. Letters that he sent to friends in the 1760s reflected a near despair with the system. As early as 1765 he complained to I.I. Bazylevyč that his colleagues "preach incessantly in schools and temples, exhorting and confusing young students by means of unenlightened and narrow opinions...."[11] He admired the objective of the preaching, that is, to instill a love for Christ in the youngsters, but objected to the way in which instructors intimidated and baffled their pupils. A few years later he expressed his alarm to Kovalins'kyj on hearing that the young man had decided to become a school teacher. Such an occupation, he warned, might lead to "moral ruin,"[12] which suggests that any respect he might once have had for the profession was dissipating. He was concerned also about the conditions of service in noble households.

Thus, Skovoroda came to a personal crossroads that saw the end of his institutional teaching career at the very time when Catherine II and Beckoj were in the midst of almost frenetic efforts to provide a comprehensive school system for her subjects. So much attention was given to education from the very first year of Catherine's reign that the European *philosophe* Baron Melchior von Grimm—a friend of both Catherine and Beckoj—noted in 1762 that writing on education was the rage in St. Petersburg.[13] Beckoj took the first practical step in 1763 by planning Foundling Homes for orphans and illegitimate children as a means of instructing a new class of citizens who were not bound by the limiting traditions of either the noble or peasant classes. A detailed programme outlined an education for both boys and girls covering religion, civics and a basic knowledge of language and mathematics. Beckoj gave strict guidance on their diet, clothing and health, and teachers were admonished to be pious, serene, and virtuous, and to develop a loving relationship between themselves and their young charges. The next year saw the publication in St. Petersburg of his famous *General Statutes on the Education of the Youth of Both Sexes*, which called for a systematic network of schools for all of Catherine's subjects. The *Statutes* were

---

10. See Petrov, "K biografii ukrainskago filosofa Grigorija Saviča Skovorody," *Kievskaja starina*, no. 4 (1903):14-16; Bendrikov, 45-7; Kovalinskij, 459. The textbook, which Skovoroda reworked in 1780, was titled "Načal'naja dver' ko xristianskomu dobronraviju." It is included in *PZT* I:144-53. For Catherine's decree of 1765 that called for a wide extension of the Xarkiv syllabus, to include also French, German, mathematics, geography, and drawing, see *Polnoe sobranie zakonov Rossijskoj imperii*, no. 12.430 (6 July 1765), 187-8 (hereafter *PSZRI*).
11. Letter of 18 April 1765, *PZT* II:390.
12. Skovoroda, *Tvory v dvox tomax* (Kiev, 1961), II:219 (hereafter *TDT*).
13. For general information on Catherinian education policy in the 1760s, see M.I. Demkov, *Istorija russkoj pedagogii* (St. Petersburg, 1897) II:234-55, 306-17, and J.L. Black, *Citizens for the Fatherland: Education, Educators, and Pedagogical Ideals in Eighteenth Century Russia* (Boulder, Colo., 1979). Beckoj and Grimm met in the 1750s at the salon of Madame Geoffrin in Paris.

followed by the opening of special schools for noble and bourgeois girls and the reorganization of the elitist Land Cadet Corps College.[14]

Skovoroda's countrymen in Ukraine were also caught up in the fever over education. Those same years saw the first meetings of Catherine's Legislative Commission. Ukrainian delegates clamoured for new educational facilities similar to those being constructed in St. Petersburg and Moscow by Beckoj. Above all, they requested a Cadet Corps College and a university[15] so that their sons would be able to compete for positions in service on an equal footing with Russians.[16] One group went so far as to proclaim that expanded educational services would soon rid all Imperial Russia of its moral and religious ills.[17] In the meantime, Skovoroda became an itinerant preacher of morality, common sense, and the word of God. After 1766, he wandered from district to district in Ukraine, carrying with him a copy of the Bible and living a spartan existence. He discoursed with gentry and peasantry on the need for man to seek spiritual rather than material things in life. According to Lubjanovskij, who heard Skovoroda speak at Xarkiv in the early 1790s, the old man's school was any place he happened to be and his audience was anyone who wished to listen.[18]

The epistemological dualism that was central to Skovoroda's philosophy[19] and prompted him to say that good and evil were present in every person resembled the notions of most eighteenth-century educators, who insisted that teachers and parents must take youth in hand almost from their infancy (as in Locke's *tabula rasa*) in order to assure that they would be guided toward the good. Herein lay the starting point of Catherinian thinking about education as well. Skovoroda was in the mainstream of Russian pedagogical thought in another way, too, for, according to Kovalins'kyj, he "taught that all ranks are good and that God, in separating the various members of society, offended none of them. He laid a curse only upon those rebellious sons who...aspire after various ranks and positions under the urging of the passions."[20] Thus Skovoroda repeated almost verbatim the message contained in the two most widely read

---

14. On Beckoj, see P.M. Majkov, *I.I. Beckoj: opyt ego biografii* (St. Petersburg, 1904).

15. *Sbornik imp. Russkago Istoričeskago obščestva* XLIII (1885):142-3, 230 (hereafter *SIRIO*). An effort had been made to found a university at Baturyn in 1760, but to no avail. See D. Dorošenko, "Education in XVIII Century Ukraine," *Forum*, no. 25 (1974):8-13.

16. *SIRIO* IV (1868):170; LXVIII (1889):236, 130, 193.

17. Ibid., LXVIII (1889):276.

18. "Vospominanija Fedora Petroviča Lubjanovskago," 106-7.

19. See V.V. Zenkovsky, *A History of Russian Philosophy*, trans. G.L. Kline (New York, 1953), I:59-61.

20. Kovalinskij, 450; see also Skovoroda, "Razgovor, nazyvaemyj alfavit, ili bukvar' mira," *PZT* I:428, "...in all ranks can be found happiness and unhappiness, order and disorder, swaggerers and despondent people...."

citizenship texts of eighteenth-century Russia: Prokopovyč's *First Primer for Youth* (1720), the themes of which were expounded from Russia's pulpits until well after mid-century, and Fedor Jankovič's adaptation from J.I. Felbiger, *Book on the Duties of Man and Citizen* (1783), which Catherine insisted should be read by all her young subjects.[21] The same lessons permeated the writings of Moscow's Freemasons, as well as those of the two most famous lay intellectuals whose careers overlapped Skovoroda's, Nikolaj Novikov (1744-1818) and Nikolaj Karamzin (1766-1826).[22]

But Skovoroda was well apart from the practicing pedagogues on other crucial issues, and for that reason cannot be considered part of any school of pedagogical thought. Although an advocate of book learning, he insisted that "true" learning was really a higher cognition that could not be attained by normal empirical methods. One must seek knowledge of oneself first ("If you have not measured yourself first, what benefit will you gain from measuring other creatures?"). In his first philosophical dialogue, "Narcissus," written between 1769 and 1771, just after he had left the teaching profession, he wrote that ultimate knowledge is spiritual and is found in one's inner "true" spirit.[23] He concluded that men of his century relied unduly upon personal experience and observation. Kovalins'kyj said that Skovoroda rejected "bookishness" as something less important than teaching children a "love of hard work and a willingness to discharge obligations."[24] In that, of course, he was hardly unique among eighteenth-century educators.

Of all the groups in Russia interested in education, it was with the Freemasons that Skovoroda seemed to have the most in common. The similarity was by no means accidental, for Böhme and German Pietism were the wellsprings of notions taken up by Russian Freemasons. They were committed to improving society by leading exemplary lives themselves, and by sponsoring morality and education in others. Concerned with the dignity of the individual, they fostered an intellectual commitment to making the lot of the peasantry more endurable. Their dedication went beyond rhetoric, for they opened libraries, organized

---

21. On the use of Prokopovyč's *Pervoe učenie otrokam* (St. Petersburg, 1720; Engl. trans. by J.F. Philippe, *The Russian Catechism*, London, 1723), see James Cracraft, *The Church Reform of Peter the Great* (Bristol, 1971), 276-90, and Max Okenfuss, *The Discovery of Childhood in Russia: The Evidence of The Slavic Primer* (Newtonville, Mass., 1980), 49-52. Jankovič's *Kniga o dolžnostjax čeloveka i graždanina* (St. Petersburg, 1783) has been translated into English by Elizabeth Gorky and is included in Black, *Citizens for the Fatherland*, 209-66.

22. See Novikov, "O vospitanii i nastavlenii detej" (1783), in *Izbrannye sočinenija* (Moscow and Leningrad, 1951), 417-506; and Karamzin, *Razgovor o ščastii* (Moscow, 1797).

23. Skovoroda, "Narkiss: Razglagol o tom: uznaj sebe," *PZT* I:154-200, esp. 154-7. In this essay too he attacked the superstitious idol-worshipping features of organized religion.

24. Kovalinskij, 449.

schools of their own, and built hospitals, all in the hope that the gentry might change their habits in relationship to the peasantry and that the peasants themselves would learn to be content with their lowly station on earth. They seem to have believed with sincerity that happiness was a matter for the heart and not of material possessions. Catherine's school system offered the same fundamental lesson, if for somewhat different reasons, for that was an explicit message of Jankovič's *Book on the Duties of Man and Citizen*.[25] Skovoroda could have no argument with any of this. Indeed, he went so far as to proclaim that "the task of wisdom was to explain of what happiness consists."[26] He was one with the Freemasons and later mystics in his constant search for the spiritual meaning of life. But he was cautious about associating with Freemasons, and with some justification suggested that many of them should practice personally a little more of what they preached: "I do not know the Martinists [branch of Freemasons], neither their reason nor their studies. If they adopt special rules and rituals in order to appear wise, then I do not wish to know them. If they philosophize with pure hearts to be useful citizens of society, then I respect them ...."[27]

There were two quite distinct stages in the evolution of Catherine's educational policy. In the 1760s and 70s Beckoj tried to apply his eclectic gleanings from the writings of the contemporary *philosophes* on learning to build a system which would allow youngsters to develop along lines that suited their particular talents. He assumed that education was best served in a relaxed atmosphere, with little emphasis upon discipline or rigorous academic pursuits. Like so many other eighteenth-century intellectuals, he put character-building far ahead of learning as the main purpose of school curricula. His efforts were noteworthy for their lack of success, and so his place as Catherine's administrator of educational projects was taken in 1783 by Jankovič, who brought to Russia the centrally controlled system that he had been instrumental in bringing to the Serbian population of the Habsburg Empire. From 1783 to 1786 Jankovič worked out a programme that called for a carefully structured prospectus, uniform teaching methodology, and a reliance upon the dicta of textbooks. Memorization by rote, weekly reports by teachers to area supervisors, and the absolute prohibition of lessons not assigned by a commission in St. Petersburg assured that instruction, rather than independent thinking, was to be the essence of the imperial public school system that was officially announced in 1786.[28]

---

25. *Kniga o dolžnostjax čeloveka i graždanina*, 1-5. "True happiness lies within ourselves. When our soul is well, free of unruly desires, and the body is healthy, then man is happy."
26. Skovoroda, "Razgovor pjati putnikov," *PZT* I:334-5; see also his fable no. 27, "Pčela i seršen'," *PZT* I:126-7.
27. Kovalinskij, 468. For the German Pietists and Russian Freemasons, see David, 51-5.
28. For the wide selection of plans discussed by Catherine in the 1760s, see S.V. Roždestvenskij, ed., *Materialy dlja istorii učebnyx reform v Rossii v XVIII-XIX vekax* (St. Petersburg, 1910), 1-257;

It was with Beckoj that Skovoroda had the most in common, though they reached their conclusions about education quite independently from each other. A detailed comparison between them might well find many more dissimilarities than likenesses, but their overall visions were remarkably alike. The keynote of their mutuality was the conviction that school systems must encourage the natural proclivities of each student. Skovoroda said several times, and in several different ways, that "Education...flows from [one's own] nature," an idea that was well in keeping with Beckoj's *General Statutes*.[29] Like Beckoj (and England's John Locke, whose work Beckoj studied), Skovoroda saw four interdependent components to education: physical, mental, moral, and aesthetic training. Physical development is the first responsibility of parents. It must begin from the child's birth and, indeed, from the care that must be taken of its mother's health during her pregnancy. Such training should encompass a proper diet and the inculcation of good personal habits such as tidiness, cleanliness, and moderation in everything. In this opinion, Skovoroda concurred with recommendations written by Beckoj for the curricula of Russia's special schools. Moreover, similar suggestions were often made in the most widely read journal of mid-century Russia, the *Monthly Compositions*, which had education as one of its frequent subjects.[30] Skovoroda agreed with Beckoj, too, in his conviction that women should be educated to the same level as men. In this, at least, they stood together practically alone among Imperial Russia's pedagogues, and apart from most leading West European educators.[31]

When it came to intellectual education, Skovoroda emphasized the inseparable nature of mental, moral and behavioural growth. Personal habits reflect the degree to which one knows himself, so that people who behave properly are products of sound mental development. Knowledge enables a man to find his rightful niche in life. Therefore, books are a man's best friend. From books came the formal content of education. Mathematics, geometry, physics, astronomy,

---

for those of the 1780s see Peter Polz, "Theodor Jankovic und die Schulreform in Russland," in *Die Aufklärung in Ost- und Südosteuropa* (Cologne, 1972), 119-74.
29. Beckoj, "General'noe učreždenie o vospitanii oboego pola junošestva," *PSZRI*, 12.103 (24 March 1764), 670; Skovoroda, "Blagodarnyj Erodij," *PZT* II:104; see also I:420; his fable no. 6, "Kolesa časovii," I:111; and Fable no. 18, "Sobaka i kobyla," I:117. Kovalins'kyj reports that, in response to E.A. Ščerbinin's (Governor of Xarkiv) query, why he did not seek higher posts himself, Skovoroda replied: "...I have learned from many tests that I cannot play well...any role besides a low, simple, carefree and solitary one...work that suits one's inclinations is satisfying," *PZT* II:457-8.
30. The *Ežemesjačnye sočinenija* (1755-63) was edited by G.F. Müller. The twelve essays in it about education were almost all translations from contemporary European educators. There is no evidence to show that Skovoroda read the journal.
31. Ern (p. 319) cites I. Sreznevskij, a famous Slavist at the University of Xarkiv in the 1830s, on Skovoroda's concern for educating women. See also J.L. Black, "Educating Women in Eighteenth-Century Russia: Myths and Realities," *Canadian Slavonic Papers* 20:1 (1978), 23-43.

chemistry, economics, history, philosophy, logic, ethics, jurisprudence, and music were all disciplines of which man must have some knowledge in order to be considered learned.[32] Since all science originates from experience, he said, one must study a long time in order to teach others.[33]

Although he had the same faith in learning as a potential panacea for social ills that the Freemasons and Beckoj had, Skovoroda still cast aspersions on the awe with which so many of his westernized contemporaries regarded their own century and the hallowed place science had in it. "Every day brings new experiments and marvellous inventions. Is there anything that we cannot conceive of or carry out? But the sad thing is that in all of this greatness is lacking."[34] In "The Circle" (1773-4), he called empirical knowledge "mean thought and elemental comprehension," and the "beginning of all evil and malice," because it did not allow thinkers to see through to a spiritual knowledge.[35] Elsewhere he recounted a fable in which an illiterate man was welcomed into heaven because he had led a pure life, concluding that "understanding is not generated by books, but books by understanding."[36] Skovoroda cautioned readers not to forget that in all things the sciences were merely "handmaidens" of Christian philosophy.[37]

The third ingredient of Skovoroda's definition of education was moral instruction. He constantly admonished teachers and parents to educate the heart, for "without a kernel, a nut is nothing, like a man without a heart," or, as he put it elsewhere, "of what use is angelic language without a good heart?"[38] Among the lessons that he included in moral education were patriotism, brotherly love, industriousness, frugality, manliness, dignity and a distaste for luxury.[39] Catherine, Beckoj and Jankovič certainly could have no quarrel with these assertions; indeed, the preamble to Beckoj's *General Statutes* carried the same sentiments and Catherine quoted them from Beckoj for her *Nakaz* of 1767.[40]

---

32. Skovoroda, letter to Kovalins'kyj, *TDT* II:245; see also "Razgovor pjati putnikov," *PZT* I:322-3.
33. Skovoroda, "Razgovor, nazyvaemyj alfavit, ili bukvar' mira," *TDT* I:353; and Fable no. 18, "Sobaka i kobyla," where he says, "experience is the father of art, authority, and habit. From it is born all science, both books and art. This is the main and only means by which a bird learns to fly and a fish to swim," *PZT* I:117.
34. Skovoroda, "Razgovor pjati putnikov," *PZT* I:335-6.
35. Skovoroda, "Kol'co," *PZT* I:363. In this instance, he cited Solomon.
36. Skovoroda, "Razgovor pjati putnikov," ibid., 346.
37. Ibid., 336.
38. Skovoroda, "Blagodarnyj Erodij," *PZT* II:99; letter to Ivan Vasil'evič, 23 January 1787, *PZT* II:406.
39. See letters to Artem Dorofeevič, 19 February 1779, *PZT* II:398, and to Kovalins'kyj, no date, *TDT* II:307.
40. In her *Nakaz*, Catherine quoted directly from Beckoj in a paragraph that contains the essence of Catherinian pedagogy in the 1760s: "An Instruction to every Private Person...[and] a general Rule

Skovoroda further echoed the creators of Russia's formal school systems in his conviction that it was in labour that the genesis of all human good was to be found. Accepting as an axiom the biblical warning that idleness was the source of all evil, a phrase that Catherine repeated in almost all her school charters and in the *Nakaz*, Skovoroda said that from toil came mental strength, pleasure and human happiness.

The final component of Skovoroda's pedagogy was aesthetic education, by which he meant the development of sensitivity and artistic taste. Without that special sense which allows one to view art and listen to music with appreciation, he said, humans are robbed of a profound source of pleasure. In this Skovoroda's viewpoint coincided with Beckoj's once again, but certainly not with Jankovič's. An accomplished musician himself and a writer of songs, many of which were popular, Skovoroda was very much in favour of policies that made music part of the school curriculum. For his part, Beckoj sponsored a school for young artists and architects at the Imperial Academy of Fine Arts and encouraged the study of writing, drama and music at both the girls' schools and the Land Cadet Corps College.[41]

Beckoj wrote much about the characteristics and training of good teachers, for in the 1760s he had to provide them for Catherine's embryonic school systems. The type of teacher he sought was exactly the kind idealized by Skovoroda. As the person after whom youngsters were most likely to model themselves, a teacher was expected to lead a praiseworthy life. He must demonstrate a love for his people, a regard for the dignity of the individual, and always practice what he preached.[42] Indeed, the ability to set good examples was a standard of excel-

---

of Education shall be:
> It is necessary to instill into youth the fear of God, to settle their hearts in laudable dispositions, to teach them the essential rules which are suitable to their situation, to kindle in them the love of industry and the abhorrence of idleness as the source of all evil and error, to teach them a proper behaviour in their actions and conventions, courtesy, good manners, compassion for the poor and the unfortunate, and an aversion to everything audacious, to teach them private economy in all its minute parts, and as much of it as is useful, to deter them from dissipation, and particularly to ingraft in them a habit of decency and cleanliness, as well in their own persons, as in what belongs to them. In a word, to endow them with all those virtues and qualifications which belong to good education, by which in our time they become true citizens and useful and ornamental members of society.

Catherine the Great's (NAKAZ) Instruction to the Legislative Commission, 1767, ed. Paul Dukes (Newtonville, 1977), 90-91.

41. For the programme of Beckoj's school for young artists, see *PSZRI*, no. 12.275 (4 November 1764), 948-60.

42. Skovoroda, "Razgovor, nazyvaemyj alfavit, ili bukvar' mira," *PZT* I:440-41. Skovoroda did not have the same sense of national identity that many of his contemporaries had, but he spoke of Ukraine, by which he meant the area east of the Hetmanate, as his "Aunt" *(tetka)*. The Hetmanate,

lence included in almost all eighteenth-century pedagogical theories about good teaching. Likewise, the importance of pre-school influences upon children was generally acknowledged, and parents were warned to demonstrate proper moral and civic behaviour to their offspring. Prokopovyč had been Russia's chief exponent of this in the 1720s, and his *Primer* opened with a reminder to parents that their children's well-being depended entirely upon what they were taught in their first years. The European educators whose works were read most commonly in Russia, Comenius, Locke and Fénelon, said the same thing. Beckoj went so far as to write that the process of good education started from the moment when a mother decided whether or not to nurse her own child.[43]

Skovoroda and Beckoj expressed similar opinions on most criteria for good teaching. That Beckoj was just as opposed as Skovoroda to rigorous and formal pedagogy was evinced in his *Discourse* of 1766, which was a blueprint for the reorganization of the Land Cadet Corps College. There he spoke against "pedantism," saying that "if one must select from the lesser of two evils, then it is better to take the teacher who has some deficiencies in learning than a pedant, who is so unbearable by his haughty manner as to warrant only laughter."[44] The main difference between them in the matter of teachers lay in the fact that Beckoj, and Catherine, had no faith whatsoever in the ability of the gentry to inculcate in their children the values that the empress felt they should have. Beckoj's solution to this dilemma was to separate children from their parents at an early age and place them in boarding schools, where the state could take their instruction in hand. In his turn, Skovoroda was quite optimistic about education at home. In one of his clearest expositions on education, "Grateful Erodius" (1787), Skovoroda presented alternatives in the form of a discussion between a monkey named Pišek and a stork called Erodius. Pišek hotly defended the existing structured education, and Erodius argued the merits of a simple but careful home upbringing in basic morality.

On hearing that Erodius was concerned about the welfare of his parents, Pišek cynically exclaimed about the novelty of such sentiments. He was shocked when he discovered that Erodius and his siblings had been educated at home by their father: "O my God! Good schools flourish everywhere in which they teach one to speak many languages. What could he teach you, since he is without education himself?" Erodius replied that together his parents had taught him to respect learning, to understand that nothing is better than a good education, and to make

---

or Little Russia, he called his "Mother"; see letter to Kovalins'kyj, 26 September 1790, *PZT* II:356; see also Kovalinskij, 457. Fuhrmann goes to somewhat exaggerated lengths to treat him as a Russian.

43. Beckoj, *General'noj plan Imperatorskago vospitatel'nago doma v Moskve* (St. Petersburg, 1763), 5.

44. Beckoj, *Razsužděnija služaščija rukovodstvom k novomu ustanovleniju Šljaxetnago kadeckago korpusa* (St. Petersburg, 1766), in *PSZRI*, no. 12.741 (11 September 1766), 975.

the most of his own talents.[45] Pišek's increasingly feeble protestations in favour of formalistic schooling were met with pithy homilies to the effect that man should be allowed to learn naturally: "Do not teach the apple tree to bear apples; nature itself has already done that. Simply protect it from the swine, cut down the weeds, chase away the geese, and block off the impure water...," said Erodius, thereby claiming that children will learn naturally if they are encouraged and remain healthy. He continued, "From nature, as from a mother, learning matures easily by itself. This is the universal, true Academy—and the only one. You can quickly teach the falcon to fly, but not the turtle."[46]

All in all, Erodius's part of the dialogue was a harsh condemnation of strict instruction by rote, reliance upon foreign tutors, and the current fashion of learning Greek and Latin. Simultaneously, he argued on behalf of education by sense impression, that is, visual aids, models, and the "learning by doing" method. In fact, several writers have suggested that Skovoroda might have been influenced in that direction by Rousseau, and the Ukrainian's desire to "educate the heart" has been equated with Rousseau's emphasis on nurturing a child's conscience. But it is very unlikely that the connection was anything but coincidental. Skovoroda returned from Europe in 1753, long before *Emile* (1762), Rousseau's most important pedagogical piece, was published. One year after it was written, the book was banned in Russia anyway,[47] and by that time Skovoroda's disappointment with formalistic training was well established. He had stressed the naturalistic approach to education as early as 1754, when, according to Kovalins'kyj, he sought "to cultivate the heart of his pupil [Tamara] and, examining his natural inclinations, merely to help in its development with mild and tender imperceptible direction, not burdening his premature reason with learning."[48]

* * *

The question of Skorovoda's educational legacy is a moot one, for there is little record of actual accomplishment. His letters and papers were not collected until a year after his death, when Kovalins'kyj, who inherited them, compiled a short biography of his mentor. The first publication of any of his writing came only in 1798.[49] But many of the master's songs, poems and dialogues had long since been circulated throughout the homes of the Ukrainian gentry, and in peasant

---

45. Skovoroda, "Blagodarnyj Erodij," *PZT* II:101-2: "Nothing is better than a good education..., neither rank, nor wealth, nor family, nor the tenderness of landlords, nor good health."
46. Ibid., 104. He said exactly the same thing, even to the sentence about birds and turtles, in "Razgovor, nazyvaemyj alfavit, ili bukvar' mira," *PZT* I:438.
47. *SIRIO*, VII (1870), 318. *Emile* was translated into Russian in abridged form in 1779.
48. Kovalinskij, *PZT* II:442; see also Ėrn, 316-17.
49. Skovoroda, *Družeskija besedy. Beseda pervaja o poznanii sebja*, in *Biblioteka duxovnaja* (St. Petersburg, 1798).

villages, in oral and handwritten form. So had his manual on good conduct, which was first published in 1806.⁵⁰ In that same year some of his work appeared in *Sionskij vestnik* (Zion Herald), which was edited by the Masonic mystic, A.F. Labzin, conference secretary of the Academy of Arts. Appropriately, the journal, which survived for only a year, also included translations from Jakob Böhme. Skovoroda had personal contact with many young people in whose homes he lived and taught briefly, so that he became a legend in his own time.

His reputation was such that in 1787, shortly after she announced the opening of Russia's first public school system, Catherine II was said to have visited him in Ukraine. She had already invited Skovoroda to live in St. Petersburg, where he might both contribute to and profit from the active intellectual community.⁵¹ By that time, however, his views on education were even more distant from hers and from those of her new adviser on education, Janković.

The degree to which he fostered a moral revival is uncertain, but Skovoroda undoubtedly contributed to the growing dissatisfaction with the cynical if superficial anti-clericalism and flippancy that many Russians called "Voltaireanism." His ideas and life-style both mirrored and helped shape a trend among intellectuals toward individual mysticism and the personalization of religious life. His open criticism of institutionalized piety, as well as the fact that the official church had become an arm of the state by the 1720s and so lost much of its sense of spiritual mission, reinforced this tendency.

Traces of Skovoroda's influence can be seen in the growth of educational facilities in Ukraine, for there he was directly responsible for much of the philanthropy on behalf of schooling. Even the founding of the University at Xarkiv in 1805, generally attributed to the persuasiveness of a former Skovoroda student, V. N. Karazyn, was underwritten financially (400,000 rubles) mainly by persons who had once been friendly to or students of Skovoroda.⁵² The Ukrainian writers and educators O.V. Duxnovyč (1803-65), I.P. Kotljarevs'kyj (1769-1838), and H.F. Kvitka (1778-1843) all acknowledged the importance to them of Skovoroda's ideas on moral instruction.⁵³ Kostomarov gained his love

---

50. *PZT* I:496. According to Fuhrmann, some copies of the manual even reached Bulgaria, Romania, and Poland; Fuhrmann, 62. The distribution of his manuscripts and the oral transmission of his poems was so widespread that they came to resemble folklore; see Kostomarov, *Sočinenija* (Kyiv, 1901), I:412-16.

51. Fuhrmann, 44, accepts the connection with Catherine II as fact; Maxnovec' (203-4) rejects it.

52. Medinskij, *Istorija russkoj pedagogiki*, 103-4. See especially D.I. Bagalej, *Opyt istorii Xar'kovskago universiteta* (Xarkiv, 1878), I:25-33. Other sources say that the sum was 618,000 rubles; see T. Tixij, "V.N. Karazin: Ego žizn' i obščestvennaja dejatel'nost'," *Kievskaja starina* 88, no. 1 (1905):39-40; no. 2 (1905):263.

53. M.F. Šabaeva, *Očerki istorii školy i pedagogičeskoj mysli narodov SSSR, XVIII v.-pervaja polovina XIX v.* (Moscow, 1973), 414-18.

and understanding of Ukrainian culture and history at the University of Xarkiv in the 1830s, especially through his association with the Slavist I.I. Sreznevskij, another admirer of Skovoroda. They and other intellectuals were products of a small but vital humanitarian milieu that the itinerant teacher had helped create. Even the great Russian philosopher of a later generation, Vladimir S. Solov'ev (1853– 1900), recalled vividly the Skovoroda aphorisms that his mother often had quoted to him when he was a youth. In fact, he was a descendent of Skovoroda's, through his mother's family.[54]

The intellectual environment of Imperial Russia in the eighteenth century was anarchic at best. Scepticism influenced by the *philosophes* existed side by side with Masonic-mystical leanings, pulling thinking students in several directions and prompting doubt and intellectual insecurity. Skovoroda's consistency as a teacher of moral reforms who retained a deep religious conviction, and as a devotee of wisdom for its own sake, was not unique. But his life remained as a symbol of perfection that no one among his fellow countrymen was able to match. Among other things, he was a model of dedication to ideals which Beckoj hoped, vainly, that his professional teachers would adopt as their own. Sometimes referred to as Russia's, though more accurately Ukraine's Socrates,[55] Skovoroda had at the root of his ideals a "know thyself" philosophy. He lived the lessons he preached, and therein lies the strength and resilience of his pedagogy.

---

54. Cited in P.M. Allen, *Vladimir Solov'ev: Russian Mystic* (New York, 1978), 10-14, 300-1.
55. See, for example, A. Xir'jakov, "Ukrainskij Sokrat (Po povodu 175-letija so dnja roždenija Grigorija Saviča Skovorody)," *Obrazovanie: Pedagogičeskij i naučno-populjarnyj žurnal*, no. 9 (September 1897): 129-34.

Part Two

Skovoroda and Literature

Prolegomena to Studies of Skovoroda's Language and Style

George Y. Shevelov

The number of articles that deal with the language of Skovoroda's writings is large. No monograph exists, however. The combined results of these inquiries into the problems to date are disappointingly meagre. The consensus is that (excluding his works in Latin) Skovoroda used three languages in a peculiar mixture in his texts: Church Slavonic, Russian, and Ukrainian (hereafter ChSl, R, and U). One does not have to be a linguist to make such a statement: it is quite obvious. The fairly large number of West-Europeanisms in his writings is usually accorded little attention. Similarly, Latin and Greek—the languages of most of Skovoroda's extant letters—appear throughout his Slavic texts in the form of quotations and as occasional words and phrases, but these are ignored by the commentators. When one moves from enumerative statements to general characterizations, the sluice gates open wide and mutually contradictory, entirely subjective evaluations pour out. These include: 1) outright condemnation— "Skovoroda wrote in a heavy, obscure and strange language...worthy of a seminarian, clumsy [*topornyj*] and often unclear" [G. Danilevskij, *Sočinenija* 21 (St. Petersburg, 1901), pp. 26, 85]; 2) condescending pity—"We must take into account the historical circumstances that prevented him from achieving a completely popular literary language and only allowed him to take the first steps in this direction" [I. Pil'huk, *Hryhorij Skovoroda* (Kyiv, 1971), 254]. One should recall that such contemporaries and countrymen as V. Kapnist wrote in good Russian; and 3) a fanfare in honour of the first pioneer in the formation of the modern Ukrainian literary language—"This outstanding enlightener prepared the ground and, in a way, determined the direction and the further development of the Ukrainian literary language on a popular foundation" [F. Medvedjev in

Akademijia Nauk UkRSR, *Hryhorij Skovoroda 250* (Kyiv, 1975), 203]. Pages could be filled with similar meaningless platitudes.

The authors of these and other statements are all guilty of premature and unfounded generalizations. They may, perhaps, claim extenuating circumstances. To elaborate a satisfactory general characterization of Skovoroda's language one needs to engage in a considerable amount of spade work in his writings as a whole. This has not yet been done. A lack of knowledge, often accompanied by certain preconceived ideas, is particularly harmful in three problem areas. No adequate picture of Skovoroda's language may be obtained unless and until clarity has been brought to these problems. The following remarks constitute an attempt at probing these three areas.

1

"Hlava že vsěm Biblija."
"But the Bible stands at the head of everything."
M. Kovalins'kyj, "Žizn' Hrihorija Skovorody," 1794

Skovoroda measured with his feet the roads from Kyiv to the Donec' and from Kursk to Taganrog, not counting his frequent rambles in the vast expanse of *Slobožanščyna*, later a *naměstničestvo* governed from Xarkiv. Wherever he walked, a heavy copy of the Bible is said to have been in his bag. If his general reading was extensive, his reading of the Bible never stopped. No doubt he knew by heart many long passages of Holy Writ and he thought and spoke in ideas, images, and expressions taken from Scripture. Before his years of roaming began, the instruction he gave was based on the Bible. He had begun to read and study the Bible at the latest toward the end of the nearly fifteen years that he spent intermittently at the Kyiv Academy. He sang church songs that were linguistically and stylistically dependent on Scripture during the two years he spent at the Court choir of the Empress Elizabeth, as well as during the nearly five years at the church of the Russian mission in Tokay, Hungary. The Bible was the companion of both his solitary and his social life. His reading of the Fathers of the Church (he mentions Basil the Great, John Chrysostom, Gregory of Nazianzus, Ambrose, Jerome, Augustine, Gregory the Great, et al.) (ŽL-80, 406[1]) also led him to the Bible. In a sense virtually all his writings are com-

---

1. References to Skovoroda's writings are given by their abbreviated titles followed by the presumed year of their creation, with the omission of the century, which is always the eighteenth, followed in turn by the page in the edition Hryhorij Skovoroda, *Tvory v dvox tomax* (Kyiv, 1961). If the quotation is taken from volume 2, this is indicated by inserting the volume number between the year and the page. Thus ND-68, 15 means "Načal'naja dver' ko xristianskomu dobronraviju," 1768, vol. 1, p. 15; reference to "Basni Xar'kovskija," 1759, vol. 2, p. 103 is given as BX-59, 2, 103. The later edition, *Povne zibrannja tvoriv*, 1-2 (Kyiv, 1973) was used for those works that were not

ments on these biblical and patristic texts. It was not without reason that he described his relation to the Bible in the terminology of erotic love. He wrote: *"Samye prazdnye v nej* [in the Bible] *tonkosti dlja menja kažutsja očen' važnymi: tak vsehda dumaet vljubyvšijsja"* and he concluded: *"Těm ščastlivěe* [my] *sožitel'stvo s seju vozljublennoju v ženax"* (PP-73, 246-7).

No wonder, then, that not only images but innumerable quotations from the Bible permeate all the writings of Skovoroda. He who would characterize Skovoroda's own contribution to the language in his writings must first eliminate all the biblical quotations. This is particularly crucial in the question of the ChSl components in his language. Did he have them only, or predominantly, as taken from the ChSl Bible? Was he, to any degree, original and personal in their selection? Were they an active component of his style(s)? Such a screening of Skovoroda's biblical quotations (as well as quotations from other ecclesiastical sources such as treatises, sermons, hymns, and prayers of the Fathers of the Church) has never been done. Moreover, it could not be done in the UkRSR until now owing to political restraints on the one hand and to simple ignorance on the other. There are hardly any men in the research institutions who are sufficiently acquainted with these sources. It comes, then, as no surprise that there is no commentary of that kind in either of the recent editions of his work. We cannot ignore the fact that a substantial part of Skovoroda's texts was not composed by him out of nothing, but was simply taken from ecclesiastical works. However, as of today we are not able to determine what part of the texts that bear his name is indeed his own and in what proportion.[2]

---

included in the 1961 edition (especially Obs 1 and 2) and for a few corrections in other texts, as well as in dating Skovoroda's letters. The list of abbreviated titles of Skovoroda's writings is at the end of this article, p. 132.

As for the rendition of Skovoroda's texts in the Roman alphabet, no transliteration can do justice to his actual pronunciation, because he constantly vacillated between U and R. This is evident, e.g., in his rhyming of *ě* sometimes with *i* and *y* (e.g., *žiti* : *sěti* : *nesytyj*—BE-87, 500; *blaholěpnyj* : *neusypnyj*—UŽ-87, 532), and sometimes with *e* (e.g., *děvě* : *Evě*—BA-83, 447, *cvětet* : *nět*—454, *nedělju* : *xmelju*—455), in his confusion of the letters *i* and *y*, *i* and *ě*, *e* and *ě*, etc. When Skovoroda decided to distinguish graphically *mir* 'world' and *mir* 'peace,' he suggested that the first be spelled with a *y* (L78-90, 2, 387), which clearly shows that he made no distinction between *i* and *y* in his pronunciation. Ideally, the transliteration should constantly switch from R to U and back, but this would be utterly impractical and, in addition, more often than not one cannot say which one is to be applied in a particular textual segment. Therefore, purely arbitrarily, a transliteration closer to R is applied here, with *i* rendering Cyrillic i and и and with *y* rendering Cyrillic ы; *jat'* (ѣ) is rendered with a non-committal *ě*; but г is rendered in the U way as *h* not only because this was, likely, Skovoroda's actual pronunciation, but also to dramatize the conventionality of the transliteration, in this case making it neither completely R nor U.

2. Metropolitan Ilarion (Ohijenko) in his "Nove akademične vydannja tvoriv Hryhorija Skovorody" (*Vira i kul'tura* 12, 1962, 14ff.) gives a restrained but devastating criticism of that aspect of the new publications of Skovoroda's texts in Kyiv (as well as the often misleading use of small letters at the

Skovoroda himself offers little assistance in this respect. His audience was well versed in these matters and could perceive the quotations at once, as well as allusions to quotations and the associations they carried with them. He did not foresee the generations of entirely secularized ignoramuses that were to come. To begin with a technicality, if one may judge on the basis of several pages reproduced from Skovoroda's original manuscripts, he did not use quotation marks. Instead he introduced biblical texts with an indentation preceded by an asterisk, but the end of the quotation was not marked at all (see, e.g., a reproduction from Ns-69, 65, or from YZ-75, 397).[3] However, the same punctuation was applied to sentences and phrases under emphasis, whatever their origin, even if they were his own (e.g., in AM-74 as reproduced in 1, 347: *"Ne ravnoe vsěm ravenstvo"*). In fact, the indentation with an asterisk in all likelihood was for Skovoroda simply a mark of emphasis; if quotations are often introduced in this way, it is not because they were quotations but because they carried the main thrust of Skovoroda's thought.

Sometimes Skovoroda indicated the source of his quotation in full, giving the reference to the book, the chapter, and the verse (e.g., *"Vzhljan' na Ieremiju v hl. 17-j, v stixě 9-tom"*—Ns-69, 35); sometimes he referred to the book alone (e.g., *"Urazuměeš sie Ieremiino..."*—As-69, 138); and sometimes a quotation was given without any reference whatever to its source (e.g., *"...hrěšnikov, o koix pišetsja: 'Běžit nečestivyj, nikomu že honjaščuʻ"*— Ns-69, 67). There are also quotations interrupted in the middle of a sentence, only hinting at the whole because, obviously, this whole was fully understood by Skovoroda's immediate audience. For example, see the quotations in K-74, 254: *"Vot č'e dělo sie est': 'Kol' krasny nohi blahověstvujščix...' Sim-to oběščano: 'Sjadete na prestolěx...' Vsěm blaženstvo, vsem mir nužen, dlja toho skazano: 'Sudjaščem oboim na desjati kolenom Izrailevym'."* It must be added that such quotations often appear

---

beginning of words whose sacredness was marked in Skovoroda's manuscripts by the use of capital letters). He does not, however, discuss the impact of these editorial shortcomings on the study of Skovoroda's language.

3.   Thus, in both Kyiv editions of Skovoroda all concluding quotation marks are the editors' and should not be blindly relied upon, e.g., in PP-73, 245: "*O sem-to Pavel ščastlivcě vopiet: 'Elicy pravilam sim žitelstvujut, mir na nix i milost'. Skaži, požaluj, čem zaměšaetsja tot, kto soveršenno znaet, čto ničevo pohibnut' ne možet, no vse v načalě svoem věcno i nevredimo prebyvaet?'*" it is obvious that the quotation marks should be closed after *milost'*. Cf. also K-74, 255. This punctuation practice of Skovoroda's was not unique in his time. In printed sermons quotations normally were singled out by the use of italics or spacing. On this, see, e.g., L. Kjellberg, *La langue de Gedeon Krinovskij, prédicateur russe du XVIIIe siècle*, 1 (Uppsala, 1957), 79f. The collation of the two editions of Krinovskij's sermons (1755-9 and 1760), as demonstrated by Kjellberg, also shows growing precision in quoting the Bible. In the first edition renarrated passages are often quoted entirely in italics, in the second one only those words that are quoted unchanged. Skovoroda was closer to the technique of Krinovskij's first edition.

in long series, sometimes united by a single word that is repeated in them, peculiar concordance-type sequences aimed at showing common symbolic meaning in many and various occurrences of the word (such as the sequences on 'there' (*tamo*) and 'mountain' (*hora*)—As-69, 106f.; 'nose'—As, 120; 'stag'— As, 125; 'teeth'—As, 126f.; 'calf'—As, 148 ff., and many more). In other cases these series do not hinge on a single word but supposedly convey the same idea or develop a certain idea. Such strings of quotations—Skovoroda apparently called them symphonies—may be indefinitely long. One in ŽL-80, 409 has 51 links, many of them unfinished, none with a reference to the source and, of course, with no guarantee that all actually do come from the Bible. They often contain obscure logical (or symbolic) connections, so that Skovoroda rightly concludes this parade with an avowal that the meaning of the suite can be open only to the initiated:

Kto razvjažet xot' odnu svjaz',
V tom bleščit izrailskij hlaz. (411)

No less entangled is the sequence of quotations in Skovoroda's commentary to SBP 28, 2, 53. Of its thirteen lines only one has an explicit reference (to Augustine) and quite a few are abruptly interrupted. The reader may find other examples, say, in Ns-69, 66; As-69, 95; BD-72, 174; PP-73, 232; and many more. Some biblical quotations are freely rendered ("*Ix zabluždenie, skazat' Ieremĕennymi slovami, napisano na nohtĕ adamantovom*"—PP-73, 218; "*Počemu ž Pavel nazyvaet vsjak um ili ponjatie prevosxodjaščim?*"—-PP, 227). In such cases the boundary between the author's speech and the Bible text is very much erased.

Thinking and speaking in biblical quotations was so natural to Skovoroda (and probably to his listeners) that even the Devil in PB-83 builds mosaics from fragments of biblical texts, not in order to polemicize with them, but as a manifestation of a natural manner of thought and speech (p. 474). As mentioned, not necessarily all the quotations in such mosaics come from the Bible. Fragments from other sources may easily be incorporated. This was made explicit by Skovoroda in BA-83, 466f., where segments from Laščevs'kyj, Prokopovyč, and an "ancient Little Russian song" immediately follow an explosion of biblical quotations. In other cases, however, particularly if all the sources were ecclesiastical, this could have taken place without any direct indication. Furthermore, going from bad to worse, even when Skovoroda does give references, they are not always correct. Apparently Skovoroda occasionally quoted from memory. Sometimes an effort is required to elucidate the situation. For example, in Ns-69, 49, as published, the text reads: "*Pomnju slovo Ieremiino sie: 'Hluboko serdce čelovĕku, pače vsĕx, i ono-to istinnyj čelovĕk est'...*'" Because of the typical editorial error discussed above, the closing quotation mark indicates that everything preceding it belongs to the quotation. But the actual text in Jeremiah 17:9

in the Synodal Bible of 1757 is: *'Gluboko serdce pače vsěx, i čelověk est'*," i.e., the words "*ono-to istinnyj*" are Skovoroda's.[4] To cap it all, in Jeremiah this verse (to the extent that it is there) is not original, but rather paraphrases Psalm 64:6. In the Revised Standard Version of the Bible it is rendered: "For the inward mind and heart of a man are deep!" (In the Synodal Bible it reads: "*Pristupit čelověk i srdce gluboko.*") Thus, what is found in Skovoroda is a blend of the two biblical quotations, plus his own insert.

In general, Skovoroda was not very scrupulous in matters of quotation. When he cited (BA-83, 467) Teofan Prokopovyč's "*Epynykyon syest pěsn' pobědnaja*," he not only changed the aorist *pryjat'* and the participle *vozvraščennyj* to *prijal* and *vozvrativsja*, but also replaced *otstupnyk* and *otečestva vrah*—which clearly referred to Mazepa—by *antixrist* and *domašnij vrah* respectively, thus eliminating political overtones and giving the text, instead, a generalized, philosophical tinge.[5]

To come back to those of Skovoroda's quotations that are specifically taken from the Bible, a student of his language has a complicated task. A necessary prerequisite for his work would be to establish what was quoted from the Bible, including even the small allusions that Čyževs'kyj adroitly calls "Biblischer Sand,"[6] in order to put this material aside and not consider it Skovoroda's own. This sorting and disentangling is of the utmost difficulty, Skovoroda's texts being what they are (and being, in addition, so poorly edited).[7] The next step must be

---

4. The Revised Standard Version of the Bible has quite a different text: "The heart is deceitful above all things and desperately corrupt; who can understand it?"

5. Prokopovyč's text quoted here from Feofan Prokopovič, *Sočinenija*, ed. I. Eremin (Moscow and Leningrad, 1961), 209. Skovoroda also slightly modernized Prokopovyč's language: *množajšaja luča* became *silnějšii luči, so soboju* — *za soboju* and *i* — *on*.

6. Dm. Tschižewskij, *Skovoroda: Dichter, Denker, Mystiker* (Munich, 1974), 222.

7. In fact, this is not only a prerequisite for studying Skovoroda's language. It is also indispensable in all studies of his ideological and aesthetic search and concepts. To limit ourselves to one example, the penetrating, erudite, and stimulating monograph by Čyževs'kyj quoted above is marred by insufficient attention to the Bible as Skovoroda's source of inspiration. Often Čyževs'kyj constructs parallels between Skovoroda's thoughts and images and more remote sources, although the similarities may more easily be explained with reference to the Bible as the common source for both Skovoroda and his posited precursor(s). After the identification of all Biblical quotations in Skovoroda, the next step would be to unearth those from the Fathers of the Church and from the church service books. Only then should connections with German mystical literature be examined. In other words, Čyževs'kyj's rich material should be accepted as typologically confrontative, rather than as pointing to the actual sources of Skovoroda's thought and imagery. Čyževs'kyj himself, from time to time, admits points of gross dissimilitude between Skovoroda and the German mystics (e.g., 98, 101, 109, 155, 174f., 203, 205), but more often he is led by his material to accept the dependence of Skovoroda. Yet the parallel he draws between Skovoroda and Valentin Weigel (*Zeitschrift für slavische Philologie* 12, 308ff.) is striking indeed. It concerns, however, apart from the ideas, the imagery and not the language proper, and it should be referred to after one has put aside the Biblical

to establish what inaccuracies Skovoroda brought into the quotations, because these are his own and constitute part of his own language.

Theoretically, Skovoroda could have dealt with three variants of the Church Slavonic Bible (or he could have made his own translations from the Greek or Hebrew text): the Ostrih edition of 1581, the Moscow edition of 1663, and the Synodal (Elizabethan) one of 1751.[8] This is only theoretically possible, though. In the specific historical conditions of the second half of the eighteenth century, Skovoroda's generation, living in the Hetman state (*Het'manščyna*) and in *Slobožanščyna*, had its ties with pre-Perejaslav Ukraine drastically cut, and the writings of the time of the Church Union were virtually forgotten.[9] On the other hand, in 1663 (and the years that followed), when the Moscow Bible was printed (incidentally, leaning heavily on the Bible of Ostrih), Muscovy remained another state and clearly another nation. Consequently, this edition of the Bible gained no popularity in the Ukraine at that time. The situation was radically different in the mid-eighteenth century, when the colonial status of the Ukraine was obvious, and administratively as well as culturally the country was undergoing rapid change and becoming a Russian province, a process that took formal shape with the destruction of the Sich in 1775 and the division of the country into *naměstničestva*, in *Slobožanščyna* in 1780 and in the Hetman state, or, more correctly, the former Hetman state, in 1782. The Synodal Bible was mandatory in the church in Ukraine. It was the only easily available edition, and it is this version that one must assume was known and used by Skovoroda. An empirical verification has confirmed these general considerations beyond any doubt. For such a verification 28 quotations of Skovoroda's taken at random from the Bible have been checked with the three editions in question. It proved, as expected, that Skovoroda's source, when there were differences among the three editions, was the Bible of 1751/1757 in all his writings in all periods of his activity from which we have his texts.

It would be cumbersome and superfluous to cite here all the collations made. It will suffice to refer to one of them, a somewhat longer one, as cited in As-69, 91:

---

and general ecclesiastical components in Skovoroda's work. Purely linguistically, this would still be Skovoroda's own contribution.

8. Its second edition, of 1757, was available to me while I was preparing this article.

9. Hence parallels between Skovoroda and, say, Ivan Vyšens'kyj (fashionable with some Soviet historians of literature, e.g., A. Pašuk in Akademija Nauk UkRSR, Instytut filosofiji, *Hryhorij Skovoroda 250* [Kyiv, 1975], 124ff.), are entirely fictitious (unless one takes them typologically).

Skovoroda	Ostrih 1581[10]	Moscow 1663[11]	Synodal 1757
Smirennaja i koleblemaja ne iměla esi utěšenija. Se az uhotovljaju tebě anfraks, kamen' tvoj, i na osnovanie tvoe sapfir; i položu zabrala tvoja iaspis, i vrata tvoja kamenie kristalla, i ohraždenie tvoe kamenie izbrannaja.	Mylujaj tja smyrennaho y rasȳpanaho se outěšyšysja. Se az ouhotovlju tebě anfraks kamȳk tvoj y osnovanyju tvoemu sapfyr y zabralom tvoym yaspys, y vratom tvoym kamȳk krystal', y ohraženyju tvoemu kamȳk yzbrannȳy.	Milujaj tja smirenago i razsypanago: se outěšišisja. Se az ougotovaju tebě anfraks kamyk tvoj, i osnovaniju tvoemu sapfir, i zabralom tvoim iaspis, i vratom tvoim kamyk kristal', i ograždeniju tvoemu kamyk izbrannyj.	Smirennaja i koleblemaja, ne iměla esi utěšenija. Se az ugotovljaju tebě anfraks, kamen' tvoj, i na osnovanie tvoe sapfir; i položu zabrala tvoja iaspis i vrata tvoja kamenija izbrannaja.

(Here Skovoroda has a fairly long—unmarked—cut in his quotation.)

Se prišelcy prijdut k tebě mnoju, i vseljatsja u tebe, i k tebě priběhnut. Se az sozdax tja, ne jako že kuznec, razduvajaj uhlija i iznosja sosud na dělo. Az že sozdax tja ne na pahubu, eže istliti.	Se pryxody pryydut tebě mnoju y k tebě pryběhnut. Se az sъhražu tja ne jako kuznec razdȳmaja hlavnja y yznosja sъsud na dělo. Az bo sъhradyx tja ne na pahubu rasȳpaty.	Se prixodi priidut tebě mnoju i k tebě priběgnut. Se az sogražu tja ne jako kuznec razdymaja glavni i iznosja sosud na dělo. Az bo sogradix tja ne na pagubu razsypati.	Se prišelcy priidut k tebě mnoju, i vseljatsja ou tebe, i k tebě priběgnut. Se az sozdax tja, ne jakože kuznec razduvajaj ouglija i iznosja sosud na dělo. Az že sozdax tja ne na pagubu, eže istliti.

While the Ostrih and Moscow editions are the same except for a few details of spelling, the Synodal Bible and Skovoroda are identical even in this, the only difference being that instead of the plural *kamenija* Skovoroda used the collective *kamenie* (leaving, however, the adjective in the plural, *izbrannaja*!). Since the outcome of the collation in all remaining cases is the same (a qualification to be introduced below), it can be taken as proven that Skovoroda used the Synodal Bible as the source of his quotations. This agrees with Maxnovec''s assumption that Skovoroda's studies at the Kyiv Academy came to an end in 1753,[12] when that version of the biblical text was new and approved by the Academy. It also

---

10. In this transliteration *y* renders Cyrillic и, i, and ï; *ȳ*—ery; *o*—o and omega; *ja*—jus malyj; word-final *jer* (tverdyj znak) is omitted.

11. In this transliteration *i* renders и, i, ï; *y*—ery; *o*—o and omega; *ja*—jus malyj; word-final *jer* (tverdyj znak) is omitted.

12. Leonid Maxnovec', *Hryhorij Skovoroda: Biohrafija* (Kyiv, 1972), 73. In light of these collations one must put in doubt the legend (accepted uncritically by V. Ėrn, *Grigorij Savvič Skovoroda: Žizn' i učenie* [Moscow, 1912], 144) that on all his journeys Skovoroda carried with him the Hebrew Bible. (According to Bahalij, in his introduction to Skovoroda's *Sočinenija* [Xarkiv, 1894], lxxiv, it was a Hebrew *or* a Greek Bible.) Of course, a definitive solution to the problem of whether Skovoroda occasionally translated Biblical passages cannot be given until all his quotations from the Bible have been identified and verified. Yet in the group of texts analyzed during the preparation of this article there are few if any traces of his independent translations. The idea that Skovoroda constantly carried with him two or three copies of the Bible (including the Greek one) is implausible, if only because of the mere physical weight of such a load.

agrees with Skovoroda's own statement: "*Bibliju načal [ja] čitat' okolo tridcati lĕt roždenija moeho*" (PP-73, 246), i.e., around 1752.

This fact is indispensable for any study of the Church Slavonic components in Skovoroda's work. Passages drawn from the Synodal Bible cannot be taken as Skovoroda's personal lexical choice. On the other hand, wherever he deviated from a particular text, he did manifest his choice, e.g., note the departure alluded to above: *kamenie* instead of *kamenija*. This is a minor variant, possibly an oversight (although it is used twice). Are there more substantive departures? Some U baroque writers of the seventeenth century were quite liberal in this respect. As shown by Simovyč in his careful and meticulous study,[13] Ioanikij Galjatovs'kyj, for example, "twisted" (*vyvoročal*) the Bible to his and his audience's pleasure quite freely, partly following the Polish translation by Wujek and partly through the dictates of his own taste. Galjatovs'kyj, no doubt, was not alone in this practice. A positive general statement would be premature as long as we do not have detailed studies on various writers of the time, but a tentative assumption may be advanced that Baroque Ukraine enjoyed fairly great freedom in this respect before the authority of the rigidly dogmatic Russian church was firmly established.

If this is correct, Skovoroda's position was between the relative freedom of the U Baroque and the later trend toward strictness, but closer to the former. More is at stake here than minor grammatical changes (as *kamenie* above) or unmarked cuts in the text (as also observed in the above quotation) or omissions of some auxiliary words ("*Člověk zrit na lice, a Boh zrit na serdce*"—Ns-69, 41 vs. "*Člověk zrit na lice, Bog že zrit na serdce*"—Samuel I:16, 7; "*Obydoša tja bolězni, jako raždajuščija*"—As-69, 92 vs. "*Obydoša tja bolězni, aki raždajuščija*"—Micah 4:9; "*Včera i dnes' toj že vo věki*"—PP-73, 214 vs. "*Iis Xrsts včera i dnes' toj že i vo věki*"—Hebrews 13:8). These examples suffice to show that Skovoroda did not consider it vital to adhere to every letter of his underlying text. This impression is strengthened by the departures from spelling as observed in the Bible of 1757, e.g., "*Dast' dožd' zemlě...rannij i pozdnyj*"—As-69, 99 vs. "*Dast dožd' zemli...rannyj i pozdnyj*"—Moses 5:11, 14; "*jako smarahd*"—As, 143 vs. "*jako že smirit*"—Job 41:15. Some of these deviations can be ascribed to copyists. But apart from such slight departures there are others, of far greater magnitude:

a) The omission of full-fledged words: "*Gluboko serdce [čelověku] pače vsěx, i člověk est', i kto poznaet ego*"—Jeremiah 17:9, as shown above, is rendered: "*Hluboko serdce čelověku...i člověk est'*"—AM-74, 342. "*Erodia na nbsi pozna*

---

13. Vasyl' Simovyč, "Sproby perekladu Sv. Pys'ma u tvorax J. Galjatovs'koho," offprint, p. 3 pass. (from *Zapysky Naukovoho Tovarystva im. Ševčenka* 99, 1930). Reprinted in his *Ukrajins'ke movoznavstvo: Rozvidky j statti* (Ottawa, 1981), 121ff.

vremja svoe: gorlica i lastovica sel'naja, vrabija soxraniša vremena vxodov svoix: ljudie že moi sii ne poznaša sudeb Gdnix"—Jeremiah 8:7 in BE-87, 491 is rendered without all the underlined words (and without any indication of such an omission).

b) The replacement of some words: *"Byst' dux in v nem"*—Moses 4:14, 23 is rendered in Ns-69, 56: *"Byst' dux Moj v nem"*; *"Da ne razširitsja serdce tvoe"*— Moses 5:11, 16 in As-69, 99 is cited: *"Da ne obmanitsja serdce tvoe"*;[14] in the quotation from Jeremiah 8:7 given above under (a), the final part: *"ljudie že moi sii ne poznaša sudeb Gdnix"* in Skovoroda is rendered: *"Izrail' že mene ne pozna."*

c) The addition of words and images (which can also originate in the Bible, but which are not included in the particular passage quoted or in the proximate context), e.g., Psalm 55:6 has: *"I rěx: kto dast mi krilě jako golubině"*; this is quoted in Ns-69, 64 as follows: *"Kto dast mně krilě? "Da čtoby oni takovy byli, kakovyi iměet sija holubica, to est' posrebrenny,"* etc.[15] In all 23 verses of the psalm there is nothing on the silver quality of the dove's wings. A similar example is found in Skovoroda's letter to Kovalins'kyj (dated 1762 by Maxnovec'). Skovoroda quotes: *"Honju že, ašče i postihnu, to est' osoblivo postihnu"* (2, 297); the Bible has: *"Gonju že ašče i postignu, o nem že i postižen byx ot Xrsta Iisa"* (Philippians 3:12).

d) What is given by Skovoroda looks like a quotation with omissions marked by dots: *"Ptica obrěte sebě xraminu...osnovana bo bě na kameně...kamen' že bě Xristos...iže est' mir naš...duša naša, jako ptica, izbavisja, i sět' sokrušisja...kto dast mně krilě"* (PP-73, 243). The last part, it is clear, is from Psalm 55:6; the immediately preceding part is from Psalm 124:7, slightly edited by Skovoroda: *"Duša naša jako ptica izbavisja ot sěti lovjaščix: sět' sokrušisja."* Needless to say, there is not the slightest hint at the rest of the fragment in either of the psalms cited. It may be a mosaic made up of citations from other biblical sources or an original text of Skovoroda's or both. Skovoroda enjoyed composing such mosaics from the most heterogeneous texts. His thinking was panchronic, i.e., essentially a- and anti-historical. Truth, in his vision of God and the world, was revealed out of time and historical context. It was eternal and general, hence everything could be combined with anything.

e) Often Skovoroda freely retells a biblical passage. It may look like a quota-

---

14. Incidentally, Skovoroda's variant is here closer to the Greek text: μήποτε πλανηθῇ ἡ καρδίασας; one of the meanings of Gr. πλανάω is "to mislead, to deceive." Is it possible that he compared the text of the Synodal Bible with the underlying Greek (or Hebrew?) and corrected the former? In any case, this would not apply to the next example, from Jeremiah 8:7, where his version does not correspond to the Greek text: ὁ δὲ λαός μου γνωρίζει τὴν κρίσιν τοῦ κυρίου.

15. In Skovoroda's edition the quotation mark stands after *krilě*, but it was shown above that the closing quotation marks are added by the editor.

tion, but it is not, or, more often, it combines fragments of the biblical text with Skovoroda's own. Such examples are numerous. *"Esli de ne uznaeš' sebe, o dobraja ženo, tohda pasi kozly tvoi vozlě šalašej pastušskix. Ja de tebě ne muž, ne pastyr i ne hospodin. Ne vidiš' mene potomu, čto sebe ne znaeš'. Pojdi iz moix očej i ne javlajsja!"* (Ns-69, 48) is based on the Song of Songs 1:7: *"Ašče ne ouvěsi samuju tebe, dobraja v ženax, izydi ty v pjatax pastv, i pasi kozlišča tvoja ou kuščej pastyrskix."* John I:4, 8, *"Bg ljuby est'"* is rendered *"Boh—ljubov est'"* (PP-73, 214), which is a translation rather than a quotation. The Book of Genesis has: *"Vozleg ousnul esi jako lev i jako skimen"* (49:9). It continues in verses 11 and 12: *"Privjazuj k lozě žrebja svoe, i k vinničiju žrebca osljate svoego, isperet vinom odeždu svoju, i kroviju grozdija odějanie svoe. Radostotvorny oči jego pače vina."* The counterpart in Skovoroda (K-74, 279) is: *"Vot odin ščenok l'vov, skimen l'vov Iuda...no iměet li oči lice sie l'vovo? Iměet, no dlja věrnyx, vot oni: 'Radostotvorny oči eho pače vina...'"* Two images are left from the initial part of the passage; the central part is entirely Skovoroda's, with only the end a genuine quotation.

The purpose of such manipulations was manifold. They instill a double meaning into the text, often transforming it into the expression of Skovoroda's symbolic manner of thinking. They slightly modify the text stylistically, bringing it closer to the colloquial language. Occasionally they introduce, as synonyms, the real translations of ChSl words (cf. above *ščenok = skimen*). There are retellings in which the latter becomes the primary purpose. St. Paul is "quoted" as saying: *"Vstan' de mertvec i voskresni ot mertvyx!"*, which in the Bible reads: *"Vostani spjaj i voskresni ot mertvyx i osvětit tja Xrstos"* (Ephesians 5:14). Or: *"Nesut i vedut za nim kivot s sokrušennym vnutr' zavětom Hospoda sil v zamok Eho Sion, a David pred nim pljašet. 'Konečno, on spilsja ili ot melanxolii s uma sošel,'—hovorit, smotrja v okoško, Melxola, doč' Saulova"* (K-74, 260), which is the counterpart of Samuel II:6, 16: *"I byst' kivotu prinosimu ko gradu Dvdovu, i Melxola dšči Saulova prinicaše okoncem."* This, in Skovoroda, is continued as *"u Melxoly, dščeri Saula, ne byst' dětišča do dne smerti eja,"* which is a genuine quotation (disregarding grammatical changes: the Bible has *"dščeri Sauli"*— Samuel II:6, 23).

Of course the "lowered" language clearly suggests that the fragments in question are not actual quotations. But it is precisely here that the student in search of biblical Church Slavonicisms is in particular danger and must redouble his vigilance. In these apparent nonquotations, elements of real quotations may be and often are scattered throughout. After all, for all their earnestness and sincerity, Skovoroda's works, especially his dialogues, are also a cat-and-mouse game of guessing where one is dealing with quotations from the Bible and what their immediate source is (in fact, that is one of the features that make them such fun, even for those readers who do not take Skovoroda's philosophy too much to heart). It is not fortuitous that in some of the dialogues or parts thereof the principle of their composition is not so much to move the thought forward through conflicts of opposing views but rather, in a process of amplification, to cover a quotation or an allusion to a quotation from one book of the Holy Scriptures with another, paralleling one from the same book or another one as a trump covers an ordinary card. In this game the ground is strewn with traps, and if Skovoroda's contemporaries were often ensnared and at a loss, modern readers are in a particularly perilous position (as the woeful inadequacy of modern editors of Skovoroda clearly shows).

At this point in our reasoning the reader is, I hope, ready and willing to share the thesis stated at the outset of this section, namely, that the question of Church Slavonicisms in Skovoroda's work cannot find a reliable, adequate answer unless one eliminates all the biblical quotations (we can now say quotations from the Synodal Bible of 1751-7) from the linguistic corpus that constitutes the full body of his work. Until then one can only guess what would remain, i.e., what actually is Skovoroda's own text. At the present stage of research all judgements on the Church Slavonic components of Skovoroda's language are necessarily impressionistic and often subjective. The present writer's hypothesis would be: Church Slavonicisms in Skovoroda do not occur only in his biblical quotations, but those that do not spring from that source are not, as a rule, introduced by the poet:[16] they are usually part and parcel of the eighteenth-century Russian language and therefore bear no function of a personal stylistic device. This is tantamount to saying—tentatively, to be sure—that Church Slavonicisms in Skovoroda are devoid of a specific stylistic function beyond the (admittedly, important) one of signalling biblical connotations. Otherwise they constitute the neutral stylistic background of his language.

Herein lies a substantial difference between Skovoroda and his predecessor (in time!) Teofan Prokopovyč. In his rejection of baroque poetics and stylistics, Prokopovyč rejected the very principle of contrastiveness in style. But in striving for stylistic homogeneity in his language he did not turn to the vernacular. Whatever his other reasons, one is obvious: he could not sermonize without biblical quotations. Such quotations were in Church Slavonic; hence, in order to avoid a multi-layered vocabulary, he had no choice but to Church Slavonicize his entire text. As a typical example one can take Prokopovyč's sermon on Peter I's return from a voyage (1717). The subject is entirely secular. The text consists of two parts. In the first half the preacher comments on a quotation from St. Luke's Gospel. This part, according to the tradition of the Russian church, should have been entirely in Church Slavonic, and so it is, with the characteristic (as Kjell-

---

16. For the present writer, all Skovoroda's texts, whether poems or so-called philosophical treatises and dialogues, are to be taken as poetry. (This point is made in a little more detail in section 3 below.) For this reason the right is reserved to call him a poet and to apply this characterization to his entire *oeuvre*.

berg rightly points out)[17] set of conjunctions (*poneže, ašče, egda, aki, ibo*, etc.) and the use of the aorist and the imperfect in the verb (*sovokupi, sogna*, etc.) as the most conspicuous indicators of that choice.[18] The second part of the text is entirely political. It deals with the strengthening of Russian power under Peter I. Its stylistic key could have been quite different, but it is not. Except for the moderate use of some West European loan words, it does not differ from the first part either in choice of vocabulary and grammatical forms or in word order and syntax in general: "*Čto že, egda ešče v živoj, jako že rex, škole sej političeskoj, v mnogostrannoj peregrinacii vjaščšago i vjaščšago iskusstva navykati tščimsja! To bo voistinnu ljubomudrie: nikogda že priobretennym veščej poznaniem dovoljatisja, no bol'šago vsegda sveta poiskovati.*"[19]

Such an even style, such a balanced Church Slavonic was alien to the preachers of the Ukrainian Baroque. Typically, their sermons consist of a constant alternation of Church Slavonic "highs" and vernacular "lows," the former in quotations, the latter in the preacher's own speech. In the simplest implementation this contrastiveness appears as a switch after each sentence as, e.g., in the initial part of I. Galjatovs'kyj's sermon "*Na vozdvyženyje Čstnaho Krsta*": *(1) "Dvojakyj jest Krst'", jeden" dxovnȳj, dobrovolnoje dlja Xa outrapenje. Toj krst" spomynal Xs movjačy: (2) Ašče kto xoščet vosled" mene yty, da otveržetsja sebe y vozmet Krst" svoj y po mně hrjadet". (3) Toj Krst" dxovnȳj nosyly Apostolove, bo onȳ terpěly dlja Xa dobrovolnoe outrapenje. Tak movyt Apsl" Pavel": (4) Ukarjajemy blhoslovljaem", honymy terpym", xulymy outyšaem, (5) toj Krst" dxovnȳj nosyly mčenyky, bo onȳ dlja Xa terpěly dobrovolnoe outrapenje, muky y smrt' podymovaly...,*"[20] etc. Each odd-numbered segment of the text is in the vernacular, each even-numbered one in ChSl. The size of such segments may vary, but the principle is constant. A certain monotony induced by such recurrent language alternations is to a great extent compensated by the play of emblematic, symbolic, and imagistic elements, but their analysis is beyond the framework of this article.[21]

---

17. Kjellberg, 14.
18. Feofan Prokopovič, *Sočinenija*, ed. I. Eremin (Moscow and Leningrad, 1961), 60ff.
19. Prokopovič, 66. In this edition ě is rendered by e.
20. Y. Galjatovs'kyj, *Ključ razuměnyja*, 1659, as reprinted by K. Bida in his *Ioanikij Galjatovs'kyj i joho "Ključ Razuměnija*" (Rome, 1975), 476. Accents are omitted in this quotation.
21. There are U Baroque sermons that contain far more complicated structures of intertwining ChSl and other (native) vocabulary components (also in Galjatovs'kyj's own writings), e.g., in Dmytro Tuptalo's sermon on "Bran' Svjataho Arxystratyha Myxayla" (1697) (in a brief and simplified presentation) the layer that consists of the literary variant of the U intellectuals' colloquial language is much more prominent, the number of Biblical quotations is much smaller, and they are scattered irregularly throughout the text; Church Slavonicisms appear in quotations other than Biblical ones (e.g., in the description of the Archangels, as "*Selafyyl—služytel' jest božestvennȳx mol'b, vȳnu k Bohu o rodě čelověčestěm moljajsja y čelověkov userdně, bohomȳsl'ně y umylenně molytysja poučajaj*

In the contrast between the Enlightener's "monolinguality" (or one-layeredness) of the sermons by Prokopovyč and the baroque "bilinguality" (or two-layeredness) of Galjatovs'kyj, as represented by his text on the Elevation of the Holy Cross, Skovoroda is definitely to be placed with Galjatovs'kyj, that is, in the baroque tradition. But the monotony of language juxtaposition is alien to Skovoroda. And this is so not only because the distribution of biblical quotations in his work is incomparably more whimsical (from an agglomeration of up to fifty quotations gathered together to scattered brief passages and allusive fragments of passages, as shown above), and because of the much more complicated linking of quotations with one another and with the rest of the text, but also, and primarily, because the biblical quotations in Skovoroda—a very important fact—are not the only source of his Church Slavonicisms. In his non-quotational passages Galjatovs'kyj employed the usual language of the intellectuals of his time, which was filled with Polonisms, but was almost entirely free of Church Slavonicisms. That language, for all practical purposes, did not exist for Skovoroda. Instead, as the contrastive partner to Church Slavonic, he used the Russian language (why and how is discussed in section 3), which, as is generally known, even now is filled with ChSl components and was even more so in the eighteenth century. Many examples may be quoted. Two will suffice (capitals are used to single out indubitable Church Slavonicisms):

"*Mojsejskij že, simboličeskij (tajnoobraznyj) mir est' kniha. Ona ni v čem ne trohaet OBITEL'NAHO mira, a tol'ko slědami sobrannyx ot neho tvarej PUTEVODSTVUET nas k PRISNOSUŠČNOMU načalu EDINSTVENNO, kak*

y na to vozbuždajaj" (An. Titov, *Propovedi Svjatitelja Dmitrija, Mitropolita Rostovskogo na ukrainskom narečii* [Moscow, 1909], 97). This switches the function of ChSl from a linguistically foreign body limited to quotations to that of a stylistic device conveying lofty notions, i.e., it associates them with particular subject matter. Then, however, this concept is destroyed by introducing isolated native components into the ChSl text as a factual commentary ("*Svjatýj Rafayl yzobražen šujcoju podnesennoju deržašč alavastr, al'bo sloyk lekarskyj, desnyceju že vodjašč Tovyju otroka*"— ibid., 101; the native components underlined). And finally it comes to passages in which the same event is presented twice in two different languages, ChSl and native: "*Srěte—to uže vojennaja potyčka zÿšlysja vojska, ztočylasja bran': Každo do svojej porvalsja broně, do svojeho oružyja. Bran' bÿst': Myxayl y ahhely jeho bran' sotvoryša s zmyem*" (ibid., 103; native components underlined). The two layers kept separate in Galjatovs'kyj here interpenetrate each other; a mixture ensues, stylistic functions cross and lose their contours; the listener (or reader) is immersed in this peculiar atmosphere, which is usual and unusual, native and non-native, home and temple at the same time.

On the other hand, Prokopovyč also had his precursors in the U Baroque tradition in terms of striving toward a consistently pure ChSl vocabulary with no admission of heterogeneous components. Such was the attitude of Lazar Baranovyč, e.g., his "Slovo na prenesenye moščej stÿx strstoterpec Knzej Rossyjskyx Borysa y Hlěba" (*Truby sloves propovědnÿx* [Kyiv, 1674], 204ff.) in this respect could have been a work by Prokopovyč, except that the ChSl of Baranovyč has a more archaic flavour (problems of symbolism and imagery aside). As there is basic English, so Prokopovyč's was, so to speak, basic ChSl. Baranovyč sought a more exquisite, more flowery ChSl.

mahnitnaja strěla, VZIRAJA na věčnuju TVERD' eho" (YZ-76, 384);
  "Naposlědok sim putem ěxal v kolesnicě evnux caricy Kandakii i poznalsja SO Filippom. Filipp otkryl emu v čelověke čelověka, v ESTESTVĚ—ESTESTVO, BLAHOUXANIE Xristovo i novym BLAHOVĚSTIEM, AKI čudnym fimiamom, nakadil emu serdce, omyl eho netlěnnoju sverx ot stixijnyja vody vodoju i otpustil eho v dom svoj" (BA-83, 451).

This may be archaic Russian for that time (although not more archaic than, say, in A. Radiščev's *Putešestvie iz Peterburga v Moskvu,* 1790!), but it is Russian. In the Russian of the time obvious Church Slavonicisms operated with a specific stylistic function. But the paradox of Skovoroda's language is that in his writings it was Russian that had a special stylistic function, as will be shown below. Thus, Russian Church Slavonicisms primarily fulfilled the function of being Russian; their own stylistic function either withered away or was at least substantially weakened. To use a comparison, a barbarism in French may function as a peculiar stylistic feature, but when L. Tolstoj used French in his Russian novel *War and Peace,* this stylistic function within French was, for a Russian reader, neutralized and probably non-existent.[22] In other words, there were at least (but see below) two types of Church Slavonicisms in Skovoroda: biblical and Russian. The former had a clear-cut stylistic function or purpose; the latter were neutral or nearly so, unless they were, in certain cases, infected, so to speak, with stylistic value from the former. Thus, the interplay of the two types of Church Slavonicisms in Skovoroda created a complicated configuration of which even the most refined stylists of the preceding Ukrainian Baroque could not dream. In that respect, therefore, Skovoroda represents the culmination of Ukrainian Baroque, which may be called the High Baroque. (This fully applies to his emblematics, symbolism, and imagery as well, but these problems are not to be treated here.)

The strangest thing is that such an unusually sophisticated effect was attained by means that apparently involved no personal effort. Neither type of Church Slavonicism was newly introduced by Skovoroda; they apparently did not spring from his own creative activity. They had in common the fact that they were both, in a sense, quoted—literally so in the case of his biblical reminiscences and, in a broader sense, in his use of Russian. To the final part of this statement the objection might be raised that Skovoroda could have selected Russian without

---

22. This is why, in many cases, predominantly Russian passages in Skovoroda flow without any external motivation into ChSl (e.g., SBP 19, 2, 33) or, conversely, ChSl suddenly appears in basically Russian dialogues (e.g., in BD-72, 167 in the rejoinder of Naeman). When Russian proper and ChSl elements that had been absorbed into Russian produced doublets, they occasionally caused Skovoroda to introduce some differentiation, but then it was mostly semantic, as in the following attempt at defining the meaning of a word (arbitrary though it was): "*Žitie značit: rodit'sja, kormit'sja, rasti i umaljat'sja, a žizn' est' plodoprinošenie ot zerna istiny*" (YZ-76, 372).

Church Slavonicisms, hence there was a free choice on his part if he still used Russian with numerous Church Slavonicisms. This objection is only partly correct. True, Skovoroda could have utilized fewer Church Slavonicisms, but a variant of Russian free of them simply did not exist.

One question remains. While most Church Slavonicisms in Skovoroda are quotational, in the broad sense of the word, did he still have at least some deliberate, function-loaded Church Slavonicisms of his own choice or even of his own coinage? Given our present state of knowledge, this question cannot be definitively answered. Moreover, it probably will never be answered in full, in application to every particular instance that may pertain to this problem, for it often borders on the unanswerable question: what did Skovoroda think and feel in choosing a particular word? In preparing the ground for at least a partial elucidation of this problem, we can only present some material.

To begin with, in at least a few cases Skovoroda was aware of ChSl vocabulary as opposed to other layers of his word supply. In BA-83, 449 he uses four synonyms for "stomach": *sirišče*, *črevo*, *utroba* and *želudok*. To the first of these he gives a footnote: "*Sirišče est' hlas vetxoslavenskij, značit...želudok.*" It is to be inferred that he did make a distinction between ChSl vs. R. Of course, this does not imply that he was able to make the distinction in every particular instance, nor does it show that he assigned the distinction a stylistic value. Yet *sirišče*, *črevo*, and *utroba* are used in the text, and *želudok* only in a commentary outside the text. This was hardly a matter of chance.

In non-quotational parts of his work (better, parts not identified with quotations) Skovoroda employs ChSl conjunctions, particles, and the like. In my lexical inventory on cards I have *daby* 5x, *ašče* 2x, *jako* and *kako* 4x each, *ubo* 3x, *potol'*—*pokol'* 2x, *poneže* 1x, *eliko*—*toliko* 1x, *kamo* 1x. It is certainly not a complete count. Yet, even if doubled, it is a very low frequency for more than one thousand pages of Skovoroda's writings. In verbal forms aorists are rare (on my cards I have 10 instances), imperfects still rarer (in my file 4x). This is a negligible quantity. Archaic forms of participles (the types *pomohajaj*—1, 54, *pověsivyj*—2, 81, *začenšyj*—1, 447) are much more frequent, especially the active present tense participles in *-aj*.[23] In declension, the only ChSl form frequently used is the gen sg fem of adj in *-yja* ("*ponjatie věčnyja natury*"— PZ-90, 536), whereas the alternation of velars in the dat-loc subst is almost entirely absent (*v čelověcě*—SBP-11, 2, 22 is unique).[24] In syntax I noticed only

---

23. According to V. Zamkova, *Slavjanizm kak stilističeskaja kategorija v russkom literaturnom jazyke XVIII v.* (Leningrad, 1975), 119, participles in *-aj* are not typical of mid-eighteenth-century poetic Russian, except in a few deviating authors.

24. This configuration of declensional features also occurs in Russian at the very end of the eighteenth c. Cf., e.g., "*proistekali iz edinyja prirody*" in a letter of a Moscow Mason, A. Kutuzov, 1791 (Ja. Barskov, *Perepiska moskovskix masonov XVIII-go veka* [Petrograd, 1915], 71).

one instance of the dative absolute ("*Hrěx...ujazvljaet dušu, pokryvajuščej tmě i naxodjaščiu straxu*"—BE-87, 505). Thus, a tentative statement may be attempted to the effect that Skovoroda knew what Church Slavonicisms were but, beyond his quotations, exploited them in a very limited way.

The situation seems to change if one proceeds to word formation. Skovoroda often indulged in using certain types of words which, at least nowadays, give the impression of having been newly formed by him on the ChSl pattern. Three main types deserve consideration:

a) The compounding of stems, generating mostly adjectives, less often substantives. Adjectives: *krasnozračnyja lěsa* (SBP-6, 2, 15), *nebo temnozračno, xolm vysokoměstnoj* (F—60s, 2, 67), *tupookij, lehkoparnyj, bystrozračnyj* (As-69, 155), *sladkoteplyj ohn'* (BD-72, 177), *zlatožaždnyj* (BD, 182), *durnomudryja děvy* (BD, 185), *blahosěnnolistvennyj dub* (DM-72, 187),[25] *ostrodalnozritelnoj...Hlaz* (PP-73, 210), *načalorodnoj tmy* (PP, 211),[26] *ravnomolnijnoe...stremlenie* (PP, 239), *bystrozornaho orla* (K-74, 292), *krovokapljuščija rany* (AM-74, 349), *dom...sedmipiramidnyj* (ŽL-80, 425), *sennopismennaho mraka* (ŽL, 436), *bljadolěpnyja lavry* (BA-83, 455), *bljadokrasujuščajasja [žena]* (BA, 459), *iaspisošarnyja krila* (BA, 460), *tonkoplotnoe nebo* (BA, 462), *bezstrannopriimnyj...Kavkaz* (BA, 468), *sladkozdravuju pišču* (PB-83, 476), *blahodvoeobrazna* (PB, 488), *krovopotnye trudy* (PZ-90, 554). Substantives: *liceljubcy* (Ns-69, 29), *ljuboprax* (Ns, 45), *plododějstvie* (Ns, 58), *naružnosteljubcy* (As-69, 152), *zoroterem* (BD-72, 185), *hradomati* (BD, 186), *raznoformie* (DM-72, 192), *knihospletec* (YZ-76, 376), *pis'mozvonstvo* (ŽL-88, 436), *suxputstvo* (Od-85, 2, 156).

b) Prefixation generating adjectives and substantives: *těn' bezbytnaja* (Ns-69, 37), *vo vsevselenněj* (BD-72, 179), *protivostrastie* (ŽL-80, 429), *knižniki bezminervnyi* (PZ-90, 566). This derivational mechanism is much less frequent in Skovoroda than compounding. Still less frequent—and less bound to ChSl patterns—is the nominal derivation by suffixation: *hlavnost'* (Ns-69, 33),[27] *zemlennost'* (Ns, 45), *těnnyj...mir* (DM-72, 192), *ceremonisty serdjatsja* (K-74, 267), *prilahatel'* (YZ-76, 394),[28] *nasmorklivym devam* (ŽL-80, 424).

c) Derivation of verbs from nouns by suffixation, occasionally in combination with a prefix. The favourite suffixes here are *-stvova-* and *-niča-*. The latter is,

---

25. Z. Petrova quotes *blagosennolistvennyj* and *legkoparjaščij* from V. Trediakovskij (AN SSSR, Institut russkogo jazyka, *Processy formirovanija leksiki russkogo literaturnogo jazyka*, ed. Ju. Sorokin [Moscow and Leningrad, 1966], 185, 189).

26. The word appears in F. Polikarpov's *Leksikon trejazyčnyj* (Moscow, 1704), s.v.

27. Mal'ceva quotes *glavnost'* from Trediakovskij. See I. Mal'ceva, A. Molotkov, Z. Petrova, *Leksičeskie novoobrazovanija v russkom jazyke XVIII v.* (Leningrad, 1975), 12, 311.

28. For eighteenth-century Russian parallels with this suffix, see Zamkova, 85; the word is also recorded in Polikarpov's *Leksikon*, s.v.

in the Russian language of the time, characterized as native Russian, i.e., not used in ChSl words and word forms.[29] This is clearly not the case in Skovoroda's writings, for he uses it with ChSl stems (as well as with other ones): *putevodničat'* (As-69, 116), *kovarničit* (PP-73, 221), *okoldunil* (BD-72, 164), *voobrazitsja (v nas Xristos)* (DM-72, 199), [*krasota...vsju tvar'...*] *osuščestvujuščaja* (AM-74, 332), *mjatežit* (C-70s, 2, 161).[30]

Most of the words listed here are ChSl in their components and patterns; if they were really created by Skovoroda, this would testify to his active, and not only quotational, use of the ChSl heritage. But one must not be hasty in positing such a conclusion.

There are more words of the above types in his writings, words that in their derivational patterns do not differ from those cited above either grammatically or stylistically, but about which we may be sure that they were not created by Skovoroda, for one simple reason: they are all listed in Miklošič's dictionary of Middle ChSl (except the verbs in *-ničat'*).[31] Here are specimens classified according to the categories above:

aa) *povsemstvennoe estestvo Božie* (ND-66, 20), *rosonosnyj* (Ns-69, 29), *dobrorodnymi zubami, radostotvorny oči* (As-69, 125), *dobrovzornaja ptička* (As, 158), *pravolučnyja strely* (BD-72, 171), *trub zvězdozornyx* (BD, 185), *vserodnaja nauka* (PP-73, 225), *idoloběšenstvo* (PP, 244. Miklošič: *idoloběsie*), *hnoejadec* (K-74, 265), *pěšešestvie* (K, 270. Miklošič: *pěšešъstvovati*), *sěnnopisannyj mrak* (K, 295), *na blahokruhlom lukě (BA-83, 447), pravolučnuju strělu* (BA, 460).

bb) *bezsovětie* (PP-73, 215), *prěbyval'naho hrada* (UŽ-87, 527. Miklošič: *prěbyvalьnikъ*), *pirovnoe izobilie* (PP-73, 219), *hlaholov potopnyx* (ŽL-80, 414), *tkateljax* (YZ-76, 376. Miklošič: *tъkatelьnica*).

cc) *putevodstvujut* (BD-72, 171), *kovarničit* (PP-73. Miklošič: *kovarьnikъ*), *sokroviščestvujut* (PP, 207), *prepobědit'* (YZ-76, 380), *plotomudrstvujuščija skoty* (ŽL-80, 408. Miklošič: *plъtomǫdrije*).

Most of the words listed under (aa)—(cc) were rarely used. As a rule, Miklošič has only one citation for each of them. Nevertheless, they cannot be taken as newly created by Skovoroda. Their appearance in his writings only implies that he was indeed well read in the Fathers of the Church. What is rare for Miklošič and for us was not necessarily so for him. In fact, time and again he not only thought in their thoughts and imagined in their images, but also thought and imagined in their vocabulary. This established, one cannot help but

---

29. Cf. Zamkova, 83.
30. A brief list of Skovoroda's neologisms was compiled by P. Buzuk, "Mova i pravopys v tvorax H.S. Skovorody," *Pamjaty H.S. Skovorody (1722-1922)* (Odessa, 1923), 79.
31. Fr. Miklošič, *Lexicon palaeoslovenico-graeco-latinum* (Vienna, 1862-5). If Miklošič gives a slightly different morphological variant, this is adduced in parentheses after the page reference in Skovoroda.

question whether all the words cited here under (a) to (c) were really Skovoroda's neologisms.[32] Two circumstances make plausible the supposition that some or many of them may not have been invented by him, but taken over from ChSl texts. The types of words in (a) to (c) are absolutely identical to those in (aa) to (cc), and while Miklošič's *Lexicon* is still the most comprehensive dictionary of Middle ChSl, it is far from exhaustive.

If one accepts this possibility, he is taken back to the beginning of this section. Directly, or through the mediation of the Church Fathers, the ChSl layer in Skovoroda's writings brings us to one crucial source, the Bible: "*Hlava že vsěm Biblija*." Neither of the two groups of his Church Slavonicisms, biblical and "Russian," had a stylistic function similar to that of Lomonosov's notorious *vysokij stil'*. The function of the bulk of Skovoroda's Church Slavonicisms (the first group) was to signal a quotation. It can be said, somewhat tongue in cheek, that they served as peculiar quotation marks otherwise apparently absent from his manuscripts. The second group, the "Russian Church Slavonicisms," was discussed above.

Let us state the preceding tentative conclusion in another way. Lomonosov's theory of three styles, which—whether followed, disrupted, or rejected—was the stylistic backbone of Russian rhetoric and literature in the middle of the eighteenth century (with high style based on Church Slavonicisms), simply does not apply to Skovoroda. This theory is devoid of justification and pointless in application to his writings. The stratification of his vocabulary seems to have been based on different principles.

At this juncture the reader should not, however, be oblivious of what was said at the beginning of this essay. Any conclusion concerning Skovoroda's language will be tentative and provisional until *all* quotations in his works have been established and traced to their sources, so that we are able to deal with the pure corpus of what is really his own linguistic material. Then it may prove, contrary to the suggested conclusions, that some of his "ChSl neologisms" actually were of his own making and consequently did play a stylistic part in his writings.

---

32. Parallels from Trediakovskij and Polikarpov were adduced above. Two more of the words listed under (a) to (c) find their parallels in I. Sreznevskij, *Materialy dlja slovarja drevnerusskogo jazyka*, 1-3 (St. Petersburg, 1893, 1912): *vъsobražati se* and *sěnьnopisanyi*.

2

"Samonužnost' est povseměstnaja i věčnaja. Boh i premudrost' beznačal'ny. A to samaja drjan', čto včera s hribami rodilos'."
H. Skovoroda, *"Kol'co,"* 1774

We noted that Skovoroda's image and concept of the world was motionless and ahistorical. Time did not exist or was to be disregarded. Moses was treated as a contemporary of Jesus Christ and King David "sang" along with St. Paul. Changes were for him only superficial and/or imaginary. Historical events and upheavals of his time, such as the destruction of Ukrainian autonomy, the liquidation of the Zaporozhian Sich, the uprisings of the *Hajdamaky*, the enslavement of the peasants, the regicides in St. Petersburg, the Turkish and the Seven-Year Wars, the fall of the Crimea, etc. found no reflection in his writings. All this was *"samaja drjan'."* Ontologically all historical changes, indeed, change in general, were irrelevant to him and of no interest whatsoever. Skovoroda was in no way a precursor of the nineteenth-century historical method. Political passions and involvement were alien to him.

As if deliberately acting in the spirit of Skovoroda's world outlook, the authors who wrote on his language took it as a whole and paid no attention to the question of changes in it. Every one of these authors described it by means of a summary characterization, whether he viewed it as Russian, bookish Ukrainian, a misbegotten monster, or a necessary stage on the road from the literary language of the post-Meletian era to modern standard Ukrainian. Such a generalization was, it must be admitted, also applied in the first part of this triptych. There is some justification for such treatment. Skovoroda created an inimitable, personal language and was, or so it seems, faithful to it for a long time. A reader can easily have the impression of an overall stability, especially from the vantage point of two centuries later. But Skovoroda wrote over a period of forty years. Did his language really undergo no changes in all these long years? Was it not subject to any development, not to mention crises or revolutions?

One really cannot obtain an adequate idea of Skovoroda's language if the question of its evolution is not studied, that is, if we do not know which aspects of it were actually stable and which were not. Moreover, one may posit that changes in Skovoroda's language were due not only to "natural," subconscious causes (like every man, he was subject to changes caused by growth and aging, just as handwriting is not the same at age twenty and at age seventy), but were also due to the fact that Skovoroda was style-conscious and liked experimentation in genres, style, and language. In 1762 he wrote to the young Kovalins'kyj: *"Usus per errores ducit nos ad elegantiam scribendi"* (2, 241) and it would be a mistake to apply this striving for elegance to his writings in Latin only. Admittedly, a year later he sent a piece of advice to the same friend that seems to be in contradiction with the preceding one: "*Tu interim perpende, non verborum, quae prope nulla est, elegantiam, sed utrum nos satis pie cogitavimus, vim sententiarum; et nucleum, non corticem degusta*" (2, 311). But the contradiction is only apparent: as everything is *dvoje* for Skovoroda, so is *elegantia*. He rejects elegance that is purely formal; he welcomes that which conveys wisdom and God's truth.

In his own practice he had a taste for the unusual ("*Vozljubil esi strannost'*," the Demon reproached him—*Dajmon*, his best critic, invented by Skovoroda himself, because otherwise he had no critics able to understand him—PB-83, 479). He compares the experimental stream of his imagery with the intricacy of a cobweb: the same *Dajmon* addresses him: "*Dušo, ispolnena paučiny! Ne poučajuščaja, no paučajuščaja*" (PB, 470). This was an expression of Skovoroda's remorse for allowing himself perhaps too much verbal experimentation. In reality, however, once again there is no contradiction between his thought and his stylistic experimentation, just as there was none between thought and elegance of style. Skovoroda teaches and preaches (*poučaet*) through stylistic experiments that he so lovingly and carefully spins (*paučaet*).

When freed from these doubts and pangs of conscience, Skovoroda realized that, as he saw it, there was no abyss, indeed, no sharp division between prophecy and poetry, because it is in both that verbal experimentation conveys the ultimate truth, and the web of words becomes an adequate means to express the wealth and intricacy of God's manifestations in the visible world: "*Sie to est' inoskazanie i istinnaja ona ποίητις, sirěč tvorenie, položit' v plotskuju pustoš zlato Božie i zdělat' duxom iz ploti... Vot istinnye piity, sirěč tvorcy i proroki*" (BD-72, 167). Skovoroda returned to the same identification of prophets and (true) poets in another work. "*Ty mně Božiix prorokov poděal piitami*," the earthly Afanasij reproves him in Obs-72, 285. Seven years before his death Skovoroda confessed that for him fun was a necessary ingredient of life and of life's bliss, that life contains elements of sport, and that play is one source of the enjoyment of life. In BE-87 a story is told of a monk who spent a thousand years trying to catch a beautiful bird. Erodij admits: "*On znal, čto ee vověki ne ulovit,*" and, to Pišek's objection: "*Dlja čeho ž sebe pusto trudil?*" answers: "*Kak pusto, kohda zabavljalsja. Ljude zabavu kupujut. Zabava est' vračestvo i oživotvorenie serdca*" (509). Here the sixty-five-year-old poet-prophet confessed what he had been doing in various ways throughout his literary life: playing with words, experimenting in style. This was his form of *zabava*.

Experiment loses its experimental character if it repeats itself. It is no longer fun, no more *zabava*. The requirement of constant innovation is contained in the notion of literary writing (or, to be more precise, at least one aspect of such writing) as game.

To demonstrate the changes in Skovoroda's language and imagery, his search for new and more convincing means throughout his entire creative life, would require a book or a series of articles. The modest purpose of this essay is only to demonstrate that this investigation should be undertaken. To give only a superficial idea of his constant impulse toward literary experimentation, to offer a brief survey of the most striking changes in genre and general stylistic orientation, let us undertake a kind of quick march through Skovoroda's major works in chronological order.

It is generally known that he began as a poet between 1750 and 1753, but it has never been emphasized strongly enough that his poems vary in genre from religious ode and rhymed sermon to stylized folk song, to satire and joke, to personal lyricism, to friendly epistle, to heraldic panegyric, to idyll, to anecdote, to marketplace interlude (F2-60s, 2, 74) and fables (BEz-60, 96) along the way. The poetic work of Skovoroda, which in scope does not amount to more than 90 pages, is one constant experiment in genres, as if it were a kind of *ars poetica* without the theoretical part, poetics represented by illustrations alone, and an experimental poetics withal. Then there were two cycles of prose fables, BX of 1759 (1-19) and of 1774 (20-30). Again, how different the two cycles are. The first is an experiment in laconicism and terseness. In the second, the principle of conciseness is maintained only in the narrative parts, while the moral (*sila*) varies from extended publicism (e.g., Fable 24) to a sermon with a moralistic purpose, abounding in biblical quotations and permeated with philosophy, popularly presented (e.g., Fable 30), sometimes even in a vulgar variety of Russian (Fables 28, 29).

In terms of genre, ND-68 is a conspectus for an academic course. Definitions and rules lie at its heart. It proceeds in the catechetical form of questions and answers leading to definitions and commandments, but it is adorned with restrained imagery, clearly pursuing the pedagogical intention of making abstractions more palatable to students. Skovoroda probably had more writings in this genre, but this is the only extant specimen.

Ns-69 is Skovoroda's first experiment in dialogue. He does not yet build a consistent conversation from the beginning to the end of the work; it is rather a series of relatively brief, disconnected dialogues with little continuity as to the participants, interrupted by "*simfonii*" or clusters of biblical quotations. Unconnected parts are brought into a unity by the general idea and by the recurrent image of the character Narkiss. The language is mostly RChSl with several brief admixtures of very colloquial Russian, which occasionally bring the lofty abstractions of the philosophical discussion down to earth.

As-69 is Skovoroda's first attempt at a thoroughgoing dialogue with the same participants throughout. But he has not yet acquired mastery of this form, and it is broken from time to time by material that is technically assigned to a collocutor, but is in reality Skovoroda's own treatise, the soliloquizing character of which is betrayed by its very length (e.g., *Druh*'s speech is seventeen pages long—104ff.). Stylistically, As is quite different from Ns in spite of the fact that the topic (self-knowledge) is almost identical. In Ns it was rather a collection of quiet, philosophical symposia. Here rhetorical prophecy prevails, thrust and parry. Hence, we find here rhetorical figures of the anaphoristic type that were virtually absent from Ns. Hence also lapses into the use of the second person plural in addressing (though this is not stated) rather an audience of a preacher than a friend or two in private conversation. Ub and DL-66 (?) probably were experimental fragments in Skovoroda's work on the genre represented by As. The impression of Skovoroda's most recent editors that they were sermons (1, 583) is justified, although Maxnovec' (p. 205) is quite right in stating that, technically, a layman like Skovoroda could never have delivered or even prepared actual sermons.

BD-72 goes rather farther in imitating a real dialogue. Its participants are the same through the entire work and it is virtually free of intermittent excessive soliloquizing. At the same time, it is a further step toward the elevation and poeticization of the speakers' rejoinders. Ukrainian components are drastically reduced, R and ChSl are blended in a unity, not a contrast, quotations in Greek and Latin increase, and foreign words of recent vintage modernize the essentially biblical subject and language. While in Ns and As the constantly recurring images were those of the main characters named in the titles, Narkiss and Asxan', here such an image is that of various birds taken figuratively (complicated by reference to animals), which lays emphasis on emblematic structures. Through the parts assigned to different speakers Skovoroda manages to ensure a gradual accumulation of lyricism and, further along, ecstasy, culminating in what is tantamount to a hymn. This is possible because, structurally, this dialogue is for the most part not an alternation of statements and counter-statements, but consists of additions and variations. Each successive speaker supports and develops what was said by his predecessor(s). Such an additive structure of dialogue was a means of transforming what outwardly was a conversation into a peculiar piece of lyricism. (This innovative device was not understood even by those Skovoroda scholars who had the deepest insight into his style, e.g., Tschižewskij 204 sees in it the sheer lack of command of the dialogue form in Skovoroda!)

In DM-72 Skovoroda retreats from the ecstasy of BD to a more informal and apparently realistic "conversation among friends," hence the number of Ukrainianisms is slightly increased, although complex ChSl vocabulary is broadly used. There are recurrent images, but mostly they organize only certain parts of the work.

PP-73 is built on a contrast between the first half of the dialogue, essentially in colloquial Russian, and the second half, which explodes with ChSl biblical quotations interpreted symbolically. This leads to an obscuring of the logical ties between the parts, in turn generating a protest on the part of some of the participants in the dialogue. "*Temno hovoriš*"—"*Ty tol' zahustil rěč tvoju biblejnym laskut'em, čto nělzja razumět'"*—246). This is a peculiar laying bare of a literary device that makes the contrast between an abstract dialogue and an everyday, "real" conversation especially obvious.

In K-74, Skovoroda seems to have recognized the incompatibility of a "real" dialogue with the topic of commenting on the Bible as a collection of symbolical and emblematic images. The work opens with a twenty-four-page-long monologue, actually a lecture by *Hryhorij*, clearly an *alter ego* of Skovoroda, which, after a very brief dialogue, is followed by another lecture, this time by Lonhin (14 pages). Only after this point does the similarity to a dialogue begin. But this likeness is actually again a monologue, distributed fairly arbitrarily among the three participants. Each of them continues what the preceding speaker began, and the only real dialogue structure is brought in by brief remarks of Afanasij, who appears as a kind of Sancho Panza in the company of three Don Quixotes. He interrupts the other speakers with his down-to-earth, blunt, skeptical remarks, which break the monotony of what otherwise is just a disguised monologue. Thus, Afanasij makes it a little livelier, but his part in the development of ideas and imagery is near zero. If Afanasij's remarks are excluded and the names of the other participants erased, K-74 may be considered a non-dialogue.

The same five characters appear in AM-74; it was probably written in the same year. The final part of this dialogue is close in style to K-74. It is an accumulation of biblical quotations, only this time with a much more developed system of semantic switches (which indeed reflect Skovoroda's philosophy that all things are the same in their higher aspect and deep essence, i.e., God). But all the preceding sections of the dialogue are conducted in quite a different key, basically in neutral everyday educated Russian, in complete agreement with the subject of that dialogue, which is designed, according to its title, as a survey of attitudes and conditions of human life on earth, a primer of this world. Such a style appeared in earlier works by Skovoroda as short diversifying sprinkles. Here for the first time they constitute the kernel of the dialogue as such. This, then, is Skovoroda's newest experiment, another of his innovations.

In YZ-76, after a break of eight years, Skovoroda returns from dialogues to the prose (in the proper sense) previously practised by him in ND-68. Like ND, YZ consists of short chapters, each devoted to the interpretation of a specific symbol as used—in Skovoroda's view—in the Bible. Yet stylistically YZ is quite different. The apparent fragmentation of the composition is overcome by an intricate structure of repeated words and images, of semantic switches and superpositions (which in cinematography would be called "fade-ins"). Altogether such a structure of intertwining repetitions constitutes a peculiar verbal fugue comparable, perhaps, in music, to some of the works of J.S. Bach, Skovoroda's earlier contemporary. The contrapuntal fugue, in its artistic structure, again, ideally reflects Skovoroda's world-view, according to which everything flows into everything and all "things" grasped by the human senses are but manifestations of the omnipresence of the unfathomable God. By the end of YZ the semantic and imagistic fugue grows into an ecstatic poem in praise of God which, in turn, is somewhat reminiscent of Bach's chorales. YZ is the pinnacle of this esoteric mastery of Skovoroda.

This mastery in creating, through semantic shifts, a peculiar metalanguage of his own finds its continuation in ŽL-80. Its metalanguage is constructed from the building material of the regular language, but the purpose is to take the reader away from the surface of all things and of the entire visible world and to transcend all that is sensually graspable so as to create a superimage of the supreme identity of everything, which opens the way to God, who is not an image now and not a notion but rather a hidden sense of all being. At this juncture a comparison suggests itself with the well-known summary of a similar philosophy in Goethe, a younger contemporary of Skovoroda, in the concluding *Chorus Mysticus* of "Faust": "*Alles Vergängliche ist nur ein Gleichnis.*"[33] But Skovoroda seems to go even farther than Goethe, because for him the road to God begins not with understanding the profound essence of things but with the destruction of things—destruction not in a physical sense, of course (Skovoroda never preached genocide or ruin; on the contrary, he advised the acceptance of the material and social reality of his, or any, time and of everyone's social condition)—but in the spiritual sense, for, according to Skovoroda, God only reveals Himself through this spiritual destruction, while accepting and even blessing the material surface of this world.

This brief and superficial summary of some of Skovoroda's ideas was necessary at this point because they determined his approach to semantics. Normal meanings of words are accepted, yet at the same time they are destroyed by adding new and newer meanings so that, in the end, the most horrendous equations of meaning (from the point of view of the language as currently used by speakers and fixed by lexicographers) arise: their wildness finds its parallel perhaps best of all in drawings and pictures by other contemporaries of Skovoroda, Francisco Goya and William Blake. Thus, the visible world (in this case the "normal" word meanings) continues to exist, and simultaneously it is destroyed, thereby opening vistas to the unusual and the essential, i.e., to God. In so doing, Skovoroda moves in ŽL even farther than in YZ, written four years earlier.

But it seems to this writer that syntactically YZ is more monolithic. YZ proceeds gradually from the simple to the more complicated, culminating in a kind of high poetry. In ŽL the conciseness of a sentence typical of YZ is lost,

---

33. This comparison also appears in Ėrn, 233, in Tschižewskij, 45, etc. But it has not been noticed that the other concluding image of "Faust," "*Das Ewig-Weibliche zieht uns hinan*," was also anticipated by Skovoroda in his treatment of Biblical female images from Eve on in ŽL, a series that found its completion in the image of "*vdova, brodjaščaja po zemlě, oblačenna v temnyja rizy, imuščaja roditi Syna*" in BA-83, 462 ff., which followed ŽL chronologically. Cf. also Ėrn, 282.

as is the syntactic and image-bearing curve that leads to an acme. In ŽL syntactic laconicism changes into hypotactic and/or parallelistic complication so freely and so often that no single line of ascent is given an opportunity to take full shape. This may have been the reason why, for more than seven years, Skovoroda was unable to force himself to finish the work, though he tried several times (1, 626). He could not find an artistically convincing finale to the work. Semantic shifts could have gone on without end, and syntactically (as well as compositionally) any movement upward was precluded. It is in this respect that ŽL seems inferior to YZ. The lack of an ending, which is inherent in the genre of additive dialogue as such (and overcome in YZ, as befits a work which is *one* piece of prose), returned to Skovoroda in ŽL, although this was not a dialogue.

It may be hypothesized that the failure of ŽL as a streamlined piece of prose made Skovoroda return to the form of the dialogue. But the dialogue of his next essay, BA-83, is a completely new type of dialogue in the corpus of his work. All his preceding dialogues were conducted among "live" characters who existed in the concrete surroundings of a *Slobožanščyna* rural estate. It is hardly a matter of chance that Skovoroda scholars succeeded in identifying at least some of those characters with real acquaintances of Skovoroda and addressees of his letters in the cultural circles of Ostrogožsk, of Babaji, et al. (Hryhorij, later Daniil—Skovoroda; Afanasij—Panas Pankov; Jakov—Jakov Dovhans'kyj; Naeman—the Rev. N. Petrovyč; Farra—Jakov Pravyc'kyj—according to Maxnovec', 219f., 235f.). The here-and-now background of those earlier dialogues could often have seemed to be removed and cast into oblivion by the abstract, elevated, and esoteric subjects of the discussions. Nevertheless, it was constantly there. This is no longer so in BA. The collocutors here are Satan and five Archangels and the setting is the world behind the visible world, i.e., nowhere, if one wishes, from the point of view of "real" life. Because the dialogue takes place nowhere and everywhere, the framework of the conventional settings falls away, as does the consistency of a dialogue. Hence one finds easy switches to narration, an ultimate freedom to include poems and songs, Skovoroda's own and those of other authors (Laščevs'kyj, Prokopovyč). Hence, also, on the other hand, the reduction of the colloquial element in the language and an increase in the use of ChSl and bookish components. The dreamlike quality of this dialogue, in which characters appear and disappear at will, enables Skovoroda to build as finale a grandiose apotheosis, an ecstatic vision of God's mighty Caucasus. Thus, the problem left unsolved in ŽL is quite naturally and facilely resolved here. (Incidentally, the symbol of *Kavkaz* as an image of the substantial world as opposed to a visible one—the flat northern shore of the Caspian Sea—was introduced and made clear in ŽL, not here, but this does not matter much in a work in which accessories of time and place are in any case lifted.)

PB-83 is another abstract dialogue between Skovoroda (*Varsava*) and Demon (*Dajmon*), and constitutes dialogue as a vision. Accordingly, its staccato sentences, its heavy ChSl coloration (with the aorist, the ChSl conjunctions, 2 sg in -*ši*, gen sg fem adj in -*yja*, etc.), and its Goya-like dualistic imagery serve as a means of building up summits of ecstasy. PB is a further elaboration of what was found in BA. The novelty of this one in comparison with Skovoroda's earlier dialogues is its very structure. It is now not additive but conflictive. The two participants do not speak in unison; they cross swords.

Having achieved the ultimate freedom of the abstract dialogue, Skovoroda could, from this position, go farther in his experimentation. In BE-87 he entered the new area of (at least partly) humorous dialogue. It is still abstract, but the characters are now a stork and a monkey, with many human and even temporally conditioned human features. The *finale* is, accordingly, ironic and frivolous. In a sense, Skovoroda returned here to the principles of his fables, but greatly enlarged and modified them. In the language, logically, colloquial elements are on the rise and Ukrainianisms become perceptible.

This trend is continued in UŽ, a work of the same year. The participants are a lark, a black grouse, and a woodpecker. The dialogue is interrupted by pieces of narration (stories within the story) and concludes with a song. The satire is still there, but an idyllic attitude predominates. The work is essentially a village idyll, but in no concrete village. The setting and the entire dialogue remain abstract. In UŽ Skovoroda achieved an amazing lightness, especially obvious in comparison with his "heavy" works of the 1770s, such as K.

PZ-90, the last major work of Skovoroda, is his ninth symphony. Basically, it is also an abstract dialogue (between Spirit and Soul), but its final sections are narrative. It is a synthesis of Skovoroda's symbolism. Symbols redound, flowing into one another. Logic becomes inconsequential. The work freely incorporates symbols and emblems developed in his earlier work (in fact, it includes entire fragments from his earlier essays) and, consequently, it returns to the "heaviness" of his earlier writings. The work is overloaded with quotations and the determining element in the language is ChSl. This was for Skovoroda, in all likelihood, an attempt to build his spiritual home, for which his preceding works constituted construction material. The ultimate balance was not achieved here by Skovoroda. There are many layers in the work, both ideologically and stylistically, combined in an "art of the fugue," but they are often not harmonized among themselves. Maybe Skovoroda was now too old to complete such an edifice; maybe his life-long search was too diversified for a final synthesis; maybe his world-view was too poetic and subjective to be brought into one harmonious and universal unity. Whatever the reason, in this sense his ninth symphony remained incomplete (it was brought to an end externally), like Bruckner's, not Beethoven's.

The above survey of Skovoroda's work has been, no doubt, incomplete, impressionistic, and superficial. The present writer hopes to return, in special articles, to the subjects only touched upon here, such as Skovoroda's semantics and semantic shifts and the use of the three language systems familiar to Skovoroda—the Ukrainian of his childhood, the Russian of his new environment, and the Church Slavonic of his school years and life-long reading—as they changed throughout his career. But the purpose of the above brief review was modest: to ascertain the fact of constant change and an unabated spirit of experimentation throughout Skovoroda's life. For this purpose the proposed survey, with all its shortcomings and lacunae, seems to be sufficient.

Establishing distinct periods in Skovoroda's work is difficult because of the constant experimentation that marked all he wrote (and did). One is tempted to consider nearly every successive major work as a period in itself, as above. Tentatively, with a great deal of simplification, the following division into four periods may be suggested.

1) Prior to 1769. This was a period of verse and academic prose. The bulk of SBP, the first cycle of BX and ND-68 were created. Biographically these were the years of his conflict with the educational system of the time and encompassed several interruptions in his teaching, but basically Skovoroda was still committed to an academic career. Most works were written in or near Perejaslav and Xarkiv, a few of the earlier ones possibly in Kyiv. (If he was active literarily as a student, his works of that time are not extant.) When he was fired from the *Pribavočnye klassy* of Xarkiv College in 1768, his pedagogical aspirations ended. Ideologically, these were Skovoroda's formative years.

2) 1769-1776. A period of additive dialogues in a realistic setting. Ns and As, both written in 1769, show a search for the ideal dialogue form. The Babaji and Xarkiv and particularly the Ostrogožsk circles of friends and followers supplied Skovoroda with characters and setting. The additive dialogue is represented by BD, Obs, DM, PP, and K. One of the dialogues has the title *Razhovor pjati putnikov*. This could apply to most of them if "wayfarers" is understood not only concretely but rather figuratively, i.e., spiritually. The form, however, did not satisfy Skovoroda, hence his outbreaks of harangue in K. The search for a more satisfying form is also visible in the second cycle of BX-74, with their overgrowth of the explanatory part (*sila*) of the fables. Biographically, this is the time of Skovoroda's stay with various landlords on their estates and in their town residences, most often probably with Tevjašov near and at Ostrogožsk.

3) 1776-1780. This was a period of searching for a spiritual metalanguage, mainly by means of semantic upheavals. Generically, it was the time of Skovoroda's return to prose. YZ and ŽL were written in those years. Biographically, the greater part of these years was spent at the Burluk estate of Donec'-Zaxarževs'kyj, at the Sošal's'kyjs' village of Husynka and at Babaji.

4) 1783-1790. This was a period of abstract, conflictive dialogue, with elements of poetry and narratives admitted: BA, PB, BE, UŽ, PZ. Biographically, Skovoroda was to be found mostly in Husynka and Burluk, but he also wandered extensively about the countryside.

No new work is known from the last four years of Skovoroda's life.[34]

Like every schematic periodization, this one is open to criticism. It certainly may be made more precise, possibly revised. But an inadequate periodization is better than a complete disregard of the very fact of development, typical of the static view of Skovoroda's language that has prevailed hitherto. The negator of historicism, Skovoroda can be properly understood only through a historical approach.

3

"Ptica možet naučit'sja letat'—ne čerepaxa."
H. Skovoroda, *"Razhovor, nazyvaemyj*
Alfavit, ili bukvar' mira," 1774

There is a myth concerning Skovoroda that prevents any objective study of his life and work. It presents him as a *narodnyj filosof*, a description that cannot be adequately translated into English (or any other language), because logically it means nothing. Somehow it makes the reader feel some vague connotations which suggest that Skovoroda originated from the peasantry (which is true), that he was a philosopher for the peasantry (teacher of peasants?), and that he was an ideologist (a mouthpiece) of the peasantry, both of which are wrong. I shall render it literally as "people's philosopher" in the hope that the very clumsiness of the phrase will properly emphasize its meaninglessness.

The foundations of the Skovoroda myth were laid by Romantics. As in many other countries, in Ukraine they needed a mouthpiece of the "national spirit." It would have been better to have had an Ossian. But there was none at hand. Ševčenko had to create an entirely imaginary Perebendja as late as 1839. The second choice was to have a new Socrates, a people's philosopher. G. Gess de-Kal've, A. Xiždeu, I. Snegirev, and I. Sreznevskij all filled that gap with Skovoroda. The first publications on Skovoroda, which appeared between 1817

---

34. Biographical references in this survey are based primarily on Maxnovec'. The proposed periodization has as its foundation the form of Skovoroda's writings. It seems that a periodization on the basis of the development of problems and ideas in Skovoroda's world-view would to some degree parallel the suggested periodization (the search for the inner man, for the sense of the Bible, for the essence of God; application of findings to various aspects of earthly life, as, for example, education; acceptance of this world as one of three worlds (man, the Bible, God)—its rejection with ascetic ardor—new acceptance as the image of God, etc.; attempts to interpret everything in the Bible, even the most concrete prescriptions concerning food and the treatment of animals, symbolically [according to Tschižewskij, 154, a borrowing from Philo] in the second period; rejection of the "trash" in the Bible at a later time, etc.). Ėrn, 174, was ready to speak of three periods in Skovoroda's work, only to reject this idea by saying: *"Vrjad li možno konstatirovat' kakuju-nibud' èvoljuciju vo vzgljadax Skovorody"* (Ėrn's emphasis). But these problems must be left to specialists in the history of philosophy.

and 1836, came from their pens.[35] They created the legend of a Skovoroda who repudiated the rich and the educated and went to live with the poor and the simple and to teach them. In 1840 Archimandrite Gavriil summarized the Skovoroda-as-Socrates legend in his *Istorija russkoj filosofii* by saying: "Like Socrates, notwithstanding time and place, he taught at crossroads, at markets, at cemeteries, on church porches," and: "Moving among the common people, he strove to learn their nature, their will, their language, and their customs."[36] Several decades later, this image, predominant by then, was restated by Danilevskij. Skovoroda, he says, "*stal dejstvovat' v pole, na sxodkax, v derevnjax, u kurenej otdel'nyx pasek, v domax bogatyx predrassudkami vsjakogo roda togdašnix pomeščikov, na gorodskix ploščadjax i v bednyx izbax poseljan.*"[37]

Such a legend could not fail to please later generations of populists, though for a different reason. They were interested not in the national spirit but in the oppressed lower classes, especially the peasants. The allegedly Socratic side of Skovoroda was forgotten, while his alleged renunciation of the rich and his allegiance with the poor were emphasized. A. Efimenko entitled her essay on Skovoroda "*Filosof iz naroda*" (1894) and in the same year S. Rusova entitled her article "*Grigorij Savvič Skovoroda, ukrainskij narodnyj učitel' i filosof.*" Paradoxically—or was it?—both revolutionary ladies followed in the footsteps of the earlier extreme reactionary, Askočenskij, to whom Skovoroda was "*naš narodnyj filosof.*"[38] The image was so persistent that even V. Èrn, a man of the Russian symbolist period, in which concern for social conflict was absent, a man who succeeded in showing the high degree of sophistication of Skovoroda's work, even he succumbed to the tradition by saying at the end of his book on Skovoroda (342): "Skovoroda has the specific charm of a primitive." The 250th anniversary of Skovoroda's birth was celebrated in 1976 in Ukraine according to the old trends. What was called "the Marxist history of literature" there proved to be just a vulgarized populism that perpetuated the earlier tradition. One quotation from a certain Hromjak suffices to demonstrate this. In his words, Skovoroda wanted to write so that his works "would be better understood by listeners from among the people, whom the philosopher addressed."[39]

It was left to a Russian *barin* and, what is more, one of Germanic descent (as often happened in Russia) to speak the simple truth. Špet called Skovoroda "*mnimo-narodnyj filosof*" and stated bluntly that Skovoroda wandered not among

---

35. Bibliography in O. Bilec'kyj, ed., *Ukrajins'ki pys'mennyky. Bio-bibliohrafičnyj slovnyk* 1, by L. Maxnovec' (Kyiv, 1960), 521, 525.
36. Quoted from G.P. Danilevskij, *Sočinenija* 21 (St. Petersburg, 1901), 90.
37. First published in 1862. Here quoted from *Sočinenija* 21:27.
38. V. Askočenskij, *Kiev s drevnejšim ego učiliščem Akademieju*, II (Kyiv, 1856), p. 129.
39. In AN UkRSR, Instytut filosofiji, *Hryhorij Skovoroda 250* (Kyiv, 1975), 145.

the peasants but *"po pomeščič'im usad'bam druzej."*[40] Špet's condescending tone may be unpleasant, but what has been quoted here is true. Neither Skovoroda's work nor his biography give the slightest confirmation of the romantic-populist-"Marxist" legend about him.

Here is a short statistical account of the addressees of Skovoroda's letters: to landlords 10; to priests and high-ranking monks 5; to rich merchants 4; to high officials 2; to artists 1; to unknown persons 3; but none to a peasant. Not only are there no peasant addressees of the letters, but there is no mention of peasants either. Skovoroda's closest friend, Kovalins'kyj, was born a priest's son; later he was a tutor of Count K. Rozumovskij, the heir of the most influential family in the Russian Empire, second only to the dynasty; still later he was the governor of the Rjazan' *naměstničestvo*, the curator of the Moscow University, and, of course, a landowner.

Only a fraction of Skovoroda's letters have been preserved. Perhaps those lost would change the picture. The following is what we know about his hosts during the twenty-five years of his wanderings.[41] He stayed with the landowners S. Tevjašov in Tavoloz'ka near Ostrogožsk; V. Zembors'kyj in Hužvyns'ke; H. Sošal's'kyj in Manačynivka; O. Sošal's'kyj in Husynka; Ja. Donec'-Zaxarževs'kyj in Burluk; F. Kvitka near Xarkiv; P. Ščerbinin in Dovžyk; A. Kovalevs'kyj in Ivanivka; F. Dys'kyj in Dys'kivka; I. Mečnikov near Kupjanka; Ol. Avksentiev in Lypci; M. Kovalins'kyj in Xotetovo; with the priest Ja. Pravyc'kyj in Babaji; and in numerous monasteries, such as Transfiguration in Kurjaž, Holy Trinity in Oxtyrka, Old Xarkiv, Xarkiv *učiliščnyj*, Sumy, Svjati Hory near Slovjans'k, Sinne, Kytajiv, and Pečers'kyj in Kyiv, etc. Again, we do not find a single peasant household mentioned. No doubt, Skovoroda must have stayed overnight in peasants' houses during his many trips on foot. But this was comparable to lodging for the night in a hotel. There is no information about dwelling at length with any peasant's family. What the known facts show is only that, while staying with a landlord, Skovoroda preferred not to be put up in the owner's house but in some subsidiary building in the courtyard, in a wood, often at an apiary. But this is not a testimony of his passionate love for "people"; it

---

40. Gustav Špet, *Očerk razvitija russkoj filosofii* (Petrograd, 1922), 68, 69. The *narodnist'* of Skovoroda was also occasionally denied earlier, but only on the basis of his language, without an understanding of his contacts with the upper classes. Thus, e.g., T. Ševčenko ("In spite of all, Burns was a poet for the people and a great one. Our Skovoroda would also have been such were it not that Latin and later the Russian language diverted him") and P. Žytec'kyj, 1899 (*Kievskaja starina* 67, no. 11, p. 151).
41. The list is compiled from I. Ivan'o in AN UkRSR, Instytut filosofiji, *Filosofija Hryhorija Skovorody* (Kyiv, 1972), 41; M. Kovalins'kyj in 2, 520; Maxnovec', 230ff.; Ju. Loščic, *Skovoroda* (Moscow, 1972), 127ff. Soviet publications for the most part play down Skovoroda's contacts with landlords, high-ranking officials, merchants, etc. The usual method is to name places without mentioning the owners and vice versa.

simply shows that he liked solitude and introspection.

All of the foregoing does not imply that Skovoroda despised the peasants or that he did not talk with them. His attitude is explained explicitly in his AM-74. This is his theory of *"neravnoe vsěm ravenstvo"* (345) and, more specifically, when addressed to the lower classes: *"Ostan'sja ž v prirodnom tvoem zvanii, skol'ko ono ni podloe"* (330). He respected peasants as long as they remained peasants, but he simply did not belong to them. He did not look for the rich; he wanted the educated. Education was to be found, however, among the rich, and that was decisive.[42]

The same conclusion is inevitable if we examine the dedications of Skovoroda's works. ND was written for *"molodoe šljaxetstvo"* (14); As, DM, ŽL, BA, and PZ were dedicated to Kovalins'kyj; K, AM, YZ, and C to Tevjašov; BE to S. Djatliv; UŽ to Dys'kyj; and Pl to Donec'-Zaxarževs'kyj. None of these men was a peasant. All the characters of Skovoroda's dialogues who have been identified were either landlords or priests, with one of them an artist.

There is no evidence that Skovoroda ever preached on the streets and in the markets, that he ever preached to crowds, or to any peasants. Vasilij Žukovskij, who was born in Russia eleven years before Skovoroda's death, published his own poems in a few copies under the title *Für Wenige*. Skovoroda took this self-isolation much further: he never published his works at all and we are not aware of a single attempt of his to do so. A few hand-written copies sufficed to satisfy the interest of those who were curious and/or had an understanding of his words and ideas. Their number hardly exceeded a score at any given moment. If he had been moved to give a title to his writings in Žukovskij's manner, it would probably have been something like *Für weniger als Wenige*.

So much for Skovoroda's writing for the people as borne out by the external evidence. In spite of all that, he gained popularity among the peasants of Slobožanščyna. But this was hardly on account of his ideas and even less so because of the style of his writings. Men and women of the lower classes were struck by the image of Skovoroda as a person. They were influenced by his repudiation of an academic career and wealth (he never accepted or carried any money), by his wanderings on foot, his moderation in food and drink, his vegetarianism, his preference for solitude, his clothes (reportedly the peasant *svyta*), perhaps even by his singing of his own *pěsni* and his piping, etc. That is how the folkloric

---

42. In Son-58, 2, 474 Skovoroda gives expression to an overtly critical attitude toward the peasants, not because they are peasants, but because they are devoid—in his evaluation—of spiritual life (in which respect, Skovoroda states, they do not differ from most of the rich): *"Ony išli uliceju..., kak obiknovenno v prostoj černě byvaet; tak že i amurnii děla srodnim sebě obrazom, kak-to v rjad odin postavivši žensk, a v druhoj mužsk pol. Xto xoroš, xto na koho poxož i komu dostoin byt' mužem ili ženoju,—s sladostiju otpravljali."* (Underlining is mine.)

legend of Skovoroda arose.[43] But even this should not be exaggerated. Some minor details show that his life-style never became completely identical with that of the peasants. A very minor detail can be cited as an example. There is a recurrent sentence in Kovalins'kyj's letters to Skovoroda: "*Ja poslal vam syr, trubku i knigi*" (2, 536); "*Posylaju syru parmazanu i galanskago*" (2, 537 and again 538 and 541). A diminutive, insignificant fact, of course. But clearly these cheeses were not items on a peasant's menu, whether he was free or serf.

For all those who imagined Skovoroda as a people's philosopher, an insuperable stumbling-block was his language. If he philosophized for peasants, why did he not use the Ukrainian vernacular, the only idiom that was fully understandable to them? Some tried to excuse him in this by pointing to the "bad" influence of his education and the unfavourable historical circumstances of the time. ("*Ukrajins'ka narodna mova do toho času šče ne praktykuvalasja dlja vyslovlennja skladnyx filosofs'kyx dumok. Krim toho, Skovoroda pysav svoji tvory ne til'ky dlja ukrajins'koho, ale j dlja rosijs'koho čytača*"[44]); more often he was accused of backwardness and a lack of understanding of problems and the situation of the time: ("*Školi ty, mov sekti mertvij, Strašennu slovom dan' platyv: Ty cvit uma v neznanij žertvi, Mov skoplenyj, zanapastyv*"—P. Kuliš; "*Vyxovannja v kyjivs'kij akademiji pereplatyv Skovoroda strašnoju movoju svojix pysan', tjažkoju, dyvačnoju, zaputanoju, tjažko zrozumiloju mišanynoju moskovščyny j cerkovščyny z čužozemnymy rečennjamy j vyslovamy j ridšym abo častišym ukrajins'kym elementom*"—M. Voznjak[45] and a host of others afterwards). But the first to anticipate such verdicts was Skovoroda himself. In Obs-72 the following characterization of Skovoroda's manner of writing is put into Afanasij's mouth: "*Ty kak sam strannymi i krutymi dyšeš mysljamy, tak i edinomyslenniki tvoi dikija dumy strannym otryhajut jazykom*" (293). He was, thus, aware of how odd his language and style were. But he did not alter them after making that self-accusation. Moreover, he defended his language. He derived it from the Bible, and to one of his critics he answered in As-69: "*Učiš'? Ne smysliš! Razberi sam sebe polučše! I ne bud' nahl v oxuždenii biblejnaho*

---

43. Danilevskij, 86, already was aware of this: "Skovoroda affected the people by his personality more strongly than by any prose or rhymed works of his." S. Jefremov brilliantly (but with a populist exaggeration) summarized this view: "*Možna smilyvo skazaty, ščo sered tvoriv Skovorody, sered usix vikopomnyx dil joho—najbil'šym buv taky vin sam, joho osoba, joho žyttja na tli obstavyn toho času, sered hurtu sučasnykiv*" ("Skovoroda na tli sučasnosty," ZNTŠ 141-143, 1925, 1).

44. P. Popov, *Hryhorij Skovoroda* (Kyiv, 1969), 66.

45. P. Kuliš, *Tvory* 2 (L'viv, 1909), 321; M. Voznjak, *Istorija ukrajins'koji literatury* 3 (L'viv, 1924), 84. Peculiarly, even Tschižewskij, 201, 218, joins this camp when he speaks of Skovoroda's "*absichtlich sprunghaft und bewusst dunkel geschriebenen Werke*" and especially "*ästhetisch totes Nachlasswerk.*"

štilja!" (138).[46] The implication of these facts is self-evident: Skovoroda never intended to write for peasants, nor in fact for broader groups of average readers. He wrote *"für weniger als Wenige."*

The myth of the "people's philosopher," then, can be laid aside definitively and forever. There still remain, however, many unanswered questions. Which reader of his time and space could properly appreciate his references to, say Boethius (2, 378), to Seneca (2, 408), to St. Maxim the Confessor (2, 422), to Augustine (2, 454) and so on? How many were capable of perceiving the exquisitely spun lace of biblical quotations? Who could follow Skovoroda in polylingual passages of his writings, with quotations in Latin and Greek, occasionally in Hebrew and other languages as well?[47] Who could readily grasp the

---

46. In the edition of Skovoroda's work after *učiš'* stands an exclamation mark that seems to be a mistake. *Nahl* is used here in the U meaning "quick," not R "insolent."

47. Polylinguality in Skovoroda's writings deserves a special study. Here a few hints at its technique and functions may be given.

Often Skovoroda gives a foreign word, phrase, or sentence and translates it, e.g., "*Erodij na nebesi pozna vremja svoe... U drevnix slavjan ona* [the bird] *erodij; u ellinov—pelarhos, u rimljan— kikonia, u poljakov—bojcan, u malorossian—hajster, —sxoža na žuravlja. Erodij značit boholjubnyj, esli slovo ellinskoe*" (BD-72, 172). The function of this excursion into comparative lexicology is evident. It is, besides introducing a certain degree of ornamentality, to call the reader's attention to one of the central images. This is even more obvious in the dedication to DM-72. The central point here is the interpretation of religion as a spiritual game, and the polylinguality concentrates attention on that: "*Veseljusja o Bože, Spasě moem... Zabava, rimski—oblectatio, ellinski—diatriba, slavenski— hlum, ili hlumlenie, est' korifa, i verx, i cvět i zerno čelověčeskija žizni*" (187). Realizing, however, that this was an ornamentation, Skovoroda hastened to deny any importance to the external aspect of his polylingual word plays. The above quotation from BD is followed by the passage: "*No čto v tom nuždy? Bros' těn', spěši ko istině.*"

Sometimes, polylinguality appears in an attempt, through a comparison of Biblical texts in various languages, to come closer to the appropriate understanding of the passage. In BD-72, 178, after having found in the Slavonic Bible the word *skverno*, Skovoroda continues: "*skverno—v rimskom že ležit—commune, ellinski—koinon, razuměj—coenum, sireč' blato, hrjaz', merzkoe, mirskoe.*" Needless to say, this is a commentary, not a translation. Elsewhere the point of the use of polylinguality is to show the universal identity of the ultimate truth in all its historical manifestations: "*Božestvennaja v čelověkě sila, pobuždajuščaja eho k srodnosti, nazyvalas' u drevnix ehiptjan Isys, Isis, u ellin—'Αθηνᾶ, Athena, u rimljan—Minerva, sireč' natura. Priroda nazyvalasja γένιος, genius—anhel prirody, nazyvalasja tož θεός — Boh*" (AM-74, 331).

But there are cases where the foreign expression comes to Skovoroda's mind first and he uses it directly because it is actually untranslatable ("*Vynyrnulo by, skazat' po-rimsku, mobile perpetuum*"—PZ-90, 552) or because the Slavic word does not come to the author's mind: "*Zděs' stolp značit ne toe, čto u rimljan columna, no to, čto u nix turris, a u ellinov πύργος, sireč', vozvyšennoe zdanie po obrazu kruhlaho ili kvadratnaho stolpa.*" But here he recovers the native equivalents and goes on: "*U nas nazyvaetsja bašnja, bojnica (propugnaculum), ili terem, kak vidno iz malorusskoj pěsni*" (PZ, 564)—however, here again with a Latin parallel!

Skovoroda leaves literary quotations from classical authors without translation (e.g., in AM-74, 346) or even without conclusion (cf. his reference to Ovid in the dedication to PZ-90, 533), but this happens in addressing a specific person fluent in Latin and knowledgeable of its literary tradition.

meandering currents and undercurrents of his semantic switches? Even for the present-day editors of Skovoroda, the professors and doctors of philosophy at the Institute of Philosophy of the Academy of Sciences, more often than not these matters are, to say the least, difficult. Were there, in his time, such *"weniger als Wenige,"* or was he entirely opaque and lonely? And last but not least, what essentially was the language of Skovoroda after the elimination of biblical (and similar) quotations on the one hand and Ukrainianisms (in many works inadvertent) on the other?

There is no brief and simple answer to these and similar questions. True, in the past, as has been noted above, answers were given too readily when what was needed was a real study in depth. The present writer intends to devote a special study to the functions of the three languages (ChSl, R, U) in Skovoroda's work. Here only a few remarks will be made on the reason for Skovoroda's use of Russian, peculiar version though it was, in the hope that this will also shed light on some of the other questions raised in the preceding paragraph.

First of all, one must realize that Skovoroda's choice of language was not haphazard and did not result from his "faulty education,"[48] or inadequate training, least of all from some sort of involuntary confusion.[49] The latter point in particular should be emphatically rejected. Skovoroda was not a maniac who prophesied in a trance, indifferent to the wording of what he was saying or

---

Also, a commentary may be given without recourse to a strict translation: *"'Pobědit' v pěsni.' Sirěč' vzojtit' tuda, kuda Božija muza vedet. Tak i rimljane hovarivali: Ascendere, superare mortem"* (ŽL-80, 427). More often, however, common expressions are translated (e.g., BD-72, 174, 176; BA-83, 438; PB-83, 470). Twice polylinguality is used as a humorous device to render it either with "low words" (*"T'fu! Putatem te cornua habere"*—PB, 438) or the colloquial and/or ecclesiastical ones ("Pišek: ...*Radujsja! Mir tebě! Χαῖρε! Salam ali kjum!—Erodij: A-a! Vsemilostivaja hosudarynja! Bonžur! Kali imera! Den' dobryj! Gehorsamer Diener! Daj Boh radovat'sja! Salve! Spasajsja vo Hospodě!"*—BE-87, 491).

Thus, polylinguality in Skovoroda is polyfunctional. It is never an ostentation, an intentional demonstration of the author's education and conversance with ancient literature; but, involuntarily, it shows that and makes the text remoter from the colloquial language of any social group which then existed in *Slobožanščyna*.

48. Ern, 64f., was right in pointing to Skovoroda's knowledge of a great many authors who were not on the curriculum of the Academy, so that in spite of his long stay there he was to a great extent a self-taught person. Besides that, we know nothing of what he studied (if anything) during his travels in Central Europe, who were the *"ljudi učenye i znanijami otlično slavimye"* (Kovalins'kyj, 2, 489) whom he contacted in Austria and possibly in Germany, and whether he took any more-or-less regular courses there. Maxnovec', 58, suggests a three-year stay in Halle, but this is only a conjecture.

49. As suggested by P. Žytec'kyj: *"Podčinjajas' raznoobraznym vlijanijam reči, to knižnoj, to razgovornoj, to gorodskoj, to sel'skoj, on kak by <u>utratil samoe čuvstvo ee</u>"* and: *"<u>Bessoznatel'no dlja samogo sebja</u> pisatel' delaet vse, čtoby vyrazit' mysl' svoju samym neestestvennym obrazom, upotrebljaja slova to cerkovnoslavjanskie, to malorusskie, to velikorusskie"* (*Kievskaja starina* 67, 1899, 149f. Emphasis is mine).

unable to control this wording. If he was captivated by his ideas, he was no less involved in the problems of a poetical form for these ideas. As shown above, in section 2, he was a poet who constantly and consciously experimented. (Remember his recurrent equation of the prophet and the poet!) The customary division of his work into poetry and philosophical treatises is unwarranted. In his "prose" he was no less a poet than in his poems, and he was philosophical in his poetry. Incidentally, his prose, in its genesis, was closer to the sermon—a genre that borders on poetry—than it was to philosophical inquiry. One should rather speak of rhymed vs. unrhymed poetry. In his unquestionable awareness of form and style, his first task was to face the necessity of choosing his language. Instruction in the Kyiv Academy at the time when he was a student there was given in Latin. Skovoroda was fluent in Latin. He wrote several short poems in that language. According to Èrn (59), his Latin was excellent; Korž points to some deviations into late colloquial Latin,[50] but these are found in his fables and might have been deliberate. He certainly could have written in good Church Slavonic as well. Finally, he knew Ukrainian, both the older, literary idiom and the contemporary vernacular, his native language, which, as he stated on many occasions, he loved dearly.

None of these possibilities was used by Skovoroda. (His poems in Latin were few and were written as experiments and/or with a pedagogical purpose.) Compared with what was done in and around the Kyiv Academy, Skovoroda made a linguistic revolution. He repudiated the Academy traditions unreservedly. But his linguistic revolution was carried out not in favour of colloquial Ukrainian or standard Russian. He decided to conduct his entire poetic experimentation, to create nearly his entire literary output, in a language that incorporated much from Church Slavonic, Ukrainian, standard Russian, and certain elements from Latin, Greek, and other languages of both East and West, but which was not identical with any of these and which so far has eluded any strict definition. For this, as we saw, he was bitterly reproached in the nineteenth and twentieth centuries.

The fact of the matter is, however, that Skovoroda's linguistic revolution, setting aside his biblical quotations and a great many of his poetic experiments, consisted of introducing a colloquial language into literature. This language was R as it was then used in Xarkiv and *Slobožanščyna* by educated landowners and the upper class in general.[51] To the extent that he had listeners and followers,

---

50. N. Korž, "Latyns'ki viršovani tvory H.S. Skovorody" in AN UkRSR, *Hryhorij Skovoroda 250* (Kyiv, 1975), 180.
51. Buzuk, 80, speaks of two sources of Russian in Skovoroda's work: Russian literature of the time and the language used by the population of Xarkiv and other towns of Ukraine. However, the influence of standard Russian—if any—was of a subordinate character. Skovoroda was not an assiduous reader of Russian literature. Besides many references to classical and ecclesiastical writers scattered throughout Skovoroda's works and letters there is, characteristically, none to even one

they came—as we saw above—from those social groups. It is to them that Skovoroda wrote (and made copies of) his works. It was their customary language that became, alongside and often in contrast to the biblical and like quotations, the backbone of Skovoroda's linguistic structure. It could not have been Ukrainian, because they did not speak Ukrainian any longer, except for special purposes. It was not identical with the "real" Russian of St. Petersburg and Moscow, because in Skovoroda's time the Russian language of the Ukrainian landowners in *Slobožanščyna*, although evolving from Ukrainian toward standard Russian, which was then in the making in the centres of the Empire, had not yet reached the final point of its development, i.e., complete identity with the language of the court and the capitals of Russia. It was a peculiar Russian that grew up on the Ukrainian substratum.

This is the key to the problem of Skovoroda's choice of his basic language. This, of course, does not imply that he simply recorded the language of his *Slobožanščyna* environment: he was a poet and a genius in poetry. The language of such writers, needless to say, is not and can never be the same as the colloquial. To repeat what has been said: the ingredients of Skovoroda's language were many and various, but now we are speaking of the foundation of his language. The edifice he erected on this foundation was highly personal, the more so since, stylistically, Skovoroda represented the High Baroque, a style that never accepted the reality of life and the reality of the [spoken] language in a literary work. If Skovoroda's language proved to be dead for the generations that followed, this is not because it was dead in Skovoroda's time. It was perceived as dead later, when the colloquial language of the landowners, merchants, upper clergy, and intellectuals of *Slobožanščyna* had moved farther along toward a nearly complete merger with Standard (i.e., Central) Russian, and, on the other hand, when the secularization of life and language had advanced rapidly.

At this point some evidence must be adduced to show that the language of the *Slobožanščyna* upper classes during Skovoroda's life, i.e., between the years 1759, when he moved to Xarkiv, and 1794, was already Russian, even if peculiar in type. This is not commonly accepted. In 1858 P. Kuliš wrote about the late eighteenth century, around 1780, in Xarkiv as follows: "*Otže u tiji časy, desjatkiv sim čy visim rik nazad, panstvo kruhom Xarkova žylo sobi prosto, po-staro-svits'ki, po-kozači, i naš pysatel'* [H. Kvitka, born 1778] *zmalku čuv u otec'kij*

Russian writer. As for the idea that Skovoroda learned the "real" Russian language during his stays in Russia (as Tschižewskij, 218, contends), this is not borne out by facts of his biography. For the time Skovoroda spent in St. Petersburg when he belonged to the Court choir (33 months), Maxnovec', 91, is right when he says that the choir consisted predominantly of Ukrainians and Skovoroda was among his countrymen and spoke Ukrainian. The reference to his trip to Moscow is not to be taken seriously at all: this trip only lasted about one month (Maxnovec', 124, 127). Skovoroda's Russian must have been learned in Ukraine, not in Russia!

hospodi i vsjudy po okolyci ščyru ukrajins'ku movu, prymazanu til'ko v slučajax ceremoniji dejakymy moskovs'kymy slovamy."[52] The use of the Ukrainian language in the *okolycja*, i.e., by the low and middle classes, for those years, is beyond any doubt. As for the landowners (*hospody*), it is not so obvious. Kuliš was a man from *Het'manščyna*; *Slobožanščyna* was not known to him from first-hand experience. Linguistic Russification in *Het'manščyna* proceeded much more slowly than in *Slobožanščyna*. This was conditioned chiefly by two circumstances. *Het'manščyna* preserved its autonomy and then some remnants of it until 1782, when the regular Russian *naměstničestva* were introduced there. Also, this territory was populated almost entirely by Ukrainians. Russian infiltration on a larger scale began only after 1720. *Slobožanščyna*, on the contrary, did not benefit from any autonomy and was settled not only from the west, by Ukrainians, but also, in much smaller numbers, from the north, by Russians, starting in the late seventeenth century. Its upper administration made no pretence of being other than overtly Russian, and *Slobožanščyna* was made a Russian *gubernija* in 1765 (a *naměstničestvo* in 1780).

We possess precious little information for a direct characterization of the colloquial language used by the upper classes in the towns and estates of *Slobožanščyna* in the eighteenth century. More data come from *Het'manščyna*. Several men from the *staršyna*, later the nobility, wrote their intimate diaries, which are extant. From these we can see the beginnings of the transition to Russian, soon after 1720, first in a language mixture with Ukrainian predominant, then with more Russian, and finally written in a language quite close to standard Russian. Private letters of the mid-eighteenth century were, as a rule, written in Russian (if not in French), even if they came from the pens of persons close to Ukrainian autonomists and conspirators like P. Myrovyč.[53]

A quotation from the diary of Ja. Markovyč gives a good idea of the situation in 1735: *"Den' byl i noč podobnie prežnim. Rano ezdil **do** knjazja, hde i obědal, a po obědě ezdil **do** Hureva i pozdravljal eho novoroždennim snom i **červonca** dal. Za povorotom ottol ihral u pěket z bratom i p. Mixajlom dolho. Pisal pismo **do** Zaruckoho v S. Pburx, čtob kupil Priměčanija vsě na 1734 hod, takže hazet francužskix ot septevr: i paru čašok farforovix. Da **do** Karataeva pisal o prisilkě pečej **trox**, a ne **dvox**, rumok kristalnix malix i bolšix, po djužině.*"[54] Markovyč still cannot discern R *y* and *i*, and he pronounces *ě* as *i* (*pěket*), but grammatically and lexically the text is mixed. Words, word forms, and constructions not used in Ukrainian (i.e., R) are underlined. Words, word forms, and constructions

---

52. "Hryhorij Kvitka i joho povisti." Quoted from P. Kuliš, *Tvory* 6 (L'viv, 1910), 464.
53. See the publication of M. Horban', *Ukrajina*, 1927, 5.
54. Entry of January 4, 1735. Published by V. Modzalevs'kyj in *Žerela do istoriji Ukrajiny-Rusy* 22 (L'viv, 1935), 1.

inadmissible in Russian (i.e., clearly U) are in bold type. (The changes *o>i* and *l>v* are not marked in writing by Markovyč according to the typical spelling of the time. The absence of such *i* and *v* is not necessarily a Russianism.)

If the Russification of a member of the ruling class in *Het'manščyna* had advanced to this extent, then for families of a somewhat lower status in *Slobožanščyna* twenty-five to sixty years later, no doubt, a much stronger advance in switch to, and command of, Russian must be admitted. One can assume a priori that the local standard of the colloquial language was Russian, though with quite a few Ukrainianisms still present, just as it may be assumed, on the other hand, that even settlers from Russia switched to the local variety of Russian, with all its Ukrainianisms.[55] In fact, the writings of Skovoroda, especially his non-Latin letters, should be critically used as documents of the *Slobožanščyna* colloquial language of the educated class in the last third of the eighteenth century—even though this argument is clearly circular in the present article.

In summary, the language of Skovoroda, minus its many biblical and ecclesiastical, political and personal features is, in its foundation, the *Slobožanščyna* variety of standard Russian as used by the educated. Skovoroda constantly communicated with these circles, and the readers and followers he had belonged there. Skovoroda was materially dependent on them. This was his milieu, not that of peasants. Unless we understand that, we shall be forever puzzled by his language and consider it a wild perversion.

The glasses of romanticism and populism must be removed from our eyes.

***

The intention of this triptych was not to characterize Skovoroda's language in all its peculiarities. It only aimed at pointing out what must be done before any adequate study of this subject can begin (unfortunately, it has not yet begun in a serious and exhaustive way). In brief, one must put aside, i.e., exclude from examination, all of the quoted material, biblical and near-biblical (ecclesiastical). One must also view Skovoroda's language dynamically, in its development. Finally, students must free themselves of romantic and/or populist illusions about Skovoroda as a people's philosopher and about his language as being in contradiction with his views.

---

55. Compare, e.g., such addressees of Skovoroda's letters as Kurdjumov in Izjum and the Xarkiv merchants Ermolov and Urjupin. The latter was called *druh* (friend) by Skovoroda and addressed as *ty* (2, 443).

Abbreviations of the titles of Skovoroda's works

AM—Alfavit, ili bukvar' mira, 1774; As—Asxan', 1769; BA—Bran' Arxistratiha Mixaila, 1783/88; BD—Besěda narečennaja dvoe, 1772; BE—Blahodarnyj Erodij, 1787; BEz—Basnja Ezopova, 1760; BX—Basni Xar'kovskija, 1759, 1774; C—Cicero, O starosti, 1770s; DL—Da lobžet mja, 1765/66; DLb—De libertate, 1757/58; DM-Razhlahol o drevnem mirě, 1772; EQ—Est quaedam, 1760s; F—Fabula (Fales), 1763/69; F2—Fabula (Filaret), 1760s; FT—Fabula de Tantalo, 1760s; K—Kol'co, 1773/74; L—Letter (by numbers); ND—Načal'naja dver' ko xristianskomu dobronraviju, 1768; NJ—In natalem Jesu, 1760s; Ns—Narkiss, 1769; Obs—Observatorium, 1772; Od—Oda, ca. 1785; OS—O seljanskij milyj, 1758/59; P—Pěsnja, 1761; PA—Poxvala astronomii, ca. 1760; PB—Prja běsu so Varsavoju, 1783; Pl—Knižečka Plutarxova, 1790; PP—Razhovor pjati putnikov, 1773; PZ—Potop zmiin, ca. 1790; RP—Razhovor o premudrosti, 1758/59; SBP—Sad božestvennyx pěsnej, 1753-85 (by numbers); Sim—Similitudo clamantis, 1760s; Ub—Ubuždšesja viděša, 1765/66; UŽ—Ubohij žajvoronok, 1787; YZ—Izrailskij zmij, 1775/76; ŽL—Žena Lotova, 1780.

The Poetry of Skovoroda

Karen L. Black

In our century, Hryhorij Skovoroda is known chiefly as a philosopher. In the West, at least, many who know him by that reputation quite often are surprised to hear that he wrote poetry at all, or have read only one or two of the poems that reveal important aspects of his philosophy. In Skovoroda's lifetime, however, his poems had at least as wide a currency as his philosophical writings. None of his works, whether prose or poetry, was printed during his lifetime, circulating instead among his friends in manuscript; but many of the poems also passed among the people of the Ukrainian countryside in the form of songs, and to some degree they acquired the status of folk songs.[1] Moreover, formal Skovoroda studies (remaining as they have, particularly in the West, in the hands of a passionate few) have focused largely on his philosophy, even in the present conditions of a reviving interest in his work.

It is a pity that so little attention has been devoted to the poems. Just as Skovoroda's philosophy tickles the curiosity, challenges accustomed attitudes, and marks him on one's first reading as an original and unfettered thinker, so his poems are apt to come as a surprise. Their language is rich and unexpected, a bit difficult, though not impenetrable for anyone with a good basic knowledge of Russian or Ukrainian and a certain grounding in Scriptural Church Slavic, ranging from ironic folksiness to a nearly vatic mysticism. Their structure shows competence in the use of traditional verse patterns, combined with a willingness to make form suit content if necessary. Their imagery, as we shall see, sometimes shows the imprint of Skovoroda's forceful, maverick personality on the

---

1. V.F. Èrn, *Grigorij Savvič Skovoroda: Žizn' i učenie* (Moscow, 1912), 187.

dramatic devices of the East European Baroque and sometimes relaxes into a lucid pastorale. The poems are, to be sure, somewhat uneven in quality, but none of them is dull.

For our purposes there are some fifty significant poems. The thirty songs of the *Sad božestvennyx pěsnej* or *Garden of Divine Songs* form the greater part of Skovoroda's lyrical work: another twenty or so are occasional poems, fables in verse, or exercises in poetry of various genres for the lectures in poetics that he delivered at the *collegia* of Perejaslav and Xarkiv. Besides all these, there are four translations from Latin poems of Ovid and the sixteenth-century poet Marc-Antoine Muret, and four original poems in Latin.[2] Another twenty-five or so short poems and fragments are scattered through the prose works. Some of these were written specifically for their contexts, some are quotations from Skovoroda's own poems or from other poets such as Teofan Prokopovyč or Varlaam Laščevs'kyj, and another small group are Ukrainian or Russian proverbs. They are generally more interesting within their texts than outside them, and I make no reference to them here. Only three poems of major interest occur in the dialogues: "Alfavit, ili bukvar' mira..." contains a song and a verse fable; "Ubogij Žajvoronok" closes with a song on the birth of Christ. One other longish poem, "Xot' snačala grěx prijaten," was found among Skovoroda's papers. Its authorship is not completely beyond question, but insofar as it is suggestive of his work, it does have a place in this discussion.[3]

The *Garden of Divine Songs* contains Skovoroda's best-known poems. Its central principle is declared in the remainder of the title, "...Grown from Grains of Holy Scripture." Each of the thirty poems has a biblical epigraph, with the exception of Songs 24 and 30, which take theirs from classical authors. The scriptural epigraphs may quite simply give the poem's message, as in Song 18: "The Lord opposes the proud, but gives grace to the humble." This is then elaborated in the poem ("Oj ty, ptičko žoltoboko") to show the delights of the humble pastoral life. Other epigraphs stand in a somewhat more complicated relationship to their respective poems. They may consist of two or more apparently disconnected biblical passages:

> Воскресенію Христову. Из сего зерна: О! о!
> Бѣжите на горы! (Захарія). Востани, спяй!
> Покой даст Бог на горѣ сей (Исаіа). (Song 8)

---

2. Skovoroda's poems in Latin are accompanied by modern translations into Ukrainian in the most recent complete edition: V.I. Šynkaruk et al., eds., *Hryhorij Skovoroda: Povne zibrannja tvoriv*, 2 vols. (Kyiv: Naukova dumka, 1973), hereafter *PZT*. Poems quoted in Cyrillic in this paper follow the orthography of this edition exactly, with the exception that I have, like Skovoroda but unlike his Soviet editors, capitalized "God."

3. These four poems may be found in *PZT* I:411; I:462; II:131; and II:434, respectively.

For the resurrection of Christ. From this grain: Ho, ho, …flee to the mountains! (Zechariah) [2:6] Awake, thou that sleepest! [Ephesians 5:14] God will give peace on this mountain. (Isaiah) [25:10]

In the poem that follows this ("Ob"jali vkrug mja rany smertonosny"), no connection with the epigraph is obvious at the beginning, but in stanzas three and four Skovoroda takes up the image of the (holy) mountain, first as the refuge of the thirsting stag, then as the Hill of Golgotha, to which the poet hurries for healing. The manner of focus is one that he uses fairly often in prose as well as poetry; he surveys a concept, chooses an object associated with one of its stated or implicit images, and invests that image with the entire force of the original idea, to the point that it sometimes acquires a quite independent vigour and ends by dominating the passage or the work. With regard to the epigraphs in general, however, we know that in most cases the "ripened fruit" produced the "seed" and not vice versa, for Skovoroda added an undetermined number of the epigraphs when he assembled the *Garden* after 1785.[4]

Virtually every one of the poems exists to carry an idea, a moral message. A few are indeed purely lyrical, chiefly the *cri de coeur* poems such as Song 17:

> Видя житія сего я горе,
> Кипящее, как Чермное море,
> Вихром скорбей, напастей, бѣд,
> Разслаб, ужаснулся, поблѣд
> О горе сущим в нем!
>
> Возвратил я бѣдный бѣг мой вскорѣ,
> Чтоб не скрытись с фараоном в морѣ.
> Се к пристани тихой бѣжу
> И воплем плачевным глашу,
> Воздѣв горѣ руцѣ.
>
> О Христе! не даждь сотлѣть во адѣ!
> Даждь мнѣ в твоем жить небесном градѣ,
> Да не повлечет мя в свой слѣд,
> Блудница мір, сей темный свѣт!
> О милости бездна!

Seeing the grief of this life,/ Seething like the Red Sea,/ A whirlwind of griefs, disasters, woes,/ I weakened, was terror-struck, I paled,/ O woe to those who are in it!

I, wretched, quickly turned my course,/ So as not to vanish with Pharaoh in the

---

4. V. Šynkaruk and I. Ivan'o, Editors' Introduction to *PZT* I:27.

sea./ Lo, I make for the peaceful harbour/ And give tongue with tearful wail,/ My hands raised upward.

O Christ! Let me not rot in hell!/ Let me live in Thy heavenly city,/ That she may not draw me after her,/ (That) whore the world, this world of darkness!/ O abyss of grace!

Songs 8 and 29, and "Est quaedam maerenti..." may also be described in these terms. Another small group of poems, contemplative rather than didactic in tone, treat the mysteries of Christmas, Easter, and suffering and redemption:

>   Тайна странна и преславна!
>   Се — вертеп вмѣсто небес!
>   Дѣва херувимов главна,
>   И престолом вышним днесь.
>   А вмѣщен тот в яслѣх полно,
>   Коего есть не довольно
>   Вмѣстить и небо небес.... (Song 5)

Strange and most glorious mystery!/ Lo—a cave instead of the heavens!/ A virgin at the head of the cherubim,/ And (become) the throne of the highest./ And all enclosed in a manger is He/ Whom the heaven of heavens is not big enough to hold....

>   ...Язвы твои суровы — то моя печать,
>   Вѣнец мнѣ твой терновый — славы благодать,
>   Твой сей поносный крест —
>   Се мнѣ хвала и честь, о Іисусе!... (Song 7)

...Thy sore wounds are my seal,/ Thy crown of thorns for me the grace of glory,/ Thy shameful cross—/ This for me is praise and honour, O Jesus!...

But, with no disparagement intended to his gifts as a poet, Skovoroda is first of all an instructor in the art of living, and most of the poems are made to promote a certain view of the universe or to encourage a certain sort of conduct. His early exposure to the works of the great baroque preachers combines with an innate interest in questions of ethics to give us many statements of his chief preoccupation: how to live a peaceful, cheerful, ethically sound life in the midst of the world's many attractions, so as to be able to die without fear. A few examples, from among his best-known poems, will illustrate this:

>   ...Строит на свой тон юриста права,
>   С диспут студенту трещит голова.
>   Тѣх безпокоит Веренин амур,
>   Всякому голову мучит свой дур, —
>   А мнѣ одна только в свѣтѣ дума,
>   Как бы умерти мнѣ не без ума.
>
>   Смерте страшна, замашная косо!

> Ты не щадиш и царских волосов,
> Ты не глядиш, гдѣ мужик, а гдѣ царь, —
> Все жереш так, как солому пожар.
> Кто ж на ея плюет острую сталь?
> Тот, чія совѣсть, как чистый хрусталь...[sic] (Song 10)

The jurist interprets laws to suit himself,/ The student's head splits from disputations./ Venus' cupid troubles some,/ Every head is bothered by its own sort of nonsense./ But for me there is but one thought in the world,/ How may my death not be a senseless one.

Frightful death, sweeping scythe!/ Thou sparest not even the hairs of the royal head,/ Thou regardest not where stands peasant, where tsar,—/ Thou devourest all, as fire does straw./ Who spits with contempt on the scythe's sharp steel?/ He whose conscience is like the pure crystal... [sic]

Life is short, and we waste it:

> О дражайше жизни время,
> Коль тебя мы не щадим!
> Коль так, как излишне бремя,
> Всюду мещем, не глядим!... (Song 23)

O time, dearer than life,/ How we spare thee not!/ How we toss thee in all directions without regard, like a superfluous burden!...

Worldly glory is illusory and worthless:

> ...Нынѣ — скипетр и булава,
> Утро вставши — худа слава... (Song 14)

...Today the sceptre, the (hetman's) staff,/ Wake up tomorrow and your glory is worthless...

Happiness lies in preserving one's innocence, being content with little, and trusting God:

> ...Хочеш ли жить в сласти? Не завидь нигдѣ.
> Будь сыт з малой части, не убойся вездѣ. (Song 30)

...Would you live in sweetness? Envy no one./ Be satisfied with a small portion, be not everywhere afraid....

> Кто сердцем чист и душею,
> Не нужна тому броня,
> Не нужен и шлем на шею,
> Не нужна ему война.
> Непорочность — то его броня,
> И невинность — алмазна стѣна,
> Щит, меч и шлем ему сам Бог.... (Song 20)

He who is pure in heart and soul,/ That man needs no armour,/ Nor a helmet on his neck,/ Nor does he need war./ Innocence is his armour,/ And purity his wall of adamant,/ God Himself is his shield, sword, and helmet....

All this is most easily achieved in a rural setting:

> ...На что ж мнѣ замышляти,
> Что в селѣ родила мати?
> Нехай у тѣх мозок рвется,
> Кто высоко вгору дмется,
> А я буду себѣ тихо
> Коротати милый вѣк.
> Так минет мене все лихо,
> Щастлив буду человѣк. (Song 18)

...Why should I give it any thought/ That my mother bore me in the country?/ Let those beat their brains out/ Who are puffed up (with ambition),/ But I will peacefully/ Pass a pleasant lifetime./ Thus all evil will pass me by,/ I will be a happy man.

From the point of view of our age, these ideas can seem little more than worthy commonplaces. But there is nothing commonplace in the techniques of their formulation, for Skovoroda often casts them in startling images, adorns them with the rich rhetorical devices of a time with many stylistic choices, and occasionally adds unconventional emphases. These last account for some instances of censorship, and also (at least in part) for his works going unpublished for years after his death. The daring equation in the lines

> Так живал афинейскій, так живал и еврейскій
> Епикур —Христос. (Song 30)

...So lived the Athenian, so also the Hebrew/ Epicurus—Christ.

became, in Lysenkov's edition of 1861,

> Так живал афинейскій
> Проводил день-денской
> В садах Эпикур.[5]

...So lived the Athenian Epicurus,/ Day by day, in the gardens.

The (one would think) unexceptionable statement that kings, archbishops, and monks have to die just as poor people do ("Хоть сначала грѣх пріятен," lines 57-60) was excised in Bahalij's rather prudish and condescending edition of 1894.[6]

To demonstrate that Skovoroda's point of view was often unorthodox is, of course, to make little progress in explaining the nervous excitement of his poems.

---

5. *PZT* I:479 (ed. note).
6. *PZT* II:552-3.

Our present task is to investigate the specific methods by which his idiosyncratic views were transmuted into the patterns and symbols, conventional or unconventional, of poetry. Such a quest first requires some consideration of the standards of literary language affecting Skovoroda most directly.

The reader whose dominant or exclusive interest is Russian—even eighteenth-century Russian—encounters a diction in these poems quite different from anything he may have seen previously. The elements are familiar, to be sure; one recognizes Church Slavic and Ukrainian forms, here and there a word suggestive of Polish, words from Latin or Greek or from Western European languages. But the mixture of elements seems at times to have almost a random character, as in this passage:

>...На тверди звѣзды блеснули прекрасны,
>Как дорогіе каменья алмазни,
>Фалес закричал: «Старухо драгая!» ... ("Fabula")

>...In the firmament the lovely stars sparkled,/ Like precious diamond-stones,/ Thales shouted, "Old lady, my dear!"...

Here we see both members of an East Slavic/Church Slavic doublet pair (*dorogie/dragaja*) and a morphological Ukrainism (the vocative *Staruxo*). The mixing of forms is not surprising, however; Skovoroda is one of the last major writers to use the Ukrainian *knyžna mova* or "book language," a literary language whose evolution differed in significant respects from that of eighteenth-century Russian.

In pre-seventeenth-century Russia, the written word appeared very largely in the form of Church Slavic, by virtue of that language's use in both liturgy and religious literature. Although Church Slavic itself had undergone some changes since its arrival on Russian soil, first by the absorption of Russian features and later by the deliberate normalizing and stylistic innovations of the Second South Slavic Influence of the later fourteenth century, its status in relation to vernacular Russian remained relatively stable. Church-related vocabulary entered vernacular Russian to some degree, but Church Slavic elements had not yet begun to play a large role in neologisms or in experimental style.

Vernacular Ukrainian followed its own path of development in the centuries preceding the seventeenth. Like Russian, Ukrainian existed in close connection with Church Slavic, though it never showed nearly so great a tendency to absorb Church Slavic elements. A different influence affected Ukrainian. The customs and cultural values of the Polish state, including the Polish language and a body of Latin and European literature, brought a large number of Polonisms and words of general Western European currency into Ukrainian. On the other hand, the distinctiveness of Ukrainian in this regard was counterbalanced by the relative (in comparison to the present day) similarity of the East Slavic languages, allowing for a considerable mutual comprehensibility that provides some explanation of Skovoroda's ability in the next century to move freely among Slavic words of differing origin within a poem and frequently even within a line.

The seventeenth century, furthermore, showed shifts in the relationships between languages of the East Slavic area that were to be important to the stylistic standardizations of the eighteenth century. There were two centres of Church Slavic scholarship, Moscow and Kyiv. The latter was dominant in the seventeenth century (partly by virtue of its importance as a centre of religious publishing), and it was in Kyiv that literary Church Slavic acquired a difference of character, in comparison with Russian literary Church Slavic, which went beyond the earlier differences of localisms in phonology and morphology.

> In Kiev the rigid distinction between the literary and the non-literary language had been observed less strictly than in Moscow. The Church Slavonic of Kiev, in so far as it fulfilled strictly ecclesiastical requirements, was preserved in a remarkably pure form. But since it was employed as a literary medium for purposes not purely liturgical, it had become permeated...by elements from colloquial speech. It had absorbed not only Ukrainian but also Polish and Latin words from the vocabulary of the brilliant Polish-Latin culture.[7]

Thus this mixed literary variant of Church Slavic, the *knyžna mova*, was the language of a thriving sacred and to some extent secular literature a century or more before Skovoroda. The efflorescence of culture in seventeenth-century Ukraine produced a rhetoric used with considerable artistry in polemic and homily; it was adopted, along with the prestigious "pure" liturgical Church Slavic, by Moscow. The following century, that of Skovoroda's lifetime, saw two trends: first, the hardening of the lively and once innovative diction of the *knyžna mova* into the conservative doctrine of rhetoric taught at the Kyiv-Mohyla Academy and its daughter-schools; second, a reversal of the cultural stream that had so recently run from Kyiv to Moscow, as Russia increasingly acquired control over Ukraine.

The state of the Russian vocabulary in the eighteenth century shows a proliferation of new forms, and an increased awareness of the stylistic uses of Church Slavic and other non-Russian forms. Sorokin[8] characterizes the lexical-stylistic traits of the period as, among other things, a great deal of variability of vocabulary; many areas of clear insufficiency in word-forming resources; a tendency to return to or preserve lexical inventiveness and experimentation; the curious combination of theoretical purism and a wide acceptance of foreign borrowings; and the sharp opposition of book and colloquial languages, with a tendency to give the book language something of a caste character.

---

7. B.O. Unbegaun, "Colloquial and Literary Russian," *Oxford Slavonic Papers* I (1950):28.
8. Ju.S. Sorokin, *Processy formirovanija russkogo literaturnogo jazyka* (Moscow and Leningrad: Nauka, 1966), 20-23.

These descriptions apply only loosely to the language of Skovoroda's milieu. The *knyžna mova* was an established literary language and was not, as Russian was, in the position of requiring basic definition and normalization. It did, like Russian, make use of many archaisms, but these were a part of its customary vocabulary that had never really gone out of use; again like Russian, it displayed lexical inventiveness and experimentation, for it had many resources to draw on. But the tendency to lexical purism in the *knyžna mova* is on the whole less marked, for, after all, its Ukrainian component had a high proportion of borrowings and was not in this period the recipient of a significantly greater number of foreign words than at other times in its recent past.

The chief result of all this for Skovoroda's poetic language was a tremendous range of lexical choice. He had been educated in a highly normative rhetorical tradition, but one whose norms in the domain of lexical source and etymological overtone allowed more use of the semantic resources of other Slavic languages than would have been available to him had he been a Russian writing in Russia. He was saturated, like any other pupil of the theological schools, with scriptural Church Slavic. He had the advantages of a natural sensitivity to languages (as well as to language) and a rigorous training in Greek and Latin, and some Hebrew; he knew German very well and apparently at least some French. Two stays in Russia—one in 1742-4 when he served in the chapel choir of Elizabeth I in St. Petersburg, the other in about 1757, when he spent some time in Moscow and at the Trinity-Sergius Monastery—must have sharpened his awareness of current Great Russian issues in language and literature. He is said to have known the work of Tredijakovskij and Lomonosov, on the statement of "two respected men who knew him personally."[9] There are no clear indications, unfortunately, as to whether Skovoroda had read Lomonosov's "O pol'zě knig cerkovnyx v russkom jazykě" of 1757. It seems likely that he had, but if he chose to apply the standards in that work concerning the amounts of Church Slavic vocabulary requisite to various levels of discourse, it appears to have been only in a rather sporadic way; whatever his awareness of the developing theories of literary language in Russia, his actual practice in assembling words of scriptural or vernacular origin *in a given poem* rests on the broader standards of acceptability of the *knyžna mova*, and moreover depends quite often (as in the passage from "Fabula" quoted above, with its use of *dorogie* and *dragaja*) on the exigencies of syllable count, as well as on the stylistic appropriateness of Church Slavic versus vernacular in Lomonosov's terms, assuming that Skovoroda in fact knew Lomonosov's work.

Another set of facts might be construed as cutting across the above observations. It appears that, at least in terms of the proportion of forms taken by

---

9. Snegirev, in *Otečestvennye zapiski* 42 (1832), quoted by Èrn, 69.

language origin, the vocabulary of Skovoroda's poetry (taken as a body) is clearly more similar to that of a sample of Deržavin's poetry, selected for comparable dating and subject matter, than it is to a sample of Skovoroda's own prose.[10] The similarity obtains in three areas, one of which is core vocabulary, "pan-Slavic" words of Common Slavic origin; this might be expected. The other areas of resemblance are Church Slavic vocabulary, and vocabulary of non-Slavic origin, for the most part Greek, Latin, and Western European. This material must be approached with care. It is, after all, the interaction of forms within a particular poem that is significant to determining a poet's stylistic sense: Skovoroda might have written a certain percentage of his poems in the purest Church Slavic and a certain percentage in relatively secular language, and the material could still yield the same results. But that the two bodies of poetry should stand in such clear contrast to Skovoroda's own prose suggests at least that the Russian and the Ukrainian literary traditions may at this time have been closer, in their assumptions as to what constitutes a suitable lexicon, in the realm of poetry than in the realm of prose.[11]

The results of Skovoroda's belonging to a tradition are in some ways as obvious as the effects of his willingness to step outside it. His training in the *knyžna mova* led him at times into the involuted patterns of syntax carried over from the fifteenth-century hagiographers and the baroque homiletic tradition. The separation of a possessive pronoun or an attributive adjective from its noun by some other word or clause, not an uncommon device for the time, is frequent:

...Так африканскій страждет елень скорый;
Он птиц быстрѣе пить спѣшит на горы,...
Даждь спасительну мнѣ цѣльбу в сей страсти... (Song 8)

...Thus suffers the swift stag of Africa;/ Faster than the birds he rushes to the mountains to drink,/ ... / Grant me Thy saving healing in this torment...

...О, се златых вѣк лѣт!(Song 1)

...O, behold the age of golden years!

Other inversions show phrase components so thoroughly dislocated as to require several readings:

...Ты людских видиш, сидяй высоко,
Разных толь мнѣній безщетну смѣсь. (Song 9)

...Thou, sitting on high, seest the uncountable mixture of such varied human opinions....

---

10. Karen L. Black, "The Sources of the Poetic Vocabulary of Grigorij Skovoroda" (Ph.D. dissertation, Bryn Mawr College, 1975).
11. An abbreviated table of the figures from this study is appended.

> ...Будь твоя Господь с Давидом часть... (Song 22)

...May thy portion, as David's, be the Lord...

> ...Как мусикійскій сличный слух,
> Сладостю тѣло и движет дух... (Song 26)

...Like the lovely sound of music,/ It moves body and soul with its sweetness...

> ...Он путь управит до небес,
> Преднося Христовых свѣт словес.
> В нем весь духовный узриш плод,
> Как в чистовидных зерцалѣ вод,
> Агнцу, послѣдуя Христу,
> Кротко очистит нечистоту.... (Song 26)

...He shows the way to heaven,/ Offering the light of Christ's words./ In him you shall see the whole fruit of the spirit,/ As in a mirror of clear waters./ Following Christ the Lamb,/ He will meekly purge uncleanness....

Most of the poems have only a few such inversions, perhaps two or three apiece; some have none. Curiously, the Songs numbered 22 through 27 show a considerably higher number, several extending over two or more lines. One possible explanation is that three of these (25, 26, and 27) are occasional poems. The Kyiv-Mohyla Academy had an old and glorious reputation in the writing of panegyrics,[12] and at this time (the 1750s) Skovoroda, a young poet and no doubt more imitative than he was later, may be reflecting the Academy's standards of syntax. If this is the case, it may be that a higher number of inverted word orders is an indication of earlier composition, a possibly useful index, since most of the poems are undated.

A kind of ambiguity prevails in Skovoroda's metric practices. He is clearly influenced by the traditions of syllabic verse, even though true syllabic passages are rare; he is just as clearly aware of the techniques of syllabotonic composition; in any case he shows a continual alertness to the mechanical requirements of the line. Five of the *Garden*-poems (Songs 5, 10, 14, 18, and 28) show extremely regular syllabotonic structure, like the steady trochaic tetrameter of Song 5:

> Тайна странна и преславна!
> Се — вертеп вмѣсто небес!
> Дѣва херувимов главна,
> И престолом вышним днесь....

Strange and most glorious mystery!/ Lo—a cave instead of the heavens!/ A virgin at the head of the cherubim,/ And (become) the throne of the highest./

---

12. Šynkaruk and Ivan'o, Introduction to *PZT* I:21.

Tetrameter and the trochee dominate this group of poems, though Song 10 uses the dactyl instead:

> Всякому городу нрав и права,
> всяка имѣет свой ум голова...

Every city has its customs and laws,/ Every head has its own mind...

Rather more common than such regularity is a pattern in which some part of the stanza—perhaps a beginning quatrain or a one- or two-line refrain—has a regular syllabotonic structure, but the remainder of the stanza differs rhythmically in some way, changing either to another regular syllabotonic line or to an irregular rhythm suggestive of, if not technically definable as, syllabic verse. Consider the third stanza of Song 23:

> (1) Брось, любезный друг, бездѣлья,
> (2) Пресѣчи толикій вред,
> (3) Сей момент пріймись до дѣла:
> (4) Вот, вот, время уплывет!

Give up idleness, dear friend,/ Put a stop to such a harmful thing,/ Get down to business this very moment:/ Look, look, time is slipping away!

Thus far, regular trochaic tetrameter. Now the shift:

> (5) Не |на́ше то у|же́, что про́й|шло́ мимо |на́с,
> (6) Не |на́ше |то́, что по|ро́дит| бу́душа по|ра́,
> (7) Днешнiй| де́нь только| на́ш, а не| у́треннiй| ча́с.
> (8) Не |зна́ем,|что́ прине|се́т ве|че́рняя за|ря́.

What is past is no longer ours,/ What the future will bring forth is not ours,/ Today only is ours, and not the morning's hour./ We know not what the evening glow will bring....

In the second half of the stanza we see a mixed pattern. Lines 5 and 7 are in dactylic tetrameter:

(˘) ˘ | — ˘ ˘ | — ˘ ˘ | — ˘ ˘ | —

Lines 6 and 8, however, show a mixed-foot pattern:

˘ | — ˘ | — ˘ ˘ | — ˘ | — ˘ ˘ ˘ | —

This illustrates a very common tendency in the lyric poems: to move from Regularity A to Regularity B to Irregularity, or in the reverse direction. Such shifts often parallel changes in mood from certainty to uncertainty, from the soothing to the unsettling, or from admonishment to exhortation.

Some other poems consist entirely of lines of regularly patterned mixed feet, such as this half-stanza from the song from "Alfavit, ili bukvar' mira"[13]:

$$\overline{}\smile\overline{}\smile\overline{}\smile\smile\overline{}\smile$$
...Если ж не|правo| зрит мое| око,

$$\overline{}\smile\overline{}\smile\overline{}\smile\overline{}$$
Ты мене,| отче, на|стави| здѣсь.

$$\overline{}\smile\smile\overline{}\smile\smile\overline{}\smile\overline{}\smile$$
Ты людских| видиш,|сидяй вы|соко,

$$\overline{}\smile\smile\overline{}\smile\overline{}\smile\overline{}$$
Разных толы|мнѣний без|щетну| смѣсь....

...And if my eye sees not truly,/ Instruct Thou me here, Father./ Thou, sitting on high, seest the uncountable mixture of such varied human opinions....

In general, however, the syllabic consciousness seems to hover at Skovoroda's elbow, making real syllabotonic consistency rare. Part of a stanza, as we have noted above, may be syllabotonically regular with mixed or unmixed feet, the remainder showing outright irregularities. But (at least where the *Garden*-poems and a few others are concerned) a hypothetical model-poem would show a loosely consistent metrical structure, usually keeping the same number of lines per stanza but allowing quite a flexible arrangement of strong and weak beats in the same line of different stanzas. It is by no means unusual to find a subtly different metrical pattern for each stanza of a poem. Analysis is complicated by occasional uncertainties as to whether a Russian or a Ukrainian stress was intended, as well as by the simple acts of metrical license that any poet takes. Whatever else may change, however, it is relatively unusual to find variations in syllable count in the stanza pattern.

Skovoroda's particular sense of the quantitative integrity of the line leads him at times into choices of form in which, apparently, the demands of syllable count take precedence over the associative qualities of the word. This is especially noticeable in the case of Church Slavic-East Slavic doublet pairs, and we see juxtapositions such as the example quoted above, or:

Что то за волность? Добро в ней какое?
Ины говорят, будто *золотое*.
Ах, не *златое*, если сравнить *злато*,
Против волности еще оно блато.... ("De Libertate")

What sort of thing is freedom? What good is there in it?/ Some talk as if it were golden./ Ah, not golden; if we compare it to gold,/ That is mere mud beside freedom....

From these and similar examples we must infer that Skovoroda felt only sporadically bound by any current prescriptions on mixing Church Slavic and vernacular forms. There are, to be sure, instances of stylistic differentiation. The "city of

---

13. This poem is, in much, identical to Song 9 of the *Garden*.

God," the "heavenly city," and man as "city of the Holy Spirit" are always *grad*, as are two actual cities treated in spiritual contexts:

    ...Граде печальный Переяслав!... (Song 26)

    ...Sad city of Perejaslav!...

    ...Там под Вифлеемским градом... ("In natalem Jesu")

    ...There below the city of Bethlehem...

The ordinary secular city is always *gorod*, and furthermore is an essentially negative entity, whereas *grad* is associated with blessedness.

Skovoroda appears to have been fond of testing various rhyme schemes, though to be sure he does not go beyond the conventional possibilities. If we consider rhyme patterns, disregarding for the moment the functions and sorts of his rhymes, the dominance of certain structures is immediately obvious. The *sense* of rhymed couplet, however lined, is pervasive, occurring perhaps in consecutive lines with end rhyme (A/A/B/B):

    ...Стоит явор над горою,
    Все кивает головою.... (Song 18)

    ...A plane tree stands upon the hill,/ It keeps nodding its head....

or over a caesura (which may be omitted in some stanzas and the one line written as two) (A‖A/B‖B):

    ...Се час исполняется! Се сын посылается!
    Се лѣта пришла кончина! Се Бог посылает сына.... (Song 4)

    ...Lo, the time is fulfilled! Lo, the Son is sent!/ Lo, the year's end has come!/ Lo, God sends his Son....

or with rhyme at both caesura and end (A‖B/A‖B);

    Не пойду в город богатый. Я буду на полях жить,
    Буду вѣк мой коротати, гдѣ тихо время бѣжит.... (Song 12)

    I won't go into the wealthy city. I'll live in the fields,/ I'll pass my lifetime where time slips by peacefully....

The end-rhymed A/B/A/B quatrain is also frequent, often acquiring a tag-line that may serve as a refrain (Song 4) or may rhyme over to its counterpart in the next stanza (Song 14). Or the quatrain may be followed by a tristich, giving, for example, an A/B/A/B/C/C/D stanza (Song 15). There are some twenty to twenty-three different stanza-schemes, depending on how one counts, and these may be reduced to four basic types: A/A/B/B, A/B/A/B, and with or without caesura. Only two poems differ significantly from a general model of two- or four-line units with consistent end-rhyme. Song 27 is unique in its three-line rhyme scheme (A/B/C/A/B/C/D/D):

> ...Пастырю наш, образ Христов
> Тих, благ, кроток, милосердый,
> Зерцало чистое доброт!
> Красны неси нозѣ, готов
> Мир благовѣстить нам твердый.
> Призри на сей священ оплот;
> От тебе помощи весь он ждет,
> Сердце и руцѣ тебѣ дает....

...Our pastor, image of Christ,/ Peaceful, kind, meek, merciful,/ Clear looking-glass of virtues!/ Beautiful are thy feet; thou art prepared/ To announce to us a lasting peace./ Gaze upon this holy fortress;/ The whole (city) awaits thy aid,/ Gives thee its heart and hands....

Also atypical are the question-and-answer stanzas of "Pěsn' Roždestvu Xristovu," in which the question-quatrains show the rhyme —/A/—/A, the only instance (except for refrain-lines in some poems) where end-rhyme is systematically lacking.[14]

There are a few generally applicable differences in metre and rhyme between the poems of the *Garden of Divine Songs* and those outside it; in fact, it becomes clear that the two groups are distinct in much more than subject matter. The *Garden*-poems, on the one hand, make use of both masculine and feminine rhyme (taken in their totality, something approaching fifty-fifty, with a slight preponderance for the masculine). Pre-caesura rhymes show a preference for feminine on the order of two to one; end-rhymes favour masculine in about the same ratio. As we have already observed, the *Garden* uses various rhyme schemes and lines of varying length, some regularly syllabotonic, others not so regularly.

The non-*Garden* poems, on the other hand, incline strongly toward a fixed pattern: an eleven-syllable (or in two cases, "Quid est virtus?" and "Melodia," a thirteen-syllable) line with strictly feminine A/A/B/B rhyme: in other words, for the most part, traditional syllabic verse. Many of these instances are easily explainable by the fact of their belonging to traditional genres of the Latin-Polish-Ukrainian culture, notably the verse *fabulae* "Kak tolko sonce k večeru zapalo," "Fabula de Tantalo," "Staričok někij Filaret v pustině," and "Basnja Esopova"; the odic "De Libertate"; a two-line epigram, "Skaži mně kratko..."; and the six-line "Vse lice morščis..." "Razgovor o premudrosti," written in the style of—if not indeed as a direct contribution to—the Ukrainian school *intermediae*, keeps the rhymed-couplet structure, but shows a twelve-syllable line and strict masculine rhyme. Of the five remaining poems, two ("Similitudines" and

---

14. One could argue that these short lines could easily be relined into rhymed couplets, though the presence of A/A/B/B rhyme in one or two of the stanzas suggests that the quatrain was intentional.

"Est quaedam maerenti...") keep A/A/B/B feminine rhyme; a third ("Pĕsn' Roždestvu Xristovu") does likewise except for the final line of the refrain; but all three show more flexibility in syllable count than the others. Finally, the song from "Alfavit, ili bukvar' mira" and the long poem "Xot' snačala grĕx prijaten" are metrically distinct from the other non-*Garden* poems. The former, however, is a variant of the *Garden*'s Song 9; the latter contains syllable-count variations so untypically large as to furnish some material for those who would argue against Skovoroda's having written it.

Rhyme is an important organizing principle in the poems, but especially so in the *Garden*. Many of Skovoroda's rhymes are obvious and to a certain degree predictable: *gore/more* (Song 17), *krasnyj/jasnyj* (Song 27), *volja/dolja* (Song 14). Indeed, it happens frequently enough to constitute a pattern that the rhyme itself appears to have inspired the connection of ideas fundamental to the poem, as in Song 3's comparison of God to city and garden, arising from the rhyme *grad/sad*. Especially frequent rhymes, and consequently associations of ideas, are *čelovĕk/vĕk*, *ad/jad*, *strast'/slast'*, *svĕt/cvĕt*, and *Xrist-/čist-*. Sometimes the automatic association is the result of a paucity of rhyming choices: *nebes/očes*, *nebes/sloves*, *vremja/bremja*, *kamen'/plamen'*. Grammatical rhyme is everywhere, almost to the point of tediousness: *uzrĕt'/doletĕt'*, *s toboju/nad goroju*, and so forth.[15] But mingled with the *moj/tvoj* rhymes, and occurring often enough to prevent one's taking anything for granted, are slant rhymes, incomplete rhymes, and double rhymes, sometimes of great subtlety, and the occasional *tour de force* of consonance, assonance, and semantic manipulation.

...Зависть, печаль, страх, несыта жажда,
Ревность, мятеж, скорбь, тяжба и вражда... («Пѣснь Рождеству Христову»)

Envy, sadness, terror, insatiable craving,/ Jealousy, turbulence, grief, strife, and enmity...

...Воля! О несытый ад! Всѣ тебѣ ядь, всѣм ты яд....
...Что нужность не трудна, что трудность не нужна. (Song 28)

...Will! O insatiable hell! All (people) are fodder for thee, thou art poison to all....
...That which is a necessity is not difficult, that which is a difficulty is not necessary.

---

15. While this is not the place to discuss the phonology of Skovoroda's rhymes, it might be mentioned in passing that *e/ĕ* rhymes are rare but *i/ĕ* rhymes rather usual, and that word-final *g* rhymes sometimes with *k* and sometimes with *x*.

Onomatopoeia is not common, though it certainly does occur:
>...Тут течет поточок близко... (Song 18)
>...Here a little stream flows close by...

>...Дух, дыша, свышшь благословит.... (Song 27)
>...The spirit, breathing, blesses from above....

This *i/st* repetition suggests the hissing of flames:
>Не боится совѣсть чиста ниже Перуна огниста, ни!... (Song 1)
>...A clear conscience fears not even the fiery Perun, nay!...

Here the alternation of velar consonants with high vowels suggests a bumpy landscape:
>...Ах долины, яры,
>Круглы могилы, бугры!... (Song 13)
>...Ah vales, ravines,/ Rounded mounds, hillocks!...

The elastic but persistent bond between *f/v* and *s/z* sounds in these lines conveys the notion of something dogging one's footsteps:
>...Гдѣ ли пойду, все с тобою вездѣ всякій час.
>Ты, как рыба с водою, всегда возлѣ нас.... (Song 19)
>...No matter where I walk, I am always with thee everywhere, at every hour,/
>Thou, like fish with water, art always beside us....

There is often an intra- or interlinear resonance which is the more interesting for being somewhat erratic. In rhyme and resonance as well as in other aspects of poetic technique Skovoroda's lyrics are characterized by what might be qualified reverently as a disinclination to be bound by a set structure, less reverently as distractibility, in the sense that a rhyme, meter, or metaphor may dominate the first few stanzas of a poem and then be replaced by another as a different concept captures his attention. The poem's underlying message is always sustained, but its forms and decorations often alter, which is not so much a matter of setting the subject in contrasting lights (as any poet might choose to do) as it is the result of being pushed by the momentum of the idea itself into other attractive forms.

The progression of a typical Divine Song might be described as loosely modular. The line tends to be clause-complete, true enjambment being a rarity; the stanza tends to be idea-complete. Again and again one particular structural sequence appears (see Songs 2, 6, 7, and 8, among others). The poem begins with a catalogue of items, a series of parallel statements, often (though not always) one per line. This may extend over several stanzas. Consider the first eight lines of Song 6, apostrophizing nature, heaven, and earth:

> Вонми, небо и земля, нынѣ ужаснися!
> Море, безднами всѣми согласно двигнися!
> И ты, быстротекущій, возвратися, Іордане,
> Прійди скоро крестити Христа, Іоанне!
>
> Краснозрачныя лѣса, стези оттворите,
> Предитечу Іоанна ко Христу пустите.
> Земныи же языци, купно с нами всѣ ликуйте,
> Ангелскія хоры, вси в небѣ торжествуйте!

> Hear, heaven and earth, be now terrified!/ Sea, move all thine abysses together!/ And thou, swift-flowing Jordan, turn back,/ Come speedily to baptize Christ, John!
>
> Beautiful forests, open your paths,/ Admit John the Forerunner to Christ./ Tribes of the earth, rejoice together with us,/ Angel choruses, triumph all in heaven!

The Catalogue complete, Skovoroda then shifts, often quite abruptly, into what we shall call the Text (in the homiletic sense):

> Снійде спас во Іордан, ста в его глубинѣ,
> Се снійде на нь и дух свят в видѣ голубинѣ.
> Сей есть сын мой возлюбленны, отец из облак вѣщаше,
> Сей Мессія обновит естество все ваше.

> The Saviour went down into Jordan and stood in its depths,/ And lo, the Holy Spirit descended upon him in the form of a dove./ This is my beloved son, the Father declared from the clouds,/ This Messiah shall renew all your nature.

The Text is always scriptural. It may be a reference to one of the New Testament parables, such as that of the grain of wheat that must die in order to live again (Song 7). It may be a direct or oblique reference to any of a number of Skovoroda's favourite biblical passages, if not from the New Testament, then very often from the Song of Songs or from the Psalms. Whatever its source, the generally central placing of the Text recalls the concept of "growing from grains of Holy Scripture" of the *Garden*'s title, and the Text lines or stanza serve as a pivot, a kind of roundhouse where the poem changes its direction in one of several ways: from earthly to heavenly, from the personal to the general or from the general to the personal. It anchors the poem in Scripture and condenses one part of the poem's message; it often echoes the epigraph, though at times the connection is tenuous or obscure.

Returning to Song 6, we see another shift, now to a conclusion. Usually this has the form of an appeal, either to the reader in the form of a moral, or to God or Christ for help, blessing, or consolation:

> Освяти струи и нам, змію сотри главу,

> Духа твоего, Христе, росу даждь и славу,
> Да не потопит нас змій. И мы всѣ от земна края
> Да почити полещем до твоего рая.

Hallow the streams for us as well, crush the serpent's head,/ Give the dew and the glory of Thy spirit, Christ,/ That the serpent may not drown us. And may we all, from earth's regions,/ Come to Thy paradise to rest.

Half or more than half of the *Garden*-poems may be described in terms of this Catalogue-Text-Appeal structure. A few others (i.e., Songs 10, 13, 18) are essentially or entirely secular, apart from their epigraphs; these tend to show another structure, assigning a more nearly equal level of meaning to each stanza and being often much more suggestive of a folk song. The remaining poems of the *Garden* may make even more extensive use of scriptural reference and are just as likely to end with an Appeal; but again the shifts in direction are less obvious, the individual stanzas more apt to be structurally similar to one another—links in a chain rather than a spiritual arched bridge on which one climbs over a keystone to a conclusion on the other side.

The sense of tension present in all of Skovoroda's poems except the most serene and the purely narrative, one's impression that the poem has an independent momentum and (at the extreme) is on the point of spinning out of control, has a number of explanations. Some of these we have noted: a vocabulary that is anything but homogenous in its origins and associations; involutions of word order; sections of contrastive metric pattern; and the "modular" arrangement of ideas that so often keeps the reader in a state of alert shifting, as it were. There are other contributory characteristics. Much sense of immediacy comes from an extensive use of second person singular discourse, in combination with a good deal of apostrophe, ejaculation (*Ni! Ax! O!*) and appeal to the reader. Furthermore, many of the "thou" poems show not just one, but numerous addressees. Song 6 has no fewer than ten: the sky, the earth, the sea and abysses of the ocean, the River Jordan, John the Baptist, forests, the tribes of the earth, angel choruses, and Christ. This song, like several others, is intended as a volley of appeals, but even when a less dramatic effect is required, there are often several thou-addressees. Song 26, for example, begins as an exhortation to the new Bishop of Perejaslav:

> Поспѣшай, гостю, поспѣшай,
> Наши желанія увѣнчай!...

Hasten, o guest, hasten,/ Crown our desires!...

Then it offers encouragement to the city itself:

> ...Граде печальный Переяслав!
> Часто сиротство твое дознав,
> Измѣну вышняго смотри....

...Sad city of Perejaslav!/ Having often acknowledged thy orphanhood,/ Behold the vicar of the Highest!...

and, after listing the various benefits the Bishop will bring to the city, the poet turns to Christ for blessing:

...Христе, источник благ святой!
Ты дух на пастыря излій твой....

...Christ, holy spring of blessings!/ Pour Thy spirit out upon Thy pastor....

Song 28, similarly, speaks first to the reader, then to the negative quality of wilfulness, and finally calls on God for the gifts of peace and serenity.

Consistent use of the first person singular is confined to the few laments (e.g. Songs 8, 17, 29). Consistent use of the third person rarely occurs except in the verse fables. In general, shifts in person/addressee at fairly short intervals contribute much to that sense of changing equilibrium so characteristic of Skovoroda.

In his preoccupations—and consequently in his tropes and figures—Skovoroda writes by turns as a preacher, as an exponent of the baroque devotional lyric, as a recorder or imitator of cheerily secular songs in the folk idiom, and as a schoolmaster touched by Renaissance and Neoclassical ideals. The last tendency is minimized if we remove from discussion the poems outside the *Garden* which were written either as demonstration pieces in poetics or as contributions to traditional genres such as the fable.[16] It is certainly not unusual to find two or more of these modes in a single poem, but in general the first two predominate. The distinction between them is significant. As a preacher, Skovoroda is exhortative, prone to make extensive use of explicit or suggested scriptural reference and turn it into practical moral-philosophical instructions. As a baroque devotional lyricist, on the other hand, he is engaged as it were in private conversation with God. The characteristics of this kind of lyric are described in one source[17] as use of the present tense and an "engaged idiom—abrupt, exclamatory, and colloquial,"[18] a sense of narrator-protagonist before an audience, of being "overheard" rather than of expounding. The reader is encouraged to try these criteria on, for example, Song 7, on the text "Who shall separate me from Thy love?"

---

16. Of the non-*Garden* poems, this leaves the song from "Alfavit, ili bukvar' mira"; possibly "Est quaedam maerenti..."; "Pěsn' Roždestvu Xristovu," and "Xot' snačala grěx prijaten."
17. Frank J. Warnke, *Versions of Baroque: European Literature in the Seventeenth Century* (New Haven: Yale University Press, 1972), 136-7. This book presents a persuasive view of the nature of the baroque, and though it does not treat Slavic literature specifically, it contains many observations that are illuminating to a study of Skovoroda.
18. Warnke, loc. cit.

Certain of the central preoccupations of the baroque are prominent in the lyric poems. Foremost is Skovoroda's concern with the reasons for conflict of opposites, a kind of continuing inner debate that is expressed either directly and personally in outcries against the turbulence of life or as instructions to the listener on how to avoid being troubled by the world's contradictory demands; the moral in the latter invariably reduces to advice to withdraw into philosophical self-sufficiency, simplicity of material needs, and faith in Christ. A quintessentially Skovorodian metaphor is that of the world as stormy sea, or as the threatening and insatiable ocean abyss:

> Видя житія сего я горе,
> Кипящее, как Чермное море,
> Вихром скорбей, напастѣй, бѣд,
> Разслаб, ужаснулся, поблѣд
> О горе сущим в нем!... (Song 17)

Seeing the grief of this life,/ Seething like the Red Sea,/ A whirlwind of griefs, disasters, woes,/ I weakened, was terror-struck, I paled,/ O woe to those who are in it!

The sea and the abyss are always negative, frightening images, except in one idiosyncratic manoeuvre in which Skovoroda turns the metaphor inside out and makes Christ the abyss—not of terrors but of mercy (Song 17).[19] Song 29, one of the few poems to be built on a consistent extended metaphor, compares life to a sea that tosses the poet's small boat, and adds another characteristic metaphor of Christ as rock and harbour. The poem's final three stanzas show a typical transmutation of Christ through three representations. First he is harbour and shore:

> ...О пристанище безбѣдно,
> Тихо, сладко, безнавѣтно!
> О Маріин сыне!
> Ты буди едине
> Кораблю моему брегом....

...O safe haven,/ Peaceful, sweet, beyond reproach!/ O son of Mary!/ Thou alone be/ The shore for my ship....

Skovoroda then reverts to Scripture (the Text again; see Mark 4:38):

> ...Ты в кораблѣ моем спиши,
> Востани! Мой плач услыши!
> Ах, запрети морю...

---

19. One of his most memorable effects is this sort of inversion of image. Another instance in the Dialogues turns the sacrament of communion into an emetic, the two being similar in their purgative power.

>...Thou sleepest in my boat,/ Arise! Hear my weeping!/ Ah, forbid the sea...

Then, in the final stanza, the Appeal (addressed to Christ) concludes:

>...Спаси мя, Петра, молюся!
>
>...Save me, Peter, I pray!

—a somewhat puzzling apparent switch of person until one perceives the underlying etymological "rock" of *Petra*; this is Christ in his metaphorical function, not Peter.

Skovoroda shares with other baroque poets a preoccupation with the deceptive nature of appearances. Worldly attractions are a baited fishhook:

>...Ты удка, сладостью обвита,
>Но мы тебе жадно жрем.... («Хоть сначала грѣх пріятен»)
>
>Thou art a hook, swathed in bait,/ But we gobble thee greedily....

Sin's attractive mask conceals evil:

>...Твоя сначала личина
>Нашим кажется очам,
>Так как прекрасна картина
>Всѣм слѣпо смотрящим нам.
>Но вдруг твоя проходит краса
>И как смертоносная коса
>Устрашает наши сердца.... (Ibid.)
>
>...Thy mask at first/ Seems to our eyes/ Like a lovely picture/ To all of us, gazing blindly./ But suddenly thy beauty passes/ And like the death-bringing scythe/ Terrifies our hearts....

Many of the poems of moral instruction, though perhaps less metaphorically explicit than this, dwell to some extent on the human tendency to be attracted by appearances.

Other images that either are very common in the poems or possess a peculiar significance for Skovoroda are water—the water of the Holy Spirit or of Scripture—as cleanser, purge, and thirst-quencher; weather, as a metaphor for the state of one's soul; the city, functioning as a symbol on the one hand for the world and on the other as the "city of God"; an aggregate of concepts associated with the flesh and including weapons and wounds, disease, corruption, and burning; and a certain taste for figures of flying or rising. Images of nature—animals, birds, flowers, fruits—are generally used in a fairly concrete sense, with the exception of animal as mythological or biblical beast (tending to symbolize secular threats to the soul's welfare) or the "devouring beast" of nightmare. The biblical serpent appears repeatedly, but it is also interesting that devils or the Devil are used almost not at all, and when they are, it is only in semi-jocular or proverbial contexts:

>...Скажи: кій бѣс нам в прах мысль сѣчет? (Song 9)

...Say: what devil chops our sense to bits?

The conflicts of despair and faith, worldly involvement and Epicurean detachment, flesh and spirit, ambition and contentment, appearance and reality—all explain Skovoroda's strong predilection for those devices of conflict, oxymoron and paradox. Song 1 alone contains the phrases "living death," "Christ, my life, who died...," "I live, for Thee, death to my passions," as well as "precious trial," "heavenly flesh," and the scriptural "kindly yoke and light burden." Paradoxical locutions, some quite striking, abound. Song 7 shows these:

>...Смерть твоя — мнѣ живот,
>Желчь твоя — сластей род...

>...Язвы твои суровы — то моя печать,
>Вѣнец мнѣ твой терновый — славы благодать,
>Твой сей поносный крест —
>Се мнѣ хвала и честь...

>Под буйством твоим свѣт,
>Под смертью — жизнь без лѣт...

...Thy death is life for me,/ Thy bile the birth of sweetness...

...Thy sore wounds are my seal,/ Thy crown of thorns for me the grace of glory,/ Thy shameful cross—/ This for me is praise and honour...

...Beneath thy turbulence is light,/ Beneath death, life without end...

In Song 5, on the birth of Christ:

>...А вмѣщен тот в яслѣх полно,
>Коего есть не довольно
>Вмѣстить и небо небес....

...And all enclosed in a manger is He/ Whom the heaven of heavens is not big enough to hold....

Skovoroda's sense of oppositions is so strong that where paradox is absent, contrastive structures appear:

>...Тот непрестанно стягает грунта,
>Сей иностранны заводит скота.
>Тѣ формируют на ловлю собак,
>Сих шумит дом от гостей, как кабак, —
>А мнѣ одна только в свѣтѣ дума,
>А мнѣ одно только не йдет с ума.... (Song 10)

...That man continually grabs up land,/ This one raises foreign cattle,/ Those train dogs for the hunt,/ The house of these is noisy with guests, like a tavern./ But for me there is but one thought in the world,/ But for me only one thing never leaves my mind....

Only some of the laments and the simplest pastorales stand as uncomplicated direct statements, without inner wrench or divided vision.

Skovoroda as poet stands out in the eighteenth century for one reason that is in itself faintly paradoxical. A significant part of his unorthodox poetic vitality comes from his being anchored firmly in a tradition—one whose spiritual colouring happened to suit his personality and his preoccupations. He was the last strongly baroque-oriented poet of any stature, the final significant exemplar of a style that during his lifetime had receded abruptly with the beginnings of Russian cultural hegemony in Ukraine and increasing access to secular literature. His imitations of the classical genres are technically adroit and often witty, but it is not these that remain in our minds; we remember him instead for his sense of robust poetic individuality and his way of contemplating his own *Sturm und Drang* and assimilating it in a peculiarly congenial idiom.

He was not, in the short run, stylistically influential. His poetic language was archaic even before his death; moreover, the long delay before any of the poems were published served to increase the distance between his work and any large nineteenth-century readership. Official restrictions on native Ukrainian publication combined with an ecclesiastical censorship's distrust of Skovoroda's variety of irreverent statement and with the tendency of belletrists to sneer at this outmoded literary style (an anonymous review in *Russkoe slovo* of 1861 describes his work as "seminarists' carrion") to keep the name of Skovoroda in relative obscurity for quite some time.

But he has always had his strong partisans, both as philosopher and as poet. We on this continent welcome the opportunity to extend the range of Skovoroda studies in English—very nearly virgin soil until the past two or three decades—and to call the attention of the uninitiated to this engaging, exasperating writer.

Appendix

A Summary of the Relative Distribution of Lexical Elements from Various Languages in:
- a. the poems of Skovoroda (1797 words)
- b. Skovoroda's prose dialogue "Narkiss" (1127 words)
- c. Deržavin's poems "Bog" and "Felica" (802 words)

		Skovoroda: Poetry	Skovoroda: Prose	Deržavin
I.	"Pan-Slavic" core vocabulary	34.9%	35.7%	37.1%
II.	Church Slavic vocabulary	27.6%	36.4%	28.6%
III.	East Slavicisms	18.9%	12.3%	16.7%
IV.	Russianisms	7.8%	9.7%	10.7%
V.	Ukrainisms	3.1%	1.2%	—
VI.	Words from non-Slavic languages	7.7%	4.7%	6.9%

From Strength to Strength: Observations on Hryhorij Skovoroda and Vasyl' Barka

Bohdan Rubchak

> А я желаю Вам итить от силы в силу![1]

Hryhorij Skovoroda's influence on subsequent Ukrainian literature, from Ivan Kotljarevs'kyj to Vasyl' Stus, has been immense. A survey article would have to consist of a rapid-fire list of authors and titles, with capsule summaries. I have chosen, instead, to concentrate on a single (possibly the greatest) living Ukrainian poet or, even more narrowly, on his two major works. The poet is Vasyl' Barka (born in 1908 in the province of Poltava, and now living in Glen Spey, New York) and the works are *Okean* and *Svidok dlja soncja šestykrylyx*.[2]

Skovoroda's influence on Ukrainian literature is twofold—through his verse

---

1. "And I wish that you might go from strength to strength." Skovoroda, "Alfavit, ili bukvar' mira."
2. There are two editions of the first volume of *Okean*. The earlier edition came out as a separate volume, and was later incorporated into the current two-volume edition. Between the first and the second edition of the first volume, Barka made quite a number of changes. To my mind, some of them are unfortunate. At the risk of creating chaos, my references to the poems in the first volume are to the first edition: *Okean* (New York: Slovo, 1959). The more recent edition, incorporating the new second volume, is: *Okean: Liryka*, 2 vols. printed in one (New York: Slovo, 1979). My references to this edition deal only with quotations from the second volume. All references to the two editions will be given within the body of the text, preceded by the letter *O*. *Svidok dlja soncja šestykrylyx: Strofičnyj roman*, 4 vols. (New York: Sučasnist', 1981), is a "novel in verse," consisting of four thousand twelve-line numbered stanzas. Because the numeration of the stanzas is featured at the expense of the page numbers, references to volume and *stanza* will be given within the text, preceded by the letter *S*. Because of Barka's complex style, quotations from his poetry will be given in Ukrainian. Skovoroda will be quoted in the original only when the discussion bears on his style.

and through his prose. The influence of Skovoroda's verse is most evident in early Ukrainian poetry, beginning with Kotljarevs'kyj and flourishing during the Romantic and early Realist periods. Skovoroda's prose begins to influence later Ukrainian literature, and that influence is far more complex, multidirectional and interesting.

We should not wonder that Skovoroda's prose has engaged modern writers, including poets, more than his poetry has done. Skovoroda is much more a poet in his prose than in his poetry. One can risk the judgement that he is much more a poet than a philosopher. Together with Plato, certain baroque writers like Burton, Browne, or Pascal, or more recent philosophers like Rousseau, Kierkegaard, Nietzsche, Heidegger or Merleau-Ponty, Skovoroda expressed his ideas in the very process of their unfolding. He thought them poetically: his dialogues and treatises are closely knit tapestries of metaphors—not so much exegeses of biblical images as their poetical re-embodiments. I shall, therefore, limit my discussion to Skovoroda's central prose works, omitting his poetry altogether.[3]

Skovoroda's profile of poet-philosopher tempts poets more than it does prose writers. Particularly in Barka's case we have an example of surprisingly close kinship with a spiritual forebear, a pure "elective affinity" of the kind that is found but rarely in literary history, all the more so since it has nothing to do with direct imitation. Not only is Barka aware of this relationship, but he carefully cultivates it. He has written an essay on Skovoroda[4] and frequently discusses or mentions him not only in his critical prose and fiction, but also in his poetry.[5]

Barka, in fact, has established for himself a poetical genealogy in Ukrainian literature: "Slovo o polku Ihorevi," Skovoroda, Ševčenko, Tyčyna.[6] I find it difficult to assimilate the "Slovo" in this context, but as for Ševčenko and Tyčyna, there can be no doubt—both poets owe much to Skovoroda.[7] In several

---

3. They are contained in the first volume of: *Tvory v dvox tomax*, ed. O.I. Bilec'kyj et al. (Kyiv: AN URSR, 1961). I refer to the following dialogues: "Narkiss. Rozhlahol o tom: uznaj sebe," abbreviating it in the body of the text as NAR; "Simfonia, narečennaja kniha Asxan', o poznanii samaho sebe"—ASK; "Razhovor pjati putnikov o istinnom ščastii v žizni"—PJA; "Kol'co"—KOL; "Razhovor, nazyvaemyj alfavit, ili bukvar' mira"—ALF; "Knižečka nazyvaemaja Silenus Alkiviadis, sireč' Ikona Alkiviadskaja"—IKO; "Dialoh. Imja emu—Potop zmiin"—POT.
4. "Apostoličnyj starčyk," *Zemlja sadivnyčyx: Eseji* (New York: Sučasnist', 1977), 99-111.
5. In Barka's poetry, we meet Skovoroda in *Svidok*, 1:613-15. An allusive portrait of Skovoroda facing death is found in *Okean*, 2:22.
6. See *Zemlja sadivnyčyx*, 59.
7. Ševčenko describes his encounter with Skovoroda in a lyrical poem, "A.O. Kozačkovs'komu," *Povne vydannja tvoriv*, 14 vols. (Chicago: Mykola Denysiuk, 1962), 3:44. He mentions Skovoroda several times in his Russian-language prose work. See *Povne vydannja*, where that short work appears in a Ukrainian translation as *Blyznjata*, 8:17, 19, 20, 27, 67. On p. 67 he is not altogether kind to the philosopher's memory. In his Preface to the "Second *Kobzar*," he praises Robert Burns as a great folk

essays on Ševčenko and Tyčyna,[8] and in book-length studies of the two poets,[9] Barka repeatedly links their work with Skovoroda's thought and art. Without Skovoroda, Barka insists in one passage on Tyčyna, "the brightest stream of light" in Tyčyna's central collection *Sonjašni kljarnety* would have been impossible;[10] in another, he calls Skovoroda Tyčyna's teacher.[11] As for Ševčenko, Barka calls him "in the main, a Skovorodian (*Skovorodjanec'*)."[12] His monograph on Ševčenko is grounded in that hypothesis so pervasively that it is in danger of distorting Ševčenko's image: Ševčenko is presented as an "evangelical" poet, an apostle of peace and passivity.

It is, however, Vasyl' Barka who remains the most consistent and the profoundest "Skovorodian" in Ukrainian literature. Skovoroda and Barka are poet-thinkers, expressing themselves both in poetry and prose, the difference being that Skovoroda's best work happens to be cast in prose, and that of Barka in poetry. Both have a well-structured view of the world that is almost a "closed system" and that (with a few important exceptions) is remarkably consistent within each writer's *oeuvre*. Both use language in similar ways: language is primarily metaphor, frequently imaging lived speech. This holds true even for so formal a poet as Barka: he manages to convey the typically Skovorodian dynamic, turbulent discourse, with its ellipses, colloquialisms, idioms, invective, and occasional humour, in his rigorously structured stanzas. It is in Barka's prose (both fiction and essays, although in Barka's case the line between the two is vague) that the similarity of his own style to that of Skovoroda becomes most apparent. Both men are similar even in their ways of life: they model themselves after *starčyky* (*starčyk*—which can be translated as "pious recluse" or "wandering

---

poet, and writes that Skovoroda could have been such a poet if he had not been deflected from his destiny by the Latin and Russian languages. See *Povne vydannja*, 2:138. Historical and critical discussions of Ševčenko's relationship to Skovoroda are far too numerous to list here. Tyčyna was much more generous to Skovoroda than Ševčenko had been. He edited Skovoroda's fables in Ukrainian translation, edited a collection of articles in his honour, dedicated his own politically "unsafe" collection *Zamist' sonetiv i oktav* (1920) to Skovoroda's memory, wrote a number of articles on him, generously peppered with references to Engels and Lenin (see, for example, *Tvory*, 5 vols. [Kyiv: Deržavne vydavnyctvo xudožn'oi literatury, 1962], 138-49, and 271-80), and worked for forty years on a controversial long poem about him, which remained unfinished at his death. See *Skovoroda: Symfonija* (Kyiv: Radjans'kyj pys'mennyk, 1971). For interesting reportage on Tyčyna's troubles with that poem, see Jurij Lavrinenko, *Pavlo Tyčyna i joho poema "Skovoroda" na tli epoxy: Spohady i sposterežennja* (New York: Sučasnist', 1980).

8. *Zemlja sadivnyčyx*: "Rečnyk obnovy," 36-41; "Vidxid Tyčyny," 58-70; "Kobzar i Biblija," 173-6.

9. *Pravda Kobzarja* (New York: Proloh, 1961) on Ševčenko, and *Xliborobs'kyj Orfej, abo Kljarnetyzm* (New York: Sučasnist', 1961), on Tyčyna.

10. *Orfej*, 57.

11. *Zemlja sadivnyčyx*, 66.

12. Ibid., 103.

holy man"—is Barka's favourite "epithet" for Skovoroda), shunning the noisy, turbulent high roads of the world and making do with the bare minimum of worldly goods.

Barka's references to Skovoroda are so numerous and so vivid that they comprise a composite, mosaic portrait of the philosopher. To my mind, that portrait is not entirely accurate. In Barka's near-identification with Skovoroda, the poet gives almost as much as he takes, mirroring his own image in the philosopher's texts and personality; Skovoroda comes out too "evangelical," too angelic even—too much a *starčyk*. He also comes out as too much a grave mystic of the apocalyptic type. Barka seems to miss his forebear's robust sense of humour, the "dancing" of his thought, which occasionally borders on the deliberately donned mask of a "holy fool," and, generally, his sense of play and open enjoyment of life—a life virtually teeming and boiling in his texts (*veselije i kuraž*). Although the image of Skovoroda as a holy man may be seen as a healthy counterbalance to deliberate Soviet misrepresentations of Skovoroda as a teacher of a proto-materialistic philosophy and a prophet of the classless society, it threatens to be a distortion in its own right—not a deliberate ideological ploy (directly opposing Skovoroda's "materialism"), but a "misprision" in Harold Bloom's sense—a more or less unconscious "misreading" of a literary "father" with whom the writer must wrestle for his place in the sun, as a real son must compete with his real father. As we have already seen in the case of Ševčenko, Barka has a proclivity for such self-mirrorings in other writers' texts; needless to say, he shares this tendency with many other great writers and critics. Ultimately, there is nothing wrong with that: we all read texts as best we can, and that means re-experiencing them, re-embodying them in our own consciousness.

As I approach a more detailed discussion of the two writers, I should warn that many aspects of their view of the world, which may appear to result from Skovoroda's direct influence on Barka, actually stem from their common intellectual sources. Both are immensely learned men; in addition, much of their learning is esoteric, not readily accessible to the reader of our time. When Barka, in a passing reference to *On the Divine Names* by Dionysis the Areopagite, takes his reader's thorough familiarity with that text and its author for granted, he surely presumes too much.[13] Skovoroda, for his part, does not even bother to

---

13. *Zemlja sadivnyčyx*, 7. Sometimes such references in Barka are so casual as to be inaccurate. Barka writes that the text is attributed to Dionysius, who was a student of St. Paul. Although that philosopher himself claimed to be the same Dionysius Areopagite whom Paul mentions in Acts xvii, and hence indeed the Apostle's disciple (thus managing to deceive Christianity for a thousand years), he actually lived around AD 500 and was a student of the Neoplatonists Plotinus and Proclus. He is, therefore, often referred to as Pseudo-Dionysius. Even without recalling this detail, Barka should have distinguished between Paul's intellectual atmosphere and Dionysius' poetic, almost pagan, Neo-

attribute his casually dropped Latin and Greek quotations, with which his "Slavonic" texts are heavily peppered. We can manage, nevertheless, to point out a few obvious texts in which the two writers meet. In Barka's case, one may be surprised that such intertextual use of philosophical and theological texts occurs in poetry. Barka's *Svidok*, however, is not a romantic poem; more like a baroque work, it is openly an integral part of the "universe of texts."

The outstanding intertextual source that comes to mind, next to the Bible, is Plato. He is reflected in our two writers both directly and as he was filtered through the early Christian and medieval tradition. Like Skovoroda and Barka, Plato is a poet-philosopher; more than that, "Plato is a philosopher *because* he is a poet."[14]

Much has been written on Skovoroda's "Socratic dialogues," including warnings about their subtle differences from Plato. Barka's *Svidok* contains many similar dialogues, especially between the hero, Fedir Ozovynec', and the numerous teachers or "guides" who enter his life one by one, taking turns to lead him ever upward to the mystical fulfillment of his destiny. Another kind of dialogue in the poem is the sharp and philosophically elaborate political dispute, usually between the Christian protagonists and various representatives of the Soviet state, including Lenin, some "Old-Guard" revolutionaries, and Stalin. Although the poem contains many dialogues of another type—"natural" and casual conversations (which, as I have mentioned, are surprisingly lively, considering the rigorous structure of Barka's intricate twelve-line stanza)—these dialogues are much more studied, deliberate, and self-conscious. They are "set pieces," relentlessly pursuing a single philosophical (usually metaphysical) issue. They interrupt the narrative, frequently throwing it off balance, especially because Barka does not even attempt to integrate them into his plot. Much of their subject matter is similar to Plato's and Skovoroda's, revolving as it does around the duality of the visible and the invisible.

Both Skovoroda and Barka mention Plato with a great deal of fondness and respect. For Skovoroda, Plato's Socrates prefigures Christianity because he taught about Divine Love—the source of all happiness. He even had his own guardian angel (ALF 1:333). In a brief theological essay on the nature of truth, Barka also regards Plato's thought as a prefiguration of the teachings of Christ.[15] In *Svidok*, Plato's philosophy is discussed at length as the crown of idealism: its single,

---

platonist thought. See Anders Nygren, *Agape and Eros* (New York: Harper Torchbooks, 1969), 576-93.

14. John Herman Randall, Jr., *Plato: Dramatist of the Life of Reason* (New York: Columbia University Press, 1970), 3. Randall goes on to say that "true philosophy is poetry—poetic insight and vision, the imaginative enhancement of life." See further G.M.A. Grube, *The Greek and Roman Critics* (London: Methuen, 1965), 54.

15. "Ščo jest' istyna," *Veršnyk neba* (New York: Naša bat'kivščyna, 1965), 16-18.

although serious, drawback is that it lacks the grace of Christ. One of Fedir's early teachers is an atheistic Platonist: his heart is in the right place, but his visions of "platonic" (more accurately, pseudo-platonic) utopian communities for peasants—similar to Myxajlo Drahomanov's *hromady*, or to reformist dreams of gentlemen-populists like Tadej Ryl's'kyj, on whom that character might be based—are not only impractical but even somewhat silly (*S* 1:364-70). Prayer within the righteous soul of a peasant is finally stronger than that teacher's Platonic "bookishness," as the author himself calls it (*S* 1:658).

Another family of texts that serve as inspirational sources for our two writers are those medieval philosophies that carry the Platonic traditions into Christianity. It is precisely the Platonic (most frequently, specifically *Neoplatonic*) line, as opposed to the Aristotelian-Thomistic direction, that Skovoroda and Barka favour—the line that adapted the pagan Eros to the Judaeo-Christian and particularly Pauline tradition of Divine Love, as Bonaventura did. Augustine is the stronghold of that direction: "Augustine's view of love," as one commentator puts it, "has exercised by far the greatest influence in the whole history of the Christian idea of love.... Ever since his time the meaning of Christian love has generally been expressed in the categories he created, and even the emotional quality which it bears is largely due to him."[16]

The central text in the world-view of Skovoroda and Barka is the Bible. Because I shall allude to this source throughout the rest of my article, I will not discuss its influence on our two writers here. Suffice it to say for the present that the Bible serves them not only as philosophical ground but as a generous wellspring of their extraordinarily rich and frequently mysterious poetic imagery. David's Psalms and the Song of Songs from the Old Testament are the texts mentioned and used most frequently by the two writers; as for the New Testament, the Book of Revelation is of paramount importance for the imagery and stylization of their vitriolic, vituperative, and polemical passages. St. Paul is the centre not so much of their imagery as of their theology, particularly when it comes to the doctrine of Divine Love; we should remind ourselves, however, that it is, more often than not, a St. Paul viewed through the tinted lenses of Neoplatonism.[17] It might be worth mentioning that Skovoroda pays much more

---

16. Nygren, 450.
17. On St. Paul, see Barka's short essays "Polum"ja Damasku" and "Blahovisnyk neba," in *Veršnyk neba*, 64-6; 67-8. In *Svidok* Paul is favourably compared to Shakespeare as a much more important writer (1:177). Barka also claims that Skovoroda's thought stems directly from St. Paul. See *Zemlja sadivnyčyx*, 103. Also see Barka's interesting commentary on the central symbols of Revelation in "Orlyna knyha," *Veršnyk neba*, 91-114. He calls Revelation the crown of poetry of all ages (114). The conclusion of *Svidok* borrows heavily from Apocalyptic imagery, and stylizations of such imagery are dispersed throughout Barka's *oeuvre*. As for Skovoroda, he mentions St. Paul in a number of his works. Also, Apocalyptic imagery abounds in them, and some of the very titles of his

attention to the Old Testament than Barka does: a more "evangelical," soteriological thinker, Barka uses the Old Testament sparingly, most often as a source of his imagery.

It is the Slavic, and more specifically the Ukrainian, ethos that most consistently permeates the works of the two writers. One may even speak of a certain Slavophilism in both of them. The *Pečers'kyj Pateryk* (Paterikon), for example, serves both of them, more or less distantly, in their descriptions of the cult of *sxyma* and the already mentioned *starčyky*. In "Alfavit," Afanasij asks the "raisonneur" Lonhin: "And so, your poor preachers remain beggars?", and Lonhin answers: "Thorough beggars, so as to be ready" (ALF 1:361). Barka gives us powerful portraits of *starčyky* in *Svidok*, especially at the beginning of the poem. In connection with *starčestvo*, we might mention Paisij Velyčkovs'kyj, whom Barka in an essay directly links with Skovoroda.[18] Ukrainian folklore also has a decisive influence on both writers, particularly on the level of style. Like Ševčenko, they even manage to "Ukrainize" or "folklorize" some of the numerous foreign influences that enter their writing, mainly by stylistic manipulation.

The foundation of Skovoroda's and Barka's view of the world is the Platonic-Augustinian division of reality into the visible and the invisible. Skovoroda's central definition of that duality is formulated by Druh in "Narkiss": "The whole world consists of two *natures*: one visible and the other invisible. The visible nature is called 'creature' and the invisible—'God'. This invisible *nature* or *God* permeates and maintains the creature world" (NAR 1:57). The seeming absence of the invisible becomes true Presence, while the illusory presence of the visible becomes absence ("you see in yourself that which is nothing, and therefore you see nothing". NAR 1:32).

This idea crops up everywhere in Barka's prose. Speaking about works of sculpture, for example, he says: "The flesh, being only the 'shell' of the eternal spirit, suffers its tightness."[19] But it is embodied much more strongly and convincingly in his poetry, where the very structure of metaphors implies the world's unity-within-division. *Okean* is structured around the division of love and the beloved into the visible (which here means erotic) and the invisible (divine); Barka makes conspicuous use of the poets of *Hohe Minne*, Dante, and the

---

works are based on it. For the origin of "Potop zmiin," for example, see Revelation, 12:15-17.

18. *Zemlja sadivnyčyx*, 103. Velyčkovs'kyj (1722-94) was the son of the poet Ivan. He studied at the Kyiv Academy, but became dissatisfied with it, choosing the strict and ascetic life of a monk—*sxymnyk*. He became an influential theologian, preaching the return of the Orthodox church to the simple and "pure" faith of the Fathers of the Church. He lived on Mount Athos in Greece and then in Moldova. The ideology of *starčestvo* is based on him. His obvious influence on Dostoevskij clamours for thorough investigation.

19. Ibid., 145.

Petrarchan tradition.[20]

The double nature of reality is expanded and intensified in *Svidok*:

...через світ видимого кипіння
сама незримість неба проступила,
розсипавши огонь жемчужний. *S* 1:21

Through the world of visible teeming,/ the invisibility of the sky [heaven] itself penetrated,/ scattering a diamond fire.

The whole universe of that work (presented in four 500-page volumes) exists on a double level; not only love but friendship, war, work, art, politics, economics, etc., have their "other," essential being, overseen by angelic orders. Toward the end of the work, when Fedir and his beloved Sanna—now forced labourers in Nazi Germany—are about to die, they observe a German city set ablaze by Allied bombs. Almost imperceptibly, a real wartime situation is elevated to an apocalyptic "invisible" symbol:

"—Гляди на знак! пожари кольорові...
дозволено нам, Санно, як в пророцтві,
відчути потойбічні сили".
Дивилися, весь небозвід збагровів,
з вінечністю: вселенському кострові! —
навкруг, немов з окрас весільних.
"—Чого то сполох, ніби крильми орлій?" —
питає Санна, й очі їй спрозорить
від дива огняного відблиск. (*S* 4:3935)

"Look at the sign! Colourful flames.../ Sanna, we are permitted, as in the prophecy,/ to feel the otherwordly powers."/ They looked, and the vault of the sky became red/ with garlanding—for the universal pyre!—/ all around, as if with wedding decorations./ —"Why is there fright, as if eagle-like, because of its wings?"—/ Sanna asks, while her eyes become transparent/ with reflections of the fiery wonder.

In the burning buildings the couple sees the invisible miracle of their own *Liebestod*, which itself is raised to an even higher vision of the Revelation, with the Apocalyptic image of the fiery Serpent and the fleeing woman: "And to the woman were given two wings of a great eagle, that she might fly into the wilderness...from the force of the serpent" (Revelation 12:14).

Skovoroda teaches that if the visible and mortal (*tlinnoe*) were to exist without the invisible and timeless, if the visible did not contain in itself the hidden and the mysterious, "flattery would exist alone, without truth, and cruelty without

---

20. On these traditions in *Okean*, see my "Rozkrylenist' hlybyn i gotyčne serce," *Terem* 6 (May 1979):21-60.

kindness, and old age without youth, and darkness without light, and floods without dry land" (NAR 1:69-70). In *Svidok*, monks who forget the invisible because they spend all their time working hard so as not to starve complain:

> ...відвернувшися, сидим:
> потоплені серцями в грішну сутінь. (*S* 1:22)
>
> ...turned away, we sit,/ our hearts sunk in sinful halfshade.

They, like Skovoroda's "sensualists," must live only in shadow, with no hope of light. The detail that the monks have *turned away* from the light is also significant; such "turning away" is represented by Skovoroda's image of the visible (particularly the corporeal) as the heel of a foot or a tail (NAR 1:32, 33, et passim).

Both authors make much of the medieval *topos* of the visible, and especially the human body, as *shadow*, which itself is a Christian reading of Plato. Skovoroda sums it up succinctly in his rather baroque "negative catalogue": "You have no ears, nor nostrils, nor eyes, nor yourself, except only for your shadows" (NAR 1:33). In an alliterative line from "Narkiss," Druh admonishes Luka: "Ty-to ten', t'ma i tlen'!" ("You are shadow, darkness and decay!" (NAR 1:37). And here is a startling greeting: "Druh: 'Dead shadow, how are you!' Luka: 'How are you, Thought! Spirit! Heart!'" (NAR 1:37).

Barka's *Svidok*, too, contains a number of images of body-as-shadow. The hero Fedir, for example, not unlike a baroque poet, meditates on the passage of a woman's beauty into the ugliness and decay of old age, and finally into death. He associates such gloomy thoughts with his absent beloved, Sanna:

> Страшить примара кістякова;
> то — Саннина! то — тінь, немов морозом
> побілена в скелет... (*S* 2:1637)
>
> A spectre of a skeleton frightens him; it is that of Sanna!/ It is a shadow, whitewashed into a skeleton,/ as if with frost...

But these meditations are quickly dispelled by the sudden realization that the body is organized and ennobled by the spirit, which comes both from inside and from above (*S* 2:1638). The strongest passages dealing with the body as shadow and decay (Skovoroda's *tin'* and *tlin'*) are contained in a number of stanzas on the hero's first reading of the parable of Lazarus and the tremendous impression that this makes on him—as once, I might add, it affected another confused and searching youth, Rodion Raskolnikov (*S* 2:1882-1912; 1945-1948). In rather elaborate, baroque detail, the poet describes the advanced decay of Lazarus' corpse (the hero's technical argument with himself as to the scientific possibility of such a resurrection provides the opportunity), in order to make Christ's miraculous call and gesture that much more dramatic.

Barka's pervasive love of life, however, does not permit him to dwell on such images. The "lowly outer shadow of existence" (*S* 2:1752) serves to mirror the light of higher Being, just as a humble church structure mirrors heaven, or visible symbols mirror the profoundest mystery of creation:

> Світ символів! мов свічі від хоромів —
> до шлюбу, звістить світ недовідомий:
> врочисто з скатертю неділь...
> він — тінь від творчости: від Світла-Слова... (*S* 1:716)

The world of symbols! As candles, lit in a mansion/ [proclaim] a wedding, so it will proclaim the unknown world/ triumphantly, together with the tablecloth of Sundays.../ It is a shadow of creativity—of the Light-Word....

Compare this with Skovoroda's "world of symbols," described in *Ikona* (IK0 1:389 et passim).

It is interesting how Ovid uses the *topos* of shadow not as an image of the body but as something opposed and inferior to the temple of the body in his rendition of the myth of Narcissus. The following passage alone, incidentally, is sufficient to convince us that Skovoroda knew Ovid well when he was writing his "Narkiss," but deliberately "misread" the pagan poet for his own purposes. For example, he theologically interpreted the "shadow-substance" dichotomy, so widespread in classical thought, exactly as the medieval thinkers had done.

> ...As he tried
> To quench his thirst, inside him, deep within him,
> Another thirst was growing, for he saw
> An image in the pool, and fell in love
> In that unbodied hope, and found a substance
> In what was only shadow.[21]

For the Christian, the body has to be "lifted up" to the invisible in order to change from shadow into substance—a process almost opposite to that described by Ovid, where the "unbodied hope" is an illusion and is located *below* the face. Barka writes in a love poem in *Okean*:

> А тайна поривання в небі синя
> і в тіні — ми в привітнім місті.
> Кривавлять губи гострого цвітіння,
> але твій скарб, як квітка, чистий. (*O* 1:40)

---

21. Ovid, *Metamorphoses*, trans. Rolfe Humphries (Bloomington: Indiana University Press, 1964), 70. For a good discussion of Narcissus' sameness and otherness, see Hermann Frankel, *Ovid: A Poet between Two Worlds* (Berkeley: California University Press, 1945), 82-5. For Ovid's Narcissus in medieval poetry, see Frederick Goldin, *The Mirror of Narcissus in the Courtly Love Lyric* (Ithaca: Cornell University Press, 1967).

And the blue mystery of striving is in heaven [sky]/ and in the shadow. We are in a friendly city./ The lips of sharp blossoming bleed,/ but your treasure remains as pure as a flower.

We recall that Barka dwells on the visible and invisible aspects of erotic love and the beloved. Because in this thematic area Barka is particularly firmly rooted in the Neoplatonic tradition, he does not reject outright the pleasures of physical love, as he cannot afford to reject the beauty of the world; physical love, however, being "wholly visible," must be permeated with the "invisibility" of spirituality. In *Okean* an intense love affair between the lyrical hero and his beloved, described with unabashed erotic overtones, runs adrift when the hero begins to see only the visibility of the woman. The invisible aura of her essential being wanes, causing her cupidity and cruelty to come to the fore; she becomes a Petrarchan "sweet enemy" (*dolce nemica*), torturing the lover. When she leaves him to go "across the ocean," only her reflection in the hero's pool of memories remains; it is that reflection which recaptures her near-saintly essence, combating and negating the woman's visible nature. In an instance of the Neoplatonic "ladder," the lyrical hero's reflections on her reflection become more and more removed from her physical being, until she becomes a pure symbol of transcendence. In the second volume of the cycle she is all but forgotten; she has served her function as the gate into the realm of the invisible where the lyrical hero now dwells, contemplating the suffering, the love, and the perpetual transfiguration of Jesus Christ.

The visible and invisible spheres of erotic love are even more pronounced and more dramatically rendered in *Svidok*. When Fedir is forced to leave his "true bride," Sanna—whom he found literally by means of the mystical "elective affinity," preordained in heaven, and through whose angelic (and, in literary terms, rather sentimentalized) visibility the invisible shines bright—he befriends another woman, Klavdija, who is Sanna's double (S 3:2351ff.). She appears when Sanna becomes physically "invisible," and only memories of her remain. Her uncanny "visible" similarity to Sanna, and even the fact that she, like Sanna, is a musician, does not at all mean that she possesses Sanna's divine "invisibility." Quite the contrary, she is Sanna's *intense* "shadow," exhibiting the mundane cupidity and carnality that Sanna herself lacks altogether, or perhaps possesses only potentially. (Sanna and Klavdija, incidentally, are reminiscent of romantic doubles and, on a more complex level, of the medieval *topos* of the two Venuses—the first representing divine harmony and the second earthly desires.)[22] The implied "humanistic" immorality of Fedir's behaviour when he

---

22. See Joan M. Ferrante, *Woman as Image in Medieval Literature: From the Twelfth Century to Dante* (New York: Columbia University Press, 1957), 154.

woos and lives with a woman just because she reminds him of another, making her thoroughly miserable in the process, does not seem to trouble either him or his author; such insignificant errors of judgment are shrugged off and forgiven in the hero's determined climbing of the shining ladder toward Divine Love, while the blame is pushed onto Klavdija's mortal shoulders. As in *Hohe Minne*, in Barka it is not the visibility or even the invisibility of the woman that really matters, but the hero's own progress toward self-perfection and ultimately toward God. This, incidentally, is a very good example of Jean-Paul Sartre's notion of *mauvaise foi* ("bad faith"), especially since the two women are not even human, but serve as veiled allegorical symbols, thus substituting metaphysical evasions for life and its responsibilities.

In the elevation of the visible to the high level of the invisible, an interesting two-directional process of imaging occurs. While physical love is embodied in increasingly disembodied and "pure" imagery, "invisible" spheres are embodied in imagery that is often coquettishly erotic and even openly sexual. This phenomenon frequently appears in the Bible, Plato, and medieval literature, and has to do with the nature of mystical thought itself—the union of the sexes symbolizes the transcendent unity of the universe. Plato, for example, likes to dwell on the impregnation of ideas so that the soul might conceive, on the ensuing pregnancy of the soul, and on the near-sexual intercourse in the discourse of kindred spirits.[23] As for the Bible, the imagery of *The Songs of Songs* is of a richly erotic nature, its mysticism doubtless exaggerated by medieval hermeneutical exegeses. Note that in medieval thought as such (not, in this case, necessarily restricted to mysticism) it is women and not men who become vehicles of allegorical constructs. Considering this tradition, therefore, it is not surprising that we find traces of it in our two writers.

When we read Skovoroda's self-indulgent, almost narcissistic prose account of Narcissus falling in love with his own image (NAR 1:27-28)—a prose whose veiled innuendos far surpass not only Ovid himself but also such embarrassingly erotic descriptions of Narcissus as Rilke's poem "Narcissus"[24]—we might explain such sensuality as the stylistic embodiment of the visible that sinfully "falls in love" with its own image (we recall that in the Dialogue, Narcissus represents the visible, while the biblical David serves as his invisible counterpart). And yet, it is as if the message of Skovoroda's askesis were deconstructing itself by the voluptuous language in which it is stated. Here is a brief example:

Наркісс мой, правда, что жжется, ражжигаясь угліем любви, ревнуя, рвется, мечется и мучится, ласкосердствует, печется

---

23. See *Republic* 490 a; *Symposium* 206 c–207 b, 208 e–209 c, 212 a; *Phaedrus* 2466ff., 251 a–252 e.
24. See *Sämtliche Werke*, 6 vols. (Frankfurt am Main: Insel, 1955), 2:101.

> и молвит всѣми молвами, а не о многом же, ни о пустом чем-либо, но о себѣ, про себе и в себе. (NAR 1:28)

> My Narcissus is the truth that burns up [or, "indeed burns up"], inflaming itself [himself] with the embers of love; being jealous, it [he] tears itself [himself] to pieces, flings itself [himself] about, and tortures itself [himself], becomes affectionate with itself [himself], worries and speaks in all languages, but not about many and frivolous things, but about himself, for himself, and in himself.

Our surprise increases when we realize that the author actually approves of Narcissus' behaviour; as in the case of Fedir's climbing the ladder of self-perfection, Narcissus' love for his own reflection—his intense concentration on himself, even if that self still belongs to the shadowy realm of the visible—is the first step toward self-knowledge.

But how should we take the following passage from *Potop zmiin* that describes Lot's daughter on the way to her father? Spirit is talking to Soul: "She goes straight…to her father. Love has inflamed her. She burns with the desire to enjoy herself with him and drink…new wine… She goes to Lot… She wants to sleep with the father. Just like the young girls with David (POT 1:562)." This, as Spirit soon makes certain to explain, is the image of the soul wanting to join her God. We see here Skovoroda the dancer, playing with language and ideas, dangerously teetering above the precipice of blasphemy, much like some early medieval philosophers, such as Origen—probably showing us how foolish the Bible can be if we read its visibility alone, without proper penetration of the surface veil that hides the invisible.

There is no such Zen-like play in the more serious Barka: his mystical-erotic images are much more elevated and "poetic," although they are no less sensuous for that. Their eroticism, in fact, is heightened by the thematic ambiguity between physical love and mystery which, as we have seen, is central in *Okean* and quite important in *Svidok*. They are, on occasion, even faintly redolent of decadence, thus courting danger in their own way. Look again at the stanza from *Okean* quoted above. And here are some other examples. In *Okean*, sexual passion is frequently represented by the orchid:

> …ніби орхідеїне з стеблини
> сіяння — пристрасть то твоя…
> простерлася до уст мені і нині,
> пожежа так не просія. (O 1:40)

> Like an orchid-like light/ on a stem—such is your passion…/ even today it stretches up to my lips,/ a conflagration cannot be so bright.

This "conflagration" is negated by another sensuous, but here also mystical, image:

> На грудях пахощами рідна вишні —
> недужа ніжністю душа…

це й не відвертість орхідеї грішна,
як сонце ласку приспіша. (*O* 1:40)

On the breast/ related to the cherry tree by its fragrance—/ the soul, ill with tenderness.../ This is not even the sinful openness of the orchid,/ when the sun hurries down its kindness.[25]

Barka deals with fictional models of living women which, as we recall, can be read as allegorical symbols. In Skovoroda such ambiguities do not exist—his females are immediate allegories of the soul, the Bible, and other more or less abstract entities. The vehicles of such allegories are frequently female personages from the Old Testament—themselves, more often than not, already erotically charged when they appear in the Bible. As we have seen in the startling example with Lot's daughters, Skovoroda transfers the erotic energy from mimetic representations in the Bible to abstract notions, thus charging such abstract notions sexually, to make them come to life. This, of course, is a technique often encountered in medieval literature.

In my discussion of the antithetical notions of the visible and the invisible in Skovoroda and Barka, I have attempted to imply the actual or potential unity of these two spheres of existence. Such unity is indeed central in both writers; in spite of the shadow/light opposition, frequently encountered in their texts, neither of them has anything to do with the irreconcilable dualities of Manichaeism. With a few minor exceptions in Skovoroda, neither author wants to shed the visible and to escape from it into the amorphous regions of pure spirit. As we shall soon see in greater detail, both of them talk about the heart more frequently than about the soul.

The presence of the invisible within the visible is imagined by our authors in one of two ways—by mirroring and by enfoldment. Although both sets of images are present in each writer (in Skovoroda, for example, even in a single sentence: "The husk contains a seed and the mother-of-pearl a pearl, and the moon throws back the sunlight," IKO 1:388)—Barka seems to favour mirroring, while Skovoroda concentrates on enfoldment. The reason for this might be that, with many exceptions, Barka seems to see the invisible as a realm apart, coming *down* to the visible as a ray of light, and reflecting upon its surfaces, as God's love *descends* upon us in St. Paul. (We are also reminded here of Jakob Böhme's ecstasy upon seeing sunshine reflected in a silver dish; this granted him a spiritual illumination so intense that it seemed to enlighten for him all invisible mysteries.) For Skovoroda—again, with many exceptions—the invisible seems

---

25. My prose translations of Barka's stanzas are so awkward because they attempt to convey at least some of the many maddening ambiguities of the originals, especially when such ambiguities bear on my discussion. The terribly un-English syntax of the present translation has provoked this explanation and apology.

to dwell within the visible, illuminating its surfaces from within. In this, Skovoroda seems more modern than Barka, prefiguring the way that the romantic Idealists were to think about the Idea some years after his death, while Barka seems to remain more faithful to the pure Platonic-Pauline model.[26]

In Skovoroda's "Narkiss," which is generally about mirroring, we have the following observation:

> When you behold God with a new and true eye, then you have seen in Him, as in a wellspring or in a mirror, *that* which has always been in Him and which you never saw... And so, you now see *two*—the old and the new, the visible and the mysterious. (NAR 1:52)

(Note that in the original the very language "mirrors" pairs by the device of near-rhymes: "*dvoe*—staroe i novoe, javnoe i tajnoe"). In Barka's *Okean* there is a whole system of mirroring that is much too elaborate to describe here in detail.[27] I shall restrict myself to a few examples. It is usually the sky, the sun, or *light* that descends to the things of this world, mirroring itself in them:

> Сьогодні мирне світло: все подвоїть
> при березі казок, де ти. (*O* 1:94)
>
> Today the light is tranquil: it will double everything/ near the shore of fairy tales, where you are.

A more complex structuring occurs in what Barka calls *poxreščennja* ("crossing," "pruning," with a possible pun on "blessing" and "relationship by christening"), where the nature of metaphor, and especially metonymy, itself is utilized as a thematic device. The sun, for example, becomes a flower ("svjati peljustky soncja"—"the holy petals of the sun," *O* 1:54); the sun becomes a bird ("Obtrusyt' sonce bilja raju pirja"—"near Paradise, the sun will shake its feathers," *O* 1:89); the sun has eyes and weeps ("Sl'oza nesvits'ka na vijax soncja pospadala"—"An unworldly tear fell from the sun's eyelashes," *O* 1:48). In another poet's work, such magnificent poetic metonymies could stand for themselves, without necessarily having to prove anything outside themselves; in Barka, however, they become integral parts of a complex philosophical system, and therefore may serve as examples of that system. We see such *poxreščennja* in Skovoroda also, when, for example, he asks: "Is not the sun similar to the ear of wheat? Why do you need purses when in them you find the same gold?" (IKO 1:393). Skovoroda even offers a theoretical explanation when he writes that a symbol is built of two or three figures that signify mortality and eternity (IKO

---

26. Reflections in mirrors and in water are a device by which Plato explains the function of images throughout his works. One's eyes would be ruined if one looked at the sun directly instead of observing its reflections in water.
27. I have attempted to describe it at some length in my "Rozkrylenist' hlybyn," 29-49.

1:387). "Ikona," incidentally, is an interesting theoretical treatise dealing with imaging and symbolization.

There are many examples of the idea of enfoldment of the invisible within the visible in both writers, but they are especially abundant and suggestive in Skovoroda. "Does not God contain everything?... In a tree He is the true tree, in grass—grass, in music—music, in a house—a house, in our earthly body He is the new body..." (NAR 1:40). Note in this quotation the interesting ambiguity between the inside and the outside, centering on the word "contains" or "maintains" (*soderzhit*)—God is in a tree, while at the same time the tree is in God. There are literally hundreds of such passages throughout Skovoroda's work.

Somewhat like Barka in his metaphors of *dzerkalennja* (mirroring) and *poxreščennja* ("crossing"), quoted above, Skovoroda uses oxymoron-like paradoxes that by their very form would symbolize the unity-within-diversity of existence. In contrast to Barka's images, which imply mirroring, each part of Skovoroda's paradox seems not so much to *mirror* its opposite as to *issue* from it. Beginning with a familiar thought from Ecclesiastes, but obviously taking it further than the Bible does, Skovoroda writes:

> Weep! But understand and differentiate between the time of tears and the time of laughter. Know: just as time exists, over it there is also a time of times, therefore, halftime and the blessed other time... blessedtime... Weeping leads to laughter, and laughter is hidden in weeping... These two halves comprise *a unity*; just as food is created by hunger and satiety, winter and summer create fruits, light and darkness—day, death and life—all kinds of creatures, good and evil—poverty and wealth God created [them] and stuck them together into *a unity*. (POT 1:567-8)

There is an almost imperceptible progression in this passage. First we have to *understand* the separation of laughter and weeping in *our* time, but soon we must *know* (note the contrast between *razumej* and *znaj*) that *our* time is contained within "that other time" (*onoe vremia*)—time transcended in eternity. From the perspective of "that other time," we shall behold the truth that oppositions are indispensable for the creation of everything—not only on the exalted levels of life and death, or darkness and light, but also on the mundane levels of food, fruits, and wealth. This is because everything is contained in the unity that God has created, and that unity must have both the hidden mystery, which is light, and the revealed shadow that implies the light (ALF 1:344). Note the joining of the words that denote time, with the resulting neologisms "halftime" (*poluvremja*) and "blessedtime" or "goodtime" (*blahovremja*), and the untranslatable ambiguity created by the absence of punctuation between "wealth" and "God." Here Skovoroda, like a poet, makes his form speak out his content.

We find the idea that opposites create unities (which, in their turn, create a transcendent universal unity) expressed more plainly in the following:

> You will not find a day without darkness and light and a year without winter

and warmth. Neither will you find a condition in which bitterness [a pun on "grief"] and sweetness are not mixed. Thus all the world stands. [In the original, there is a play on the words *sostojanie* [condition] and *stoit* (stands).] The opposite aids the opposite. Sweetness rewards bitterness, and bitterness is the mother of sweetness. (ALF 1:354)

And here is the central passage of envelopment, expressed in a series of oppositions:

> And then I see in this entire world two worlds, creating one world: the visible world and the invisible, the living and the dead, the whole and the scattered. This one is the mantle and that—the body, this one—the shadow and that one—the tree... And so, a world within a world means eternity in decay, life in death, awakening in sleep, light in darkness, in a lie—the truth, in weeping—joy, in despair—hope. (IKO 1:381-2)

One of Skovoroda's frequent images of the unity of the universe is a coiled snake (serpent) holding its tail in its mouth. This is his emblem for the blessed unified nature (TRA 1:214), the sun (POT 1:550), the Bible (KOL 1:258-9), Christ (KOL 1:258-9), and finally God (POT 1:558). The snake belongs to the emblem family of the circle, the ring, the garland (TRA 1:214); together with those symbols, it embodies the mystical idea of unity within diversity (POT 1:558), of the beginning within the end, and the end within the beginning: "And the snake, holding its tail in its mouth, illuminates the fact that the endless *beginning* and the beginningless end ends by beginning and begins by ending" (IKO 1:383). The snake, therefore, is both good and evil at once, and these qualities, too, relate to the beginning and the end: "If the snake in the grass tempts our hearts away from paradise, let the snake, which has now arisen from the earth, return them there" (KOL 1:258). Like God Himself, the snake is "lying and truthful. A fool and all-wise. Evil, it is also good" (POT 558). Although the coiled snake as a symbol of the highest mysteries occurs in many civilizations, it is particularly powerful in Gnosticism, as the symbol of the Ouroboros. One-half of its body is light, the other dark. It is the base of the world, providing it with materials and energy, developing as reason and imagination, and also figuring as a force of darkness. Some Gnostics believed that the coiled snake lived in all objects and in all beings.[28]

Barka's snake or serpent, which makes its appearance in *Okean*, and particularly frequently in *Svidok*, seems to be actually opposed to the idea of universal unity. More a proper serpent than a snake, it is all evil, symbolizing disjunction, disorder, and ultimately the end of the world, but not its beginning. It stems, in fact, directly from The Book of Revelation, where it is represented as the Ruler of the Bottomless Pit, the fallen angel Apolyon, bringing the fire of destruction

---

28. See J.E. Cirlot, *A Dictionary of Symbols* (New York: Philosophical Library, 1962), 274.

upon the world (Revelation 9:11ff.). At times Barka's serpent is reminiscent of the dragon of medieval legend, thus reinforcing a possible interpretation of *Svidok* as a quest romance. In *Svidok*, peasants claim to have seen a dragon stealing a maiden (*S* 1:710ff.), which symbolizes Sanna leaving Fedir for distant cities, her spiritual battle with atheistic communism, and the impending famine of 1933. (In Barka's novel, *Žovtyj knjaz'*, the famine is consistently symbolized by images from The Book of Revelation.) The dragon as a symbol of Sanna's plight is revealed at the end of the work, when—the lovers having been reunited after a long separation—she tells Fedir that she escaped from the mouth of the dragon (*S* 4:3843). I found one image of coiled snakes in Barka's *Okean*, but it too has evil reverberations, without reference to the *alpha* and *omega* of Being; more precisely, it suggests Being as a negative, shadowy unity:

> І прокинувши гілля далеке,
> в сторону, де вмерла юність:
> ти погас, мов гнотик, білоклене! —
> серед змій, вінцем отруйних. (*O* 2:16)

> And extending distant branches/ toward the region [direction] where youth has died: you extinguished yourself like a wick, o white maple,/ among snakes, poisonous in their garland.

Nevertheless, the emblems of garland (*vinec'*, with a pun on "crown" and "end"), circle, ring, which in Skovoroda belong to the same family as the coiled snake, abound in Barka's work. In addition to a direct symbolization of the unity of existence, the garland and the ring (*persten'*), or more specifically the wedding ring (*obručka*), which is an important component of the love motif in both works, symbolize for Barka marriage as the highest mystical consummation of a union of the sexes (which in its turn symbolizes the union of opposites within the universe), with its roots as romantic love in the sphere of the visible. The symbols of the garland (also a wedding symbol) and the ring reach the highest levels of mystery in the second volume of *Okean*:

> Голосами в колосках прибратись
> тайні! — зв'язана, як перстень. (*O* 2:49)

> The mystery in the ears of wheat should dress itself in [adorn itself with] voices!/ It is bound like a ring.

And here is an example of the transfiguration of Christ's crown of thorns (*vinec'*) into the sun-like crown (*vinec'*) of triumphant universal unity:

> Скрізь: свічення вінця, трисвітле в сплесках
> скрізь: на горі за нас розп'яте,
> що кров від терну — вмерла і воскресла,
> скрапаючи, в рятунок звати. (*O* 1:233)

> Everywhere: the light of the garland, three-lighted in waves,/ everywhere:

crucified for us on a hill [or "up high"],/ so that the blood, dripping from the thorns, would die and be resurrected,/ to call us into salvation.

As I have mentioned, it is Divine Love that becomes the energy of unity in both writers.[29]

While dividing the universe "vertically" into the two halves of the visible and the invisible, Skovoroda divides it "horizontally" into the microcosm, the macrocosm, and the symbolic level of the Bible (POT 1:536 et passim). The divisions of the macrocosm, occurring within the all-pervasive unity, are reflected in the microcosm; it is there that our two writers like to dwell. Following Christ, Skovoroda teaches that our happiness, our world, our paradise, and our God are inside us (ALF 1:328), shining from within, just as the invisible shines forth through all visible surfaces. But because man has a will, he can choose either to accept or to reject that inner light: "It is true that everything is done according to God's will, but because I agree with it, it is now my will." (TRA 1:231). Man has to will to find that inner light of the invisible within himself—hence the Delphic-Platonic motto: "*Know* thyself" (TRA 1:224 et passim). It is only in oneself that one can see the *alpha* and *omega* of existence, which is ultimately one and the same (ASK 1:96).

When one knows oneself, one knows one's *srodnost'*, which is perhaps the most familiar notion in Skovoroda's philosophy, and needs no elaboration. *Srodnost'* is the embodiment of the divine law that governs all life—"the similar flows toward the similar." A function of knowing oneself is the ability to recognize what in one's soul *responds* to a chosen task out in the world (ALF 1:343). It is such a response that becomes a true *calling*. By recognizing one's inner being, one knows one's destiny, which in this case means the direction of one's perfectibility. In opposition to animals, which have no will—there is no need for flying turtles (ALF 1:344)—man can easily be blind to his *srodnost'* and be led astray in the visible world; no matter what worldly successes he then reaps, he will remain unhappy (ALF 1:326, 329). Education can perfect a *srodnost'*, but it cannot help one if one has missed one's *srodnost'*. When education and *srodnost'* go hand in hand, learning is easy and pleasant. For the student, nothing that is difficult to learn is really necessary (ALF 328-9, 337).

The plot of Barka's *Svidok* revolves, in the main, around the hero Fedir's misjudging his *srodnost'* in his youth, and then searching for it within himself and "*without* himself." At the very beginning of the poem, he is near it but not really with it: he is a metaphysical rebel—Ivan Karamazov's twin brother—who

---

29. On the duality-in-unity of the universe and the importance of the accompanying symbol of light, so very crucial to our two writers, see Mircea Eliade, *The Two and the One* (New York: Harper Torchbooks, 1969). Specifically on Biblical symbols and St. Paul as they relate to that theme, see pp. 55-66.

is angry with God because people's wounds hurt him, while he sees immorality ruling the church. As in Dostoevskij, although he is in opposition to God, that opposition is *dialectical*, the Negative of metaphysical rebellion bearing within it the potential Positive of faith. Subsequently he becomes a student, reads many books, writes poetry, teaches, does odd jobs, and joins the army, but nothing brings him peace. It is only after he recognizes his *srodnost'*, which he had known as a child but subsequently lost, that he becomes happy:

...маленьким я про схиму мріяв,
а от забрала райдугу зневіра,
руїну в грудях тінить крук. (*S* 1:184)

As a boy I dreamed of being a monk/ but disillusionment took away my rainbow/ and now a crow casts a shadow on the ruin in my breast.

Fedir finds himself only after he musters sufficient courage to declare himself a lay monk in Soviet society. His beloved Sanna, being more blessed than he is, never leaves her *srodnost'* with music, because in her breast that *calling* is wedded to her profound religious faith. She, however, strays temporarily when she leaves her native parts (something that Skovoroda never tires of warning us against) and follows her calling away from her land and her beloved.

Srodnosti are frequently implied in other contexts of the poem. For example, an episodic character, a painter, has genius because he:

...звик з посиленістю відкривати
первинні вдачі, всюди — вряд. (*S* 1:244)

...is used to uncover with verve/ primary natures in everything.

Even more Platonic than the *srodnosti* that deal directly with individual striving are those that help one find the right friends. To intuit the affinity that links two friends is very much a part of *srodnost'*. A "native" (*rodnyj*, playing on *srodnost'*) road to unhappiness is to marry somebody against one's *srodnost'*, or to make such "uncongenial" friends (ALF 1:322). Skovoroda directly connects this phase of *srodnosti* with Plato when he writes that goodness lives only in beauty, and that God leads like to like (ALF 1:132). While two people, as in Plato, are attracted to each other by the outer covering of beauty, it is the inner core of goodness in each of them that ultimately strives toward union. Friendship "on high levels" is not chosen by us, but depends on a higher destiny (ALF 1:332).

Not without the direct influence of the romantic doctrine of "elective affinities" (which also comes from Plato's notion that like and like seek each other out), Barka constructs his elaborate love motifs both in *Okean* and *Svidok* around such "interpersonal" *srodnosti*. It is only when love is based on "native" affinities that it becomes "true love" and can lead to the highest levels of Divine Love.

At the very beginning of *Okean* we find that the two lovers are destined (*sudženi*) to be joined by the light of the invisible, no matter how strenuously the world of the visible attempts to keep them apart: "Bo serce den' vid sercja čulo" (because one heart felt the day in another heart [*O* 1:117]). Throughout the cycle, the lyrical hero reminds himself and his beloved (especially in her "visible" fickle and cruel mask, which is the disruptive work of the world) of that bright truth. In *Svidok* Fedir and Sanna develop their own heavenly "affinity" much more elaborately. It is Sanna—whose visibility and invisibility (as opposed to the nameless woman in *Okean*) are not split but remain in perfect balance—who declares her love to Fedir and who reveals to him the bright flame of their *srodnost'*:

> Ми зріднені серцями! — в безконеччя:
> між їх дзеркальця свічечка свячена
>   в два відблиски палахкотить...
> обом на безліч повторя в глибинах
> незнаний огник! і живуть обидва
>   від нього, ставши в світ простий. (*S* 1:58)

Our hearts are related!—into [for] infinity:/ between their little mirrors a blessed candle/ burns with two reflections.../ the unknown little flame gives them/ countless repetitions in the depths, and they both/ live by it, standing in the simple world.

In this passage the "simple world" of the visible and the mysterious "unknown" light of the invisible are clearly embodied, as romantic love becomes a "microcosm" of universal mirroring. Fedir answers Sanna:

> "— Що ти побачила від ясновиддя:
> найкраще! доля — душі споріднила,
>   колись при висоті ненашій...
> де два світила, як зоря подвійна,
> ведуть в життя в терпіннях і надіях —
>   аби розлуки ми не знали". (*S* 1:59)

That which you saw in your illumination [revelation]:/ is the most beautiful!/ fate related our souls,/ a long time ago, in a height that is not ours.../ where two lights, like a double star,/ lead us into a life of suffering and hope—/ so that we will never know parting [let us hope that we will never part].

The lives of the lovers are indeed *translated* or repeated by mysterious lights in the realm of the invisible that shone long before the lovers' embodiment. The motif of Fedir and Sanna's "fated love" emerges throughout the poem, especially when the lovers have to live apart (*S* 1:261, 1:357, 2:1277, 3:2240, et passim).

The centre of the microcosm and the wellspring of the energy of love that has the power to unite the Universe is the heart. It is in the heart that the *srodnosti* are born; it is the heart that joins the beginning and the end of the individual. A central symbol of Skovoroda's philosophy, it is also at the centre of Barka's poetry.

For Skovoroda the heart not only defines but contains the individual. The frequently repeated motif in "Narkiss" is: "Vsjak est' tem, čie serdce v nem" (NAR 1:29) (Everyone is that whose heart is in him). We again note that the concept of the individual and the heart are linked formally by the device of rhyme. The heart and not the head is the organ of thought, ruling the whole man: "Your heart is the head of your interior. And if your heart is your head, you yourself are your heart. And if you do not approximate and unite with that which is *the head* of your head, you will remain a dead shadow and a corpse" (NAR 1:42). Skovoroda warns that vain passions may betray and ultimately destroy the heart. Such "death of the heart" is the only real sin against the self, equal to suicide (KOL 1:257). In a prophetic voice, he pronounces the following moving warning, stylized as an image of passionate, excited speech: "Syne! Xrany serdce tvoe!... Znaj sebe. Smotry sebe. Bud' v domĕ tvoem. Berežy sebe. Slyš! Berehy serdce." (0 Son! Save your heart!... Know yourself. Watch yourself. Live in your own house. Guard yourself. Listen! Guard your heart. NAR 1:47).

The lyrical hero of Barka's *Okean* lives in his heart as in his own house; the word "heart" seems to appear in almost every poem of that 600-page cycle. Indeed, the hero *is* his heart: it is his heart that reacts to all the joy and grief that the world holds in store for him.

> І я, що серце від півоній дужих
> поломеніє до весни,
> шепчу... (*O* 1:28)

And I, [who am] the heart that flames from the strong peonies to the spring, whisper...

These lines are almost untranslatable, precisely because of the ambiguity between "I" and "heart," created by a complex syntactical displacement. They can be translated in two ways: "And I that am the heart flaming toward spring, and away from the strong peonies," or "And I, whose heart flames toward spring..." I am certain that the formal ambiguity between "I" and "heart" is intentional.

The essential being of the lyrical hero's beloved is also contained in her heart, and occasionally she is *his* heart; exploiting the Ukrainian idiom, equivalent to "dear heart," the lyrical hero addresses her:

> О, рідне серце! — все при тій святині,
> де я з тобою міг радіти. (*O* 1:45)

O, native heart!—all by that temple/ where you and I were able to know joy.

When the beloved, in her visible worldly profile, begins to torment the lyrical hero, it is his heart that she tortures, perhaps because this heart is "in communion" with the invisible world that she is betraying:

> Над мак новонароджений все серце
> причасністю палахкотить.
> Від нього з сміхом на цеглиння стерте
> і рвеш, і губиш пелюстки... (*O* 1:18)

Higher than newborn poppies, my whole heart/ flames with communion./ Laughing, you tear off its petals, and lose them along a worn brick road.

Suffering the insults of his beloved, the hero begins to be afraid that he is not "guarding" his heart properly by dedicating it to visible love and its turbulent passions (*O* 2:5). But his fears are in vain: the heart, if it is in communion with the invisible, has the power to renew itself, to resurrect itself.

In its renewal, the "new heart" (another Christian *topos* of long standing) rededicates itself to faith, as it also does for Skovoroda. In *Svidok*, a monk predicts the atheist-rebel Fedir's future:

> "— А от, коли з посіяної іскри
> на серці дано вірі розігрітись..." (*S* 1:116)

And so, when from a sown spark/ faith will be destined to take flame upon the heart...

When the heart is ignited by the flame of faith, it becomes elevated to mystical heights. In *Okean* we read:

> І не спиниться на мить, не стихне
> серце, в славлення палавши... (*O* 2:27)

And the heart will not stop for a moment, will not be quiet,/ flaming into praise.

The hero's heart becomes Christ's flaming heart:

> То прикмета: до безсмертя кличе
> серце — від розп'яття в жертві. (*O* 2:45)

This is a sign: the heart calls to immortality—/ from the crucifixion in sacrifice/

The heart, finally, becomes the "carrier of God" (*bohonosec'* [*0* 2:27]).

In both Skovoroda and Barka, the heart steps out into the macrocosm and becomes something much vaster than the centre of the individual (the microcosm), although it does not cease to reflect that microcosm. We see this particularly in metaphors that cross the image of the heart with those of the sun and the ocean. In its macrocosmic being, the heart is most frequently compared to the sun, which is the heart of the macrocosm. Skovoroda compares the sun to the heart in "Potop zmiin" when he discusses the visible and the invisible—just as there is a sun within a sun, so there is a heart within a heart (POT 1:539). Comparisons of the heart with the sun are especially abundant in Barka's *Okean*; the poet fortifies the affinity by frequently exploiting the sonic similarity between the two Ukrainian words (*sonce—serce*). In one poem the sun is called "the heart of the sky" (*O* 2:6). In another, Barka writes:

> Бившися, як серце з болю — сонце,
> чисте в грудях яблуневих. (*O* 2:88)

Beating in pain like a heart, the sun,/ pure in the breasts of apple trees.

In both writers the heart, so to speak, internalizes the sun, as the sun externalizes the heart.

The ocean *has* a heart and the heart *is* the ocean: again we see universal "mirroring" or "crossing" of heights and depths in the microcosm of metaphor. In "Narkiss" Skovoroda seems to address "the heart of the sea" (NAR 1:28); also in that dialogue the heart becomes deeper than the ocean: "O heart, bottomlessness, wider than all the waters and skies... How deep you are! You embrace and hold everything, and nothing can contain you" (NAR 1:42). Barka "formulates" the following "equation": "The heart is an ocean" (*O* 2:99). In another poem he calls the heart "a mighty ocean" (*O* 1:43) and claims that the sea "sings with its golden heart," perhaps embodying in this image the sun's reflection upon the water (*O* 1:75). Note that in addition to the obvious visual metaphor of unity, we have here a "confounding of the senses" ("synaesthesia"), which implies unity on an even subtler formal level. Also consider the title of the work.

Finally, I would like to discuss the *topos* of the Book, as our two writers develop it; that *topos* is indeed very important in their work. First of all, the Bible represents for Skovoroda the highest, symbolic level of existence, and it is also central in Barka's view of the world. And second, both writers are vitally interested in other texts, as well as in the process of writing and reading itself. For all their numerous formal images of lived speech, both are intensely "literary" writers. One can go on to say, with Northrop Frye and the later deconstructionists, that every great text, as part of the "order of words" of literature, a "universe" of literature, reflects other texts rather than "life."[30]

It may come as a surprise to us, therefore, that both Skovoroda and Barka warn against reading too much. Skovoroda admonishes: "Read little and chew well. Oh, what sublime taste!" (ASK 1:126). Intellectual greed dulls our sense of taste, bloats our consciousness and ends in boredom and depression (IKO 1:400).[31] In "Alfavit" we find a line that seems to be appropriate for sherry parties even in our time, and is worthy of quotation in the original: "Dovelos' byt' v hostjax i napast' na šajku učonyx" ("I happened to be a guest and happened to meet a gang of scholars" [ALF 1:320]).

---

30. See his *Anatomy of Criticism: Four Essays* (Princeton: Princeton University Press, 1957), 16-18, 352-4, et passim.
31. Søren Kierkegaard warns against similar dangers in many places of his *oeuvre*.

We find similar "attacks" on reading Barka's *Svidok*. In his search for his *srodnost'*, Fedir undergoes a period of voracious reading, not at all to the benefit of his spiritual health. He is searching for a book of revelation, without yet having found the Book of Revelation:

> Якби розвиднилось і в найдревнішій
> і в свіжій книзі: звідки руки ширить
>   духовне сонце — всіх обняти....
> я гризтиму сухар і на горищі,
> чи на цепу в льохах, де щур ошкірився,
>   аби мені книжки багаті. (*S* 1:445)

If only it dawned in a most ancient/ and in a fresh book, where the spiritual sun/ would spread his arms to embrace everybody…/ I would even gnaw dry bread in an attic,/ or on a chain in a cellar where a rat bares its teeth,/ if I could only get rich books.

Soon, however, Fedir finds that he has been "contaminated" by books (*S* 2:1491, 1496); nevertheless, he cannot leave his reading—in each crisis, in each moment of grief, he returns to his books as if they were a narcotic (*S* 3:2827). He begins to lead a monk-like existence with them, but realizes that this is a false monkhood. Eventually he finds his literary *srodnost'* in the Bible. Incidentally, the fact that the hero read many books before his "conversion," and now condemns this practice as a vice of youth, strongly reminds us of Augustine's *Confessions*.

It should be obvious by now that for both our writers there are "good" books and "bad" books, and that the quality of books is determined neither by literary reviewers nor by best-seller lists. It is religious faith that hovers like an intermediary between the book and the reader. Skovoroda has no doubt that only the "Good Book" is worth reading slowly and deeply, although he manages to be very learned and erudite for that. For Barka as for Skovoroda, there are books, both ancient and new, which either prefigure the New Testament or are under its aegis. Barka frequently alludes to this in his poetry (see, for example, *S* 4:3372) and develops it at length in his critical essays.

In both Skovoroda and Barka, we find "battles of books." Skovoroda's "Narkiss" is a consistent dialogue between two texts: pagan classicism, particularly Ovid, with its worship of the body, and David's Psalms. More distantly, he counterposes the Bible and some of its exegetes. In "Asxan'", for example, a *starčyk* becomes prophetically irate in his attack against those interpreters of the Bible who read it too literally and fail to see the spirit behind the words:

> They have torn everything apart, gobbled up everything, chewed everything with the iron teeth of their father [Daniel's monster], without leaving anything. Where are your leftovers [in the original, *ostanok*—a pun on "end" and, more distantly, "salvation"]? Oh! You have trampled your leftovers ["end," "salva-

tion"]! Behold a sinful tongue! The serpent's seed! (1:128).

The "leftovers," in Skovoroda's paradoxical thought, are those ineffable overtones of the text in which the light of authentic signification is to be found.

The "battle of books" in Barka is more of a worldly philosophical bent, because generally he is by far more politically aware than Skovoroda. The mighty antagonists in *Svidok* are the Bible and Marx. Moreover, the Soviet Union, it seems, was born of texts—the wrong texts, "paper schemes," in the maze of which human imagination has withered and died (1:488). Like Skovoroda's "wrong" texts, in Barka the "wrong" texts of Marxism and atheism are seeds of the serpent—the lying serpent from the Old and New Testaments:

> Бо з порожнечі книжної зміїнець
> підман — самотне серце, нерозмінне,
> вкусив! і жала муку вносять. (*S* 1:985)

From the bookish void a petty serpent/ a lie—bit the lonely, honest heart,/ and his sting is pouring suffering into it.

Finally, the Bible enters into battle against itself. This is particularly evident in Skovoroda; for him the Bible, like the microcosm and the macrocosm, is split into the visible and the invisible. Skovoroda's very bold, and occasionally quite nasty, paradoxical attacks on the visible nature of the Bible are well known (the story of Lot's daughters, quoted earlier, may serve as an example of this; even more shockingly, he calls the words "And God created Heaven and earth" a lie, POT 1:551). We have the alternating images of the Bible as its body and as its secret, sacred, authentic content (its "leftovers"), which is the thought of its heart. Hence the Bible is "like a single man or Adam. His clay and body is visible to anyone, but his heart is hidden, and the spirit of life is invisible in him" (ALF 1:342, cf. KOL 1:267). Woe to him who takes the Bible at its "face" value and interprets it thus. Skovoroda's attack on the "wrong" exegetes, quoted above, refers to the sin of such interpretations. The reason is that the Bible is more than a text; it is also the symbolic embodiment of God, Christ and the serpent (POT 1:550, KOL 258), and *this* is its secret. After all, God's nature is the greatest secret of all.

This, of course, is not new. For example, medieval and early Renaissance thinkers, explaining the nature of allegory, thought of the Bible as a river that is both shallow and deep at once (compare this with Skovoroda's image of the Bible being like a river or like the sea, deep in some places, shallow in others, NAR 1:77). The difference between most such opinions and Skovoroda's is that Skovoroda does not believe in extended and complex exegeses: one should "understand" the secret meanings of the Bible intuitively and all at once, as one "sees," in a flash, a poetic metaphor.[32] This is why Skovoroda speaks like a poet, rather than an "explainer," building metaphors that would parallel and reflect those of the Bible. This procedure, incidentally (with obvious differences of intent), is somewhat similar to that of philosophers like Heidegger and literary critics like the "deconstructionists."[33]

Barka also believes in the double nature of the Bible, although in his poetry this is not stated so directly and originally as it is in Skovoroda. What is more important to me here is that Barka's "interpretations" of the Bible proceed by Skovoroda's method. Although this is evident in his short essays on the Bible collected in *Veršnyk neba*, it is incomparably more effective in his poetry. Much of his poetry, in fact, may be read as a "synchronic interpretation" of the Bible, proceeding from one arresting metaphor to another. What is even more interesting is that the "obscurity" of his poetry, about which critics have been complaining for many years, is a deliberate "mimesis" or imaging of the invisible nature of the Bible and sacred writing. His stanzas, with such ravishing surfaces and yet such deeply hidden "hearts," are meant to reveal by concealing and, perhaps, to conceal by revealing. It is probably in this that Barka is Skovoroda's closest student.

The question of Barka as Skovoroda's "student" is broad and interesting: I have hardly begun to broach it here. For example, the numerous similarities in their language and style—idiomatic expressions that do not shy away from vulgarity, satire, invective, word games and puns, conceits; the general rootedness of both in the baroque tradition—all this would need another long article. Such an article should also touch upon the numerous differences between the two writers—the fact that not only Barka's interpretation of Skovoroda in his essays, but also Skovoroda's shadow (or, rather, his light) in Barka's poetical lines may be the result of a "misreading," a "misprision," perhaps even a wilfully determined one.

---

32. For an interesting discussion of the "visible" and the "invisible" meanings in the Bible, as they apply to contemporary literary theory, see Gerald L. Bruns, *Inventions: Writing, Textuality, and Understanding* (New Haven: Yale University Press, 1982), 17-43. See further Frank Kermode, *The Genesis of Secrecy: The Charles Eliot Norton Lectures 1977-1978* (Cambridge, Mass.: Harvard University Press, 1979). Bruns points out that some medieval exegeses were meant not so much to disclose Biblical mysteries as to "reveal" them in the mystical sense, by refusing to violate their hiddenness and even by hiding them more deeply.

33. Much has been written on this question in recent years. Perhaps the best theorist (and, incidentally, practitioner) of the "visible" and the "invisible" in a text is the Heideggerian "deconstructionist" Paul de Man. See his *Blindness and Insight: Essays in the Rhetoric of Contemporary Criticism* (New York: Oxford University Press, 1971; 2nd, rev. ed., Minneapolis: University of Minnesota Press, 1983), *Allegories of Reading: Figural Language in Rousseau, Nietzsche, Rilke and Proust* (New Haven: Yale University Press, 1979), and other works.

Gogol' and H.S. Skovoroda: The Problem of the "External Man"

Mikhail Weiskopf

> Пусть судит всякий, как хочет, а по мне так философ Хома стоит философа Сковороды!
> В. Белинский. "О русской повести и повестях Гоголя".

Thoughts on the possible influence of Skovoroda on the works of Gogol', expressed half a century ago by D. Čyževs'kyj, have not been developed further in specialized literature. To some extent, this involves the difficulties inherent in any discussion of the interdependence of ideology and poetics. In this particular case, the difficulty is aggravated by the fact that Skovoroda's ideological legacy comprises an eclectic transposition of diverse mystical doctrines,[1] the imprints of which are abundant in the works of Gogol' as well. Čyževs'kyj himself had already come up against this problem in drawing a parallel, in his excellent article on "The Overcoat", between the collection of "passions" in *Dead Souls* and many other works of Gogol', and Skovoroda's well-known line, "Each city

---

1. See the rich collection of sources in Čyževs'kyj's book, *Skovoroda: Dichter, Denker, Mystiker* (Munich, 1974). In his lecture, "Musagim v'smalim kabaliim v'shabtaim b'ktavav shel Grigorij Skovoroda" (Cabbalistic and Sabbatarian Concepts and Symbols in the Works of Hryhorij Skovoroda), read on 24 March 1987 at the Israeli National Academy of Sciences, Prof. Shlomo Pines illustrated the dependence of the later works of Skovoroda on Jewish mystical studies. For the genesis of Skovoroda's ethics, see G. Špet, *Očerk razvitija russkoj filosofii* (St. Petersburg, 1922), Part One, 68-83; on the source of Skovoroda's symbolism, see, for example, D.P. Kyryk, "Svit symvoliv H. S. Skovorody", *in Vid Vyšens'koho do Skovorody. Z istoriji filosofs'koji dumky na Ukrajini XVI-XVII st.* (Kyiv, 1972), 116-17.

has its own customs and rules."[2] In fact, the theme of "passions"—the fatal inclinations of the flesh—is universal, not only in baroque, but also in all mystical literature, modified to some degree by the influence of Gnosticism. In asserting, in terms of this theme, that Skovoroda was Gogol''s direct predecessor, Čyževs'kyj ought to have demonstrated some evidence of semantic-stylistic relationship between the juxtaposed texts. This, however, is lacking. In 1968 he returned to this question and, once again comparing Gogol''s "passions" with Skovoroda's verse-line, he simply presented a collection of additional examples, adding as sources *Vladimir of the Third Degree*, *The Inspector-General*, the second volume of *Dead Souls*, etc.[3] The list proved truly inexhaustible, but it brought Čyževs'kyj no closer to Skovoroda's text. The question was losing its focus and, in the end, Čyževs'kyj had to give it up. Having referred to the typological similarity between the religio-ethical views of Gogol' and Skovoroda, he in fact ended his analysis on a pessimistic note:

"It would be possible to assume the extensive influence of Skovoroda on Gogol'—it would be possible if it were not clear that both of them, the Ukrainian writer and the Ukrainian philosopher, were inspired by common sources—the writings of the Church Fathers and, albeit to different degrees, the didactic literature of the Kyiv School of the seventeenth century."[4]

In his definitive work on Skovoroda, published in 1974, Čyževs'kyj does not treat this problem at all and is, moreover, sceptical about any attention paid by Gogol' and other Ukrainian romantic writers to the work of their countryman. He even speaks of their ignorance and undervaluing of Skovoroda. He explains the thematic connection with Gogol''s work by convergence.[5]

Nonetheless, the problem of "Skovoroda and Gogol'" is susceptible of a solution, but in a different form, which was noted by Čyževs'kyj himself. Astutely indicating the link between Gogol''s Christian mysticism and the *Philokalia*, he understands the "passions" to include those often trivial tricks by which a person is enticed by the external world: for Akakij Akakievič the role of just such a fatal, trivial "temptation" is played by the overcoat. It is appropriate to bring certain clarifications to Čyževs'kyj's explanation, in order to reveal the genesis and function of the "passions" both in the plot of "The Overcoat" and in the idea of the "exterior life" in the works of Gogol' in general.

According to the gnostic view adopted by the Church Fathers, in the bodily

---

2. Dm. Čiževskij, "O 'Shineli' Gogolia," *Sovremennye zapiski* LXVII (1938):189-90.
3. D. Tschižewskij, "Skovoroda—Gogol'," *Die Welt der Slaven* XIII, Heft 1 (1968):322-3. See also the later edition of his article, "Komposition von Gogols "Mantel," *Gogol, Turgenev, Dostoevskij, Tolstoj. Zur russischen Literatur des 19. Jahrhunderts* (Forum Slavicum, 1966, B. 12):113-14.
4. D. Tschižewskij, "Skovoroda—Gogol'," 323-4.
5. D. Tschižewskij, *Skovoroda: Dichter, Denker, Mystiker,* 122.

prison, the spirit becomes encompassed by trivial appetites and passions.[6] Their total complex, identified with the flesh as the "clothing" of the spirit, represents a sleeping or dead soul; the "psyche" as opposed to the "pneuma," the "inner man" of St. Paul. The notion of the "dead soul" appears in Skovoroda's dialogue "Alfavit, ili bukvar' mira,"[7] and comes, apparently, from Western patristic writing, which is permeated with gnostic elements. Gogol' most likely borrowed the title of his *poema* not from Skovoroda, but from this common source. In the *Philokalia*, St. Gregory Palamas says, "Know...that the soul can also die, even though it is by nature immortal...hence the Lord called dead those who live according to the vain world... The Lord called those dead who, although they live, are dead in their souls. Because...the separation of the soul from God is the death of the soul."[8]

Skovoroda, obsessed by the idea of visible and invisible natures, ceaselessly exposed, in great detail, the "external," spiritually dead man. It is precisely in this sense that Gogol' stands closest to the mystic prophet, with his hypermaterial poetics and his gift for concretization, and it is here that clear points of convergence can be demonstrated between the two authors. In this new form, the problem retains its fascination within the framework of the historico-literary context, from the point of view of the theme of "the Ukrainian Gogol'," and also in terms of the ideological and semiotic structure of his works. Furthermore, it is doubtful that so colourful and, in the context of eighteenth-century Ukraine, so grand a figure as Skovoroda would go unnoticed by Gogol'. Nonetheless, a positive answer to the question that occupied Čyževs'kyj can be given only when clear and concrete parallels with Skovoroda are found in Gogol''s texts, parallels that can be traced on both the thematic and the semantic level.

Attention to Skovoroda in Russian literary journalism and criticism rose sharply in the 1830s in particular. While in the first quarter of the nineteenth century publications about him were relatively rare (more or less complete biographies appeared in 1817 and 1823), in 1833, Izmail Sreznevskij, editor of *Zaporožskaja starina*, included Aleksandr Xiždeu's notes concerning Skovoroda in this publication.[9] Gogol', who corresponded with Sreznevskij about their mutual interest in Ukrainian history, expressed his delight with the contents of

---

6. Hans Jonas, *The Gnostic Religion. The Message of the Alien God and the Beginning of Christianity* (Boston, 1958), 44.
7. Hryhorij Skovoroda, *Povne zibrannja tvoriv u dvox tomax* (Kyiv, 1973), I:420. All citations are from this edition, with volume and page numbers indicated in the text. In all excerpts, italics are mine (M.W.), with the exception of designated places.
8. *Dobrotoljubie* (Philokalia) (Moscow, 1889), 5:278.
9. See N.V. Gogol', *Polnoe sobranie sočinenij v 14 tomax* (Moscow, 1937-52), X:480. All citations are from this edition, with volume and page numbers indicated in the text.

this issue.[10] Sreznevskij then also published a comprehensive work on Skovoroda with excerpts from his texts in *Utrennjaja zvezda* (Xarkiv). In 1834, his article on Ukrainian oral literature appeared in *Učenye zapiski Moskovskogo universiteta*, in which he named "the sage Skovoroda" as one of its leading exponents, followed in 1836 by the biographical tale about "Grigorij Savvič the Wanderer" entitled "Major, major!" in *Moskovskij nabljudatel'*. Xiždeu published a lengthy panegyric in two issues of *Teleskop* in 1835. In the following year, Nadeždin, having already published three songs of Skovoroda, also published in *Teleskop* the article "Europeanism and National Consciousness in Relation to Russian Literature," in which he valued the "sage of the Russian people" highly.[11] The first issue of *Literaturnye pribavlenija k Russkomu Invalidu*, appearing in January 1837, opened with an article by the editor, Andrej Kraevskij, "Thoughts concerning Russia," in which Skovoroda is called the "prophet of Russian national philosophy," standing opposed to the godless rationalism of the West. This programmatic article made a "great impression on many writers" according to Ivan Panaev, and it was approved by Gogol''s friend, Petr Pletnev.[12] Gogol' also knew about this article, judging by his letter of 25 January 1837 to Nikolaj Prokopovič. And finally, in 1840 in "Istorija filosofii v Rossii", Archimandrite Gavriil demonstrated Skovoroda's learning with numerous excerpts and ranked him among the leading national philosophers.[13] In this same decade, several of Skovoroda's own works were published.

Such circumstances could naturally have stimulated Gogol''s interest in his famous countryman. It is noteworthy, however, that his interest had arisen earlier, at the beginning of the 30s, when the creator of the "Evenings" began a thorough study of sources for Ukrainian history and ethnography that continued through the whole first decade of his creative life. I will attempt to base my assertions on three Gogolian cycles—"Evenings," "Mirgorod" and the St. Petersburg tales, each of which will be represented here by one illustrative tale.

In the first of these, "The Terrible Vengeance," signs of familiarity with Skovoroda's dialogue "Narkiss" are clearly evident. The dialogue was published, anonymously in fact, in 1798 in St. Petersburg and, before that, was circulated in manuscript.

In Gogol''s tale, the sorcerer begs his daughter to free him from the dungeon:

---

10. "You have already done me a great service by publishing *Zaporožskaja starina*. Where did you dig up so many treasures?" (X:298).
11. See F.M. Poliščuk, *Hryhorij Skovoroda. Seminarij* (Kyiv, 1972), 11-16; Ju. Barabaš, "...Sii...raznorodnye o nem suždenija." Grigorij Skovoroda v ocenkax i sporax," *Voprosy literatury* 3 (1985):98-9; A. Lavrov, "Andrej Belyj and Hryhorij Skovoroda" in this volume.
12. Vl. Orlov, *Puti i sud'by. Literaturnye očerki* (Leningrad, 1971), 471-3.
13. See G.P. Danilevskij, "Grigorij Savvič Skovoroda," *Sočinenija v 24 tomax* (St. Petersburg, 1901), 21:88.

He went up to the window to see whether his daughter would pass by. She was meek and gentle as a dove... It is she! He pressed more closely to the window. Here she was, already coming nearer... Kateryna! Daughter! Have pity!.. If only I could get out of here, I would give up everything. I will repent:... Day and night I will pray to God... I would not even fear these walls and would pass through them, but...they were built by a holy hermit, and no unclean force can free a prisoner from here without unlocking the doors with the very same key that the saint used to lock his cell. (I:261-3)

In comparison, the following passage from "Narkiss":

He knew that there was no way to escape the darkness...except through these gates... He knew that no bird, and no human wisdom, no matter how quick, had the power to carry him out of the chasm except that pure dove... So charmed was he by this lovely dove, so captivated by her that, like Magdalene at the tomb, he would always sit at the window of his beloved. He begged and pleaded that she open the door for him, that she end his sufferings. (I:185)

Gogol''s description of the subsequent flight of the "worst of sinners" into the mountains also clearly recalls "Narkiss":

The road itself seemed to be pursuing him... Everything seemed confused somehow... He rode straight for Kaniv... The road was the same, yet this was not Kaniv, but Šums'k. The sorcerer was amazed to find that he was in quite another part of the country. He raced back to Kyiv and a day later a city appeared, but it was Halyč, not Kyiv... Not knowing what to do, he turned his horse back again, but felt once more that he was going in the opposite direction, yet always forward... He shuddered to see the Carpathian mountains rising not far ahead of him...and his horse galloped on and was already plunging through the mountains. Suddenly the clouds lifted, and there before him appeared the horseman in all his terrible grandeur. (I:276-8)

Compare the following from "Narkiss":

It is written: "The sinner runs, chased by no one...feeling the danger of his path, he runs like a harried rabbit to these hills, finding himself in the confusion of his poor reasoning, which previously seemed to him to be perfectly correct. But when the light from the divine hills, shining on his face, shows him how he has been deceived, then he himself destroys his path like St. Paul on the road to Damascus. (I:186)

The analogy to Paul is included in Gogol''s text. The sorcerer says to Kateryna, "Have you heard about the Apostle Paul—what a sinful person he was, and how he later repented and became a saint" (I:262). Borrowing the subject of the repentant sinner from Skovoroda, Gogol' inverts the situation, rendering it hopeless; where Skovoroda tells of a symbolic resurrection from the dead, Gogol' speaks of a terrible existence beyond the grave. I have in mind the following lines from "Narkiss":

> What a terrible thing it is to sit and be a prisoner in a dungeon [compare the first punishment meted out to the sorcerer. M.W.], but it is even worse to be in the company of those whom Paul awakens: "Stand up, sleepers, and arise from the dead... *Break the sleep of your eyes,* o unhappy corpse: *Get up on your feet!*" (I:189)

and the fate of the sorcerer in "The Terrible Vengeance":

> In an instant the sorcerer died and *after death he opened his eyes.* But he was already a corpse and saw like a corpse. Neither the living nor the resurrected look in such a terrible way. He rolled his dead eyes from side to side and saw the dead getting up...and they all looked just like him." (I:278)

The central theme of "Narkiss"—self-knowledge, the revelation in oneself of the inner, spiritual man as a condition of salvation—is nuanced by contrast in Gogol''s text. In "The Terrible Vengeance" the sorcerer sees only his corporeal doubles—his godless ancestors. And while Skovoroda, addressing the external, earth-bound man, exclaims: "And now *eat the earth,* love your own heel, crawl on the earth" (I:134), Gogol''s dead Petro literally eats "the earth like a madman" (I:281). Thus, the fundamental line of correspondence between Gogol' and the Ukrainian mystic develops through Gogol''s unilaterally negative realization of Skovoroda's subjects.

Unfortunately, further analysis of this question is hindered by a serious methodological obstacle. Unlike "Narkiss" and those pieces that were published in the 1830s, many of Skovoroda's works appeared in print only after Gogol''s death and, while they circulated in manuscript, it is impossible to make an accurate assessment of their accessibility to the writer. The dialogue "Asxan'," published only in 1912 but known in manuscripts of the end of the eighteenth century, can serve here as a corroborative example. Again, in "The Terrible Vengeance," in his description of how "the dead eat the dead" and "gnaw their own bones," Gogol' is concretizing a metaphor from "Asxan'": "Will you not arise from the sleep of your graves? We are eating flesh, but our own, and with our own teeth we tear our own carrion" (I:237).

If we assume that Gogol' knew "Asxan'," then what was the case with the other texts? Skovoroda's dialogue "Razgovor družeskij o duševnom mire" (in contemporary editions "Razgovor pjati putnikov o istinnom sčastii v žizni") was first published in 1837. Does it follow that Gogol' could not have become familiar with its contents earlier—in 1833, for example, when, intending to publish "Istorija Malorossiji," he occupied himself profitably with the search for old Ukrainian manuscripts?[14] In December he read to Puškin "Povest' o tom

---

14. See his letter to Puškin, 23 December 1833 (X:291). See also the commentary on p. 470. As G. Shapiro has kindly informed me, Skovoroda's writings were in Troščyns'kyj's library, to which Gogol' had access as a young man.

kak possorilsja Ivan Ivanovič s Ivanom Nikiforovičem," in which he responds to the leading theme of Skovoroda's "Razgovor."

Recounting the material, technical achievements of mankind—"we have measured the sea, the earth, the air and the skies and troubled the belly of the earth for the sake of metals...we have found an incalculable number of worlds, we build incomprehensible machines, fill up chasms, subdue and impel the force of waters, daily new experiments and wild inventions"— Skovoroda's character then exclaims, "My God, what can we not do! Of what are we incapable! But it is grievous that, with all this, it seems something great is lacking. We lack that which we cannot even express. We know only one thing—that something is lacking, but what it is we do not understand" (I:335-6).

The hero of Gogol''s "Povest'" muses in the same manner, "My God, what a master I am! What do I lack? Birds, buildings, granaries, every comfort, berry vodka, pears in the orchard, plums; in the garden poppies, cabbage, peas... What do I lack?... I would like to know, what do I lack?" (II:228).

According to Skovoroda, man is destroyed by pagan "frenzied idolatry"—the attraction to visible and palpable existence, to the fleeting and corruptible "nature of the flesh" (I:354). The flesh is "coloured filth and filthy paint (colour)," clothing a "threadbare robe" or a shadow obscuring the invisible essence. In its pursuit of illusory riches, the world "litigates, betrays ... builds, destroys, obscures," so that often "the very smallest demon threatens our undefended town" (I:357). True happiness exists in the spiritual world, and peace in accordance with God (I:343).

Gogol' opposed "Razgovor o mire" with "Povest' o tom kak possorilsja ...." The conflict, arising because of a gun, is anticipated in the scene in which Ivan Ivanovič contemplates his neighbour's clothing, which is hanging outside (this wardrobe, by the way, entirely in the spirit of Skovoroda, is identified with its owner, Ivan Nikiforovič).[15] A sham life is imparted to the clothing and it is compared to a "puppet theatre," which is a further metaphor for illusory being. The wide pants "took up almost half the yard" and their shadow "almost the whole court." The shadows of things envelop Mirgorod.

The path of salvation, according to Skovoroda, leads from the "worldly world" to the genuine world—the spiritual. Allegorically transforming the folkloric theme of accord, barred to the crippled and the blind by their fellow wanderers, the author of "Razgovor" describes with pathos their return to the Heavenly Father, who "lives in a mountain fortress called Mirgorod." He goes on to say, "Blessed are those who, day by day, climb higher up the mountain of this most

---

15. "What a stupid woman!" thought Ivan Ivanovič: "She will be airing out Ivan Nikiforovič himself next! *And in fact, Ivan Ivanovič was not entirely mistaken in his guess.* Five minutes later the nankeen trousers of Ivan Nikiforovič moved out" (II:229-30).

illumined Mirgorod. This is Pasxa or the crossing over to Jerusalem: understand, to the city of peace and to its keep, Zion" (I:343).

In other words, Skovoroda's "Mirgorod" is a translation of the word "Jerusalem" through its popular etymology: Yerushalayim—ir shalom. The ascent, according to Skovoroda, is accomplished "from baseness up the mountain...from the *filthy wallows of swine* to mountain springs" (I:347). "O, let us risk all so that we may enter into the peace of God on the feast of the Lord's day, at the very least on the Sabbath, if not on the most holy Sabbath of Sabbaths and Feast of Feasts" (I:349).

Gogol''s reality is the swine and filthy wallow; instead of a mountain Zion, a church is presented to which, "on Sundays" (days of resurrection; see Skovoroda's Feast of Feasts above), Ivan Ivanovič and Ivan Nikiforovič go in friendly harmony, as though parodying the crippled wandering companions in Skovoroda's text:

> And if Ivan Ivanovič, whose eyes were exceedingly sharp, was the first to notice a puddle, or some kind of dirt in the middle of the street (which happens from time to time in Mirgorod), then he always said to Ivan Nikiforovič, "Take care, don't step here, because it is unpleasant" (II:239).

Following Skovoroda, Gogol' deliberately neutralizes and effaces the difference between "mir"—accord and "mir"—society.[16] At the conclusion of the "Povest'" Mirgorod, fallen and in the grip of its passions, with its empty *festive* church, anticipates the symbolic "earthly Jerusalem": "It is dull on this earth, gentlemen!" This symbol of an earthly city, transferred from the last tale of the cycle to its title, itself colours the entire collection.

An equally negative, if not polemical, assimilation of the central motifs of Skovoroda is evident in "The Overcoat."

In an interesting article, Anthony Hippisley demonstrated the use of biblical and gospel semantics of clothing in this story, in particular, the analogy between the changing of Akakij Akakievič's clothes and spiritual resurrection.[17] There is, however, a significant basis for presuming that the religious theme of clothing and, moreover, its symbolic relationship to the name of the hero was suggested to Gogol' directly by Skovoroda's works, in particular by the dialogue "Beseda o tom, čto blažennym byt' legko," published in 1837 by the committee "Čelovekoljubivoe obščestvo." Gogol' began working on "The Overcoat" in the fall of 1839 and finished in the first months of 1841. In the concluding section of the "Beseda," entitled "The Lord's Gates into a New Land, into the Eternal Realm," we read:

---

16. In "Razgovor," Skovoroda writes мір with an и as in мир.
17. Antony Hippisley, "Gogol's 'The Overcoat': A Further Interpretation," *Slavic and East European Review* 20 (Summer 1976):124-5.

But who sowed this evil seed in you, that it is difficult to be holy? Was it not enemies, sirens?...
Farra: Yes, yes, they! From them comes this guttural voice (saying) *"Xalepa ta kala."* "Goodness is difficult..."
Naeman: ...Expel that spirit of falsehood hence. And put this precious stone in your heart: *"Xalepa ta kaka."* "It is difficult to be evil." (I:274)

Against the corruptible clothing of the flesh, Skovoroda counterposes an ark, the spiritual "robes of salvation," vested in which a person finds God in himself: "This is a cloak from the flood! This very ark is the cloak not made by human hands...that covers better than a *mantle*. Il'ja's coat (*šinel'*) gazes from a distance at this garment... And where can you get Il'ja's cloak? *'Xalepa ta kaka'"* (I:277).

Although the name of Akakij was probably taken from *"Xalepa ta kaka,"* it has taken on an additional and complex symbolism inherent in the semantic and stylistic structure of the story, in which Gogol' deals with the problem of external material man. The semantic dynamics of "The Overcoat" consist of a sequential concretization of images in the transposition from the general and undefined to the given and specific, from the external to the internal, from physical, material contours to the hidden psychic essence. On every level the theme unfolds by way of narrowing and assimilation, and is fixed in the words "kakoj," "kakoj-to," "takoj," "kak," "tak" (I counted no less than 330 of these), and added to these are attributes such as "vsjakij," "častnyj," "odin," etc. From a murky, diffuse background, from "kak" and "tak," issues the name of the hero:

The mother was presented with the choice of three names (*kakoe* ona xočet)... "No," thought his late mother, "the names are all so... (*takie*). "This is such a punishment...what awful names (*kakie*)... I have really never heard such names (*takix*)... It is clear that such is his fate (*takaja*). If it is so (*tak*), let him be called by his father's name (*kak*). His father was Akakij, so (*tak*) let the son be Akakij. In this way (*takim* obrazom), he came to be Akakij Akakievič. (III:342)[18]

Just as the pseudo-individuality of the hero is revealed through his attitude to things and focused in the motif of the overcoat, so the choice of the surname Bašmačkin is conditioned by apparent contrast to the fact that "absolutely all the Bašmačkins wore boots." In the works of Skovoroda, the corruption and wretchedness of despised material existence are signalled in the image of feet and heels—the closest analogy to clothing. See in "Narkiss": "What is evil counsel and the seed of the serpent?... In all things to love and approve *the empty*

---

18. Rancour-Laferriere interprets this passage differently, as a phonological anticipation of the name, which suggests, in the spirit of psychoanalysis, a fecal and therefore anal symbolism. Daniel Rancour-Laferriere, *Out from Gogol's Overcoat. A Psychoanalytic Study* (Ann Arbor, 1982), 97.

exterior or the heel" (I:171).

The motif of the heel and of shoes is more fully developed in the dialogue "Asxan'":

> You will see that that which you call a foot is nothing but bare superficial dust...formed from the earth like a corrupt wooden figure, and your feet are like *boots*...and all the dust, like your *boot*, is put on the wearer's foot... The heart is the root. In it lives your true foot, and the external dust is its shoe (*bašmak*). (I:242-3)

This passage clarifies both the genesis of the hero's surname and its functional tie with the main theme of the story. See further: "Not only the foot, but also... all your external self, all the puppet-like parts, are nothing more than *clothing*" (I:243).

In direct relationship with this symbolism, a correlation is established in the story between the foot, the shoe, and the overcoat. Petrovič advises Bašmačkin to make himself some "footcloths" out of his old coat, "because stockings don't keep one warm" (III:151). In the drafts, the old coat was lined with fur, like that "which is used to line winter boots" (III:450). Preparing to acquire his new coat, the hero walks "almost on tiptoe" in order not to scuff his soles.

The "heel" in Skovoroda's work is invariably associated with damaged and partial vision, with "the eye of the flesh," which is capable of seeing only the external man. See again in "Narkiss":

> Our eye watches our heel and is found in the most external place, bereft of its strength, its purpose, its head. (I:165)
> This *eye of yours is a heel*, or a tail in your eye... But the true eye itself, the main and primal eye—where is it? (I:159-60).

This, strictly speaking, is the source of Bašmačkin's weakened sight, which catches Petrovič's big toe with its hideous nail, "thick and strong like a turtle shell."[19] At the home of the assistant to the director, who lived "*on his big foot*" [i.e., in a showy way; tr. note], he immediately notices "on the floor whole rows of galoshes" (III:159). This connects with another of Skovoroda's pervasive themes—the loss of sensations of taste, also symbolizing soullessness. Bašmačkin eats "without noticing the taste at all" (III:145). Compare with "Narkiss":

> Know that we lack whole personhood and we must say, "Lord, we do not have a person..." What is the use of having and not understanding? *To eat and not perceive taste?*... We perceive people *as though someone were showing only a human foot or heel*, having covered the rest of the body and head... Is it possible to recognize a person from his heel only? (I:159)

---

19. See in Skovoroda: "The thought or the heart is that spirit which is the lord of the body, the master of the house. And the body? It is an *oyster shell*." "Žena Lotova," 2:52.

In the same vein, Gogol''s hypothetical observer suffers from a comparable spiritual blindness; the young functionary who is contrasted externally with Bašmačkin "refines the acuteness of his eagle eye to such an extent that he can even notice who has a torn bootstrap on the other side of the sidewalk" (III:145).

But, Gogol' emphasizes, crooked Petrovič also examines Akakij Akakievič's frock coat first. That he has one eye is a sign of carnal and therefore damaged vision—a symbol that is, of course, founded on a complex of images from folkloric demonology, but is not exclusively limited to it. It is especially characteristic that Petrovič's demonism is interwoven with a paradoxical, fully pagan piety—faithfulness to ancestral customs. Compare Skovoroda's symbolic treatment of one eye:

> I admit that this word "faith" in my filthy lips longs for only one thing, but I perceive no taste in it...
> Drug: Know that faith looks at that which *your empty eye* cannot see.
> Luka: What is this empty eye?
> Drug: It has been said that all flesh is emptiness.
> Luka: Oh, yes! In the whole world I see nothing but what is visible, or, in your terms, flesh.
> Drug: And thus you are a faithless heathen and idol-worshipper...*you require another eye* in order also to see the invisible... A true eye and faith are one.[20]
> (I:162)

In terms of "The Overcoat," the treatment so favoured by Freudians of shoes and feet as erotic symbols retains a certain conviction for the simple reason that, besides the semantic system demonstrated above, the foot and shoes are directly associated by Gogol' with kinetic and volitional impulses. The foot in "The Overcoat" is a sign of determined desire, and furthermore, desire negatively judged—the image of the lowest vain inclinations. In the works of Skovoroda, the foot also indicates "inclination, love, and grasping desire" (I:241), including "appetite," i.e., the erotic impulse in a broader sense than the merely sexual. Free voluntary action must be ennobled, inspired—for the new paths, says Skovoroda, one needs "new feet." At the same time, the difference between flesh and spirit is understood with absolute clarity: the external person is like a cover over the inner man:

> You have already heard that your exterior foot is not a foot, but only a mere covering for your foot?... What nonsense! Is the foot healed by bandaging the boot?... Go, beginning with your foot, along all the edges of your false self...then you may find out that...your external self is nothing but your mask covering each of your parts. (I:243-4)

---

20. See in this context the concupiscence of Xoma Brut in "Vij" and his death from an "earthly" glance.

The expected enlightenment and liberation from the flesh are equivalent to the removal of shrouds: "Take the scab from your eye...*take the boot* from your foot, and you will see whence your external self is growing" (I:242).

Gogol' transforms this call to *remove one's shoes* into a concrete situation, definitively changing the symbolic value. In "The Overcoat," removing clothing and taking off shoes is the means of exposing the illusory quality of the vain physical world. Scholars have already noted the correlation between the picture of the woman kicking off her shoe, which so mesmerized Bašmačkin's imagination, and the scene in which the robbed hero meets his "bride"—an undressed old woman "with only one shoe on"[21] (III:162). The motif of the wedding is played on throughout the accumulation of episodes; youth and old age join the course of the general theme of the fleeting and illusory world. Compare the overcoming of temptation at the end of the dialogue "Beseda": "Farewell forever, foolish girls, sweet-voiced sirens with your smoldering eyes, *with your aging youth, with your youthful age*, and with your harbour filled with weeping" (I:281).

While working precisely along this line, Gogol' nonetheless removes the perspective of salvation that is opened up in Skovoroda's "Beseda." Thus, in the representation of Petrovič, Gogol' rejects Skovoroda, making a travesty of his characteristic theme of refuge, the theme of St. *Peter* the Pardoner.[22] In the "Beseda" the principle of *xalepa ta kaka* is indicated by the foundation *stone* and by the *keys* of salvation personified in the Apostle Peter (I:274): "We are given the keys: *xalepa ta kaka*; rejoice, my Peter, my haven!... You are opening for me the gates to the blessed kingdom, the bright lands" (I:281).

According to the profound insight of Čyževs'kyj, false salvation in "The Overcoat" is given as the acquisition of external, not essential, being. The external and the internal relate in the story as sign and meaning. But the paths from the first to the second are hidden from the heroes of "The Overcoat" because their perception is clouded. See the preceding description of the damaging of vision and taste; to this may be added hearing—cf. "Petrovič was hard of hearing;" Akakij Akakievič spoke, "not trying to hear the words spoken by Petrovič"—and, what is more important, the damaging of speech, hindering communication.

But in these signs themselves, stress is placed on the external plane, on the "material cover." All of Akakij Akakievič's life consists of the senseless

---

21. See F.C. Driessen, *Gogol as a Short Story Writer* (The Hague, 1965), 192. It may be that the episode with the old woman has some connection with the biblical custom of refusing betrothal and the baring of one foot. Deut. 25:7-10.

22. For more detail on the connection between Petrovič and the Apostle Peter in Gogol''s work, see Daniel Rancour-Laferriere, op. cit., 59.

recopying of letters. Although without doubt the theme of dead letters comes from the dictum of the Apostle Paul (II Cor. 3:6-8), the nearest source, it seems, is once again Skovoroda. See "Narkiss":

> "If someone sees the colours of words but cannot read the letters, what do you think? Does he see the letters?"
> Luka: He sees with his eye of the flesh only complete emptiness or the colour of the words, but he cannot understand the characters; he sees only the heel, not the head...
> Drug: 'As a picture is in colours, so a figure is in letters." (I:164)

Even more clearly in "Alfavit, ili bukvar' mira," the heathens called matter being, "as a viewer looks at a painting, concentrating his sight on a colourful smudge, but not his mind on the ethereal image carrying the colours of the picture, or like an illiterate fixing his mortal eye on a piece of paper and the ink of the letters but not his mind on understanding the force concealed beneath the letters. And these words did not even enter their minds: 'The flesh is nothing, the spirit gives life'." (I:426).

All the above-mentioned motifs in Skovoroda grow together in Gogol''s work into a unified complex; it is as though the images in "The Overcoat" were foretold by the Ukrainian mystic's formula: *"Tasteless food, sightless eyes, senseless speech...godless life* is the same as building without measuring, *sewing without a pattern, painting without a sketch*, dancing without rhythm...." (I:428).

The most significant movement in "The Overcoat" consists in the auditory and semantic treatment of his graphic imaging.[23] To the second category belongs the general with his "face wrapped in paper" who is pictured on the lid of Petrovič's tobacco box and who, according to O. Ronen and F. Driessen, is later transformed into the "significant face."[24] In Skovoroda's terms, this interpretation may be considered to mark the passage from "the heel" (the general's coat) to "the head" (face) as a physical, external expression of "the strength concealed

---

23. See "Teatral'nyj raz"ezd": "The inner sense is always apparent later. And the more lively, the more bright the images in which it is enveloped...the more general attention fixes upon the images. Only by putting them together can you find the essence and sense of a work. But not everyone can take these letters apart and put them quickly back together again. And until then, they will *see only the letters*" (V:161). See the analysis of letters in the article by Charles C. Bernheimer, "Cloaking the Self: The Literary Space in Gogol's' 'Overcoat'," PMLA 90 (January 1975):56. Ju.N. Tyn'janov paid attention to the importance of the "graphological gesture" in his work on the film of "The Overcoat." See Ju.G. Tsiv'jan, "Paleogrammy v fil'me 'Shinel'," *Tyn'janovskij sbornik. Vtorye Tyn'janovskie čtenija* (Riga, 1986), 22-3. With reference to the "hidden force" of letters in Skovoroda himself, see I.Z. Serman, "M.V. Lomonosov, G.S. Skovoroda i bor'ba napravlenij v russkoj i ukrainskoj literaturax XVIII v.," *Russkaja literatura XVIII veka i slavjanskie literatury. Issledovanija i materialy* (Moscow and Leningrad, 1963), 76.

24. See F.C. Driessen, op. cit., 206-7; also D. Rancour-Laferriere, op. cit., 188-92; M. Weiskopf, "Poètika peterburgskix povestej Gogolja," *Slavica Hierosolymitana* III (1978):41-2.

beneath the letters," expressing the motif of significance or, more precisely, meaning. However, the semantics of representation turn out to be fatal for Gogol''s hero. Here we come directly to the point of divergence between Gogol' and Skovoroda, who sheds light on the semiotic construction of Gogol''s tale. In order to find the way to the hidden spiritual person, it has to be dissociated from its "rank and name"; its shroud must be torn away—"every kind of fur and leather with which people have thought to cover themselves" (III:169). Nonetheless, because of the plastic vividness of his poetics, Gogol' was able to represent the inner man only by objectifying his psychic condition; he could render the invisible only by means of the visible, the physically tangible. In the process of revelation, a face invariably took on a new material image, the next in a series of masks.[25] Bašmačkin only gradually changes his physical coverings from the *kapot* to the general's overcoat. His wanderings, both earthly and beyond, and equally, the very idea of the "luminous guest" and "the pleasant companion of life," were in fact defined by Gogol''s manner of representation, the dynamics of ceaselessly changing masks, directed toward an unreachable goal. But the hidden, conceptual motive for these is found in Skovoroda's "Narkiss":

> Do not be surprised, my soul! We are all lovers of dust! He who has fallen in love with his own visible flesh cannot help but chase after that which is visible throughout all heaven and earth. But why does he love it? Is it not because he perceives in it *light and pleasantness, life*, beauty, and strength? But isn't it all the same? One can consider an idol alive and confer life on it, but it must die. (I:170)

And further:

> Can dust lying in the grave rise up and admit that there is still the invisible, that there is still spirit? It cannot... (I:177)

As a result, the principle *xalepa ta kaka*—"it is difficult to be evil"—acquires a paradoxical refraction in Gogol''s work: his hero overcomes this difficulty, so to speak.

"Can it be that you are making Christ your caftan and flesh?" asks Skovoroda, offering thereby precisely that way of life which was followed by Akakij before the idea of the overcoat dawned on him. "Reject evil, leave the shadows... Flee idle talk, embrace solitude, love poverty, embrace wisdom, befriend patience, live with humility... This yoke is exceedingly blessed and light. But to live unnaturally in a masquerade—is this not a burden? Yea, it is hard to bear because it is foolish and useless. I say '*xalepa ta kaka*'." (I:277).

Taking this burden upon himself, Akakij chooses evil. However, Čyževs'kyj's

---

25. See the psychological interpretation of Gogol''s "masking" in "The Overcoat" in Charles C. Bernheimer, op. cit., 60.

opinion that the overcoat is a "temptation" for Bašmačkin seems to me not entirely justified. "The Overcoat" was the most precise compromise between the positive socially grounded ideology of the later Gogol' and the particular poetics that bound him to a negative treatment of images. By concretizing abstract ideas, Gogol' was able to embody representations of Christian ethics in his tale to the extent of making them immediately, materially convincing.[26] But in order to do this he had to equate a person with a thing, or, in Skovoroda's terms, to reduce a person to a "heel" and a "robe." The profound, essential reality of the representation was nil, so that the author's lament at the death of his hero—"And Petersburg was left without Akakij Akakievič, as though he had never been in it" (III:169)—repeats the maxim of "Narkiss": "In short, you never were on earth, because the earth, dust, shadow, and nothingness are all one" (I:175).[27]

---

26. According to R.-D. Keil, the sermon on "brotherhood" in the story is inspired by the saying of Jesus, "As you have done it to the least of these my brothers, you have done it to Me," Matt. 25:40. Rolf-Dietrich Keil, "Gogol und Paulus," *Die Welt der Slaven* XXXI, Heft 1 (1986):98. It is worth noting that this call for sympathy in the Gospel is full of graphic images of reality that are picked up by Gogol: "I was naked and you did not clothe Me; I was sick and in prison, and you did not visit Me" (25:43). Note that none of his co-workers visits the dying Bašmačkin—the department custodian comes in only after his death.

27. See my article, "Nos v Kazanskom sobore: O genezise religioznoi temy u Gogolia," *Wiener Slawistischer Almanach* 19 (1987):25-46 for possible traces of Skovoroda in another tale of the St. Petersburg cycle.

Andrej Belyj and Hryhorij Skovoroda

Aleksandr Lavrov

In the epilogue to Andrej Belyj's novel *Petersburg* (1911-13), there is a description of the travels of the hero, Nikolaj Apollonovič Ableuxov, who, following an agonizing spiritual crisis, journeys through North Africa and Palestine and subsequently returns to Russia. The novel ends with the words:

> During the year 1913, Nikolaj Apollonovič continued to spend his days strolling through fields, meadows, and forests, observing the farm work with gloomy indolence. He wore a visored cap and a long-waisted, camel-coloured coat. His boots creaked. A golden, spade-like beard strikingly altered his appearance, and his shock of hair was set off by a distinct streak of pure silver. (This streak had appeared suddenly.) He had experienced an eye illness while in Egypt, and had begun to wear blue-tinted glasses. His voice had hoarsened, and his face had become deeply tanned. His accustomed swiftness of movement had failed. He lived alone. He did not invite anyone to visit him and did not go out to others. He was often seen in church. People reported that he had taken to reading the philosopher Skovoroda. His parents had died.[1]

It is clear that the allusion to Skovoroda in the last lines of the novel, dedicated to the fate of the main, authorial hero, is very important to the understanding of *Petersburg*. All the same, Belyj, usually so generous in specifying the role played by one thinker or another in his own creative development, did not render any elaborate judgement about Hryhorij Skovoroda.

Belyj became acquainted with the personality and world-view of the Ukrainian

---

1. A. Belyj, *Peterburg. Roman v vos'mi glavax s prologom i èpilogom* (Petrograd, 1916), 276 (third pagination).

philosopher thanks to V.F. Èrn's monographic work on Skovoroda.[2] The author of the book, Vladimir Francevič Èrn (1881-1917), was a Russian religious philosopher, a follower of the Slavophiles and of Vladimir Solov'ev. Belyj had been very familiar with Èrn's work from his youth, and was quite sympathetic to the direction of Èrn's thought.[3] Èrn's work appeared at the end of 1912, when a large portion of Belyj's novel had already been written, but without a doubt, Belyj already had some notion of Skovoroda's personality and Èrn's interpretation of it. Èrn's article, "The Russian Socrates," his first work on Skovoroda, appeared as early as 1908 and bore witness to the admiration he felt for the philosopher, who "with his whole life served some great liturgy and knew the joys of ecstasy and the supreme rapture of the spirit."[4] In 1911 Èrn published two lengthy articles on Skovoroda[5] that subsequently formed the basis of his monograph. Skovoroda's name also figured in Èrn's article "On the Logos: Russian Philosophy and Scholarship," with which Belyj polemicized.[6]

In his monograph on Skovoroda, Èrn developed the basic premise of his

---

2. V. Èrn, *Grigorij Savvič Skovoroda: Žizn' i učenie* (Moscow: Put', 1912). (Reference to this edition will be made later in the text by indicating the page numbers in parenthesis). For evidence of this knowledge, see A. Belyj, "Vospominanija o Bloke," *Èpopeja*, no. 2 (1922):156; A. Belyj, *Meždu dvux revoljucij* (Leningrad, 1934), 17, 305. There is no evidence that Belyj was acquainted with Skovoroda's works (if one does not take into account the extensive and numerous quotations from them in Èrn's monograph).
3. See A. Belyj, *Načalo veka* (Moscow and Leningrad, 1933), 270-75, 305, 452-4.
4. V. Èrn, "Russkij Sokrat," *Severnoe sijanie*, no. 1 (November 1908):64. There is reason to believe that Belyj knew of this issue of the journal, which also included articles by Belyj's friends V.V. Vladimirov and G.A. Račinskij, as well as a series of other materials of Symbolist content. The editor of the journal was A.M. Pocco (who also later became an anthroposophist), the husband of N.A. Turgeneva (sister of A.A. Turgeneva, Belyj's first wife), to whom Belyj dedicated several poems in the collection *Zvezda*.
5. V. Èrn, "Žizn' iličnost' Grigorija Savviča Skovorody," *Voprosy filosofii i psixologii*, Book 107, no. 2 (March-April 1911):126-66; V. Èrn, "Očerk teoretičeskoj filosofii G.S. Skovorody," *Voprosy filosofii i psixologii*, Book 110, no. 5 (November-December 1911):645-80.
6. Èrn's article "Nečto o Logose, russkoj filosofii i naučnosti" (*Moskovskij eženedel'nik*, nos. 29-32, 24 July - 14 August 1910) was written apropos of the new philosophical journal *Logos*, the organ of the neo-Kantians, and presented a sharp rebuke to "philosophical goods of recent manufacture." It defends the traditions of Russian religious philosophy. Belyj, who in 1910 still had a lively interest in Kant and his followers, and who in addition to this was close to the editors of *Logos*, came to the defence of the philosophical journal with his article "Neoslavjanofil'stvo i zapadničestvo v sovremennoj russkoj filosofskoj mysli" (*Utro Rossii*, no. 274, 15 October 1910). "The fact that Russian philosophical thought is connected to Western tradition does not at all mean that Russian thought is a slave to foreign forms," objected Belyj, emphasizing at the same time that Èrn, who opposed "pure philosophy," confused problems of philosophy and religion. Belyj's article, which seems partly to represent a relapse into the mood prevailing in his consciousness in 1904-8, points to the distance between him and the extreme neo-Slavophile tendencies represented by Èrn. In the republished version of his article, Èrn answered some of Belyj's critical remarks (V. Èrn, "Bor'ba za Logos," *Opyty filosofskie i kritičeskie* [Moscow, 1911], 77-8, 90-91).

philosophy, namely, the idea of the crisis of European thought, which had chosen the path of rationalism, "in essence, *a denial of Nature as the Essential*" and a transformation of nature into "an inanimate *mechanism*" (p. 14). In contrast, he considered the tendencies of Russian religio-philosophical thought fruitful, for they were based on "the logic of Eastern Christian speculation" (p. 22).[7] According to Ėrn, Skovoroda was the precursor of this philosophical tradition:

> Skovoroda is the natural, national element that facilitates the germination of the godly seed of Logos, which fertilizes our national soul (p. 332). The birth of philosophical reason in Russia originates in the person of Skovoroda, and through these first murmurings, new unfamiliar notes sound in a new Europe... Skovoroda made the first furrow with a heavenly plough; for the first time the wild and free Russian black soil is turned. And in this black soil, in the earthy, national nature of Skovoroda, we see with surprise the basic features that characterized all subsequent Russian thought. (p. 333)

It should be emphasized that the interpretation of Skovoroda's personality and works developed by Ėrn is of a rather arbitrary character. Only Ėrn's like-minded contemporaries accepted his book.[8] Others concluded, not without justification, that Ėrn made Skovoroda fit his conception by stretching interpretations in a manner incompatible with objective research. The neo-Kantian philosopher B.V. Jakovenko noted Ėrn's "methodological subjectivism."[9] D.V. Filosofov judged him even more concretely:

> Mr. Ėrn's book is thoroughly tendentious. It is interesting for a determination of the *Weltanschauung* of Mr. Ėrn himself. He is a representative of contemporary Orthodox theological thought, but as far as providing an unbiased study of Skovoroda or acquainting us with his unclear and tongue-tied philosophy, the book is practically worthless. Ėrn obscured the modest Skovoroda with his own broad shadow."[10]

---

7. According to Ėrn's definition, "λογος is a slogan calling upon philosophy to turn away from scholasticism and abstractness and to return to *life*, not mere schemata of life, but on the contrary to *heed it*; to become an inspired and sensitive interpreter of its divine *meaning*, its hidden joy, its great tasks" (V. Ėrn, "Bor'ba za Logos," viii).
8. Thus, S.N. Durylin wrote in a review of Ėrn's book: "This book is essential for anyone who is interested in Skovoroda, not only because it is beautifully written and pervaded by a special love for the thinker herein portrayed and his thoughts, but also because Skovoroda's language is difficult to understand without the help of a dictionary, and only by first becoming acquainted through Ėrn's exposition is it possible to get to know Skovoroda's works well" (*Put'*, no. 2 [1913]:64).
9. B. Jakovenko, "Novaja kniga o Skovorode," *Russkie vedomosti*, no. 42, 20 February 1913. Jakovenko especially objected to Ėrn's assertion that the line of philosophical succession derived from Skovoroda: "If some later Russian thinkers leaned toward the same ideas as Skovoroda, this was derived not from him, but from the direct study of the Fathers of the Church. Therefore, there can be no question of any genuine succession constituting a line of independent Russian philosophy."
10. D. Filosofov, "G. S. Skovoroda," *Reč*, no. 135, 20 May 1913.

A few years later, upon returning to Ėrn's research, G.G. Špet justly noted:

> The book is an inflated literary work, and not historico-philosophical research. Written with great uplifting feeling and inspiration, this book provides an excellent expression of the world-view of the author himself, but as far as Skovoroda is concerned, it is a panegyrical song in which the latter is revealed to the reader as the author would like the first Russian philosopher to have been, but not as Skovoroda appeared in reality.[11]

Thus, Belyj's view of Skovoroda may have been formed less by historical reality than by the myth of the "first Russian philosopher" created by Ėrn.

Ėrn's ideas on Russia's "unique path" were similar in many ways to those formulated by Belyj with graphic clarity in 1911, at the time of his Eastern travels (in Tunisia, Egypt, and Palestine). Belyj's own travel impressions and experiences were reflected in an extremely direct manner in the short description of the wanderings of the hero of *Petersburg* referred to above.[12] Belyj's attitude at the time of his travels and after his return to Russia in the summer of 1911 (which he spent in Boholjuby in Volhynia) was marked by a feeling of rupture in the pattern of his life, by a sharp foreboding of the advent of purifying, fundamental changes, and by a groping, intuitive search for new spiritual stimuli. "The dawn promises many things: I feel the approach of great events...," Belyj declared at this time.[13] Belyj reminisced about the summer of 1911: "In my poems of that time there was an expectation of something great, something very close to the soul"; "the general impression of the summer was of thundering silence."[14] This feeling of approaching change was related in Belyj's mind to

---

11. G. Špet, *Očerk razvitija russkoj filosofii. Pervaja čast'* (St. Petersburg, 1922), 70. Let it also be noted that M.F. Sumcov, the Ukrainian folklorist and literary specialist, found the fundamental shortcoming of Ėrn's book to be the author's ignorance of the culture of the people from which Skovoroda emerged. He considered unfounded the designation of Skovoroda as the "first Russian philosopher" and underlined the inseparable tie between Skovoroda and Ukrainian theologians of the seventeenth century (Lazar Baranovyč, Ioanikij Galjatovs'kyj, and others). He rejected the analogies drawn by Ėrn between Skovoroda and the latest Russian thinkers (Mykola Sumcov, "Skovoroda i Ern," *Literaturno-naukovyj vistnyk* 69 [1918], 1:41-9).

12. Belyj wrote the epilogue to *Petersburg* in Berlin in November 1913 (A. Belyj, "Material k biografii [intimnyj]...," Central'nyj gosudarstvennyj arxiv literatury i iskusstva SSSR [CGALI], f. 53, op. 2, ed. xr. 3, 1. 680-6—69). There, however, he describes his frame of mind in 1911 as inviolable by the new spiritual aspirations. Belyj saw the end of the novel as the "*remnants* of plans that had been mechanically concluded in *1912* and *1913*: *Petersburg* ends *mechanically*" (a letter of Belyj's to R.V. Ivanov-Razumnik dated 1-3 March 1927: CGALI, f. 1782, op. 1, ed. xr. 18).

13. Letter to M.K. Morozova (1911), Otdel rukopisej Gosudarstvennoj biblioteki SSSR im. Lenina [GBL], f. 171, kart. 24, ed. xr. 16.

14. A. Belyj, "Vospominanija o Bloke," *Èpopeja*, no. 4 (1923):208, 210. The poems referred to are: "Šut," "I opjat', i opjat', i opjat'...," "Golos prošlogo," and "Blizkoj" (A. Belyj, *Korolevna i rycari. Skazki* (St. Petersburg, 1919), 18-45. Compare Belyj's admission in a letter to A. Blok (June 1911,

a particular *credo* of "attachment to the soil," a belief in the redeeming quality of the "non-European" path; these were views that Belyj adopted repeatedly at various stages of his development, and that he felt with special force in 1911 in Palestine and upon his return to Russia. (Compare this with Nikolaj Apollonovič's visit to Nazareth in the epilogue of *Petersburg*.) The letters he wrote from Jerusalem in April 1911 contain decisive assertions:

> I am returning ten times more Russian; five months of relations with the Europeans, with these walking butchers of life, have angered me greatly: we, thank God, are Russians and not Europeans; we must hold high our non-Europeanness.[15]

In another letter, drawing the same conclusion ("I am returning to Russia ten times more *Russian*"), Belyj stated:

> The idea of "European culture" was thought up by Russians; in the West there are civilizations; there is *no* word for Western *culture* as we understand it; this kind of unitary culture in rudimentary form exists only in Russia... For a month now everything in me has been rebelling at the word "*Europe.*" Our pride lies in the fact that we are *not Europe*, or that we alone constitute the *authentic Europe*, etc.[16]

It follows that Belyj found a response to his mood in Ėrn's Slavophile doctrine and in his conception of Russian philosophical thought as formulated in the book on Skovoroda. The fact that Belyj perceived Skovoroda as figuring centrally in this question is also confirmed by the nature of his revisions to the poem "The Tempter" (1908), which reflected the period during which he had studied Kant's philosophy.[17] Belyj experienced its influence primarily in the years 1904-8. The subsequent years (1909-12) are characterized by a movement "away from Kant toward a search for *mystery* in a new fashion, as a *path of life*, by a striving to realize *the concrete spiritual content of life*."[18] This "path of life" was found in 1912 in the anthroposophy of Rudolph Steiner, but one of the signposts on this path was the feeling of "attachment to the soil" (*počvennik*), also recorded in the epilogue to *Petersburg*. Demonstrating his transcendence of

---

Boholjuby): "For the last two years, 1910-1911, I have had the presentiment that the forest is thinning out (there are spaces between the trees, dawn glimmers beyond the denseness in the distance), but *the main thing—the roar of the sea— is ahead* (a sure sign of the end of the forest)" (A. Blok and A. Belyj, *Perepiska* [Moscow, 1940], 263). On the feeling of the "path" in Belyj, see D.E. Maksimov, "Ideja puti v poėtičeskom soznanii Al. Bloka," *Blokovskij sbornik* (Tartu, 1972), II:44-6.

15. Letter to A.M. Kozebatkin of 12 April 1911, CGALI, f. 53, op. 3, ed. xr. 11.
16. Letter to M.K. Morozova ("Ierusalim. Xristovo Voskresen'e"), GBL, f. 171, kart. 24, ed. xr. Ib.
17. A. Belyj, *Urna. Stixotvorenija* (Moscow, 1909), 70-73.
18. From Belyj's letter of 1-3 March 1927, CGALI, f. 1782, op. 1, ed. xr. 18.

Kantianism, Belyj included the following lines in a new variant of his poem, "The Tempter" (1913-14):

> Leave me...in this volume
> We will all drown without a trace!...
> Don't speak to me of Kant!!
> What is Kant? Here...is...Skovoroda.
>
> A Russian philosopher, and not a German!!![19]

Like the hero of the poem "The Tempter," Nikolaj Apollonovič Ableuxov undergoes an analogous development from an intensive study of Kant (in the main part of the novel) to that of the "Russian philosopher" Skovoroda. Concerning the conclusion of *Petersburg*, Vjačeslav Ivanov (a close friend of Èrn's) noted in his article, "The Inspiration of Horror," "The follower of Kant...displayed an inclination first to ancient Egyptian mysticism and then to contemporary Orthodox mysticism,"[20] thereby identifying the reading of Skovoroda with an interest in contemporary religious searchings, Èrn's Slavophile-Orthodox doctrine in particular.

The last lines of *Petersburg* return in many ways to the fundamental motif of Belyj's previous novel, *The Silver Dove* (1909), on the inevitable return of Russia's prodigal sons, raised on "Western," "foreign words," to the native meadow path. "There will be, there will be an increase in the numbers of those fleeing to the fields!"[21] In this, Nikolaj Apollonovič clearly echoes Dar'jal'skij, the hero of *The Silver Dove*. Taking this parallel into account, one can see a probable supplementary meaning in the reference to Skovoroda in the epilogue to *Petersburg*. It is known that certain traits of V.S. Solov'ev, the Symbolist poet

---

19. A. Belyj, *Stixotvorenija i poemy* (Moscow and Leningrad: Biblioteka poèta, bol'šaja serija, 1966), 609-10. Compare the new stanza of the poem "Wisdom," "I harken to the speeches, enveloped by darkness..." (1908), which completes the poem in the latest revised edition.

> Once again scholar quarrels with scholar:
> In the fog of lofty questions
> We—yes, will vanish without a trace...
> Yes, gentlemen: What is Kant? The greatest
> Philosopher is Skovoroda...

(A. Belyj, *Stixotvorenija* [Berlin, St. Petersburg and Moscow, 1923]), 304. The element of irony contained in these lines by no means detracts from their conceptual meaning. We remember that even in the "(Second Dramatic) Symphony" Belyj presented his most valuable ideas in a semi-parodic manner. A similar semi-ironic reference to Skovoroda exists in an early edition of *Petersburg* (1911): "...It was in the process of their spontaneous birth that Apollon Apollonovič's thoughts were so extremely original; had he written them down at the moment of conception, we would be dealing with a second sage, a Skovoroda, our national philosopher [...]" (A. Belyj, *Peterburg* ["Nekrasovskaja" redakcija], CGALI, f. 53, op. 1, ed. xr. 18).

20. Vjačeslav Ivanov, *Rodnoe i vselenskoe* (Moscow, 1917), ed. G.A. Leman and S.I. Saxarov, 98.

21. A. Belyj, *Serebrjanyj golub'* (Moscow, 1910), 229.

and Belyj's closest friend, are reflected in the character of Dar'jal'skij. Solov'ev was, on his mother's side, a descendant of Myxajlo Ivanovyč Kovalins'kyj, the favourite pupil and friend of Skovoroda, who wrote "The Life of Hryhorij Skovoroda,"[22] the basic source of information on the philosopher's mode of life and personality, to which Èrn, too, frequently turned in his research. Having spent many summers at Didova (the estate of A.G. Kovalins'ka, S.M. Solov'ev's grandmother), Belyj knew about this connection. In his memoirs he referred to Kovalins'kyj as Solov'ev's ancestor and Skovoroda's pupil.[23] To the extent that *Petersburg* was conceived as the second part of a trilogy that began with *The Silver Dove*, and Dar'jal'skij and Nikolaj Apollonovič were particularly authorial heroes, the existence of this connection seems obvious.[24]

Analyzing Skovoroda's philosophy in detail in his book, Èrn concentrated his attention on a number of aspects that undoubtedly attracted Belyj's particular sympathy. He diligently investigated the "symbolism" of Skovoroda's ideology, which could be traced to the Bible, "a symbolic world" (pp. 222-46). He showed that the idea of the world's feminine essence (in Èrn's words, "the deepest foundation of a new, purely Russian *metaphysics*"), which subsequently became central to the philosophical system of Vladimir Solov'ev (p. 341), to which Belyj felt so partial, was close to Skovoroda as well.[25] The integrity of Skovoroda's

22. See *Sočinenija Grigorija Savviča Skovorody*, collected and edited by D.I. Bahalij (Xarkiv, 1894), [otd. I], 1-40.
23. A. Belyj, *Meždu dvux revoljucij*, 17. S.M. Solov'ev also wrote about Kovalins'kyj as his ancestor and Skovoroda's friend in his reminiscences about his mother, "Ol'ga Mixajlovna Solov'eva" (1927) (CGALI, f. 475, op. 1, ed. xr. 16, 1. 2).
24. Skovoroda's high reputation among sectarians serves as a curious parallel to the understanding of his image in connection with *The Silver Dove* (in the theme of the hero-intellectual's rapprochement with the populist mystical sect, the "Doves"); in particular, to the *Molokans* ("milk drinkers"), Skovoroda's name "is almost Apostolic" (F.V. Livanov, *Raskol'niki i ostrožniki* (St. Petersburg, 1870), II:288-99; compare Orest Novickij, *Duxoborcy, ix istorija i veroučenie* (Kyiv, 1882), 178-9. P.N. Miljukov, proceeding on the conviction that "Skovoroda was in his soul a sectarian," proves that the ideas preached by the Katerynoslav Doukhobors ("spirit-wrestlers") were identical with Skovoroda's theories (P. Miljukov, *Očerki po istorii russkoj kul'tury* [St. Petersburg, 1899], part 2, 109-13). B.D. Bonč-Bruevič also considered Skovoroda the forefather of the "spiritual Christians" (see *Sobranie sočinenij G.S. Skovorody*, I, with remarks and comments by V. Bonč-Bruevič [St. Petersburg, 1912]). Incidentally, the "fanatical Orthodox" Èrn did not share this view of Skovoroda.
25. In general, Èrn traced the deep internal kinship between the philosophical views of Solov'ev and Skovoroda. In the article "On Logos, Russian Philosophy, and Skovoroda," which was well known to Belyj, he wrote: "The amazingly integral *Weltanschauung* of the 'Russian Socrates,' G.S. Skovoroda, as well as the all-embracing, universal *Weltanschauung* of the 'Russian Plato,' V.S. Solov'ev, are both imbued with a fundamental ontologism" (V. Èrn, "Bor'ba za Logos," 93). Compare the analogous parallel in the speech by Professor I.A. Sikorskij, "The Moral Significance of Vladimir Solov'ev": "Both Solov'ev and Skovoroda have common concerns—those of self-cognizance. Both strive to awaken in people higher feelings, elevated moral aspirations. [...] Both philosophers were distinguished by an ascetic mode of life, but their asceticism did not prevent them

life and creative path, the absence of conflict between the teaching and ideal of one's comportment in life and its practical implementation were of great importance to Belyj, who always keenly experienced the problem of "life's pathway" and strove toward "life creativity." Èrn wrote:

> He who begins to study the life and teachings of Skovoroda will indeed be struck by the exceptional integrity of his nature, the consummate *unity* of his spiritual make-up. His life is the best illustration of his philosophy, and his philosophy is a wonderful speculative commentary on his life. Skovoroda graphically unites within himself a profound theoretical wisdom with its practical realization in life. He is organic, as people were in antiquity. He lives as he thinks, and thinks as he lives.[26]

Furthermore, Skovoroda's life was esteemed a more meaningful phenomenon than his philosophical legacy. "G.S. Skovoroda, full of the sacred fires of theomachy, is far more significant and far greater than his deeply original and remarkable philosophical creations," wrote Èrn.[27] Skovoroda's attempt to "imitate Christ" was seen as a great moral lesson. Although he could have been very successful in the world, the 44-year-old Skovoroda became a homeless wanderer, "a beggarly bearer of popular wisdom" (p. 137), roaming with a staff and a Bible through Ukraine and Russia until the last day of his life.

> In a simple peasant's cloak, with a hood and sack over his shoulder, with a reed flute in his belt and a gnarled stick in his hands, Skovoroda walked through the villages and educated the people in a language understood by them...[28]

The comparison made by Èrn between L.N. Tolstoj's departure prior to his death and Skovoroda's many years of wandering had an unquestionable significance for Belyj (pp. 138-9). Belyj experienced Tolstoj's departure as a "clap of thunder," a great "world" event.[29] He wrote:

> A brilliant artist of the written word has proved to be a brilliant author of personal life.... With his departure and death somewhere in the Russian fields

---

from having a joyous outlook on life, something they considered essential to maintain in themselves and in others" (*Voprosy nervno-psixičeskoj mediciny* 4 [1901], 1:6).

26. V. Èrn, "Žizn' i ličnost' Grigorija Savviča Skovorody," *Voprosy filosofii i psixologii* 107, no. 2 (March-April 1911):126. It is characteristic that as late as the 1890s Skovoroda's universality was viewed as a sign of the "primitive phase of intellectual life," in which the split between religion and philosophy had not yet occurred. (B. Nikol'skij, "Ukrainskij Sokrat," *Istoričeskij vestnik* 60, no. 4 [1895]:215-22.) At the beginning of the twentieth century, Symbolists considered Skovoroda's "syncretism" a model to be emulated.

27. V. Èrn, "Bor'ba za Logos," 95. Cf. "Skovoroda was a sage, a teacher of life, and not a scholar striving to explain the phenomena of the external and internal world" (E. Radov, *Očerk istorii russkoj filosofii* (St. Petersburg, 1920), 10.

28. V. Èrn, "Russkij Sokrat," *Severnoe sijanie*, no. 1 (1908):65.

29. See A. Belyj, "Vospominanija o Bloke," *Èpopeja*, no. 4 (1923):185.

he illuminated these poor Russian fields.... His departure and death are his best sermon, his best work of art, the best action of his life. Life, preaching, and creative work were combined in one gesture, in one moment.[30]

Èrn, however, preferred Skovoroda's example, for the latter combined "life, preaching, and creative work" not in the face of death, but at the dawn of his life, and then, in the course of subsequent decades, he lived out this creative ideal.

It is understandable that Skovoroda was one of Tolstoj's favourite thinkers.[31] Connected with Tolstoj were A.M. Dobroljubov and L.D. Semenov,[32] young Symbolist poets who shared strikingly similar fates; both broke irrevocably with their milieu and went to the people, subsequently putting into practice their moral and religious ideals and ideas of holiness. For Tolstoj, his departure was a natural solution to the tormenting conflict between preaching and his daily mode of existence, and Dobroljubov's vital choice was for him, in this sense, an obvious example. "It is not possible to preach the teaching of good while living in conflict with this teaching, as I do," wrote Tolstoj in his diary. "The only means of proving that this teaching brings good is to live according to it, as Dobroljubov does."[33] The "rebirth" of both Symbolists was an important fact for Belyj as well (he was acquainted with Dobroljubov and with the legends about him that existed among the Symbolists, and was even friendly with Semenov at one time). Thus, Skovoroda's fate seemed analogous to the quest of many at the

---

30. A. Belyj, "Lev Tolstoj," *Russkaja mysl'*, no. 1 (1911):otd. II, 93-4.
31. The critic A.A. Izmajlov cites Tolstoj's words on Skovoroda: "Much of his *Weltanschauung* is so surprisingly close to mine! I just recently reread his works. I would like to write about him. And I will do so. His biography, perhaps, is even better than his writings. But how good his writings are, too!..." (A. Izmajlov, "Dve legendy, Lev Tolstoj i Grigorij Skovoroda," *Russkoe slovo*, no. 253, 3 November 1910). Indeed, there were many common aspects in Tolstoy's and Skovoroda's positions on life: the philosophy of personal self-perfection, the exaltation of the simplicity of life close to nature, of poverty, of useful labour, etc. (See D.I. Bagalej, "G.S. Skovoroda i L.N. Tolstoj. Istoričeskaja parallel'," *Pamjati L.N. Tolstogo. Sbornik rečej* [Xarkiv, 1911], 44-51). Tolstoj's pupil N.N. Gusev wrote a short popular book on Skovoroda in which he presented an outline of Skovoroda's life and work and an exposition of "selected thoughts" of his that are strikingly analogous with Tolstoj's theory (N.N. Gusev, *Narodnyj ukrainskij mudrec Grigorij Savvič Skovoroda* [Moscow, 1906]). On the basis of this book, Tolstoj prepared an essay about Skovoroda (L.N. Tolstoj, *Polnoe sobranie sočinenij* [Moscow, 1956], 40:406-12, 510-11), and included Skovoroda's "selected thoughts" in his philosophical-religious works "Na každyj den'" (1906-10) and "Put' žizni" (1910), which constitute a collection of dicta on the most important questions of life.
32. See N.N. Gusev's comments in L.N. Tolstoj, *Polnoe sobranie sočinenij* (Moscow, 1937), 56:436-7, 486-8; V.A. Sapogov, "Lev Tolstoj i Leonid Semenov," *Učenye zapiski*, issue 20. Filologičeskaja serija (Kostroma, 1970):111-28.
33. Entry of 20 July 1907: L.N. Tolstoj, *Polnoe sobranie sočinenij*, 56:47, compare pp. 282-3.

beginning of the twentieth century.[34] For Tolstoj, as well as for the Symbolists, it appeared as the prototype of simplifying and religiously creative aspirations, a yearning for "real life" and "true" culture, in opposition to European "civilization."[35] In this respect the image of Skovoroda assumed a timely and important meaning for Belyj as well.

According to the testimony of N. Valentinov in his memoirs, the words of Skovoroda in Ėrn's book that apparently most attracted Belyj were: "I want no new sciences other than Christ's wisdom, in which the soul is sweet."[36] These words are from the twelfth song of Skovoroda's "Garden of Divine Songs," cited by Ėrn (p. 101). The theme of the song is praise of life in harmony with nature, as opposed to life in cities, which "leads to bitter bondage."

> I will not enter the wealthy city. I will live in the fields,
> I will while away my years where time flows gently.
> O oak grove! O verdure! O native mother mine!
> In you life is joyous, in you there is peace and silence![37]

These lines, too, could not help but elicit a sympathetic response from Belyj, who fully shared similar anti-urban sentiments. It is sufficient to refer to verses from the collection "Ashes," the hero of which flees the city in order to surrender himself to the "solemn rite of the fields":

> I, an exile, am forsaking you—
> You will not bind my freedom.
> I flee—a bent, pale wanderer—

---

34. It is characteristic that various authors trace both Skovoroda's and Dobroljubov's conduct to one model—St. Francis of Assisi. Ėrn cites this parallel (p. 146); compare S.N. Durylin's opinion of Skovoroda: "An external wanderer, he resurrected in many ways in eighteenth-century Ukraine traits of St. Francis of Assisi" (*Put'*, no. 2 [1913]:64). At the same time Merežkovskij, writing in his article "Revoljucija i religija" about his meeting with Dobroljubov, concludes: "I did not doubt that I was seeing before me a saint. [...] In fact, in five centuries of Christianity, what third person was there between these two—St. Francis of Assisi and Aleksandr Dobroljubov? The one is illustrious, the other unknown, but what difference does this make in the sight of God? L. Tolstoj talked, but did not practice what he preached. [...] But a poor, comical decadent, a feeble child did that which titans were unable to do" (D.S. Merežkovskij, *Ne mir, no meč. K buduščej kritike Xristianstva*, ed. M.V. Pirožkov (St. Petersburg, 1908), 104.
35. Compare G. Špet, "Očerk razvitija russkoj filosofii. Pervaja čast'," no. 69:82-4.
36. N. Valentinov, *Dva goda s simvolistami* (Stanford, 1969), 194. The quotation is cited inaccurately; in the 1894 edition of Skovoroda, which was used by Ėrn, there is a misprint: *duša* instead of *duma*. In the contemporary corrected edition: *Ne xoču i nauk novyx, krome zdravago uma,/ Krome umnostej Xristovyx, v koix sladostna duma.* (I want no new sciences other than good sense,/ Other than Christ's wisdom, in which thought is sweet.) Hryhorij Skovoroda, *Povne zibrannja tvoriv u dvox tomax* (Kyiv, 1973), 1:70.
37. Ibid., 69. In the copy of the 1894 edition of Skovoroda's works that Ėrn used (collection of N.V. Kotreleva, Moscow), the lines from the twelfth song quoted here and above are marked off (pp. 267-8).

> Between sheaves of golden grain....
>
> Touch me, tender flower.
> Drop, drop your crystal dew!
> I will rest with soul rebellious,
> A soul that has suffered much.[38]

The open-ended finale of the novel *Petersburg*, in which Nikolaj Apollonovič has been spiritually cured and has returned to "sources," stands in striking contrast to the body of the novel, which depicts a fantastic, spectral city, the focus of darkness, horror, and the delirium of a sick consciousness.[39] The hero has come to see Skovoroda as the hypostasis of the teacher, related to the "prophet of the fields" of "Ashes."

Finally, Belyj was sympathetic to Skovoroda's theme of self-knowledge, spiritual struggle, and the yawning "caves of the heart," examined in detail by Èrn (pp. 84-5). Skovoroda's suffering spirit, discovering its own "chaotic disorder," thirsted for resurrection; "He seeks to raise his own mortality to the cross in order to be healed *there*" (pp. 88-9):

> Crucify my body, nail it to the cross;
> Let me be dead without, but risen within.
> Let my outer self dry out,
> And my new self bloom within; behold life-giving death![40]

Having gone through "an internal Golgotha," Skovoroda experienced a turn-about "from darkness to light": "the destructive forces of nature...are transformed into beneficial, natural forces. Spiritual storms and tempests having passed and ended, peace and azure skies were opened in Skovoroda's soul" (p. 90). Èrn concentrated his attention on the idea of "co-crucifixion" in Skovoroda, which was intimately close to Belyj. Furthermore, in the spiritual struggles of Skovoroda, with which Belyj empathizes, there are features common to the entire artistic system of *Petersburg*. The recreation of chaos that undividedly rules the spiritual world of the heroes is one of the problems of the main part of the novel. Only in the epilogue, having gone through his own "internal Golgotha," does Nikolaj Apollonovič find enlightenment and harmony. And this condensation of Skovoroda's image again proves to be a symbol of positive values, to the realization of which Belyj brings his hero.

---

38. A. Belyj, *Pepel* (St. Petersburg, 1909), 223-4.
39. In this aspect the analogy with A.M. Dobroljubov can again be drawn. In the excerpt "*Ja vernus' k vam, polja i dorogi rodnye...*" (I will return to you, my native fields and roads..."), he declares to the city: "*Smert'ju dyšut tvoj mrak i krasa tvoix sten*" (Your darkness and the beauty of your walls exude death") and extols life "*sred' lesov v prostote i svobode*" (amid the forests in simplicity and freedom). A. Dobroljubov, *Iz knigi nevidimoj* (Moscow, 1905), 64-5.
40. Hryhorij Skovoroda, *Povne zibrannja tvoriv u dvox tomax*, 1:65.

At the time *Petersburg* was written, Skovoroda's image in Russian literature already had a certain history. Skovoroda appeared as the prototype of the "sage" Ivan in Narežnyj's novel *A Russian Gil Blas* (1814);[41] "the wanderer Grigorij Savvič" became the principal hero of I.I. Sreznevskij's *povest'* "Major, major!"[42] N.S. Leskov ("The Rabbit's Penalty")[43] and Belyj's contemporaries V.I. Narbut and A.I. Tinjakov skilfully made use of epigraphs from Skovoroda.[44] Against this background, the image of Skovoroda with which Belyj concluded his novel stands out by virtue of its remarkable, multi-layered significance; by its deep, internal ties with the creative searchings of the author; and by its relevance to the urgent problems of social thought at the beginning of the twentieth century.[45]

Translated by Esther Rider

---

41. V.T. Narežnyj, *Izbrannye sočinenija v dvux tomax* (Moscow, 1956), 1:524-59.
42. *Moskovskij nabljudatel'*, 1836, part VI:205-38, 435-68, 721-36.
43. See O.B. Ankudinova, "Leskov i Skovoroda" (on the question of the moral significance of Leskov's short story "Zajačij remiz"), *Voprosy russkoj literatury* (L'viv, 1973), 1 (21):71-7.
44. Vladimir Narbut, *Alliluija. Stixi* (St. Petersburg, 1912), 40, 44. (Epigraphs precede the verses that include Ukrainian realia, together with naturalistic depictions of stagnant life; A. Tinjakov, *Treugol'nik. Vtoraja kniga stixov* [Petersburg, 1922], 63).
45. Compare B.V. Mixajlovskij, "O romane Andreja Belogo 'Peterburg'" in *Izbrannye stat'i o literature i iskusstve* (Moscow, 1969), 455.

Textological Notes on Skovoroda's *Alphabet*

Bohdan Strumiński

When V. Bonč-Bruevič was publishing Hryhorij Skovoroda's programmatic *Discourse called Alphabet, or the World's Primer* (Разговор, называемый Алфавит, или Букварь Мира) in 1912, he had only one manuscript at his disposal, Muz. 605/3 from the Kyiv Divinity Academy (now 326 L of the Saltykov-Ščedrin State Public Library in St. Petersburg), dated by watermarks to 1788, formerly the property of Archbishop Filaret of Černihiv (1805-66). He plainly said, "We are printing this manuscript according to the only extant copy."[1] A little later, another manuscript became known—f. 86, no. 18, of the Institute of Literature, Academy of Sciences in Kyiv—originating from the late eighteenth century and once owned by I. Ljubyc'kyj. When the Ukrainian Academy of Sciences embarked on a complete new edition of Skovoroda's oeuvre after World War II to supersede the old, prerevolutionary editions, which were "textologically imperfect,"[2] the edition's collaborators discovered three more manuscripts, including Skovoroda's autograph, written in 1775 (Ščukin collection 91/193, A 394, G 4/85, State Historical Museum in Moscow). The other, secondary, manuscripts were: F. 86, no. 9, with watermarks of 1785-6, which belonged to Skovoroda's friend S. Djatlov (Institute of Literature, Academy of Sciences in Kyiv), and f. 1613, no. 2, dating from the first half of the nineteenth century (Central State Archives of Literature and the Arts in Moscow). In 1973 the Academy of Sciences in Kyiv produced another complete

---

1. "Sobranie sočinenij G.S. Skovorody," vol. I, ed. by V. Bonč-Bruevič, *Materialy k istorii i izučeniju russkogo sektantstva i staroobrjadčestva* (St. Petersburg, 1912), 5:319.
2. Hryhorij Skovoroda, *Tvory v dvox tomax* (Kyiv, 1961), I:vi.

edition of Skovoroda with "a number of corrections and improvements in precision" in comparison with the 1961 edition. This time the editors signalled the existence of another secondary manuscript of the *Alphabet,* written between 1785 and 1800 and preserved at Harvard. They also reported that its microfilm had been secured for the Saltykov-Ščedrin Library in Leningrad in 1960.[3]

In view of such a wealth of manuscripts for Skovoroda's *Alphabet* and the existence of two critical editions based on an autograph, it might seem that secondary manuscripts, such as Harvard's Kilgour M.S. Russia 22, do not deserve any particular attention. But acquaintance with the Harvard copy and a comparison of it with the two critical editions convinces one that the study of secondary copies may be of use in two ways: 1) as a check on the reliability of critical editions based on autographs or the best copies, and 2) as a demonstration of the later textological-linguistic story of the original.

The Harvard copy evidently once belonged to Jevstafij Fedorovyč Zvirjaka, probably a relative of Skovoroda's cousin, Justyn Zvirjaka. His name is written on leaf 1v (verso). Although a pencil note in pre-1917 Russian orthography on the cover says, "Hryhorij Savyč Skovoroda's own handwriting (unpublished)," the text was actually written by two other persons, one imitating Skovoroda's post-1785 orthography (without jers), and the other using the normal Slavonic-Rhossic spelling system. The manuscript was donated to Harvard's Houghton Library on 9 January 1953 by Bayard L. Kilgour, Jr., who bought many archival treasures from the Soviet authorities in 1926.

The comparison of the Zvirjaka text (hereafter Z.) with the two academic autograph-based editions (hereafter abbreviated as B. and Š., after the names of their editors-in-chief, O. Bilec'kyj and V. Šynkaruk, 1961 and 1973 respectively) shows that 1) B. is more reliable than the "corrected" Š. edition of 1973; 2) even B. is not without flaws. To prove the first point we can compare the following: мушинѣ (leaf 7_1 of the autograph, Š., I:414)—мущинѣ (B., I:319; Z., leaf 6); звае (30_2, Š. 429)—званія (B. 337, Z. 26); стршилища (31_2, Š. 429)—страшилища (B. 338, Z. 27); сдѣлала (36_1, Š. 432)—здѣлал (B. 342, Z. 31); мы (36_2, Š. 433)—ты (B. 343— Z. 31v); блаженный (42_2, Š. 437)—блаженны (B. 349, Z. 37); perticit (44_1, Š. 438)—perficit (B. 350, Z. 38v); руук (51_1, Š. 443)—руку (B. 356, Z. 45), позравленіе (61_1, Š. 451)—поздравленіе (B. 364, Z. 55). The Š. edition never corrects any mistakes of the B. edition (listed below), which indicates that the Š. editors did not consult the autograph.

The mistakes of the B. edition can be proved by the following comparisons:

1) Один в восточной, тѣ в вечерній край / Пловут (B. II:61-leaf 2_2)   Одни в' восточній, тѣ в' вечерній край / Пловут (Z. 1v)

---

3. Hryhorij Skovoroda, *Povne zibrannja tvoriv* (Kyiv, 1973), I:6, 524-5.

The Z. version is more logical and therefore probably more authentic. It can be supported by another variant of the same song, from Skovoroda's *Garden of Divine Songs* (Сад Божественных пѣсней), 1758-86, where there is a logical parallelism in singular to the former version: Тот на восточный, сей в вечерній край/Плывет (B. II:18).

2) Nunc mihi cetra quies.   Nunc mihi certa quies.
    (Now peace is certain for me.)
    (B. II:62 - 2$_2$)   (Z. 2)

3) Ἀρκήν ʽαπάντων   Αρχὴν ἀ=πάντων κϳ
    καί τέλος ποίει τεόν.   τέλος ποίει Θεόν.
    (B. I, 320 - 8$_2$)   (Z. 7)

The autograph reproduced in B. on p. 317 shows this quote from Thales in the form identical with Z. The correct one is: Ἀρχὴν ἀπάντων καὶ τέλος ποιεῖ Θεός (God makes the beginning and the end of everything.)

4) Стал странник сей   Стал странник сей разгребат'
    разгребать физыческій   физческій Пепел: находит'
    пепел, находит в нем   в' нем божественную Искру.
    божественную искру.
    (B. I:335 - 28$_2$)   (Z. 24)

In this case even the unsatisfactory Bonč-Bruevič edition had the correct находить (p. 333). The ' is the normal symbol for ь used by Skovoroda from 1785 on, on the basis of the older Slavonic script tradition.

5) они любомудрствовали   они любомудрствовали так,
    так, как медвѣдь пляшет,   как Медвѣд' пляшет:
    научен в рожкѣ.   научен в' Ропскѣ.
    (B:I:336 - 29$_1$)   (Z. 24v)

This mistake (also committed by Bonč-Bruevič, p. 334) is particularly harmful, because it gives the reader no opportunity to make his own correction or right guess (which he is able to do in the case of other mistakes in the Kyiv critical editions). Who can guess, without special study, that рожкѣ is a misreading of Ропскѣ (due to a similarity between the hand-written civic Slavonic пс and ж)? The Z. copy allows us to clarify that Skovoroda meant the town of Novyj Rops'k on the Irpa River in the Topal' Company of the Starodub Regiment, where bears were actually taught to dance in the eighteenth century. A 1781 description of that northern Ukrainian town (now in the Brjansk oblast of Russia) explains that some of its dwellers "practice bear hunting and, having obtained bears from the local estate (экономіи) and other landlords, train them with music and lead them for entertainment to Little Rhossic steppe towns, to the Province of the Ukrainian Free Communes (Слободскую Украинскую губернію), to Don

Cossack settlements and to Great Rhossia, even to Moscow, and thus make their living free of misery and pay rent to the owner. There are up to twenty homesteads of such hunters in this one town."[4]

6) непріятны горничныя   непріятны горничныя
   сгѣны   стѣны
   (В. I:340 - 33$_1$)   (Z. 28v)

The Bonč-Bruevič edition also has the correct form (p. 337).

7) А народ скуку ни во что   А народ скуку, ни во-что ставит:
   ставит и к прогнанію сего   и к' прогнанію сего непріятеля,
   непріятеля за чрезчурь   за чрез чур довол'ное оружіе
   допольное оружіе почитает   почитает: ден'гу, вино.
   деньгу, вино.
   (В. I:341 - 34$_1$)   (Z. 29v)

The correct довольное can also be found in Bonč-Bruevič (p. 337).

The other benefit of studying a secondary copy can be illustrated by a few remarks on the language change that seems to be typical of the later fate of Skovoroda's works. The copyists of Z., first of all, de-Ukrainized it by: 1) substituting и for the Ukrainian ы (Владымиру of the autograph—4$_1$—was changed into Владимиру 3, as in Filaret's copy—B. I:614; физыка 27$_2$ became физика 23v); 2) by substituting če for Ukrainian čo (собачою 27$_2$ changed to собачею 23v, чоловѣчое 29$_2$ to человѣчое 24v, changed even more in Filaret's copy: человѣчее, I:615); 3) by removing the northern Ukrainian dispalatalization of r', whose presence in Skovoroda shows a northern Ukrainian influence in his Lubni dialect[5] (мѣрали 27$_1$ replaced by мѣряли 22v, as in Filaret's copy, I:615); 4) by removing the Ukrainian morphological change of -vь into -va in feminine nouns (вѣтву 2$_2$ changed into вѣтвь 2); 5) by removing the Ukrainian contraction of feminine adjectival endings (безпечна 2$_1$ changed into безпечная 1); 6) by changing the morphological look of some other words (сунутся 30$_2$ changed to суются 26).[6] On the other hand, copyists also removed some traits of Muscovite pronunciation (not admitted to the written language) from Skovoroda's spelling (ничево 25$_2$ into ничего 22v, тово 30 into того 25v, the same change in Filaret's copy, I:615) and some Slavonic pseudo-archaisms (adverbial comparative -яе into -ѣе: миляе 21$_1$, сильняе 34$_2$, трудняе 38$_1$ into милѣе 17,

---

4. Al. Lazarevskij, *Opisanie staroj Malorossii*, vol. I, *Polk Starodubskij* (Kyiv, 1888), 426.

5. In the seventeenth and eighteenth centuries the northern hardening of r' before vowels was not infrequent in some Lubni dialects (I. Varčenko, *Ljubens'ki hovirky i dialektna sumižnist'* [Kyiv, 1963], 208).

6. Cf. remarks on the Muscoviticization of Skovoroda's Song 13, known in an autograph, by later copyists and publishers: Jar Slavutyč, "Trynadcjata pisnja H. Skovorody. Do pytannja tekstolohiji," *Juvilejnyj zbirnyk Ukrajins'koji Vil'noji Akademiji Nauk v Kanadi* (Winnipeg, 1976), 223-32.

сил'нѣе 30, труднѣе 33v).

These notes, mostly devoted to details, are certainly too long and boring for the reader. He might have been spared most of them had the Kyiv Academy of Sciences done a better job on Skovoroda's critical editions. It is to be hoped that these remarks will help it produce a better complete edition of Skovoroda on the third attempt.

Part Three

The Philosophy and Theology of Skovoroda

Skovoroda's Metaphysics

George L. Kline

When one is dealing with Skovoroda's philosophical anthropology, ethics, or social philosophy, there is a significant risk of distortion if one assumes uncritically that a given protagonist, or even the same protagonist at different stages of a given dialogue, represents Skovoroda's own position. Thus, in *A Conversation among Five Travellers concerning Life's True Happiness*, the position that Athanasius takes at the beginning is refuted by Gregory, satirized by James, and recanted by Athanasius himself about a quarter of the way through the dialogue. As the dialogue opens, Athanasius naïvely assumes that a sufficient condition for human happiness is being well-born, rich, of high rank, and resident of a luxurious and diverting city, such as Paris or Venice. But within a few pages he is laughing at his own earlier "foolishness."[1]

Fortunately, when one is dealing with Skovoroda's metaphysics, the risk of distortion is substantially reduced, partly because in the dialogues disagreements about metaphysical questions are not sharp or fundamental, and shifts of position by a given protagonist are not dramatic. I shall attempt to reduce the hermeneutical risk even further by making copious use of the letters and poems—especially those written in Latin—which seem to me to have been insufficiently studied in this connection.

---

1. "Razgovor pjati putnikov o istinnom sčastii v žizni" in H.S. Skovoroda, *Povne zibrannja tvoriv* (Kyiv, 1973), I:324, 330; English translation by George L. Kline in *Russian Philosophy*, ed. James M. Edie et al. (Chicago, 1965; Knoxville, 1976, 1984), I:26-7, 34. All subsequent references to Skovoroda's writings, unless otherwise identified, will be to the 1973 Kyiv edition: volume number in Roman numerals, followed by page number in Arabic numerals, inserted in parentheses immediately following the passage quoted.

I

Does Skovoroda's metaphysics, as Soviet commentators assert, contain the germ of a materialist ontology? Tabačnikov, who claims that Skovoroda "moved from idealism toward materialism,"[2] mentions several passages in which Skovoroda makes what are allegedly significant references to matter as an ontological category. They are a mixed metaphysical bag. In one case *hac materia* means simply 'this subject-matter' or 'this topic of discussion' (Ltr. #19, II:251; cf. II:422). In another passage *materija* means 'material' in the sense of cloth for making clothes (I:324). In yet another the opposition is between *materia* and *forma*, and these are equated, respectively, with *smert'* ('death') and *žizn'* ('life') (II:139).[3]

Equally beside the ontological point is the claim made by V. Šynkaruk and I. Ivan'o that Skovoroda's theory of knowledge contains *hlyboki materialistyčni položennja*.[4] It turns out that these "profoundly materialistic theses" amount to no more than "empiricist elements." The confusion of materialism and empiricism in epistemology, common among Marxist-Leninist authors, has its philosophical roots in the writings of Feuerbach and the young Marx.[5] Although Skovoroda himself does not use the terms *materializm, empirizm,* or *idealizm,* or indeed any '...ism' word, to designate a philosophical (or theological) position, he does, confusingly, equate sensuousness—or visibility or perceptibility—with materiality. Thus, for example, he speaks of an *obraz* ('image') as being *veščestvennyj* ('material') (II:54) when what he means is *vidimyj* ('visible') or perhaps *osjazaemyj* ('palpable').

In technical terms, this involves a confusion of phenomenalism, or "sense-datum empiricism," with materialism. In this confusion Skovoroda has distinguished company. Even if we pass over the cruder confusions of Feuerbach and Marx, there is still Aristotle's concept of *hulēs aisthetēs* ('sense-matter' or 'perceptible matter')[6] and Locke's characterization of the external objects of sense-perception as both "sensible" (i.e., 'sensuous,' 'available to the senses') and "material."[7]

---

2. I.A. Tabačnikov, *Grigorij Skovoroda*, in the series "Mysliteli prošlogo" (Moscow, 1972), 63.
3. Tabačnikov's references are to the earlier (1961) Kyiv edition, in which I:207 corresponds to I:324, and I:539 to II:139, of the 1973 edition.
4. See their introduction to H.S. Skovoroda, *Povne zibrannja tvoriv*, I:46.
5. For details see my essay, "The Myth of Marx's Materialism," in *Philosophical Sovietology*, ed. Helmut Dahm et al. (Dordrecht and Boston, 1988), 158-203, esp. 159-62.
6. *Metaphysics*, Bk. VI, ch. 1: 1025b36. Since *hulē* also means 'content' as contrasted to 'form' (*morphē*), this expression could be taken in the Kantian sense, according to which the five senses supply the "matter" (i.e., content) of experience, in contrast to the understanding, which supplies its *form* (the categories of substance, causality, relation, etc.).
7. John Locke, *An Essay Concerning Human Understanding*, Bk. II, ch. 1, §§ 2-4.

Ivan'o's entry on Skovoroda in the Soviet *Encyclopedia of Philosophy* is rather more restrained than the Šynkaruk-Ivan'o Ukrainian "Introduction." Describing Skovoroda's ontology as a form of "objective idealism," Ivan'o adds:

> Visible nature [*natura*] is the perishable covering, the shadow of the eternal tree of life, i.e., of spirit [or] invisible nature [*natura*], which represents the unfathomable life-giving foundation of changeable material nature [*priroda*], which thus is also eternal and infinite and in constant transition from one opposite to the other.[8]

The Šynkaruk-Ivan'o introduction to the *Russian* edition of Skovoroda's works also makes the vaguer and more modest claim—compared to Tabačnikov's—that Skovoroda's philosophy "reflects the historical tendency of the transition from objective idealism to materialistic pantheism."[9] As we shall see, *none* of these terms (neither 'objective idealism' nor 'materialistic' nor 'pantheism') is properly applicable to Skovoroda's metaphysics. But, for the moment, we focus on what Soviet editors and commentators have had to contribute on the question of Skovoroda's incipient "materialism."

The Moscow 1973 edition contains a number of tendentious renderings of Skovoroda's Latin, introducing the word *materija* where it has no clear counterpart in the original. Thus, the expression *divinissima matrê* ("from the most divine [or "blessed"] mother") (Ltr. #26, II:264) is mistranslated as *ot...bespodobnoj materii* (Ltr. #25, R II:218), and duly indexed under *materija* (R II:478).[10] The word *humorum* ('of humors') (Ltr. #26, II:263) is twice translated as *vlažnye materii* (Ltr. #25, R II:218).[11] Despite such clumsy attempts to make Skovoroda sound more "materialistic" in Russian than he does in Latin, Soviet commentators can claim *prima facie* textual evidence of "materialistic tendencies" in Skovoroda, namely, his assertion that *materia* is *aeterna* (II:16, 148). However, as I have already indicated, one key sense of the Latin *materia*

---

8. *Filosofskaja enciklopedija* (Moscow, 1970), V:24. Ivan'o's terminological distinction between *natura* and *priroda* would have been more helpful if he had used *priroda*, rather than *natura*, for "visible" as well as for "material" nature, reserving the term *natura* exclusively for "invisible" nature. For Skovoroda's usage of these terms, see p. 237 and n. 31 below.

9. G. Skovoroda, *Sočinenija*, ed. and trans. I.V. Ivan'o and M.V. Kašuba (Moscow, 1973), I:26. Further references to this edition will be given in the text as 'R' followed by volume number (Roman numeral) and page number (Arabic numeral). Since the numbering of Skovoroda's letters differs slightly in this edition from that of the 1973 Kyiv edition, both numbers will be given.

10. The Ukrainian translation—*najpryrodnišoi materi* (II:265)—is accurate. Since, earlier in the same letter, the expression *harum pestium matrem* ("the mother of all these disasters") is correctly rendered in the Russian edition as *materi vsex ètix bedstvij* (Ltr. #25, R II:218) and in the Ukrainian edition as *materi vsix cyx lyx* (Ltr. #26, II:265), it is possible that 'материи' is an uncorrected misprint for 'матери' and that the index entry for R II:218 is meant only for the two occurrences of *vlažnye materii* on that same page.

11. The Ukrainian rendering *volohi* (II:265) is straightforward and unmisleading.

(and the Greek *hulē*) is simply 'content.' And Skovoroda does in fact appear to mean that the same cosmic content persists through endless variations of form. Such a claim does not entail a materialist ontology, since the content might well be spirit (*dux*) or energy (*sila*) rather than matter in the narrower sense (*veščestvo*). And even in the passage where he explicitly mentions *veščestvo*, using that term to translate his own Latin *materia*, a parallel interpretation is plausible. Skovoroda writes:

> [M]ateria aeterna—"veščestvo večno est'," sireč "vse mesta i vremena napolnila"
> [M]ateria aeterna—"matter is eternal," i.e., "it has filled all spaces and [all] times" (II:148).

But again, this might mean simply that no space or time is empty, that every space and every time has some content; however, this content might be *dux* or *sila* rather than *veščestvo* in the ontological sense, assuming that Skovoroda is here using both *materia* and *veščestvo* in the sense of 'content' (*soderžanie*). Such an interpretation, while unwelcome to Soviet commentators, would be entirely consistent with Skovoroda's pervasively pejorative use of the noun 'matter' (usually *veščestvo,* but occasionally *materija* or *materia*) (I:146, 174, 180, 347, 350, 354, 361, 362; II:12, 13, 14, 16, 36, 139, 140, 148) and the adjective 'material' (usually *veščestvennyj* but occasionally *material'noj*[12]) (I:180, 329, 350, 397; II:14, 138, 139), and his pervasively honorific use of their opposites, especially the nouns 'spirit' (*dux*), 'idea' (*ideja*), and 'form' (*forma*), and the adjective 'immaterial' (*neveščestvennyj* and, in Greek, *aulos*, as a plural substantive, viz., *t'aula*). Since these nouns tend to occur in the same passages, often with the adjective, I group all the references together: I:180, 241, 347, 349, 426, 456; II:22, 58, 107, 130, 137-60, 313; Ltr. #99, II:391, and passim.[13]

In a word, the kind of matter that Skovoroda calls 'eternal' is simply cosmic content as opposed to form; matter in the contrasted sense (to be discussed in

---

12. The adjective *materoj* is not directly related to *material'noj*. Skovoroda uses it only in such expressions as *materyja zemli sušu* ('dry land of the solid earth') (I:242) and *tverduju, materuju zemlju* ('firm and solid earth') (I:277; cf. I:265; II:360).

13. The 1973 Kyiv edition of Skovoroda's works, like the 1961 Kyiv edition, has only a name index (cf. "Imennyj pokažčyk," 1973, II:561-70). The index in the 1961 edition is called a "*Predmetno-imennyj pokažčyk*" (II:601-21; italics added), but is in fact only a name index. The 1973 Moscow edition has the advantage of separate subject and name indexes in each volume. But, like those of the two Kyiv editions, its name index conspicuously omits the entries 'Jesus' and 'Christ.' And its subject indexes, although they give full references for *materija* (perhaps *too* full—see n. 10 above) and *veščestvo*, omit both *Bog* and *dux*, merely listing *duxovnyj* as a subheading under *zakon* (R I:503; II:477) and *duxovnoe* as a subheading under *telo* (R I:506; II:479). Predictably, these indexes include *tlenie* but omit *netlenie* and list *tlennaja* but not *netlennaja* as a subheading under *natura* (R I:504; II:478). The revealing cross-reference under *materija* in vol. I ("sm. takže veščestvo, tvar', *ten*'": R I:504; italics added) is unaccountably omitted from vol. II.

Section II) of what is perceptible, merely apparent, shadowy, superficial, and perishing is obviously *not* eternal. This latter sense, which might be called a 'moral' or 'axiological' sense, is quite distinct from the broad ontological or even methodological sense in which matter, as content, can be characterized as eternal.

II

Skovoroda's closest approximation to a definition of 'matter' (*veščestvo*) is cast in the form of a wholly serious philosophical pun: "Vse veščestvo est' krasnaja grjaz' i grjaznaja kraska i živopisnyj porox..." ("All matter is [but] painted mud, muddied paint, and picturesque dust") (I:354; trans. in *Russian Philosophy*, I:55-6).[14] This formulation makes three related philosophical points: (1) The fact that the *appearance* of matter is attractive, even seductive, is conveyed by the noun *kraska* and the adjectives *krasnyj* and *živopisnyj*; (2) but the fact that the *reality* of matter is base and repulsive is conveyed by the adjective *grjaznyj* and the nouns *grjaz'* and *porox*; (3) finally, the fact that the appearance of matter is indissolubly linked to its reality is conveyed by the noun-adjective pairs: *grjaz'— krasna, kraska—grjazna, porox—živopisen.*

As Čyževs'kyj has pointed out,[15] Skovoroda's "long and baroquely vivid listings of the properties of matter" are filled with harshly negative terms. Like Plotinus—to whom, by the way, he never refers directly—Skovoroda characterizes matter as 'darkness,' 'shadow,' 'evil,' 'falsehood,' and 'death.' Čyževs'kyj suggests the following plausible ordering of Skovoroda's multifarious epithets for matter:

(1) Nothingness, emptiness, mere appearance, shadow;

(2) A covering or curtain, including "painted mud";

(3) Transience or perishingness (Čyževs'kyj's *Vergänglichkeit* captures an important semantic component of Skovoroda's terms *tlen'*, *tlenie*, and *tlennost'*); matter is a "fading flower" (*iščezajuščij cvet*—I:177);

(4) Aspects of "externality" (*vnešnost'*): matter as the "heel," "back," "tail," and, one might add, "sole of the foot or shoe" (*podošva*—cf. I:294).

It is not only in his negative value judgements about the material world, or the material "elements" (see Secs. III and IV below), but also on two related theoretical points that Skovoroda's position is sharply opposed to philosophical materialism. (1) He has no interest in developing or defending a theory of material atoms, i.e., indivisible and indestructible particles of impenetrable stuff;

---

14. This is an example of what, in technical jargon, I have called a two-term (noun-adjective) permutational pun of the identifying species. See my essay, "Philosophical Puns," in *Philosophy and the Civilizing Arts: Essays Presented to Herbert W. Schneider on his Eightieth Birthday*, ed. John P. Anton and Craig Walton (Athens, Ohio, 1974), esp. 224-5.

15. Dmitrij Tschižewskij, *Skovoroda: Dichter, Denker, Mystiker* (Munich, 1974), 75-6.

and (2) for Skovoroda the *reality* of spirit, idea, or form produces the *appearance* of perceptible matter, whereas for materialists it is the *reality* of the moving atoms in varying combinations that produces the *appearance* of colours, sounds, tastes, and textures (so-called "secondary qualities"). Skovoroda's position shares only one point with that of his materialist adversaries: for him, as for them, reality is imperishable and eternal, whereas appearance is temporal and perishing. But for them the imperishable reality is that of the "eternal" material atoms, whereas for him the imperishable reality is that of spirit, thought, form, and idea (in the Platonic sense).

Typically, philosophical materialists praise matter, or the material atoms, assigning them not only ontological but also axiological priority. In sharpest contrast, Skovoroda sees *tlen', tlenie,* or *tlennost'* ('transience,' 'corruptibility,' 'perishingness') as the root property of matter. This point, like most others in his metaphysics, is biblical both in conception and in terminology. *Phthora*, the term that Plato and Aristotle used for 'perishing' or 'passing away' (the opposite of *genesis* or 'coming-to-be'), reappears in the *koinē* of the New Testament in the adjective *phthartos*, with its negative *aphthartos*, which Skovoroda renders as *tlennyj* and *netlennyj*, respectively. The idolators, according to St. Paul, "changed the glory of the incorruptible God [*aphthartou Theou*] into an image made like corruptible man [*phthartou anthropou*]" (Rom. 1:23).

According to Skovoroda's charming gloss on this passage, the Athenians of Paul's time, who "knew not God," enthroned "only perishing nature [*tlennoe estestvo*]" in their hearts. "They gaped at the machine of the world but saw in it only clay"—as an inexperienced viewer buries his bodily gaze in the bright mud of a picture's surface, not letting his mind (*um*) penetrate to the "immaterial [*neveščestvennyj*] image" carried by the colours. Or, like an illiterate person "who has fixed his corruptible eye on the paper and ink of the letters, but not his reason [*razum*] on grasping the hidden meaning [*sila*][16] of the letters" (I:426), those Athenians limited nature to the realm of the palpable (*osjazaemyj*). They considered anything impalpable to be "nonsense, superstition, and nothingness." In a word, they understood everything except what is of chief importance: God as a nonphysical and incorruptible being (I:426, 427).

Skovoroda emphasizes the corruptibility or perishingness of matter in a

---

16. Skovoroda's use of *sila* ('force') as a synonym for 'sense' or 'meaning' follows the *koinē* Greek use of *dunamis* ('power'), e.g., in the expression *tēn dunamin tēs phōnēs* ('the meaning of the voice' [KJV], 'the meaning of the language' [RSV]) (1 Cor. 14:11). Contemporary English usage also retains this sense of 'force': cf. *Webster's New International Dictionary*, 2nd unabridged edition, which defines 'force' as 'special significance or import' (sixth meaning). It is in this sense that Skovoroda speaks of the *netlennuju silu tleni seja* ('imperishable meaning of this perishingness') (II:38; cf. also I:199, 401; II:25). He also uses *sila* in the related, but distinct, sense of 'the moral of a fable' in all but one (the fourth) of his thirty *Basni Xar'kovskija*.

favoured scriptural metaphor: "[A]ll flesh *is* as grass, and all the glory of man as the flower of grass. The glory withereth and the flower thereof falleth away. But the word of the Lord endureth for ever" (1 Pet. 1:24-5; cf. Is. 40:6-8). He sometimes writes "Vsjaka plot'—trava" (e.g., I:378), literally rendering the Greek *chortos* ('grass'), but more often "Vsjaka plot'—seno" (e.g., II:25, 50), lit. "All flesh is hay." 'Flesh' is used as a metonym for 'matter,' and *seno* suggests two words for 'shadow': *sen'* and *sten'*. These, in turn, evoke *ten'*, and through it, *tlen'*, *tlennyj*, etc.[17] When Skovoroda calls the world *senovnyj* (I:386), he means, I take it, both 'haylike' (hence 'perishing') and 'shadowy.' But when he uses the unusual term *sennoobraznyj* (II:19), in the context of a discussion of day and night, light and darkness, he seems to mean simply 'shadow-like.'

The "shapes" (*figury*) of material things are characterized not only by corruptibility or perishingness (e.g., II:22), but also by "deadness" (*mertvennost'*) (II:21). Skovoroda harshly condemns the "swinishness of perishing shapes" (*svoloč tlennyx figur*) (II:18; cf. II:87), asserting that "Every...shape is death and a pagan poison if the spirit does not arise from it" (I:456). Such shapes are also shadowy. And a series of highly negative adjectives is used to modify *ten'* or *sen'*, among them 'dead' (I:191), 'deceptive' (I:291), 'elemental' (*stixijnyj*)[18] (I:271), and 'bright' or 'vivid' (*krasočnyj*) (I:287)—presumably in the sense in which Skovoroda calls matter "*painted* mud" and "*picturesque* dust."

The naïve Luke in the dialogue "Narcissus" exclaims indignantly: "But I am not a shadow [*ten'*]. I have a solid body [*korpus*]." To which his interlocutor retorts: "You are shadow, darkness, and corruptibility [*tlen'*].... You are a garment, and he [viz., the true invisible man] is the body. You are a [mere] appearance and he is truth.... You are dirt and he is your beauty, image, and plan..." (I:163). In general, for Skovoroda, the "false man" is "shadow [*sen'*], darkness, fumes, corruptibility [*tlen'*], dream" (II:43).

Skovoroda associates corruptibility or perishing (*tlen'*) with trash or rubbish (*drjan'*) and urges us to raise up our thoughts from the "low foulnesses of shadow" (*nizovye podlosti teni*) (I:336).

---

17. Passages in which the adjective *tlennyj* and the nouns *tlen'*, *tlenie*, and *tlennost'* are used with reference to matter, the flesh, the world, or the "elements," and the adjective *netlennyj* and the noun *netlenie* are applied to God, "blessed Nature," or the spirit, are to be found at I:167, 171, 179, 199, 207, 210, 211, 218, 221, 225, 249, 267, 278, 280, 305, 312, 316, 317, 350, 353, 362, 370, 380, 381, 388, 389, 394, 400, 404, 405, 414, 422, 426, 427, 432, 451, 452, 455; II:9, 10, 13, 14, 22, 26, 43, 50, 53, 58, 69, 138; Ltr. #89, II:372. Note, in particular, the punning association of *ten'* and *tlen'* or *tlenie* (I:163, 311, 313; II:43, 87) and the parallel use of the adjectives *tennyj* ('shadowy') and *tlennyj* ('perishing'), e.g., the passage in which our *tennyj i tlennyj mir* ('shadowy and perishing world') is equated with the *drevo smerti* ('tree of death') (I:312).

18. For Skovoroda's special (Pauline) pejorative use of this term, see Section IV below.

III

For the Greek philosophers *kosmos* was an honorific term; it meant 'the ordered whole of the universe.' Its opposite was 'chaos'—sheer disorder. In the *koinē* of the New Testament *kosmos* takes on a pejorative meaning, and its opposite becomes the cluster of terms 'spirit,' 'salvation,' 'Christ,' and 'God.' Consider such expressions as "the world [*kosmos*] passeth away" (1 Jn. 2:17), "the whole world lieth in wickedness" (1 Jn. 5:19), "love not the world nor the things *that are* in the world" (1 Jn. 2:15), "the world is crucified unto me and I unto the world" (Gal. 6:14), "What shall it profit a man, if he shall gain the whole world, and lose his own soul?" (Mk. 8:36; cf. Mt. 16:26), "I am the light of the world" (Jn. 8:12) (quoted by Skovoroda, e.g., at I:177), and "Peace I leave with you, my peace I give unto you: not as the world giveth, give I unto you" (Jn. 14:27) (quoted, in part, by Skovoroda, e.g., at I:335; English trans., *Russian Philosophy*, I:40).

Skovoroda uses the word 'world' ('мір' or 'мыр')[19] in this same pejorative sense; he sees the world as both corruptible and corrupting. He refers to the first characteristic when he asserts that "this world passes away..., it passes away each moment" (I:322, 323) and speaks of the "shadow of your perishing world" (I:312). He refers to the second characteristic in his celebrated epitaph: "The world laid a trap for me, but it did not catch me" (*Mir lovil menja, no ne pojmal*—quoted in Kovalins'kyj's "Life," II:473) and in references to the world as a "prostitute" (*bludnica*) (I:76). He even speaks, in an early Latin letter, of tearing away the mask from *blandissimae turpissimaeque meretrici, puta mundo huic* ("this most enchanting and most corrupt harlot, viz., this world") (Ltr. #45, II:297).

Skovoroda plays on the similarity between the words *mirskoj* ('worldly') and *merzkij* ('loathsome') (I:275) in such strong expressions as "vile, worldly, and loathsome" (*podloe, mirskoe, merzkoe*) (II:61). He sets the "malicious midnight of the world" (*zlaja mirskaja polnoč'*) (Song #5, I:63) in stark contrast to the dawn, which leads to God. In another place he evokes the "darkness and roar of the wind of the world" (II:116) and contrasts the "night of corruptibility" with the "day of resurrection [and] salvation" (I:379). Shifting the metaphor, Skovoroda characterizes the world as the "smoke of eternity" and eternity as the "fire that consumes all things" (II:33).

Skovoroda was intrigued by the similarity-in-difference of the homonyms

---

19. Heidegger has aptly noted that with the beginnings of Christianity *kosmos* came to mean "a basic type of human existence," one which was "estranged from God" and opposed to the spirit of Christ—the latter being conceived as "life," "truth," and "light." Cf. Martin Heidegger, *The Essence of Reasons* (*Vom Wesen des Grundes*, 1929), bilingual edition, trans. Terrence Mattick (Evanston, Ill., 1969), 50-53.

'мир' ('peace') and 'мір' or 'мыр' ('world'), seeing this as an instance of his general principle of the unity of opposites.[20] He sometimes makes his point by using both words in a single sentence, e.g., "Your peace [мир] is here and not in that turbulent world [мірe] of yours" (I:318). In this he follows the example of Jn. 14:27, except that in Greek the word for 'peace' (*eirēnē*) is entirely different from the word for 'world' (*kosmos*).

The Latin poetry eloquently expresses the contrast between the inward and imperishable reality of things and the perishing and shadowy surface of the world of appearances:

> *Qui latet, ille manet, quae apparent, somnium et umbra est.*
> *Ergo latere est res: ergo patere—nihil.*
> *Machina magna patet* mundi *haec, sed somnium et umbra est.*

> That which is hidden endures; the things that appear are dreams and shadows.
> Therefore, to be hidden is to be something; to appear is to be nothing.
> This great machine of the *world* appears, but it is only dreams and shadows.
> (I:102; emphasis added)

In another Latin poem the contrast is between the transience and corruptibility of the things of this world and the eternity of the human heart as a moral and spiritual reality:

> *Omnia sunt foenum, furfur, sunt pulvis et umbra.*
> *Omnia praetereunt. Cordê perennis homo.*

> All things are hay and husks, dust and shadow.
> All things pass away. The human heart is eternal
> [lit., "A human being is eternal through his/her heart]. (In Ltr. #89, II:373)

In some of the poems the vision of the "world" takes on the tones of tragedy:

> *O prelestnyj mir! Ty mne—okian, pučina.*
> *Ty—mrak, oblak, vixr, toska, kručina.*

> O lovely world! To me you are an ocean, an abyss.
> You are darkness, storm-cloud, whirlwind, yearning, sorrow. (Song 16, I:75)

The world, for Skovoroda, is but an "outward appearance" and "all outwardness is an onward-flowing river" (I:179). Moreover, "every appearance

---

20. Skovoroda not only regularly wrote 'мир' for 'peace' and either 'мір' or 'мыр' for 'world,' but also called explicit attention to this distinction: "'Древный м[ы]ір' (пишу ы, *ut differat ab illo мир*)" (Ltr. #78, II:357). The photocopies of Skovoroda's autograph manuscripts included in the 1973 Kyiv edition make it clear that in certain passages the editors—perhaps influenced by the new orthography, which erases this distinction—have put 'мир' where the sense requires, and the autograph clearly shows, 'мір' (e.g., II:14 [twice]). In a number of other passages where this edition has 'мир,' the sense seems to require 'мір,' but no photocopies of the relevant pages are available. See I:191, 273, 329, 332, 335, 339, 340, 349, 353, 363, 370, 386, 396, 398, 400; II:21, 135.

is an image, and every image is flesh, shadow, an idol, and nothingness" (I:386). The Creator of "all things [both] visible and invisible" (*ta horata [kai] ta aorata*") is "the invisible God" (*ho Theos aoratos*) (Col. 1:15), or, as Skovoroda writes, *nevidimyj Bog* (I:169). For Skovoroda the visible, i.e., perceptible,[21] world is the outward, material "garment" of the divine spirit, and specifically of the forms and ideas in the mind of God. The invisible and imperishable realities—"voice, word, will, decree, kingdom, law, force [or 'meaning'—*sila*], spirit" (I:315n.)—underlie and sustain the worldly appearances: "Earth, flesh, sand, wormwood, gall, death, darkness, malice, Hell" (I:177). Or, in another richly baroque catalogue: "blood, flesh, water, inconstancy, falsehood, fire, and destruction..., hell and death" (Ltr. #80, II:360).[22]

The world is not only perishing, but corrupt and corrupting; it is "a walnut, corrupted [*rastlen*] by a worm" and a "prisoner of the devil" (II:65). Together with the flesh and the devil, the "world" forms what Skovoroda calls an "ungodly trinity" (*bogomerzkaja trojca*) (II:62). No wonder that, in an early Latin poem, he urged the young Kovalins'kyj to leave all of this behind:

> *Nunc mihi terrenis omissis t'aula specta,*
> *Ac ex visibili nosce metaphysica.*

Now, having put aside earthly things for me, having looked upon immaterial things,
[Proceeding] from visible things, [you will] come to know things metaphysical.
(Ltr. #24, II:261)

IV

Skovoroda also follows St. Paul in associating corruption, darkness, and death with the material "elements of the world." The *koinē* Greek is *ta stoicheia tou kosmou* (e.g., Gal. 4:3), accurately rendered as *stixii mira*, e.g., in another Pauline passage, which Skovoroda quotes: "Ašče umroste so Xristom ot stixij mira, počto, aki živušče v mire, stjazaetsja?" (I:317). Although he does not identify it,

---

21. Like St. Paul—and, for that matter, Plato, who used *horatos* ('visible') as a metonym for *aisthētos* ('perceptible') (cf. *Republic*, Bk. VI, 509d)—Skovoroda takes sight as the paradigm of sense-perception, using *vidimyj, visibilis*, and *vidimost'* in the broader sense of 'perceptible' and 'perceptibility' or 'appearance', e.g., at I:145, 150, 162, 169, 170, 172, 176, 177-9, 218, 293, 354, 379, 386; Ltr. #24, II:261. He uses the terms *nevidimyj, invisibilis*, and *nevidimost'* in the sense of 'imperceptible' and 'imperceptibility', e.g., at I:145, 163, 164, 169, 170-72, 177, 179, 180, 191, 224, 313, 354-5, 385, 387, 427, 434; II:18, 68; Ltr. #35, II:282, Ltr. #49, II:304. In a few passages Skovoroda uses the form *vidnyj* rather than *vidimyj*, and *nevidnyj* rather than *nevidimyj* (cf. I:357, 431, 432, II:110).

22. Cf. Karen Black's perceptive comment that Skovoroda's poetry exhibits an "aggregate of concepts associated with the flesh and including weapons and wounds, disease, corruption, and burning" ("The Poetry of Skovoroda," this volume, p. 154).

this is in fact from Paul's Epistle to the Colossians, ch. 2, verse 20. In the King James Version it reads: "Wherefore, if ye be dead with Christ from the rudiments of the world, why, as though living in the world, are ye subject to ordinances." 'Rudiments' is misleading, as is the 'elemental spirits' of the Revised Standard Version. *Ta stoicheia tou kosmou* is a pejorative synonym for *kosmos* (itself a pejorative term, as we have seen), conceived as "composed of manifold material elements."[23] Its negative value-associations are made clear by such Pauline expressions as "bondage under the elements of the world" (Gal. 4:3; in this passage the KJV rightly uses 'elements' rather than 'rudiments'), and the contrast between living "according to the elements of the world" (*kata ta stoicheia tou kosmou*) and living "according to Christ" (*kata Christon*) (Col. 2:8-9)—misleadingly rendered as "after the rudiments of the world, and not after Christ" (KJV) and "according to the elemental spirits of the universe, and not according to Christ" (RSV). The version that Skovoroda quotes—"po stixiam mira sego, a ne po Xriste" (I:217)—is both accurate and concise.

Skovoroda's negative characterizations of *stixii* or *stixii mira* parallel those of "the world" (see Section III above). He qualifies the noun *stixii* by such adjectives as 'dead' (I:317, 350) and 'flowing-past' (II:54), and refers to fearful hearts that lie "in the elements" (*v stixijax*) (I:363), chiding the idolaters, who see in the world "nothing but the elements, which are the principle-and-beginning (*načalo*) of all evil" (I:363).

He uses the adjective *stixijnyj* to qualify a series of harshly negative terms: *sen'* and *ten'* ('shadow') (I:271, 318), *sten' i mrak* ('shadow and darkness') (I:321), *mertvennost'* ('deadness') (I:317, 319), *podlost'* ('baseness') (I:316), *burda* ('garbage') (I:317), *grjaz'* ('filth' or 'mud') (I:321), *kuča* ('[dung] heap') (I:400), and *gnil'* ('rottenness') (I:405). "Elemental understanding" *(stixijnoe razumenie)* is associated with "base thoughts" (*podloe pomyšlenie*) (I:363). In contrast, "non-elemental thought" or "thought freed from the elements of the world" (*besstixijnaja mysl'*) belongs to the realm of the imperishable and spiritual (I:349).

Moving from metaphysics toward philosophical anthropology and ethics, Skovoroda asserts that "every element [*stixija*]" represents "mourning, lamentation, and affliction" (I:322). But, confident that the human spirit can elude the entrapping elements, he urges his readers to "Soar above the elements, ...fly out with all [of your] corruptibility to the unshakable firm ground of eternity..." (II:50).

---

23. Theodor Zahn, *Introduction to the New Testament*, trans. J.M. Trout et al. (Edinburgh, 1909), I:473, n. 5.

V

Addressing the ancient metaphysical problem of "the One and the Many," broached by Heraclitus and explored by Plato, Skovoroda employs two striking and related images: (1) that of the single unchanging tree with its many shifting shadows, and (2) that of the single object reflected in many mirrors or mirror-fragments.

(1) He begins with a down-to-earth example intended to stress the difference of value between a tree and its shadow. "When you buy an orchard," Skovoroda explains, "you pay money for the apple tree, not for its shadow." And he adds: "Is not a person mad who would exchange an apple tree for its shadow?" (I:291). The world of shadows is marked by both changeableness and multiplicity. A shadow "is born, it disappears, diminishes, [and] steals away" (I:312). A single apple tree has "many thousands of shadows" (I:312). It is of the nature of such shadows to "pass away" or to "flow past" rather than to "stand firm" (I:316).

> When the sun goes down, the shadow [of the tree] disappears, and it disappears more rapidly as it grows longer. Yesterday it was one thing, today it is another, tomorrow it will appear as a third thing. It is born and it disappears. Once born, it does not stand firm, but steals away from one place to another. Yet the apple tree stands unmoving for a hundred years. (I:311)[24]

In key passages the tree with its shadows becomes the Tree of Life (*Drevo žizni*). The image remains the same: the Tree of Life is single and enduring; it stands firm forever. Its shadows are many, shifting, and perishing (cf. II:16). The related biblical image of the "shadow of death" (e.g., in the Twenty-Third Psalm, verse 4)—quoted by Skovoroda, e.g., at I:311—underlies a number of his epithets that link "shadow" and "death," among them 'dead shadow' (*ten' mertvaja*—I:163; *mertvaja ten'*—I:292).

(2) The relation of the single reflected thing to its multiple reflections is vividly evoked in one of the Latin poems:

> *Quale est si centum speculorum te orbe corones,*
> *In variis speculis, forma sed una patet.*

> Thus it is that if you are ringed about by a hundred mirrors,
> *One* form appears in [all] the different mirrors. (I:103; emphasis added)

That reflections, like shadows, are dependent for their being upon that of which they are the reflections or shadows is made clear in the passage in which Skovoroda asserts that, as soon as the mirrors are removed, all the "copies" (*kopii*)—i.e., mirror-images—of the reflected object will disappear into their

---

24. Skovoroda refers not only to apple trees but also to oak trees and their shadows (I:163; II:116). Further references to trees and shadows as symbols of reality and appearance, respectively, occur at I:152, 273, 414; II:16.

"original," like the branches of a tree retreating into the seed from which they had grown (I:113).[25]

In a related image, Skovoroda describes the one Divine Wisdom as appearing—in much the way that a single countenance is reflected in the fragments of a broken mirror—in the "Hundred-Faceted" (*Sto-Vidnyj*) and "Thousand-Faced" (*Tysjašče-Личnyj*) garments worn by tsars and peasants, ancients and moderns, rich and poor (II:55).[26]

Finally, in an eloquent gloss on Genesis, Skovoroda declares:

> The seven days [of creation] included all the creatures. And above these seven days there shines the glory of the eternal—like a single countenance [reflected] in seven mirrors, and [like] one sun [shining] on [each of the] seven days... (I:403.)

VI

I would side with Ėrn and Čyževs'kyj, who insist that "*symbolism* is a characteristic feature of Skovoroda's metaphysics," against Zen'kovskij, who claims that "ontological symbolism—especially in his doctrine of the Bible as a special world—does not go deep in Skovoroda, nor is it essential to his metaphysics."[27] In addition to the symbolism of tree and shadow, there is a series of symbols drawn from nature that Skovoroda uses in ways sharply different from the Romantic and post-Romantic uses to which we have become accustomed. Thus, we tend to think of water in general, and the sea in particular, as a symbol of life and freedom, e.g., in the poetry of Pasternak and Joseph Brodsky. But for Skovoroda water and the sea symbolize what they did for Noah, namely, darkness and death. Light and life, for Skovoroda, are symbolized by the sky, cloud (*oblak*),[28] and dry land (*suša*). He groups together "shadow, water, and misfor-

---

25. Skovoroda uses *ten'* to mean not only 'shadow,' but also 'reflection' (cf. I:291). He sometimes distinguishes between mirror-images and shadows in the strict sense by calling the former 'mirror-like shadows' (*zercalovidnye teni*) (I:313). Plato, in the Divided Line passage, includes both *skias* ('shadows') and *phantasmata* ('reflections' or 'appearances') under the general heading of *eikonas* ('images') (*Republic*, Bk. VI, 510a).
26. The editors of the 1973 Kyiv edition have written 'стовидных' and 'тысящеличных' (II:55). But Skovoroda's autograph manuscript of this page, reproduced at II:56, clearly shows the spelling 'Сто-Видных' and 'Тысяще-Личных.' I have followed Skovoroda's usage.
27. V.V. Zenkovsky, *A History of Russian Philosophy*, trans. George L. Kline (London and New York, 1953), 64. The reference is to Vladimir Ėrn, *Skovoroda* (Moscow, 1912) and D. Čyževs'kyj, *Filosofija H.S. Skovorody* (Warsaw, 1934; in Ukrainian).
28. *Oblak* is a uniquely ambiguous image or symbol in Skovoroda's usage. His other symbols are either definitely positive or definitely negative. But that of the cloud shifts with context. When grouped with such terms as *suša* and *nebo* (as at II:19), *oblak* has positive and joyous connotations, but when grouped with the terms *mrak* and *vixr* (as in Song 16, I:75, quoted above, p. 231), it takes on the negative and threatening connotations of those terms.

tune" (*ten', voda i beda*) (I:276). And not only the Ark and the sheltering harbour, but also the cliff and the rock, symbolize safety and security after a perilous voyage at sea or the perilous journey of a human life (cf. II:114; I:411).

As we have seen, eternity is a central Skovorodian concept. It is symbolized in three related but distinct sets of images: (1) Mountain peaks, the hair on a person's head (in contrast to the heel and sole of the foot, which symbolize perishing temporality), and the rays of the rising sun (I:406, 411; II:21. cf. II:54); (2) rings and circles—including the "ring of eternity" (*kolco več'nosti*) (II:41; emphasis removed) and the "infinite wheel of God's eternity" (*beskonečnoe koleso Božija večnosti*) (I:381)—and the ancient symbol of the curled snake with its tail in its mouth (I:378, 380, 383, 387); (3) dawn, the East, morning, and the spring of the year (I:201; II:19, 127).

Certain of Skovoroda's symbols for eternity are more idiosyncratic, e.g., a "wonderful, marvellous, and most beautiful bird" (II:115). The "taste" of eternity—like that of the "judgements of the Lord" in the Nineteenth Psalm, verse 10—is said to be sweeter than "honey and the honeycomb" (I:409; II:38, 114, 115). Skovoroda adds that divine grace is the "eternal seed from which grows a tree [bearing] imperishable fruits" (II:86). He speaks of the "seed of eternity" (*večnosti zerno*) (II:43) from which grows the "tree of eternity, which is always green" (II:148).

Kovalins'kyj reports that Skovoroda drew a sharp contrast between the "treasures" of eternity and the "perishing temporality [*brennaja vremennost'*][29] of bodily existence" and, more generally, between the eternal and the temporal as light *versus* darkness, good *versus* evil, and head *versus* tail (Kovalins'kyj, "Life," II:471).

VII

Skovoroda's ontology, clearly, is not materialistic, or "moving toward materialism," as Soviet commentators claim. It is spiritualistic rather than subjectively idealistic or phenomenalistic, since, as Zen'kovskij rightly notes, for Skovoroda "corporeal being, the whole of visible [i.e., perceptible] nature, is not an illusion; however, empirical reality is wholly 'sustained' and moved by God."[30] It is a "symbolist" ontology, and its symbols are, for the most part, biblical.

That which is eternal, imperishable, imperceptible, and inward (symbolized as "head," "thought," "heart," and "meaning") is the divine ground and wellspring of the "world" and of the "elements of the world"—both terms taken as Pauline pejoratives—that are temporal, perishing, perceptible, and outward (a "vanity of

---

29. There are several passages besides the one here quoted in which Skovoroda uses *brennyj* rather than *tlennyj*, his standard term for 'corruptible' or 'perishing' (cf. I:273, 274, 349).
30. Zenkovsky, *A History of Russian Philosophy*, 64.

vanities" symbolized as "shadow," "darkness," "image," "filth," "idol," and even "Goliath").

Skovoroda equates God only with eternal, invisible, inward nature. He regularly uses the terms *natura* and *estestvo* to refer to this invisible, spiritual nature, and is careful to avoid using the term *priroda* in this sense. *Priroda* refers exclusively to corruptible human and "natural" nature, in such expressions as "corrupt material nature" (I:250) and "filth of its corruptible nature" (II:13).[31] But Skovoroda sometimes, confusingly, uses the terms *natura* and *estestvo* in a broader sense that includes both "visible" and "invisible" nature (e.g., at I:145, 146, 426). In one place, he even wrote "*натуре или природе*" (I:349), where the term *priroda* makes it clear that visible, perishable nature is intended.

The honorific sense of *natura* extends to its Greek counterpart *phusis*. Thus Skovoroda translates Epicurus' expression *makaria phusei* ('blessed nature') as *Bog* ('God'), because it is this Nature which, like God, has so ordered things that what is necessary for human life and happiness is not difficult, and what is difficult is not necessary (II:76n.).[32] Skovoroda's reference to "most blessed nature [*natura*] *or* spirit" (I:146; italics added) makes the point abundantly clear.

His theological position is not a *pantheism* (the doctrine that equates the world taken as a whole with God), but rather a *panentheism* (the doctrine that the world constitutes an aspect or part, but not the whole, of God's being) (cf. I:145). For Skovoroda God is the ground and origin of all things. "[T]ruth," he declares, "is in eternity, eternity [is] in incorruptibility, incorruptibility [is] in the principle-and-beginning [*načalo*], the principle-and-beginning [is] in God" (II:19). Moreover, with respect to the "microcosm" of man, Skovoroda insists, God is that which is "immaterial in what is material, eternal in what is corruptible and perishing, single in each one of us and whole in every one; God [is] in the flesh and the flesh [is] in God" (I:180).*

---

* This essay was completed in 1989, at which time present-tense references to "*Soviet* commentators" were still appropriate. The Editors.

---

31. Skovoroda often uses *priroda* to designate those elements of human nature that impel people toward the *srodnyj trud* ('congenial labor') for which they are best suited. He is clearly playing on the root *rod*, which the words *priroda* and *srodnyj* have in common (cf. I:417, 418, and passim).
32. Čyževs'kyj is right to deny that this translation or the apparent identification of Christ with Epicurus in Song 30 (I:89) implies that Skovoroda is—as has been claimed—an "Epicurean" (i.e., hedonist), atheist, or materialist. What Epicurus and Christ have in common is simply their *Angstlosigkeit* and *Freude* in the face of the trials and sufferings of human life. (Cf. *Skovoroda: Dichter, Denker, Mystiker*, 174.)

Skovoroda's Moral Philosophy

Taras Zakydalsky

The aim of philosophy, which is worthy of the name "wisdom," is practical—to show men the way to happiness (I:326).[1] Skovoroda's view of philosophy is formulated best by his friend and pupil, Myxajlo Kovalins'kyj:

> ...philosophy, or love of wisdom, directs all its efforts to this end: to give life to our spirit, nobility to our heart, and clarity to our thoughts, which are the head of everything. When the spirit in man is gay, the thoughts calm, and the heart at peace, then everything is radiant, happy, and blessed. This is philosophy. (II:465)

Wisdom is the totality of knowledge that is necessary for happiness, and its main characteristic is usefulness. "Perfect wisdom is not knowledge of everything in the world... But to know everything that is useful to you, this is perfect wisdom" (I:132).

Since happiness is the goal of life and is unattainable without the knowledge of happiness (I:324), philosophy is the "highest science" (I:337), "the head, eye, and soul of all the sciences" (I:116). God intends all living things to be happy (I:328), hence He makes everything that is necessary for happiness available to all (I:331, 337) and easily accessible (I:144). It follows from this that the knowledge necessary for a happy life is always within men's grasp, regardless of the age or place in which they live, or the talent or social status they possess. For this reason philosophy is "the catholic, that is, universal science" (I:361). It is

---

1. The Roman numeral indicates the volume, the Arabic numeral the page of *Hryhorij Skovoroda: Povne zibrannja tvoriv*, ed. V.I. Šynkaruk, V.Ju. Jevdokymenko, L.Je. Maxnovec', I.V. Ivan'o, V.M. Ničyk, and I.A. Tabačnykov (Kyiv: Naukova dumka, 1973).

also easy to obtain, for it is "the invisible face and living word of the omnipresent divine nature that thunders secretly within each man" (I:149). And yet, few men succeed in acquiring wisdom, and so authorities in this field are rare. Many specialists in various sciences presume that they are competent in philosophy and produce catastrophic results. Only those who themselves have attained a blessed life—the apostles, prophets, priests, preachers and philosophers—are genuine authorities here (I:360, 367). Because the purpose of wisdom is happiness, it can be tested by the results it produces: what is not wisdom cannot give happiness (I:368).

To say that philosophy for Skovoroda is a practical science does not imply that his philosophy is no more than a normative morality or a collection of useful admonitions for successful living. What it does mean is that the main sections of his philosophy—metaphysics, epistemology, and anthropology—are developed not for their own sake, but for the purpose of grounding his moral principles. This explains why these sections are not elaborated in a systematic and detailed manner. Skovoroda's practical orientation also explains why he shows little interest in the natural sciences and other academic disciplines (I:70). He does not consider them essential for happiness (I:335, 361). At best they could be servants of the "queen" science that leads to happiness (I:336), and at worst they are distractions from the true purpose of life (I:290, 336, 359).

Skovoroda's favourite book, the Bible, is for him the "best and wisest means for acquiring peace" (I:369, 371, 376), but it is not the only source of wisdom. According to his doctrine of the universality of wisdom, there are wise men in all ages and among all nations. Many of their teachings have been absorbed into the common treasury of popular wisdom. Skovoroda's writings are studded with pithy sayings and proverbs from Ukrainian, Russian and other folklore. But the main source of his ideas, apart from the Bible, is ancient philosophy. He was very fond of the Greek and Roman thinkers and defended them against narrow-minded Christians (I:448, 304-5, 423). He frequently refers to such figures as Socrates, Plato, Aristotle, Thales, Pythagoras, Diogenes, Epicurus, Cicero, and Plutarch, and freely draws upon their ideas. Skovoroda's philosophy is an original synthesis of Christian concepts with Platonic, Stoic, and Epicurean doctrines, a synthesis that developed in response to his own needs and was tested in his own life.

Skovoroda's moral philosophy attempts to answer two main questions: (1) what is happiness, and (2) how is happiness to be attained, i.e., what are the necessary and sufficient conditions for happiness? Both questions presuppose that the highest good for man is happiness. This belief rests on (1) a theological premise, (2) introspection, and (3) common observation of men's behaviour. That God is good is a fundamental principle for Skovoroda, and from this he reasons that "everything is born for a good end, i.e., happiness" (I:328). By reflecting on his own consciousness, he discovers that thought is "an unceasing striving" for "sweetness and peace" (I:349), which are the same as happiness. Then, from observing men's activities, he concludes that all men, whether they realize it or not, pursue one goal—"a joyful heart" (I:324). Since "our deepest desire is to be happy" (I:324) and since God, the creator of men, implants this desire in man's nature, it is reasonable to conclude that happiness is something we not only seek, but ought to seek, i.e., that happiness is the highest good.

As many commentators have already pointed out, Skovoroda's definition of happiness is very similar to the Stoic, Epicurean, Cynic and Sceptic concepts of happiness.[2] What needs to be noticed is how much it differs from the earlier concepts. Skovoroda accepts what he takes to be Epicurus' view—that the aim of life is sweetness (*sladost'*)—but identifies sweetness not with pleasure or absence of pain, but with "the heart's gaiety" (*veselie serdca*) (II:6). Like Epicurus, he stresses that fear is incompatible with happiness (II:65) and hence identifies gaiety with boldness (*kuraž*) (II:6). Again, Skovoroda's terminology suggests a more positive mental state than *ataraxia*.

Following the Stoics, Skovoroda speaks of happiness as inner peace (I:75, 338, 361, 368), tranquillity (*pokoj*) (I:69, 70, 411), and serene (*bezmjatežnyj*) life (I:341). Then, he identifies this state with virtue (I:341), manliness (I:341) and power (*krepost'*) (I:339, 341). In contrast to the Stoics, however, he describes inner peace and power as joy (*radost'*) and gaiety (I:339, 340), suggesting a more positive psychological state than *apatheia*. This suggestion is confirmed by an explicit rejection of the Stoic concept of happiness:

> So, you will say, I demand with the Stoics that the wise man be completely passionless. On the contrary, in that case he would be a stone column, not a human being. Hence it follows that blessedness lies in conquering the passions, not in their absence. (II:283)

Happiness, for Skovoroda, must be defined positively, not as the absence of one thing or another. Furthermore, happiness is not a state of imperturbability or relaxation, but rather a state of tension. The struggle between opposites is a necessary condition of life and consciousness, and hence of happiness as well:

> To care about nothing, to be grieved by nothing means not to live, but to be dead, for care is the motion of the soul, and life consists of motion.... But where there is labour there is rest as well. Where there is care, there is joy also. (II:350)

The happy man is not without some disappointments, hardships and suffering. Realizing, however, that they are necessary, he accepts and transcends them, blessing life:

---

2. Among the most recent commentaries, see I. V. Ivan'o, "Filosofs'ko-etyčne včennja," *Filosofija Hryhorija Skovorody*, ed. V.I. Šynkaruk (Kyiv: Naukova dumka, 1972), 201-2; M. Red'ko, *Svitohljad H.S. Skovorody* (L'viv: Vydavnyctvo L'vivs'koho universytetu, 1967), 190, 206.

> The world is built in this way. One opposite promotes the other opposite. Sweetness is the reward of sorrow and sorrow is the mother of sweetness. Whoever wants to reap sweetness, let him love sorrow first. (I:441)

Skovoroda's conception of happiness as a state of tension fits nicely with his insistence upon activity as the condition of happiness.

There are further differences between Skovoroda and the Stoics, the Epicureans, and the Sceptics on how happiness can be achieved. While he admits that the most important condition for happiness is an inner one and under the individual's control, he sides with Aristotle and common sense in recognizing the importance of certain external conditions such as health and congenial work, and the material goods connected with them. But more importantly, he thinks of happiness in an Aristotelian way as *eudaemonia* (I:299-300). According to Skovoroda's doctrine of congenial work, happiness is the full realization of one's potentialities. From this point of view, the happy man is not one who shuns the world or is indifferent to it, but rather one who participates in it to actualize the divine powers concealed in it and in himself. The world is a manifestation of divinity, hence it is good and worthy of love.

To discover the necessary conditions for happiness, Skovoroda uses two principles as guidelines. First, what is needed for happiness must be universally available. Nature has "zealously and providently prepared everything that is indispensable to the happiness of the most insignificant worm, and if anything is lacking then it is, of course, unnecessary" (I:331). Secondly, what is necessary for happiness must be easily accessible. Since happiness is the easiest thing to attain (I:144), all the things that are necessary for it must be easy to obtain. The good and wise Master makes "what is necessary not difficult and what is difficult not necessary" (I:275). Both principles follow from Skovoroda's conception of God as "our most merciful Father" (I:332) and "our most merciful mother nature" (I:330), who wants all creatures, not only men, to be happy. These principles are the "touchstone" for testing what is really necessary for happiness and what is not (I:332-3).

Applying these criteria, Skovoroda rejects most of the goods that men pursue as unnecessary for happiness. Luxuries (I:69, 86), wealth (I:144, 331), honour and fame (I:76, 144, 332), high rank and prestigious profession (I:144, 439), scientific knowledge and academic learning (I:144, 290, 337, 360, 361), and health (I:144, 331) are not accessible to all men and are not easy to obtain. Hence, they are not necessary. This does not mean that people who possess any of these goods cannot be happy. It does mean that they are happy not because of these goods, but because of something else (I:421; II:347).

To be happy we must possess a certain type of knowledge, which Skovoroda calls wisdom or faith, and we must live according to this knowledge. Wisdom consists of certain metaphysical truths about God, man, and the universe, along with the practical rules that follow from these truths. By shaping our life and character according to these rules we shall attain happiness. "The task of wisdom lies in this—to comprehend in what happiness consists. This is the right wing. And virtue labours to seek it out.... This is the left wing. Without these wings it is absolutely impossible to set out and soar up to happiness" (I:326). Thus, wisdom is the primary condition of happiness, because without it virtue is impossible (I:148; II:34). But it is not the sole condition: it needs to be completed by action. A passive wisdom or faith is false and hypocritical (I:149; II:417).

The essential metaphysical doctrines that constitute wisdom can be summarized in the following way: the universe is composed of two natures—God and creature, spirit and matter, form and matter. The first is invisible, the second visible (I:145, 179; II:14, 139). The first is eternal and unchanging, the second perishable and changing (II:14, 139). Invisible nature is a force or law within the visible nature, sustaining and governing the latter (I:149, 180, 329, 342, 414, 431) as a tree supports and controls its shadow (I:311). God (or ruling nature) is good to all His creatures (I:146-7, 342) and wants all of them to be happy (I:330). Hence, He provides them with everything that is necessary for happiness (I:331). Since all events are determined by God, everything that happens is for a good purpose—the happiness of all His creatures.

Like all creatures, man is composed of an invisible nature—the true man or the heart—and a visible nature, the body (I:161, 169-70, 180, 313). The true man is immortal (I:182, 190-91). Death does not destroy the individual, but merely puts an end to his visible existence (II:138). It is a transition to freedom (II:324), not a loss (I:89). Thus, the fear of death—one of the main sources of human suffering—proves to be groundless and is expelled from the soul.

God inscribes the moral law—the Ten Commandments—on men's hearts and fills them with the virtues that make social life possible—friendship, self-restraint, generosity, justice, and mercy (I:147-8, 149; II:104). Besides these innate traits, which are common to all men, each individual's heart is stamped with a special talent or inclination for a particular role in life (I:127, 410, 421, 439). The heart is an active principle and manifests itself mainly through one's vocation or congenial work. It is also the basis of true friendship. Since like attracts like, real friends must be similar in character (II:229), inclination and talent (I:425, 122, 130).

New scientific discoveries about the universe are of no interest to the wise man, for they have no bearing on happiness. It is sufficient for the wise man to know that the visible universe is a mere shadow of the real universe. All material things are shadows of real things and, like shadows, they are changing and perishable. Hence, the human heart, which is of a spiritual and imperishable nature, cannot find satisfaction and rest in material goods (I:172, 176, 368). Like desires like: the heart can find happiness only in contemplating and loving invisible and eternal being (I:61, 369; II:74, 136).

What practical rules for attaining happiness follow from this metaphysical theory? The supreme and most general rule is: obey God (I:87, 145, 416). Since God is a good and wise ruler of the universe, it is best to accept His will in all things:

> Why seek a better judge? Rely on Him and make His holy will your will. If you accept it, then it becomes your own. Wills that agree are one soul and one heart, and what is better than friendship with the Highest Being? At such a time everything will happen according to your will, and a wise will at that. And this is to be content with everything. (I:342)

The greater the agreement between our will and God's the happier we shall be (I:343, 377). In a most imaginative way Skovoroda associates the Platonic idea of happiness as the health of the soul with this rule of obedience (I:368). Since bodily health consists in the proper ordering of the elements, and obedience to God is the proper ordering of the soul, obedience to God is the health of the soul. "Bodily health is nothing but a balance and agreement among fire, water, air and earth, while the subordination of the soul's rebellious thoughts is its health and eternal life" (I:343).

It is important to note that for Skovoroda obedience to God is based on a belief in His goodness and wisdom. Hence, although Skovoroda frequently uses the biblical phrase "fear of God," this obedience is not a grudging, coerced submission to God's power. It is rather a ready and grateful acceptance of His will (I:342). Skovoroda places strong emphasis on gratitude as the proper relation between man and God. "The fruits of a blessed life are joy, gaiety, and contentment; its root and richly leafed tree is a quiet heart, and the seed of this root is gratitude" (II:107). "Every good is concealed in gratitude (he says), as fire and light are concealed in flint" (II:109). Gratitude is the "daughter of the spirit of faith" (II:113), since without faith in a providential God it is impossible to regard all events as serving our best interest. The only ancient philosopher who appreciated the place of gratitude in a happy life was Epicurus, but in his system gratitude lacked the deeper metaphysical foundation that is found in Skovoroda.

Obedience to God is Skovoroda's "categorical imperative." It expresses what is common to all right actions and serves as the ultimate criterion of rightness (II:401). By applying this law to different contexts Skovoroda derives three more specific rules for living well: (1) live according to the Ten Commandments and the innate virtues that God has inscribed on the soul; (2) work in the vocation assigned to you by God, and (3) flee from the world, i.e., seek what is divine and eternal, not what is earthly and temporal. Skovoroda does not elaborate on the first of these rules, but discusses the last two at great length.

The doctrine of congenial work (*srodnoe delo*, II:140; *srodnoe dejstvie*, I:430;

srodnoe delanie, I:338) is Skovoroda's main contribution to philosophy.[3] The basic idea does not originate with Skovoroda. It appears in Plato's doctrine of the three metals that fit men for different social roles, in Aristotle's teachings that men are fitted by nature for different occupations and that self-realization is the goal of life, and in the Stoic injunction to follow nature. Skovoroda, however, works out this concept in greater detail and puts it to more extensive use than his predecessors. It becomes the central concept in his moral system.

According to Skovoroda, men are predisposed by nature not merely to several general types of social roles, as the Greek philosophers taught, but to very specific roles and professions. Men are by nature not merely thinkers, political leaders, warriors, farmers and artisans, but are philosophers (I:114), theologians (I:439), priests (I:422), preachers or orators (I:443), kings (II:284), state advisors or generals (I:422), musicians (I:422), painters, architects, writers or physicians (I:420), cavalry or infantry soldiers (I:442), farmers (I:436) or potters (I:422). "There are as many natural vocations (*srodnost'*) as there are stations in life (*dolžnost'*)" (I:424). The only occupations for which there are no natural inclinations are those that contravene divine or human laws—robbing, thieving, etc. (I:417, 420).

To work in one's natural vocation is the principal way of fulfilling God's will:

> When a man reflects upon himself, responds to the Holy Spirit that lives and calls within him, and follows its secret nod instead of his own whims or the advice of others, by applying himself and adhering to the station for which he was born into the world and to which he was assigned by the Highest Being Himself—this is to undertake happily one's calling with God. (I:418)

And this is the only way to happiness, for happiness "depends on the heart, the heart depends on peace, peace depends on vocation and vocation depends on God" (I:439).

The spiritual nature within each individual is an active principle, hence idleness produces boredom and suffering (I:120) as well as all other evils (II:122). Activity contrary to one's nature is even more painful than inaction (I:435). Only action in conformity with one's inner nature is enjoyable:

> Nature is the original cause and the self-moving spring of everything. It is the mother of inclination. Inclination is eagerness, disposition, motion. Inclination, as the saying goes, is stronger than captivity. It seeks work and takes joy in work as in its son. Work is the lively, tireless motion of the whole machine for as long as the task is being realized. It weaves for its agent a garland of joy. In a word, *nature* incites one to work and confirms one in one's work by making work sweet. (I:417-18)

Congenial work is its own reward and is enjoyed more than the product that it

---

3. Ivan'o, "Filosofs'ko-etyčne učennja," 221.

yields (I:126). "The natural hunter enjoys the hunt and work more than the roasted rabbit on the table" (I:430). Congenial work is preferable not only to any reward, but to all temporal goods: wealth, reputation, comfort, health, and even life itself (I:428, 430, 437, 439, 441). "Sweet is the physical labour, the physical suffering, and even physical death when the soul, the master of the body, enjoys congenial work" (I:126-7). A bee enjoys gathering honey more than consuming honey, and will keep at its task in spite of the risk of being killed for its honey (I:420). Nothing is more enjoyable in life than to work in one's natural vocation, and nothing is more tormenting than to work at an uncongenial task (I:126).

Uncongenial work turns the soul into a "dirty, smelly puddle" (I:420). The soul becomes ill, dissatisfied with the world and estranged from others. It cannot find peace or enjoyment and is torn by impossible desires. "It cannot live and does not want to die" (I:431). Death is better than a lifetime of misery in an uncongenial task (I:435). It is much better to accept a humble station in life as long as it is congenial than a lofty uncongenial one (I:420, 422). "Better be a natural cat than a lion with an ass's nature" (I:434).

Why do men assume uncongenial roles, then? Obviously, not for the work itself, but for some external reason: because of material profit or fame. Any position or task that is adopted because of its external advantages is sure to be uncongenial (I:435, 445).

To be happy is to recognize one's vocation and to work in it (I:417). But how can one discover it? Self-knowledge is necessary, since one's calling is determined by one's inner nature. "Know thyself. Heed thyself and listen to thy lord" (I:418). Self-knowledge consists of much more than introspection, however. It requires self-observation and analysis of one's behaviour. Since every inner truth is manifest in its shadow, one's hidden heart is visible to a wise man through one's behaviour (I:434). This kind of knowledge is gained only by long effort, hence, "think ceaselessly to know thyself" (I:220). In fact, it requires a lifetime (I:372). From his reading and his own experience Skovoroda realized that self-knowledge is difficult, but this conclusion conflicted with his belief in divine providence, which makes what is necessary easy to obtain. Hence, he asserts dogmatically that self-knowledge is easy (I:434) without explaining how it can be easy and yet require such long effort. Furthermore, Skovoroda seems to overemphasize the cognitive element in our choice of vocation and minimizes the volitional element. The choice, he thinks, can be completely determined by self-knowledge, and risk, which demands decisiveness, can be ignored.

Since happiness lies in fulfilling one's vocation in life, it can be attained in every station or occupation (I:420, 434). In spite of unequal natural endowment and unequal social status, all men can be equally happy. God "wrongs no one by inscribing the law of congeniality. If one man takes to one vocation, another to another, a hundredth to a hundredth, then although the vocation or trade be lowly, as long as it is not dishonourable and is thus enjoyable and useful, he will be happy" (I:433). In this way He insures "unequal equality for all" (I:435).

Men are ordained by nature to live in society. The unequal distribution of talents necessitates the division of labour, which in turn compels men to associate with each other. Men's natural vocations "constitute the fruit-bearing orchard of the church or, more exactly, of society, just as certain parts constitute a machine" (I:417). But it is not only need that drives men to form societies. There is also a natural tendency in men to associate with similar individuals, i.e., to form friendships. Like inclination toward different types of work, attraction to different people comes from God (I:130, 425). Friendship is based on equality or affinity among men's souls. It springs not from wealth, rank, descent, comeliness or cleverness, but from kinship of hearts, character, convictions, and values (I:122, 130; II:228, 250). Skovoroda regards friendship as highly as did Socrates, Plato, Aristotle, and Epicurus. Nothing is better in life than true friendship (I:130; II:349) and nothing is sweeter (II:246, 267).

The division of labour that is implanted in men's natures requires a hierarchical ordering of society. As in a living body, certain members must govern and others must support and obey them (I:111-12). Skovoroda objects not to social ranks, but to filling them with unsuitable people (I:127). Only congenial work is easy and successful (I:274-5, 437, 422), and uncongenial work has to be flawed (I:417, 422). Since society is like an intricate machine that functions well when each part is sound and performs its assigned function (I:417), uncongenial work gives rise to social disorder (I:428, 436; II:388), and can even lead to a society's downfall (I:426). It perverts and debases the professions and demoralizes the public (I:425, 426; II:106). It is, undoubtedly, the greatest social evil (I:428). Skovoroda severely criticized the society in which he lived (II:122, 429), especially its upper classes—royalty, the aristocracy, and the clergy. It is interesting to note that he had not one kind word to say about the tsars and the court, although his principle of social hierarchy is not inimical to monarchy.

The perfect society would be one in which each member performed the role for which he was born. This earthly city is not described by Skovoroda in his works. It is frequently confused with the "Kingdom of God" (I:275, 419), the "holy city" (I:78), the "heavenly city" (I:61), the "heavenly Jerusalem" (II:41), or the "heavenly republic" (II:43), in which all things are held in common, hostility is replaced by love, and no differences of age or sex exist (II:41, 51).[4] From the contexts in which these phrases appear, it is clear that Skovoroda is referring not to some future society on earth, or a transcendent society, but to a spiritual condition of the soul, a state of blessedness.

To enter the Kingdom of God one must be resurrected (I:60, 177, 190, 284)

---

4. T.A. Bilyč, *Svitohljad H.S. Skovorody* (Kyiv: Vydavnyctvo Kyjivs'koho deržavnoho universytetu, 1957), 55; Red'ko, *Svitohljad...*, 184.

or born a second time (II:43, 52, 405). By resurrection or second birth Skovoroda means a religious conversion, which consists in recognizing the dual nature of reality and accepting divine providence, and entails a moral transformation—the pursuit of new goals according to new rules. The believing heart becomes filled with a new confidence and peace.

The doctrine of congenial work is very attractive from the moral viewpoint. It demands of men an active participation in the affairs of the world, instead of passivity and escapism. It reconciles self-interest with the common good, and self-fulfillment with public service. It implies that social progress should be made through the moral improvement of individuals, not through violence or revolution. Unfortunately, the doctrine does not seem very plausible. It places too much emphasis on nature, too little on nurture. While a vague doctrine about innate capacities for certain general functions is plausible, the view that each man is naturally suited for a very specific role or job is not. Skovoroda's doctrine implies that the division of labour is a historical constant: that labour has always been highly specialized in all societies and always will be. To accommodate the fact that types of work vary with social structure, Skovoroda would have to admit that God distributes innate capacities according to the types of societies into which individuals are born. Furthermore, individuals who are to enter a rapidly changing society in which some occupations become obsolescent and new ones arise within a generation's lifetime must receive more than one vocation. Of course, God is all-powerful and can adjust His actions to historical circumstances, but traditionally He is thought to act in a uniform manner. In rejecting miracles Skovoroda places special emphasis on the principle that God acts in the same way everywhere and at all times. This makes it difficult, if not impossible, to reconcile Skovoroda's doctrine of congenial work with the fact of changing social roles and occupations.

To love material goods and worldly fame is to condemn oneself to unhappiness. "Our soul cannot be satisfied with material things;/ Only heavenly things can overcome its consuming tedium" (I:61). But this does not mean that we should hate the world and despise the body. What is necessary is useful and good: the physical world is a necessary manifestation of God (I:386), and our bodies, which are members of this world, are necessary as well (I:243-4). The body should be regarded not as an enemy, but as a servant of the soul (II:408). A healthy body is the soul's helpmate in the pursuit of wisdom (II:281). Hence, one must care for the health of the body. On the one hand one should avoid overindulgence in food and drink (II:265) and on the other excessive severity (I:277; II:285), for both are detrimental to health. Moderation is the best course. Skovoroda recognized the advantages of health and the wisdom of preserving it (II:285), although he did not consider it absolutely necessary to happiness (I:330, 331).

What are the legitimate claims of the body? According to Skovoroda, "one should submit to the body only to the extent demanded by necessity, not to the extent urged by desire—the servant of the body" (II:408). The body must be protected from cold, hunger, thirst, and illness, even if this should require much effort (I:353). The man of simplicity and poverty desires only those material goods that are necessary to health and is indifferent to what is superfluous (II:121, 128, 237). The things that Skovoroda considered necessary were things "without which life is impossible or filled with pain" (II:75n): bread and water (I:70, 82, 89, 111, 112); some simple clothes (I:353); a pair of boots for winter (II:75n). Kovalins'kyj reports that Skovoroda owned at one time only a pair of shirts, a tunic, a pair of stockings and shoes (II:442). He had only one meal a day, consisting usually of herbs, fruits or dairy products (II:446). He slept four hours a day (II:447). He never owned a home of his own, but lived with friends for various periods of time (II:464).

"Be satisfied with little" (II:108, 109) and you will banish the fear of want from your heart. Whoever is satisfied with the bare necessities of life can rest assured that God will always provide for him (I:144; II:109, 128). He who loves luxury, however, can never be sure of obtaining and keeping what he desires. Hence, he is bound to live in constant anxiety and fear (I:353, 115-16; II:64, 123). Love of luxury is the source of all hostility, crime, and social disorder (I:434; II:402). Yet Skovoroda does not condemn wealth and luxury and does not call upon the rich to give up their possessions. He advises men merely not to love or to attach themselves to earthly goods (II:128).

According to Skovoroda's optimistic outlook, the physical universe and the human body are good, although they are subordinate to the higher needs of the soul. Everything created by God is good: evil lies in the improper ordering of things by men (II:387). To indulge the body's whims and to seek material goods that are superfluous is wrong, not because this injures the soul, but because it belittles the body's master (II:409). An insulted soul cannot be happy.

Skovoroda's early writings reflect a divided mind on one key issue in his philosophy. From his earliest poem, written in 1753, he repeatedly emphasizes the idea that it is easy to be good and to attain happiness (I:60, 144; II:62, 64, 78, 84, 85, 89). This idea follows logically from his faith in a providential God who makes everything that is necessary for happiness easy to obtain. But Skovoroda concedes, probably because of his personal experience and observation of others, that it is difficult to overcome the appetites and attain virtue (I:99). In his letters to Kovalins'kyj, written in the early sixties, he admits that "divine truth is most difficult to find" (II:254), and "to learn the most noble art of living is very difficult" (II:263). In Fable 15, written probably at the end of the sixties, the moral is that the higher the good the more difficult it is to attain (I:115). In the seventies he had still not made up his mind on this issue, and admitted that peace is difficult (I:352), and that the necessities of life are hard to obtain (I:353). It was only in his late work, "Prja běsu so Varsavoju" ("The Dispute between the Devil and Varsava)" (1783), that Skovoroda definitely rejected the view that goodness is difficult and confessed that he had been wrong (II:86). His argument there is based not on experience, however, but on the doctrine of divine providence; goodness must be easy, otherwise God is not good (II:62, 64, 89). His attempt to explain away the contrary evidence derived from experience by blaming people's attachment to material things for their difficulties in attaining goodness (II:89) simply begs the question. In any case, there are no signs of further wavering on this question in the last decade of his life.

The observation that many, if not most, men are unhappy raises a problem closely connected with the previous one. If God is benevolent and happiness easy to attain, why are many men unhappy? Skovoroda's two attempts to answer this question are not successful, but this is true of all religious thinkers who pose the question in similar terms. Ignorance about God is the basic reason why men take the wrong path in life, pursue earthly goods and end up unhappy. The very word for unhappiness (*neščastie*) points to the source of unhappiness, which lies in preferring the lower part (*čast'*) to the higher part (I:416) because of blindness (I:386, 416; II:96). This solution only moves the question one step back: why are many men ignorant? The other solution places the blame on the will rather than on reason. Anyone who wants to can attain happiness (II:95), but many are distracted by the world and swayed by other people (I:340). The truth that will lead us to happiness is at hand, but men do not want to listen, some because they are born deaf but most because they were brought up badly (I:149). This answer implies that at least a few men are by nature incapable of attaining happiness, which contradicts the basic tenets of Skovoroda's philosophy. As for the others, who are incapable of happiness because they have been raised badly by their educators or society at large, the question arises why a good God permitted them to be spoiled, or how the educators and society were corrupted. The problem of evil remains unsolved in Skovoroda's system.

In spite of these difficulties, Skovoroda's moral philosophy is remarkably unified and coherent. It is the most profound and appealing part of his philosophical system. Although Skovoroda believes in the immortality of the soul, he never speculates about the afterlife. He is interested only in this life, in finding fulfillment and happiness here. Heaven and hell dwell in men's souls (I:87). Judgement occurs in this life (II:135, 470-71), for sin is its own punishment (I:376). By their nature men must be active, and congenial work confers happiness on the agent and benefit upon society. Such work requires concentration and renunciation of everything except what is necessary to one's health and vigorous activity. Skovoroda's recognition of the individual's supreme value does not lead to conflict or isolation, but to a deep and lasting unity called friendship. The happy life for Skovoroda is the most intense and creative form of life, resting on a firm faith in providence. This ideal is a synthesis of the best insights of the ancient philosophers and the Bible with the inclinations of his own inner nature.

An Introduction to the Theological Thought of Hryhorij Skovoroda

Petro B.T. Bilaniuk

Skovoroda was a most original thinker and one of the greatest minds of Eastern Europe in his day. Many Ukrainian scholars see in Skovoroda an outstanding representative of the Ukrainian psyche—a man of intense introversion, with a generous heart, displaying the domination of spiritual virtues over the intellectual, manifesting a joyful love of nature, a very keen aesthetic sense, a profound humanism and a genuine religious spirit. Therefore, many researchers of the ethnopsychology and character of the Ukrainian nation place Skovoroda alongside Taras Ševčenko as one of the most typical Ukrainians and as an ideal to be imitated in the process of the formation and education of the Ukrainian people.[1]

In addition, Skovoroda was a many-sided literary genius. He was a philosopher, a writer, a translator, a critic of culture, a poet, a mystic, a biblical scholar and a theologian. His erudition was as profound as it was diverse. He had a very good command of Latin, Greek, Hebrew and German, and was extremely well versed in classical poetry, literature, philosophy, the Church Fathers, and biblical exegesis.

Skovoroda's *Weltanschauung* may be summed up as follows: the macrocosm is the beautiful and meaningful creation of an all-wise God. Thus, ontologically, the world is good. But demonic and evil powers are at work, trying to entice and ensnare man in his striving toward true happiness. The temporal, visible, and

---

1. Cf. Jakym Jarema, *Ukrajins'ka duxovist' v jiji kul'turno-istoryčnyx vyjavax* (n.p.: Peršyj ukrajins'kyj pedagogičnyj kongres, 1935); Ivan Mirtschuk, *Geschichte der ukrainischen Kultur* (Munich: Isar Verlag, 1957), 66: "Der ukrainische Sokrates, Skovoroda, dessen geistiges Leben alle charakteristischen Züge der national-psychischen Struktur des ukrainischen Volkes wiederspiegelt,..."

material aspect of the world is worthless without an intimate conjunction with the divine, invisible, spiritual, and eternal aspect, which is of inestimable value and to which all must strive as to the source of true beatitude. The second world, or microcosm, which reflects the macrocosm, is man himself. Ontologically, again, man is a good creature of God, and must use his cognitive and volitional faculties in order to gain knowledge of the macrocosm and its Creator. The necessary prerequisite for this is self-knowledge. The Socratic maxim "Know thyself" is the first step toward philosophical and theological knowledge. However, the search for truth about oneself, God and the world is not an end in itself, but only a means that prompts men to perfect their wills, their virtues, and their hearts. A practical quest for spiritual happiness and divine beatitude, not theoretical speculation, should be the primary concern of man. Thus, the cognitive efforts of man must strive toward the ethical, and the ethical toward the ontological purpose of man. The third world is a symbolic one, namely, the Bible, in which are gathered the figures, symbols, types, and images of heavenly, earthly, and nether-worldly realities. These are monuments leading our thoughts to an understanding of eternal nature, which is mysteriously present in mortal man's nature.[2]

Part One: Skovoroda—Philosopher or Theologian?

Is the world-view described above theological or philosophical in nature? In other words, should one continue the prevailing tradition and classify Skovoroda as primarily a "philosopher," or should one depart from this tradition and classify him as essentially a theologian? After all, true scholarly research must strive to corroborate or refute accepted scholarly, scientific, or popular views by a process of constant verification and cultivation of the available information. I am convinced that in the case of Skovoroda it is necessary to perform a somewhat radical re-evaluation of conclusions concerning his classification as a "philosopher," or the "founder of the so-called philosophy of the heart."[3] If one elaborates a fuller and more exact characterization of Skovoroda and elucidates his creativity and heritage, then it will be necessary to classify him as primarily a theologian.

The fundamental distinction between theology and philosophy can be reduced to the mode of knowledge and the source of truth. The theologian speaks of the acceptance of divine self-revelation through the gift of faith and the use of human intellectual and natural knowledge. The philosopher discerns only a human, natural and intellectual knowledge that extends to the world and its

---

2. This paragraph is taken from my book review of *PZT,* which appeared in *Slavic Review* 33, no. 3 (1974):560.
3. G. Luznycky and L.D. Rudnytzky, "Ukrainian Literature," *NCE* XIV:370.

phenomena, but without the explicit intervention of divine self-revelation. In philosophy, therefore, God is only a Supreme Being, the Creator and the All-powerful Ruler of the natural world, and, thus, the Author of natural truth. True philosophy may not deny a priori the existence of God the Creator, or of the Giver of grace. On the contrary, philosophy can and should attempt to elucidate by rational arguments the existence of God the Creator and the possibility, or even probability, of divine self-revelation by the inspired word. It is, however, only the believing man who, without any apodictic or compelling arguments and under the influence of the divine light of faith, arrives at the existence of God as the giver of divine life, light, and love. Such an act of faith surpasses the merely philosophical and natural act of knowing or speculation, and attains to super-rational and salvific reality.[4]

On the basis of the above exposition, one can affirm that both the sciences of theology and philosophy are fundamental sciences which do not conflict with one another, because God is the ultimate ground of both the inner-Triadic and the extra-divine reality and truth. Moreover, history is an eloquent witness that theology constantly has used contemporary philosophy as an auxiliary source of knowledge and as an instrument for a deeper and more exact penetration and elucidation of the divinely revealed truths. This is so because divine love and salvific self-revelation are addressed to the whole man, with both body and soul, with intellect, will, and feelings, that is, with all his metaphysical and integral parts and aspects.[5]

When one applies the above elaborations, classifications and divisions to the person and heritage of Hryhorij Skovoroda, an entirely new image of this extraordinary figure emerges. First of all, those who classify Skovoroda as a philosopher would agree that he was not a systematic philosopher, that is, he did not construct a coherent system that would do justice to all branches and divisions of philosophy. They would also agree that his main interest was in the area of axiology (with an emphasis on ethics and the philosophy of religion) and in philosophy as *Weltanschauung* (with an emphasis on anthropology and theodicy). It is not sufficient to give only scant attention to Skovoroda's love for Sacred Scripture. To him the Bible was the main source of divine self-revelation, and

---

4. The First Vatican Council considered and defined these matters in a Dogmatic Constitution, *De Fide Catholica "Dei Filius,"* which was promulgated during the third session (24 April 1870); cf. H. Denzinger and A. Schönmetzer, *Enchiridion Symbolorum...* (Barcelona: Herder, 1963), 32nd ed., No. 3000-3045. The Second Vatican Council further developed these questions in a Dogmatic Constitution, *De divina Revelatione "Dei Verbum"* (18 November 1965).

5. For more exact information, see K. Rahner and H. Vorgrimler, "Philosophie und Theologie," *Kleines theologisches Wörterbuch* (Freiburg: Herder, 1963), 287-9; C.F. Van Ackeren, "Reflections on the Relation between Philosophy and Theology," *Theological Studies* 14 (1953): 527-50.

usually served as the starting point of his thinking.[6] The Bible also was to him the definitive authority and the rule of truth.[7] This indicates that Skovoroda was concerned primarily with divinely revealed truth, which to him was a gift, accessible only by divine faith.[8] Therefore, it is necessary to classify Skovoroda as primarily a theologian or a Christian thinker, and only secondarily as a philosopher, writer, poet, etc.

Skovoroda's famous "philosophy of the heart" (which some scholars consider to be his creation[9]) is not a strictly philosophical teaching on the heart, but rather a discursive theological elaboration of biblical teaching,[10] combined with philosophical elements borrowed principally from ancient Stoic thought.

One of the most eloquent witnesses to the exalted role of the Bible and theology in Skovoroda's thought and life is a quotation from an article, "Kinship to Theology," in his work, entitled *Razhovor, nazyvaemyj alfavit, ili bukvar' mira* (A Discourse Called the Alphabet, or Primer of the World):

---

6. These statements are relatively easy to prove. Almost every major work of Skovoroda begins with a short introduction or introductory chapter entitled, "the contents of the discourse," "the main subject-matter of this book," "the foundation of the dialogue," "the foundation," "this book's main subject," "main subject of the work," "the main subject and contents of the booklet," or "the foundation of the parable." Each of these introductions consists of biblical quotations that embody the main thoughts or themes, as well as the main arguments in favour of the author's conclusions. Often his work opens with an appropriate biblical quotation that serves as the guideline of the whole work in question. Also, all of his writings are rich in scriptural quotations that serve as the foundation and guideline of his dialogue and reasoning.

7. The theological thinking of Skovoroda emerges very clearly also in his works dealing with purely secular themes. The preface to *Basni Xar'kovskija* (The Tales of Xarkiv) (*TDT* II:101-50; *PZT* I:107-33), for example, bears witness to the author's theological intention. He wishes to illustrate with human examples the divine truths revealed in the Bible. As a result, the moral teaching deduced from each of the tales (the so-called "strength") is theological in nature, or at least contains a very important theological ingredient. It is also interesting to note that there, too, we find quotations from Holy Scripture, especially in the "strength" of the last tale (*TDT* II:145-50; *PZT* I:129-33).

8. Skovoroda also quite clearly distinguished between the natural and the supernatural modes of knowledge; that is, between the natural act of faith based on reason and intuition and the supernatural act of divine faith. This is clearly indicated in his work, *Načal'naja dver' ko xristianskomu dobronraviju* (The Initial Door to Christian Morality), where in Chapter Two, entitled "On Universal Faith," he writes: "Similarly, all ages and nations have always unanimously believed that there is some mystery; namely, a power that is poured out upon everything and that dominates all things" (*TDT* I:17; *PZT* I:146). Again, in the sixth chapter, entitled "On the True Faith," Skovoroda writes, "It [i.e., true faith] is a beatitude that is hidden from all counsel and that [acts] as if it were looking from afar through a telescope, with which it is also portrayed" (*TDT* I:24; *PZT* I:152). For Skovoroda, purity of heart is not a naturally acquired quality, but a "calm breathing and blowing in the soul of the Holy Spirit" (*TDT* I:26; *PZT* I:153), that is, a supernatural gift or a charisma.

9. Cf. note 3.

10. On the concept of "heart" in the Bible and theology, see P. Hoffmann and K. Rahner, "Herz," *Handbuch theologischer Grundbegriffe*, ed. H. Fries (Munich: Kösel, 1962), I:687-97; O. Schroeder, N. Adler, and A. Maxein, "Herz," *LThK*[2], V:285-7; W.E. Lynch, "Heart (in the Bible)," *NCE* VI:965.

Flee from anxiety, embrace solitude, love lowliness, kiss purity, befriend suffering, study sacred languages, learn at least one well, and become one of the scribes [=scholars] educated for the divine kingdom, of whom Christ [said]: "So then every scribe instructed in the kingdom of h[eaven is like a householder who bringeth forth from his storeroom things new and old. Matt. 13:52]..." That is why these scribes are learning languages. Be not afraid! Hunger, cold, hatred, persecution, denigration, abuse, and all effort is not only tolerable, but also sweet, provided that thou wert born for it. Thy Lord is thy strength. All this will make thee much keener and much more sublime. A torrent in nature, be it a rushing stream or a flame, courseth much more quickly through a narrow passage. Greet the ancient pagan philosophers. Converse with the universal Fathers [of the Church]. Finally, thou shalt come into the Israelite land, to Bethlehem itself, into the house of bread and wine, into the most sacred temple of the Bible, chanting with David: "I rejoiced because they said unto me: [We will go up to the house of the Lord."] (Ps. 121:1)... How cautiously one must enter this wedding hall! Be well dressed! Wash thy hands and feet. Then sit down at this immortal table. But beware! Do not push [thy hand] into the salt-dish with the host. Remember that this is not thine, nor a carnal meal, but the one of the Lord. God preserve thee! Thou shalt die if thou eatest blood. Eat the blood and the body of the Lord and not thine own. "May this be good and pleasing unto thee before thy Lord God." Receive, but only from the Lord; eat, but [only] for the Lord; be satisfied, but [only] before the Lord.[11]

This set of theological admonitions reads like an autobiographical account of Hryhorij Skovoroda himself, and quite clearly demonstrates that in the final analysis he is a theologian. The different stages of spiritual development spoken of in the foregoing are: 1. the acquisition of the necessary virtues, above all, patience and persistence; 2. the acquisition of knowledge of the sacred tongues (Hebrew, Greek, Latin); 3. an acquaintance with pagan philosophers (especially Socrates, Plato, Aristotle); 4. dialogue with the Church Fathers; and finally, 5. entrance into "the sacred temple of the Bible," which opens the door to the highest mystery of the Body and Blood of the Lord, that is, the Holy Eucharist.

This text is a close approximation of the method Skovoroda used in his work.[12] A careful scrutiny of this method reveals that he made use of sacred tongues, the pagan philosophers and the Fathers of the Church, and employed the external form of a dialogue to elucidate the theological contents of the divine mysteries depicted in the Bible in order to make them existentially accessible to his contemporaries.

On the basis of the above arguments I presented the following conclusion in

---

11. *TDT* I:352; *PZT* I:439-40.
12. On Skovoroda's method, cf. Dmytro Čyževs'kyj, *Narysy z istoriji filosofiji na Ukrajini* (Prague: Ukrajins'kyj Hromads'kyj Vydavnyčyj Fond, 1931), 41-7.

a previous publication:[13]

> The thought of Hryhorij Skovoroda is, then, almost entirely a *terra ignota* which must be investigated primarily by theologians. This is so because Skovoroda is not, strictly speaking, a philosopher, but a moral theologian and a Christian thinker. Scholars with exclusively philosophical and literary training will be confused by this great person, or will wander about aimlessly through his writings, as they have been doing ever since his own day.[14] As was to be expected, this position was wholeheartedly accepted by theologians,[15] and rejected by scholars with an exclusively philosophical and literary training, who continue to defend Skovoroda as a philosopher, a thinker, or a Christian philosopher, without any reference to his theology.[16] However, the most absurd evaluation of Skovoroda is proposed by "Soviet scholarship," which tendentiously claims that the "philosophical views of Skovoroda evolved in the direction of materialism and were characterized by an ever sharper presentation of social problems and a definite striving to liberate himself from the bondage of idealism and religion."[17]

---

13. Petro B.T. Bilaniuk, "Hryhorij Skovoroda—Philosopher or Theologian?" *The New Review* XIII, no. 1-2 (1973):50-61.
14. Ibid., 59. The above-mentioned article was also published twice in Ukrainian: "Hryhorij Skovoroda—filosof čy bohoslov?", *Bohoslovija* 34 (1970):244-53, and in *Zbirnyk naukovyx prac' na pošanu Jevhena Vertyporoxa...* (Toronto: Kanads'ke Naukove Tovarystvo im. Ševčenka, vol. XII, 1972), 55-65.
15. E.g., Msgr. Jean Rupp (Archbishop of Monaco and Apostolic Nuncio in Baghdad), "Der ukrainische Rousseau: Skovoroda und seine theologischen Ansichten," *Mitteilungen,* no. 10-11 (Munich: Arbeits- und Förderungsgemeinschaft der Ukrainischen Wissenschaften e.V., 1974):18-30.
16. E.g., Volodymyr Oleksjuk, "Hryhorij Skovoroda—Xrystyjans'kyj filosof," *Do problem doby obmanu mudrosty* (Chicago: Ukrajins'ke Katolyc'ke Akademične Objednannja "Obnova," 1975), 16.
17. D.X. Ostrjanyn et al. in an essay, "Vydatnyj ukrajins'kyj filosof i pys'mennyk," in *TDT* I:xiii. There also we read: "The representatives of the dominant classes have made an all-out effort to use the anti-feudal writings of the great protester against feudal society for the defence of the feudal-landlord system, the absolute monarchy and the church establishment. They have perverted the true views of the thinker and presented him as a mystic and a theologian. Stressing the theological form and religious phraseology, by means of which Skovoroda usually expressed his moral-ethical principles of 'universal love,' 'self-knowledge,' and 'self-perfection,' bourgeois scholars rejected or obscured the concrete social questions that were raised by the philosopher, his angry and passionate struggle against parasitism, profiteering, official religion, the clergy, the rich, the nobles and the bureaucrats; they denied the democratism of the philosopher as well as his burning patriotism." Substantially the same views were expressed by many Soviet scholars, e.g., M. Red'ko, *Svitohljad H.S. Skovorody* (L'viv: Vydavnyctvo L'vivs'koho universytetu, 1967); Ivan Pil'huk, "Poet-myslytel'. Estetyčni pohljady H. Skovorody," in H. Skovoroda, *Poeziji* (Kyiv, 1971), 3-44; Pavlo Tyčyna, "Hryhorij Skovoroda," in *Skovoroda: Symfonija* (Kyiv, 1961), 348-63; Borys Derkač, "Narodnyj filosof, poet-humanist," in Hryhorij Skovoroda, *Vybrani tvory* (Kyiv, 1971), 5-19; V.I. Šynkaruk et al., *Filosofija Hryhorija Skovorody* (Kyiv, 1972). For further bibliography on Skovoroda (i.e., works published in the Ukrainian SSR and USSR between 1945 and 1972), cf. T.A. Korčyns'ka, "Bibliohrafija filosofs'koji ta suspil'no-polityčnoji literatury pro Skovorodu H.S. (1945-1972)," *Filosofs'ka dumka,* no. 5 (1972):99-104.

Part Two: Skovoroda—A Theologian of the Alexandrine Tradition?

There can be no doubt that Skovoroda deserves the honorary title of "Bohoiskatel'" [God-seeker], who perpetually and actively sought God and His divine reality. Therefore, if somebody refuses to accept Skovoroda as a theologian, he certainly cannot refuse to acknowledge him as a "theological man" comparable to St. Francis of Assisi or many other figures in both East and West.

Further, let us investigate the Skovorodian concept of *mysl'* (roughly, "thought"), which is not a product of intellect only, i.e., an abstract and spiritual image or concept that can remain in the intellect or can be expressed externally by a symbol, writing, or a living word. *Mysl'*, in the Skovorodian sense, is a product and expression of the whole human being, i.e., intellect, will, heart, emotional apparatus, and the body of the human person, who, according to the teaching of Skovoroda, is a mystery, a microcosm and a psychosomatic unity. Therefore, *mysl'* has not only intellectual, but also moral, voluntary, artistic, sentimental, and material dimensions or aspects. Thus, *mysl'* can express itself in both theological and philosophical thought, in moral values, and in the acts of a person or of a community. It can also result in the creation of material and artistic monuments in which it can fix its permanent expression. Precisely in the case of Skovoroda, this *mysl'* is extremely important, for he was not only a great intellectual (admittedly, we can detect a certain anti-intellectual trait in his thought), but also a person of great literary talent who expressed himself in poetry, fables, philosophical and theological dialogues, treatises, sermons, and translations. However, the most important fact is that Skovoroda practised what he preached, and his virtuous and upright life was the most beautiful expression of his moral values, ideas, and strivings.[18] The Skovorodian *mysl'* has a religious and theological character, for it is oriented toward God, its object is God, the whole divinized reality and the whole of creation in its relationship to and dependence on God. All the philosophical, literary, and artistic elements of the creativity and *mysl'* of Skovoroda are subordinated to and coordinated with his theological *mysl'* in the broadest sense of the word.

But how may one classify this Skovorodian *mysl'*? Where does one look for its sources and models? Many students of Skovoroda's writings concluded that he relied on, or drew from, the ancient Alexandrine school of theology and the Alexandrine type of biblical exegesis.[19] Therefore, one may adopt the following

---

18. Cf. Myxajlo Hruševs'kyj, *Z istoriji relihijnoji dumky na Ukrajini* (Winnipeg, Munich and Detroit, 1962), 106-12.
19. E.g., Hruševs'kyj, op. cit., 111-12; Lebedev, Krasnjuk and Florovskij, cf. notes 32, 33, and 34

method: first, we shall examine the nature of theological schools in general. Second, we shall outline very briefly a comparative synthesis of the most characteristic elements of the Alexandrine and Antiochian theological schools or traditions. Third, we shall analyze the witness of Kovalins'kyj, Skovoroda's student and friend, and draw upon several examples from the works of Skovoroda. Finally, we shall draw several conclusions.

Schools of theology[20] can be described as cultural and sociological entities consisting of theological teachers and their followers, or groups of theologians, who, under a common local or personal influence, but within one Church and her one profession of faith, represent some more or less similar conceptions, orientations, trends, systems or syntheses of theology or spirituality. They have their origin in a manifold historicity, i.e., of human knowledge, of divine revelation and its theological explanation, and of homogenous evolution of dogmas. Therefore, it is legitimate to speak of the one and objective divine revelation expressed in a definite historical setting and form, and of its subjective, diversified but legitimate interpretations or schools. These schools, as a sign of healthy theological pluralism, must keep within the limits of orthodoxy set by the magisterium of the Church and avoid theological relativism and heresy. Therefore, the magisterium always distinguished between legitimate and illegitimate schools of theology.[21] Some were explicitly formed and sociologically or institutionally perpetuated by some order, school, or nation. Some were more implicit and consisted in differentiation, accentuation, and a different philosophical foundation of theological thought. While reflecting on the problem of schools of theology, the following must be kept in mind: "To wish to belong to no school would be the part of a proud and stupid man who imagines that here and now he can possess eternal truth outside historical time. To cling to a system as if it fully expressed the faith of the Church would be to deny the historicity of truth."[22]

In Christian antiquity, at the beginning of the third century, there emerged two rival schools of theology: the Alexandrine[23] and the Antiochian.[24] These two

---

below.

20. Cf. K. Rahner, "Schulen, theologische," *LThK*² IX:509-12; Y.M.J. Congar, *La foi et la théologie* (Tournai: Desclée, 1962), 197-201; J. Danielou, "Unité et pluralité en matière de théologie," *Recherches et débats* 10 (1955):11-21; J.-H. Nicolas, "La théologie et les théologies," *La vie spirituelle* 103 (1960):277-301.

21. Cf. H. Denzinger and A. Schönmetzer, *Enchiridion Symbolorum...* (Barcelona, etc.: Herder, 1963), 32nd ed., 697-8; also No.: 718, 1090, 1097, 1146, 1216, 1219, 1579, 2167, 2565, 2726, 3154-5, 3625.

22. K. Rahner and H. Vorgrimler, *Theological Dictionary* (New York: Herder and Herder, 1965), 428.

23. Cf. F. Normann, "Alexandrinische Theologenschule," *Sacramentum Mundi. Theologisches Lexikon für die Praxis* (Freiburg, etc.: Herder, 1967) I:95-101; A. Van Roey, "Alexandria, School of," *NCE* I:304-5; H. Rahner, "Alexandrinische Schule," *LThK*² I:323-5; Altaner, 167-85, 233-57.

schools elaborated two classical types of theological thought, which, to a greater or lesser degree, are with us to the present day. It is possible to say that every theologian is born as a sympathizer either of the Alexandrine or of the Antiochian theological school. In this brief description we cannot delve into the complex and, in many instances, obscure history of both schools. We can simply provide a very general summary of their salient features.

The philosophical background and substratum upon which Alexandrine theological thought grew was Neoplatonism. Therefore, both Platonic and Neoplatonic elements are dominant in it.[25] Aristotelianism dominated in the Antiochian school, for here Aristotle's works were regarded as the pinnacle and fulfillment of philosophy. And yet, even here Neoplatonic elements were sometimes used.

In the realm of biblical exegesis, the Alexandrine school distinguished itself by an allegorical and typological explanation of Sacred Scripture. Here the influence of Philo of Alexandria was considerable, and, therefore, the search for the mystical and spiritual meaning and significance of divine revelation expressed in Sacred Scripture was dominant. On the other hand, the Antiochian school continued the old Rabbinical exegesis, that is, it looked for the literal sense of the critical text of Sacred Scripture. As a result of this the Alexandrine school used deduction as its principal theological method,[26] especially in the elaboration of allegories and in its explanation in the light of faith. In contrast to this, the Antiochian school used an inductive and historico-philological or grammatical method, and by the same token tried to explain the typology of the historico-salvational acts of God and to make them accessible to the average person in the light of faith and reason.

All this contributed to the growth of two distinct types of theological thought: the Alexandrine and the Antiochian. The former was distinguished by its contemplation, metaphysical speculation and profound sense of mystery. The latter distinguished itself by positive and historical investigations. Therefore, it was no accident that at Alexandria the guiding theological principles were based on abstract metaphysical, spiritual, and supernatural reality. At Antioch the guiding theological principles were based on empirical, practical, experiential, and natural reality. At this point, it may be helpful to explain that in the tradition of Eastern

---

24. Cf. F. Normann, "Antiochenische Theologenschule," *Sacramentum Mundi. Theologisches Lexikon für die Praxis* (Freiburg, etc.: Herder, 1967) I:194-9; A. Van Roey, "Antioch, School of," *NCE* I:627-8; H. Rahner, "Antiochenische Schule," *LThK*² I:650-52; Altaner, 185, 276-306.

25. Cf. Endre v. Ivanka, *Plato Christianus. Übernahme und Umgestaltung des Platonismus durch die Väter* (Einsiedeln, 1964).

26. Cf. J. Beumer and L. Visschers, "Die theologische Methode," *Handbuch der Dogmengeschichte*, eds. M. Schmaus, A. Grillmeier, L. Scheffczyk (Freiburg, etc.: Herder, 1972), vol. I, Faszikel 6:6-9, 25-47.

Christian theology theologians do not usually jump to ultimate theological conclusions, as is often the case in the West. Rather, they usually express a certain tendency, or an orientation of their speculative thought, without necessarily drawing ultimate conclusions. In the Alexandrine school it is a thought that descends "from above to below," of a deductive type, which tries to interpret created reality from the point of view of God. In the Antiochian school, an ascending and inductive type of thought dominated, i.e., "from below to above," which tried to interpret God and things divine from the point of view of created reality.

In mystical theology, however, the situation has often been quite different. In the specifically Alexandrine cosmology and anthropology, the human being, under the attracting power of the transcendent God and by way of transfiguration and divinization, ascends vertically, step by step, through the different spheres of the world and of being to God as to its primary cause and its absolute and transcendent goal. In the Antiochian school, mysticism was considerably less developed than in the Alexandrine, and was not of a vertical, but of a horizontal type, i.e., it concentrated on the contemplation of the immanence of God in His creatures.

The most classical example of the diversity and even contrariety between the Alexandrine and the Antiochian schools was in the area of Christology.[27] Alexandrine Christology stressed the mystery of the incarnation of the Divine Logos and of the divine nature of Christ. Although it did not deny the human nature of Christ, it continued to obscure and minimize it. In the Antiochian school, Christological thought that stressed the real and perfect human nature of Christ and held His divine nature and the divine attributes to be of secondary importance was dominant.

Most certainly both schools were constantly exposed to the peril of exaggerating one of their beloved features. Therefore, the Alexandrine school was constantly criticized as holding to theological irrationalism, exaggerated mysticism and unwise asceticism based on a hostility to the body and accompanied by a Neoplatonic hostility to matter and the whole empirical and created reality generally. The Antiochian school, in its turn, was constantly in danger of theological historicism and rationalism. In the course of time both the Alexandrine and the Antiochian schools generated their own heresies, which were exaggerated forms of the theological positions described above. The Alexandrine school gave rise to monophysitism, whereas the Antiochian school generated Arianism, Nestorianism and Pelagianism. Besides these, the Alexandrine school was constantly influenced by Manichean and Gnostic tendencies, while the Antiochian

---

27. Cf. J. Liebaert, "Christologie. Von der Apostolischen Zeit bis zum Konzil von Chalcedon (451)," *Handbuch der Dogmengeschichte*, ed. M. Schmaus and A. Grillmeier (Freiburg, etc.: Herder, 1965).

was under the spell of rationalism and secular influences.

Before we proceed to examine and classify the theological thought of Skovoroda, let us hear some of the critics of this thought. In the middle of the nineteenth century Archbishop Filaret (i.e., D. Gumilevskij) objected to Skovoroda's exaggerated immanentism, which, he felt, bordered on pantheism. He very strongly accused Skovoroda of this error, and attributed it to the influence of the German mystic, Jakob Böhme.[28] It is true that such an influence cannot be excluded a priori. However, there is sufficient evidence that Skovoroda's theological thought was inspired by the Fathers of the Church of the Alexandrine tradition. According to it, the whole of creation is filled with the Divine Presence, which sanctifies, transfigures and divinizes it. And precisely this is the foundation of that pneumatic optimism which we find in both the Fathers and writers of the Alexandrine tradition and in Skovoroda.

Toward the end of the last century B. Nikol'skij levelled heavy criticism against Skovoroda.[29] To him the thought of Skovoroda appeared to be a mixture of contradictions: it was partially pantheistic, partially rationalistic, and partially mystical. However, stated Nikol'skij, Skovoroda's thought is neither simply the first nor the second nor the third. But this is so not because Skovoroda made some sort of synthesis of these views, but because he was unable to distinguish one mode of thought from another.

Nikol'skij's remark concerning Skovoroda's pantheistic tendencies is not correct. We can, however, speak of Skovoroda's panentheism, i.e., the teaching of God's intense presence to and immanence in His creatures. Most certainly there are mystical elements in Skovoroda's thought, but the charge of his rationalism is without foundation. We can, however, detect some gnostic tendencies of the Alexandrine type. Nikol'skij's observation that Skovoroda did not create some higher synthesis needs further examination. It is true that he did not create a coherent and systematically organized synthesis, but it cannot be denied that it is possible to distill from his works a coherent theological and philosophical *Weltanschauung* with a solid systematic foundation. Further, it is necessary to stress that Skovoroda was quite capable of distinguishing different philosophical and theological currents, systems and views. In his work he used not only Platonic and Neoplatonic elements, but also some Aristotelian categories and other philosophical principles and views that today are classified as Christian existentialism and personalism. We have to stress once more that different philosophies, as well as all branches of human knowledge, accepted in the light of faith, were for Skovoroda the necessary tools for an explanation of divinely

---

28. Cf. D. Gumilevskij (Archbishop Filaret), *Obzor russkoj duxovnoj literatury, 862-1858* (St. Petersburg, 1861) I:72. Cf. also F. Maliske, "Jacob Boehme," *LThK*[2] II:559-60.
29. Cf. B. Nikol'skij, "Ukrainskij Sokrat," *Istoričeskij vestnik* (1895), 222.

revealed truth, or better, of the divine self-revelation. He was truly a *Bohoiskatel'*, a God-seeker.

Toward the end of the nineteenth century F. Kudrinskij[30] attacked Skovoroda's theology, objecting to it as not truly orthodox. Further, he observed that Skovoroda's thought, especially toward the end of his life, was becoming more and more tinged with mysticism. There can be no doubt that Kudrinskij was wrong in his first charge, for the theological thought of Skovoroda was very dynamic, fully orthodox and based on the teachings of the Church Fathers of the Alexandrine tradition. (This will be elucidated below.) Besides, his theological thought was far superior to the official theology of the Russian Orthodox Church of his day, which since Peter I (1672-1725) had been oppressed by the yoke of Muscovite caesaropapism and often found itself used as a tool of Muscovite imperialism. Furthermore, the church categorically rejected all religious views and feelings that did not conform to the official model. Skovoroda, by his sincere and living theological thought, into which he integrated philosophical and secular knowledge, objected to that ecclesiastical and state establishment, for he constantly pointed to the necessity of the inner religious and moral renewal of each member of the church and of the whole church as a communal body. There is no doubt that the church of Skovoroda's time was suffocating from superficiality, ritualism and external forms, and dogmatic narrowness.

The eminent Ukrainian historian, Myxajlo Hruševʼskyj, made the following remarks concerning Skovoroda's biblical exegesis and thought:

> In these interpretations Skovoroda follows the old Christian symbolists of the Alexandrine school (Origen, Clement), whose writings he loved very much and held in high esteem. But, evidently, all these symbolic expansions by themselves were giving him nothing: they were necessary to him in order to harmonize the authority of the Bible with his moral system, with the ideas of "the viewer of God, Plato," as he called him, and with the moral teachings of Plutarch, Cicero and the other ancient moralists, whom he loved to read, to quote and to translate. Evidently these works were close to him, but he was too closely united to the ecclesiastical tradition to be able to place its books on the same level as others, in the same way as he was unable fully to escape the influence of the Mohylan learning [i.e., the scope and level of education of the Kyiv Mohyla Academy], which very often is reflected in his writings, regardless of his critical position in regard to the Mohylan church. "It is necessary first of all to demolish, break and crush much instead of erecting a new building on the old ground," he himself remarked. He was unable to perform this monumental task, and therefore his practical and moral incorporation of the moral ideal that was given by his life transcends his literary speculations.[31]

---

30. Cf. F. Kudrinskij, "Filosof bez sistemy," *Kievskaija starina*, no. 1 (1898):58.
31. Myxajlo Hruševʼskyj, *Z istoriji relihijnoji dumky na Ukrajini,* 2nd ed. (Winnipeg, Munich and

Hruševs'kyj was right concerning the Alexandrine type of Skovoroda's exegesis. All his other conclusions, however, are wrong. First of all, Skovoroda did not try "to harmonize the authority of the Bible with his moral system," but, on the contrary, tried to subject all his philosophical speculations and the writings of the ancient philosophers to the authority of divine revelation expressed in Sacred Scripture and tradition, as these were understood in the Alexandrine school. In other words, he did not philosophize and did not use the Bible as a philosophical source or tool. He examined the philosophers and the Church Fathers and measured them against the ultimate authority, Sacred Scripture. This is theology at its best. Second, Skovoroda went far beyond the horizons of the Mohylan church and learning and therefore became unintelligible to the majority of his contemporaries.

A.S. Lebedev was the first to give a correct appreciation of the stature of Skovoroda as a theologian when he wrote: "G.S. Skovoroda, who as a philosopher constitutes the pride of Ukraine, was not only a philosopher, but also a theologian, and may also be more of a theologian than a philosopher. It is true that he was a theologian of a type not completely usual for his (and also for the present) time, but in any case of an unobjectionable and non-condemnable type, who took his origins from the ancient and famous Fathers and teachers of the church."[32] Lebedev was also the first who correctly identified Skovoroda as a theologian of the Alexandrine tradition.

This assessment of Skovoroda was accepted by M. Krasnjuk[33] and Rev. Georgij Florovskij, who believed that with Skovoroda real theologizing was born in Russia.[34] In more recent literature Skovoroda has assumed a more permanent place as a philosopher, but sometimes authors make references to his religious or theological thought, e.g., Konrad Onasch calls him a "heretofore fully unknown type within orthodoxy."[35] A very welcome development of the whole question took place with the completion of Stephen Patrick Scherer's dissertation, entitled "The Life and Thought of Russia's First Lay Theologian, Grigorij Savvič Skovoroda (1722-1794)" (Ph.D. dissertation, Ohio State University, 1969). However, this dissertation and its main argument—that Skovoroda was the first Russian lay theologian—was rejected by Ekkehard Völkl as an extreme posi-

---

Detroit, 1962), 111-12.
32. A.S. Lebedev, "G.S. Skovoroda kak bogoslov," *Voprosy filosofii i psixologii* 27 (1895):170.
33. Cf. M. Krasnjuk, "Religiozno-filosofskie vozzrenija Skovorody," *Vera i razum* (1901), Book XVI.
34. Cf. Georgij Florovskij, *Puti russkogo bogoslovija* (Paris, 1937), 120-21.
35. Konrad Onasch, *Grundzüge der russischen Literaturgeschichte* (Göttingen, 1957), 110.

tion.[36] A very good survey of research on Skovoroda's religious thought was provided by Joseph T. Fuhrmann in his article, "The First Russian Philosopher's Search for the Kingdom of God."[37]

There can be no doubt that Dmytro Čyževs'kyj is the greatest interpreter of Skovoroda's life and thought. His many works[38] are concerned with disentangling the historical and objective facts from the "Skovoroda legend," which grew through both the oral and the written tradition. Further, he investigated many possible influences on Skovoroda's thought: the Bible, Philo of Alexandria, the Fathers of the Church, and the German mystics and poets (especially Jakob Böhme, Angelus Silesius, Valentin Weigel and others). Čyževs'kyj also made a successful synthesis of Skovoroda's thought and very vividly portrayed him as a poet, a thinker and a mystic. Thus, we can conclude that there is a definite revival of interest in Skovoroda's religious and theological thought.

A very important witness to the sources and method of Skovoroda's thought is M.I. Kovalins'kyj, who in his "Life of Hryhorij Skovoroda"[39] wrote the following about his teacher and friend:

> Skovoroda continued to lecture publicly on syntax and the Hellenic language, and instructed his beloved young man separately in the Greek language and the reading of ancient books, of which the more beloved by him were the following writers: Plutarch, Philo Judaeus, Cicero, Horace, Lucian, Clement of Alexandria, Origen, Nilus, Dionysius the Areopagite, Maximus the Confessor, and, of the modern [writers], those related to these; at the head of everything stood the Bible. The power, contents and goal of their learning endeavour was the heart, that is, the foundation of the blessed life.[40]

When from the above list of the favourite authors of Skovoroda and of his

---

36. Ekkehard Völkl, "Der ukrainische Philosoph Skovoroda und die Orthodoxie," *Mitteilungen* no. 10-11 (Munich: Arbeits- und Förderungsgemeinschaft der Ukrainischen Wissenschaften e.V., 1974):9.
37. Published in: *Essays on Russian Intellectual History*, ed. Leon Borden Blair (Austin and London: University of Texas Press, 1972), 33-72.
38. The most important works of Čyževs'kyj on Skovoroda are: "Filosofija H.S. Skovorody (1722-1794)," *Put'* 19 (1930):23-56; *Narysy z istoriji filosofiji na Ukrajini* (Prague: Ukrajins'kyj hromads'kyj vydavnyčyj fond, 1931), 35-63; D. Čyževs'kyj, "Skovoroda-Studien. I. Skovoroda und Angelus Silesius," *Zeitschrift für Slavische Philologie* 7 (1930):1-33; "Skovoroda-Studien. II. Skovorodas Erkenntnislehre und Philo," ibid., 10 (1933):47-60; "Skovoroda-Studien. III. Skovorodas Bibel-Interpretation der kirchenväterlichen und mystischen Tradition," ibid., 12 (1935):53-78; "Skovoroda-Studien. IV. Skovoroda und Valentin Weigel," ibid., 12 (1935):308-22; *Filosofija Skovorody* (Warsaw, 1934); D. Tschižewskij, *Skovoroda: Dichter, Denker, Mystiker* (Munich: Wilhelm Fink Verlag, 1974 = Harvard Series in Ukrainian Studies, Vol. 18); valuable material on Skovoroda may also be found in D. Čyževs'kyj, *A History of Ukrainian Literature*, trans. Dolly Ferguson et al., ed. George S.N. Luckyj (Littleton, Colo.: Ukrainian Academic Press, 1975), passim.
39. Cf. *TDT* II:487-535; *PZT* II:439-76.
40. *TDT* II:502; *PZT* II:450-51.

beloved young pupil [M.I. Kovalins'kyj himself] we eliminate the ancient classical writers Plutarch, Cicero, Horace and Lucian (whom it is difficult to identify, for there were several Lucians), then only the representatives of the Alexandrine school remain on the list. The first is Philo Judaeus (of Alexandria),[41] the most distinguished thinker of the Jewish diaspora and the founder of the allegorical, mystical and pneumatic explanation of the books of the Old Testament.

Further down the list we see Clement of Alexandria[42] and Origen,[43] who were the founders of the Christian theological school of Alexandria. Origen and Bishop Demetrius founded a catechetical school in Alexandria that was designed for the instruction of the broad masses. At the same time, several theological academies were founded in Alexandria for the instruction of the more educated classes. Among these the Didaskaleion was the most distinguished, because Origen and Clement of Alexandria taught the advanced courses on theology and biblical exegesis there.

St. Nilus[44] is next on Kovalins'kyj's list. He was a highly learned *hegumen* of the monastery in Ancyra. (Until recent times he was improperly called St. Nilus of Sinai.) In his moral and ascetical writings, destined to educate monks, St. Nilus elaborated the pneumatic aspects of the monastic life on the basis of the Alexandrine tradition, and called the monks the pneumatophores, or the carriers of the Holy Spirit.[45]

Next we see a cryptonym, *Dionysius the Areopagite*, who today is called the Pseudo-Dionysius,[46] for it has been definitively established that the works of this unknown author were not written during the missionary journeys of St. Paul,[47] but at the beginning of the sixth century, probably in Syria. However, the whole corpus of the Pseudo-Dionysius is a classical example of Alexandrine

---

41. Cf. R. Arnaldez, "Philo Judaeus," *NCE* XI:287-91; C. Mondésert, "Philon v. Alexandrien," *LThK*² VIII:470-71.

42. Cf. M. Spanneut, "Clement of Alexandria," *NCE* III:943-4; T.Th. Camelot, "Klemens v. Alexandrien," *LThK*² VI:331-2; Altaner, 169-75.

43. Cf. H. Crouzel, "Origen and Origenism," *NCE* X:767-74; H. Crouzel, "Origenes," *LThK*² VII:1230-35; Altaner, 175-85.

44. Cf. P.W. Harkins, "Nilus of Ancyra, St.," *NCE* X:470; H.C. Graef, "Neilos v. Ankyra," *LThK*² VII:870-71; Altaner, 300.

45. In the work "Prja běsu so Varsavoju" [Polemics of the Devil with Barsaba] (*TDT* I:482; *PZT* II:94) Skovoroda mentions St. Nilus in remark "b": "*Črevoneistovstvo* is a stomach-wisdom that thinks only of what sweeter sacrifices there are for its god—the stomach. So explains St. Nilus in the book on the seven devils." Thus Skovoroda attributed the work *Antirretikos* of Euagrios Ponticos to St. Nilus.

46. Cf. F.X. Murphy, "Pseudo-Dionysius," *NCE* XI:943-4; H.C. Graef, "Dionysios Areopagites," *LThK*² III:402-3; Altaner, 466-70.

47. Cf. Acts 17:34; Dionysius Areopagita, Ep. 7, 3; Div. Nom. 2, 11.

theological thought. It exercised a tremendous influence on the minds of theologians, mystics and even philosophers in both the East and West. It is true that in Skovoroda's writings one detects a profound influence of Pseudo-Dionysian thought, especially as far as the hierarchical order of beings in the world is concerned.

The last Church Father on the list is St. Maximus the Confessor (c. 580-662).[48] It is true that this holy man fought against different heresies and errors stemming from the Alexandrine school, i.e., monophysitism and monotheletism. However, in his exegetical writings he used the allegorical and moral exegesis of Sacred Scripture in the spirit of the Alexandrine school. In his ascetical and mystical works he was a representative of an Alexandrine type of spirituality with very strong Gnostic tendencies. Also in his *Mystagogy* he presented a symbolic explanation of Sacred Scripture in the spirit of the Alexandrine theological school.

Future investigators of Skovoroda must conduct a comparative study and analysis of the works of the Church Fathers and the writers enumerated by Kovalins'kyj and the works of Skovoroda in order to establish definitively the extent of their influence on his thought. I am convinced that precisely here is the key to the correct interpretation of Skovoroda's works and thought.

The first similarity between Skovorodian and Alexandrine theological thought is the philosophical background, or, more exactly, the dominance of the Neoplatonic elements.[49] Skovoroda was very well versed in the philosophy of Plato, and very often based his speculations on its principles. He mentioned Plato in his writings more than thirty times.[50] However, both Origen (and the Alexandrine school after him) and Skovoroda modified the Platonic philosophical tradition and applied it to the explanation of Christian Sacred Tradition and Sacred Scriptures. Therefore, to them God is the absolute, transcendent, eternal and stable Being. He is also the eternal Logos. The finite and created being is only a reflection or an image of part of the divine Being and a participant in His greatness and glory. Both in the Alexandrine school and in Skovoroda, there is a predominance of the idea of hierarchical order in the world, as well as an idea of the dynamic movement of the created being from God to God, i.e., from its efficient cause to the final and definitive cause. Further, there is a stress on the immortality and the immateriality of the human soul, which is directed and oriented to God. Both ethics and mysticism are resolved in *theosis* or

---

48. Cf. M. Hermaniuk, "Maximus Confessor, St.," *NCE* IX:514-16; A. Ceresa-Gastaldo, "Maximos Confessor," *LThK*² VII:208-10; Altaner, 484-6.
49. Cf. P.J. Aspell, "Plato," *NCE* XI:430-33; J.O. Riedl, "Platonism," *NCE* XI:433-8; P. Hodot, "Neo-Platonism," *NCE* X:334-6; J. Hirschberger, "Platon," *LThK*² VIII:553-4; J. Hirschberger, "Platonismus," *LThK*² VIII:555-8; E. Elorduy, "Neuplatonismus," *LThK*² VII:917-19.
50. Cf. *TDT* II:615 (Index); *PZT* II:567 (Index).

Theological Thought 267

divinization, *metamorphosis* or transfiguration, and a transformation of the whole human person into a spiritual being and its subsequent elevation to God. This is a brief list of the Neoplatonic elements that became the permanent possession of the Christian tradition and received a very special emphasis in the works of Skovoroda.

In the domain of biblical exegesis, Skovoroda is also a representative of the Alexandrine tradition. His interpretation of Sacred Scripture is allegorical and typological, for he constantly searched not for the literal but the mystical and spiritual meaning of divine revelation. The most interesting example from the Skovorodian writings in this area is the second redaction of a work entitled, "Dialoh. Imja emu—Potop zmiin" (Dialogue. Its Name—The Flood of the Serpent), in which the Soul and the Imperishable Spirit converse.[51] This is the last known work of Skovoroda, dated "In the year 1791, Aug. 16." In the preface to this work, the author signed his name "Hermit Hryh. Varsava Skovoroda,"[52] thereby clearly indicating his great sympathy for the Alexandrine tradition and the Egyptian hermits, who became the prototype of monasticism in the whole Christian world. At the beginning of Chapter Two of this work, "Spirit" teaches "Soul":

> Each [human being] born is a stranger in this world, [be he] either blind or illumined. Is this world not the most beautiful temple of the most wise God? There are three worlds. The first is the general and inhabited world, in which all born [creatures] dwell. This one consists of innumerable worlds-of-worlds and is the great world. The other two are partial and small worlds. The first is the microcosm, that is, a small world, worldlet, or a human being. The second world is a symbolic one, that is, the Bible. In any of the inhabited worlds the sun is its eye and the eye also is its sun. And as the sun is the head of the world, therefore, no wonder that the human being is called the microcosm, that is, a small world. The Bible is the symbolic world, because in it the figures of the heavenly, terrestrial and the nether-worldly creatures are gathered in order that they may be the monuments leading our thought [=*mysl'*] into the understanding of the eternal nature hidden in mortal [nature], just as a picture [is hidden] in its colours.[53]

In this text, besides the genuine Alexandrine cosmology in which the material dimensions of the world are harmoniously tied to the spiritual and pneumatic ones, we see also a strict hierarchical order of the world in which the Bible is represented as a symbolic world of figures and the source of esoteric or even gnostic knowledge. A little farther in the same work, we read:

---

51. *TDT* I:533-80; *PZT* II:135-71.
52. *TDT* I:535; *PZT* II:136.
53. *TDT* I:536; *PZT* II:137.

Spirit. The sun is an archetype, that is, a primordial and main figure, and its copies and vice-figures are innumerable and fill up the whole Bible. Such a figure was called *antitypos* (primordial image, vice-image), that is, one that was placed instead of the main figure. But all of them flow back to the sun as to their source. Such vice-figures are, for instance: the dungeon and Joseph, the small box and Moses, the pit and Daniel, Delilah and Samson, that is, sunlet, the skin and Job, body and Christ, the cave and the lion, the whale and Jonah, the manger and the babe, the sepulchre and the Resurrected one, the chains and Peter, the basket and Paul, a wife and family, Goliath and David, Eve and Adam... All this is the same as the sun and little sun—the dragon and God. The most beautiful of all and the mother of all other [figures] is the figure of the sun. It was the first one to be blessed and sanctified into the peace of God. "God blessed the seventh day." For this reason the vice-figures of other creatures are placed in its [the figure of the sun] power, [and] receive all of their existence in the days of the luminous seven-day week, for during it all creatures are born; however, it is established before all others.[54]

This quotation speaks for itself and definitively proves that in the domain of biblical exegesis Skovoroda imitated the Alexandrine school. Also, Skovoroda's works abound in the traditional Alexandrine teachings, namely, concepts and images of light and sun, archetypes, typology, transfiguration, blessedness of the human being and of creatures in general. These elements entered Alexandrine thought under the influence of the Gospel of St. John, which was probably written in Alexandria and influenced by the theological and philosophical *Weltanschauung* of a cosmopolitan Alexandrine society in which the teachings of Philo, Neoplatonic thought, and even the Buddhist tradition coexisted side by side and competed for a hearing.[55]

Symbolism constitutes a very important ingredient of Skovoroda's works. On this Semen Pohorilyj remarks: "Symbolism in Skovoroda is presented pictorially (emblems and paintings), but mostly in writing (words). There were many paintings. A great number of them were component parts of the manuscript "Alphabet, or Primer of the World" and of other works. It is very sad that they have not been published and have not even been described."[56] Some of Skovoroda's graphic symbols were published in 1973, and Čyževs'kyj made a general study of his symbols in 1932.[57] But a more detailed study has yet to be under-

---

54. *TDT* I:541; *PZT* II:141.
55. Cf. J. Edgar Bruns, *The Art and Thought of John* (New York: Herder and Herder, 1969), 116-19.
56. Semen Pohorilyj, "Symvoly u Skovorody," *Sučasnist'*, no. 3 (March 1973):19.
57. *PZT* passim. Cf. D. Čyževs'kyj, "Pro dejaki džerela symvoliky Skovorody," *Praci Ukrains'koho Vysokoho Pedagogičnoho Instytutu im M. Drahomanova u Prazi, Naukovyj Zbirnyk* 2 (Prague, 1932):1 (405)-19 (423).

taken. However, even cursory, preliminary research points to the fact that Skovoroda was closely related to Alexandrine symbolism, which goes back to ancient Egyptian symbolism and hieroglyphics. Skovoroda gives evidence of this in the preface to the "Tales of Xarkiv":

> This entertaining and figurative genre of writing was at home with the very best of the ancient lovers of wisdom. Laurel is green even during the winter. So also wise [men] are intelligent in toys and truthful in a lie. The truth to their sharp sight did not silhouette itself from a distance [as is the case with] inferior minds, but manifested itself clearly to them as in a mirror, and they, having quickly perceived its living image, compared the same to different [and] perishable figures.
>
> No colours manage to explain a rose, a lily, or a narcissus as it is in life, as the shade of heavenly and earthly images, which well and beautifully reflect in themselves the invisible divine truth. From this were born *hieroglyphica, emblemata, symbola*, mysteries, parables, fables, similes, sayings... And it is no wonder that Socrates, when his inner angel, who was a leader in all his works, ordered him to write poetry, chose the fables of Aesop. And as the most sophisticated image appears to the untrained eye to be a lie, so also it happens here.[58]

The Alexandrine type of theological thought, i.e., synthetic, deductive and descending from above, or an interpretation of the created reality from the point of view of God, is very well represented in Skovoroda's work "Ubohij žajvoronok" (The Poor Lark):

> Verily nothing is good except the pure heart; a seed [that] sprouted through heaven and earth; a mirror that contains in itself and portrays all creatures in eternal colours; a solid foundation which by its wisdom fortified wonderful heavens; a hand which with its palm engulfs the whole globe and the dust of our body. What then is more wonderful than memory, eternally representing in images the whole world, eternally hiding in its bosom the seeds of all creatures, seeing with one eye both past and future deeds, as well as contemporary ones? Tell me, my guests, what then is memory? Are you silent? I'll tell you. Yet not I, but the divine grace in me. Memory is the never-sleeping eye of the heart that oversees all creatures, the never-setting sun that illumines the whole earth. Oh, morning memory, like the indestructible wings! By thee the heart flies up into the height, into the depth, into the breadth without end, one hundred times more quickly than lightning.[59]

The last sentence of the above text constitutes an introduction to Skovoroda's mysticism, i.e., a vertical ascent of the human being to God, but through different dimensions and spheres of existence. The intimacy of mystical experience and the concept of reciprocal immanence of God and mystic is portrayed in

---

58. *TDT* II:102; *PZT* I:108.
59. *TDT* I:525; *PZT* II:127.

Skovoroda against the background of a *kenosis* of the Alexandrine type. It is the condescension and diminution of God Himself, who comes down to His people and His creatures in their hearts. This pure heart is a gift that comes from the East as a bridegroom who illumines us with his light of glory. On this Skovoroda writes in "Ubohij žajvoronok":

> Oh, to a good man each day [is] a feast day, but to a lawbreaker—not [even] the Great Day [Resurrection Sunday]... If the heart is the head and source of the whole world, is it not also a root of the feast day? The mother of the feast day is not time, but a pure heart. It is also the Lord of the Sabbath. Oh, pure heart, verily thou art not afraid either of lightning or of thunder. Thou art God's, and God is to thee thine. Thou art to Him, and He to thee a friend. It is to thee, my God, a sacrifice, and thou to it. You are two, and are one. O pure heart! Thou art the new age, eternal spring, beautiful heaven, the promised land, the intellectual paradise, joy, quietude, divine peace, Sabbath and the great day of the Pasch. Thou hast visited us from the dwellings on high of the luminous East, descended from the sun, like a bridegroom from his palace. Glory to Thee who hast shown to us Thy light. This is the day of the Lord: let us rejoice and be glad, o brothers![60]

In the same work we also find the Skovorodian theory of the contemplation of the world. In it we discover Alexandrine gnostic and dualistic tendencies, that is, an accentuation of esoteric and salvational knowledge, and the dualistic struggle between good and evil:

> The world is nothing else but a bond, or a synthesis of deeds or of creatures. And nothing else is god of this age but the earthly heart, the source and head of the world. But thou, my son, while reading the book of this visible and evil world, direct the eye of thy heart in all works toward the very head of the work, at its very heart, to its very source; then, having learned its origin and seed, thou wilt be a just judge of any work, seeing the head of the work and the very truth, and the truth shall save thee from all assaults. If there are two kinds of creatures and works, then [there are also] two hearts. If there are two hearts, then also two spirits—good and evil, truthful and full of lies...[61]

Alexandrine theological thought can easily be detected in the philosophical and theological anthropology of Skovoroda. In a work called "Narkiss" ["Narcissus"], we read:

> *Friend:* The above-mentioned imperial daughter of David, the most pure she-dove and the most beautiful virgin, leads us away from this mud, having dressed us not in muddy [wings], but in wings gilded between the shoulders and silvered by the Divine Spirit. Bewinged, we fly up with David and rest. We throw off the earthly Adam with his bread, [and] illnesses, we fly over with our

---

60. *TDT* I:525; *PZT* II:127.
61. *TDT* I:523; *PZT* II:125-6.

heart to the Pauline man, to the invisible, heavenly, to our world, not beyond the seas and forests, not above the clouds, not to other cities and centuries—it alone is eternal—but we penetrate to the very centre of our heart and our soul, and, having forsaken all foul and diluvial thoughts with all the extreme exteriority of our body, having left the whole thunderstorm and fog under his feet, we ascend by means of the above-mentioned ladders to the high ascent and descent to our life and head, to the true human being, into the ark not made by human hands and to his incorruptible and most pure body, of which our little earthly dwelling is but a faint shadow and appearance of the true, joined into one hypostasis without confluence of the divine and perishable beings. This is, then, the true *man*, equal to his eternal Father in being and power, one in all of us and whole in each of us, whose kingdom has no end...[62]

It is very difficult to describe adequately the wealth of theological thought expressed in the above quotation. Therefore, let us simply enumerate the most important elements: esoteric and supernatural knowledge, which flows from the gift of faith and transfigures the human being; the beautiful, antithetical presentation of the earthly, visible and natural human being and of the invisible, heavenly and supernatural, that is, of the true human being as he should be according to the divine design; the heavenly ladder (which reminds us of the ascetical work of John Climacus, a representative of Alexandrine spirituality) by means of which a human being ascends to his true life, a copy of which is the earthly life; finally, orthodox Christology, but of the specifically Alexandrine type, i.e., with a strong tendency toward monophysitism.

This brings us to a consideration of Skovoroda's Christology, which points to the fact that he knew theology very well in general and the Alexandrine type of Christology in particular. In "Narkiss," Skovoroda meditates on the death of the Lord Jesus Christ and exclaims:

Thou art in the darkness, Thou liest in the grave... O divine spark! A grain of mustard and of wheat! O seed of Abraham! O Son of David! O Jesus Christ! Heavenly and new man! Head and heart and light of all creatures! Point of the universe! Power, law, and kingdom of peace! Right hand of God! Our resurrection! When shall we comprehend Thee? Thou art a true man with a true body. But we do not know such a man, and those whom we know, they all die. Ah, the true man never dies. Thus, it seems that we have never seen a true man, and those whom we know, their hands, feet, and whole body turn into dust.[63]

In this text, again, we find a wealth of teaching: Christ is the archetype of a new and heavenly human being; He is the head, heart, illuminator and point of convergence of the whole universe, i.e., the classical Alexandrine teaching of the recapitulation of every creature in Christ, or *anacephalaiosis*; Christ is the

---

62. *TDT* I:72; *PZT* I:191.
63. *TDT* I:71; *PZT* I:190.

pantocrator or All-powerful Ruler of the whole universe and of all creatures. It is important to note that in this text Skovoroda centres his attention on the human nature of Christ and of each human being in relation to Christ and the world. The result of this reflection is truly Alexandrine, for on the one hand the anthropology is fully dependent on Christology, and on the other hand it is under the influence of an anthropological pessimism of a Neoplatonic type.

In another text Skovoroda portrays Christ as the original who has many copies and is an object of contemplation that transfigures the viewer:

> O Christ, sacred fountain of graces!
> Pour Thy Spirit upon the shepherd.
> Be unto him an Archetype,
> So that, gazing upon him,
> Each man of his flock may be led to act,
> And so extend his blessed life-span.[64]

Any serious thinker reveals himself best when hesitating and introducing corrections into his own works. This happened to Skovoroda in an important Christological text, "Ubuždšesja viděša slavu jeho" [Awakening, They Saw His Glory]:

> O true, incorruptible Israelite (*man*) God! Illumine us with Thy light as much as our eye can possibly bear it. In order that we might go into the light of Thy face and, insensibly transfigured into a new [creature], attain our most joyous resurrection even down to our last hair! To Thee be glory with Thy man and the Holy Spirit. Amen![65]

Leaving aside true Alexandrine symbolism, mysticism, and the metaphysics of light, as well as the teachings concerning transfiguration and resurrection, this text is important because of a correction made by Skovoroda himself. In the autograph of this text Skovoroda in his own hand struck out the word "čeloviče" [the vocative of "man"] and substituted the word "Bože" [the vocative of "God"], even though it did not fit into the context very well after the word "Israelite." This points to the fact that Skovoroda caught himself overstressing the humanity of Christ, and, according to his Alexandrine mode of thinking, stressed Christ's divinity instead. This stress becomes more apparent if one takes into account the expression "with Thy man" in the last part of the quotation. As a truly orthodox theologian, Skovoroda does not forget the human nature of Christ, but as a representative of the Alexandrine tradition he assigns it a much lower place on the scale of importance.

---

64. *TDT* II:47; *PZT* I:84.
65. *TDT* I:6; *PZT* I:138.

Conclusion

In conclusion, one must add that in all the texts quoted above one detects a profound contemplation, metaphysical speculation, and a deep sense and intuition of the beauty and dynamism of the life-giving mystery of God. Furthermore, there is a definite tendency to portray abstract, metaphysical, spiritual and supernatural reality. Here we have an example of the deductive method, for, from a general and fundamental principle, Skovoroda tries to deduce the particular and the secondary. Sometimes he describes a cause and then cites the effects. All these are typical traits of Alexandrine theological thought.

It is interesting that Skovoroda started to think in the categories of the Alexandrine tradition precisely at a time when many different theological and philosophical trends and views based on Aristotelianism and rationalism were penetrating Ukraine and the whole Russian Empire from the West. Besides, cultural achievements, various technological inventions, scientific views, and discoveries in the natural sciences were coming from the West.[66] Skovoroda did not reject these new advances, but was intent on distinguishing between positive and negative influences. In this difficult process he discovered, elaborated and applied in practice what he considered the most authentic Christian theological thought and spirituality, i.e., the Alexandrine patristic tradition. As a result of the many contradictory trends and ideas that were flowing together in Eastern Europe at the time, we can detect in the works of Skovoroda a great tension, an antithetical and dialectical mode of thought, or even a paradox. Therefore, many of his writings remind us of the writings of the father of modern existentialism, Søren Kierkegaard (1813-55), whom Skovoroda anticipated a century before his appearance on the European theological and philosophical scene.

Skovoroda was a loner and a person generally unintelligible to his age, for in many instances he was ahead of his time; it is only today that ancient Alexandria is being rediscovered as the centre of a very advanced and original culture and of profound theological thought and spirituality. Contemporary theologians and philosophers might find in Alexandrine thought many useful elements for the work of renewal of contemporary Christianity, which is undergoing one of the most profound crises in its two millennia of history. Skovoroda had a vision of the future, and many of his works were intended as a serious *memento* to his contemporaries and to future generations. Therefore, there is no doubt that the life and thought of Skovoroda can contribute to the renewal of contemporary Christian life and thought.*

* This article previously appeared in *Studies in Eastern Christianity* 2 (Toronto, 1982):159-82.

66. Cf. S.P. Scherer, "The Concept of an Unlimited Natural World in the Thought of H.S. Skovoroda (1722-94)," *The New Review* 12 (1972):33-42.

Abbreviations

Altaner = Berthold Altaner, *Patrologie. Leben, Schriften und Lehre der Kirchenväter* (Freiburg: Herder, 1958), 5th ed.

LThK^2 = *Lexikon für Theologie und Kirche*, established by Michael Buchberger, edited by Josef Höfer and Karl Rahner (Freiburg: Herder, 1957-68), 10 vols.

NCE = *New Catholic Encyclopedia*, prepared by the editorial staff at the Catholic University of America, Washington, D.C. (New York, etc.: McGraw-Hill, 1967), 15 vols.

PZT = Hryhorij Skovoroda, *Povne zibrannja tvoriv u dvox tomax*, ed. V.I. Šynkaruk et al. Akademija Nauk Ukrajins'koji RSR (Kyiv: Naukova dumka, 1973), 2 vols.

TDT = Hryhorij Skovoroda, *Tvory v dvox tomax*, ed. O.I. Bilec'kyj et al. (Kyiv: Vydavnyctvo Akademiji Nauk Ukrajins'koji RSR, 1961), 2 vols.

A Note on the Character, Orthodoxy, and Significance of Skovoroda's Thought

Stephen P. Scherer

In the two centuries since H.S. Skovoroda's death a large secondary literature devoted to his life and thought has emerged.[1] This body of work is marked by a significant area of agreement concerning Skovoroda's biographical data and life-style. Practically all who have considered his life, activities and personality have concurred on the facts of his religious inclinations, his education at the Kyiv Academy, his travels to St. Petersburg and abroad, his career as both a private tutor and seminary instructor, and his ultimate choice of the impoverished life of a wandering teacher. The reason for this consensus is that those who have concerned themselves with Skovoroda's life have based their knowledge of it, at least in part, on the biography by M.I. Kovalins'kyj, Skovoroda's student and life-long friend.[2] This biography, which reflects Kovalins'kyj's talent, as well as his love for Skovoroda, is the only extended discussion of Skovoroda's life by one who knew him personally. The biography, it is true, has its shortcomings, particularly with regard to the details and chronology of Skovoroda's youth, formal education, travel abroad, teaching career and final decision to adopt the life of a *strannik*. Still, it is the only relatively full, first-hand account of Skovo-

---

1. Some indication of the extent of this secondary literature may be gained by looking at *Ukrajins'ki pys'mennyky: Bio-bibliohrafičnyj slovnyk,* 5 vols. (Kyiv, 1960-65), I:520-36. A more complete picture of the literature can be had by examining *Hryhorij Skovoroda: Biobibliohrafija* (Xarkiv, 1968); *Hryhorij Skovoroda: Biobibliohrafija,* 2nd ed. (Xarkiv, 1972). Concerning the jubilee work on Skovoroda, see V.I. Šynkaruk et al., ed., *Hryhorij Skovoroda 250* (Kyiv, 1975), 245-53.
2. This biography has been published numerous times; for this paper I have consulted the following edition: M.I. Kovalinskij, "Žizn' Grigorija Skovorody," in Hryhorij Skovoroda, *Tvory v dvox tomax* (Kyiv, 1961), II:487-535 (hereafter cited as *TDT*).

roda's life, and so is indispensable for a study of the man.

In contrast to this general accord on Skovoroda's biography, however, there is a great deal of disagreement with respect to: 1) the character of his thought; 2) his relationship to Orthodoxy; and 3) his significance as a thinker. Such conflicts become apparent when one considers some representative opinions on these questions. Concerning the character of Skovoroda's thought, for instance, Vissarion Belinskij, the nineteenth-century Russian literary and social critic, exhibited a most negative view: "Let everyone judge for himself, but for me the philosopher Xoma[3] is as good as the philosopher Skovoroda."[4] Belinskij gave his reason for this negative evaluation of Skovoroda when he wrote sarcastically, "O incomparable master Xoma! How magnificent you are in your stoic indifference to everything earthly...."[5] Because he saw in Skovoroda an exclusive concern with spiritual matters, with the other-wordly sphere, Belinskij rejected his thought out of hand. In contrast to this adverse criticism of Skovoroda's thought, Mykola Kostomarov, the father of modern Ukrainian historiography, was constrained to take a more favourable attitude. While arguing that Skovoroda's thought was not a potent or influential force in the nineteenth century, he attacked the superficiality of those who criticized Skovoroda's works "as if he were a new writer just now appearing, when it is appropriate to view his writings as a memorial to the ideas that held sway almost one hundred years ago."[6] Kostomarov not only viewed Skovoroda's work positively in terms of the time and place in which it appeared, but also found in it a remarkable freedom of thought and practical morality.[7]

Later in the nineteenth century one can find attitudes toward Skovoroda's thought which, though they were the product of a greater knowledge than either Belinskij or Kostomarov possessed, still demonstrated discord. D.I. Bahalij, for instance, who edited Skovoroda's *Collected Works* in 1894, perceived in his thought numerous contemporary ideas, including the following:

> A straining toward the moral rebirth of the individual, an unflinching search for truth, the principle of a broad religious tolerance, the struggle against supersti-

---

3. Xoma Brut is the central character in Nikolaj Gogol's story "Vij." He was a seminarian and philosophy student in Kyiv, who, while travelling home for the summer, experienced a series of extraordinary adventures. The last of these was his face-to-face meeting with the monster, Vij, which encounter resulted in Xoma Brut's death.

4. V.G. Belinskij, *Polnoe sobranie sočinenij*, 13 vols. (Moscow, 1953-9), I:304.

5. Ibid. N.G. Černyševskij, the leading civic critic of the 1860s, enthusiastically supported Belinskij's assessment of Skovoroda's thought. N.G. Černyševskij, "Očerki Gogolevskogo perioda russkoj literatury," *Izbrannye filosofskie sočinenija* (Moscow, 1938), 482.

6. N.I. Kostomarov, "Otvet na stat'ju Vsevoloda Krestovskago," *Osnova*, no. 8 (1861):4.

7. N.I. Kostomarov, "Slovo o Skovorode," *Osnova*, no. 7 (1861):178; "Otvet na stat'ju Vsevoloda Krestovskago," *Osnova*, no. 8 (1861):9.

tion, a democratic spirit expressed in his desire to give enlightenment to the lower classes of society, and a complete accord between word and deed.[8]

Bahalij was also struck by the critical aspect of Skovoroda's thought, a criticism that was directed in the main toward the Bible and religion, but which was critical thought nonetheless.[9] The Russian essayist B. Nikol'skij, writing at about the same time as Bahalij, discerned in Skovoroda's thought neither contemporary nor critical elements. On the contrary, he argued that Skovoroda's writings were bewildering in the extreme, a hodgepodge of ill-fitting ideas. Skovoroda's thought, he wrote,

> is confused and inconsistent. While it is a little pantheistic, a little rationalistic, and a little mystical, it is neither the first, the second, nor the third: this is so not because Skovoroda reconciled these world-views into some kind of higher synthesis, but simply because he could not unravel one from the other.[10]

With regard to Skovoroda's work, one can find even more severe conflict in contemporary evaluations of it. V.V. Zen'kovskij, for instance, emphasized the "inner wholeness" of Skovoroda's thought, an inner wholeness which, he argued, "issues from the steadfast feeling that the essence of being is located beyond the limits of empirical reality."[11] On the other hand, one discovers in Soviet attitudes toward Skovoroda's work an inclination to ignore his idealism altogether or to exaggerate his materialism, even while admitting the idealist element in his thought: "In the philosophic views of Skovoroda it is characteristic that...in the last analysis the answers to the basic question of philosophy clearly expressed a materialistic tendency."[12]

> In the views of Skovoroda...there is a noticeable vacillation between materialism and idealism. He is a materialist when he asserts the eternity of matter...he stands as an idealist in his teaching about the two principles that make up the world, the outer—matter, the inner—idea.[13]

---

8. D.I. Bahalij, "Učenie, žizn' i značenie G.S. Skovorody," *Kievskaja starina*, no. 12 (1894):474.
9. D.I. Bahalij, "Ukrainskij filosof Grigorij Savvič Skovoroda," *Kievskaja starina*, no. 6 (1895):278.
10. B. Nikol'skij, "Ukrainskij Sokrat," *Istoričeskij vestnik* LX (1895):222.
11. V.V. Zen'kovskij, *Istorija russkoj filosofii*, 2 vols. (Paris, 1948-50), I:79.
12. Ja.D. Dmiterko, I.A. Tabačnikov and O.V. Traxtenberg, "Razvitie obščestvenno-političeskoj i filosofskoj mysli na Ukraine v èpoxu feodalizma," Akademija Nauk SSSR, *Očerki po istorii filosofskoj i obščestvenno-političeskoj mysli narodov SSSR*, 2 vols. (Moscow, 1955-6), I:181.
13. A.I. Beleckij, "Literatura perioda usilenija krepostničeskogo gneta i zaroždenija kapitalizma," Akademija Nauk Ukrainskoj SSR, *Istorija ukrainskoj literatury*, 2 vols. (Kyiv, 1954-7), I:117. This conventional Soviet emphasis on Skovoroda's materialism has been questioned of late. See, for instance, F.V. Konstantinov, "G. S. Skovoroda—vydajuščijsja gumanist," *Voprosy filosofii*, no. 2 (1973):146; V.I. Šynkaruk and I.V. Ivan'o, "Hryhorij Skovoroda" in Hryhorij Skovoroda, *Povne zibrannja tvoriv u dvox tomax*, ed. V.I. Šynkaruk et al., 2 vols. (Kyiv, 1973), I:37, 45-6.

The differences evident in the above evaluations of Skovoroda's thought are also manifest in various interpretations of his relationship to Orthodoxy. These conflicts have no reference to Skovoroda's ties to the official church, for Kovalins'kyj's biography and Skovoroda's own work have made abundantly clear both his criticism of the institutional church and his refusal to participate in its monastic life.[14] The concurrence, or lack thereof, between Skovoroda's thought and Orthodox dogma is, however, another matter. On this latter question D. Gumilevskij (Archbishop Filaret), the nineteenth-century cleric and scholar, argued that Skovoroda's teachings deviated from Orthodoxy when he asserted that Skovoroda was a Ukrainian thinker "who, unfortunately, tainted his thought by his familiarity with Jakob Böhme's muddle-headed mysticism."[15] Pavel Miljukov, in his classic volumes on Russian culture, concurred with Gumilevskij's contention concerning Skovoroda's deviation from Orthodoxy. He argued that Skovoroda's writings were almost perfectly in accord with the teachings of the Doukhobors, the sectarians who emerged in southern Russia and Ukraine during the middle of the eighteenth century.[16] In opposition to this argument concerning Skovoroda's departure from Orthodoxy, A.S. Lebedev, in an article on Skovoroda's theology, contended that his teachings were in complete agreement with Orthodox thought.[17]

Finally, as concerns the significance of Skovoroda's thought, there is some agreement that his intellectual influence was diffuse and oblique rather than concentrated and direct, but little accord as to his precise intellectual importance. Vladimir Èrn, a Russian philosopher of the turn of the century who was concerned with combating the increasingly mechanistic approach to life, saw in Skovoroda's thought an opposition to the growing emphasis on the object and empirical observation.[18] Because of this, he perceived Skovoroda's significance in his decision to reject the material world and empirical science. Èrn contended that subsequent thinkers had remained stubbornly faithful to this decision, even though Skovoroda did not directly influence them.[19] V.V. Zen'kovskij perceived Skovoroda's importance in his being the first representative of religious philosophy in the Russian Empire. Along with this he remarked on the "unquestionable

---

14. M.I. Kovalinskij, "Žizn' Grigorija Skovorody," *TDT* II:493, 498. See also Skovoroda, "Beseda narečennaja Dvoe," *Sobranie sočinenij* (St. Petersburg, 1912), 206.
15. D. Gumilevskij, *Obzor russkoj duxovnoj literatury, 862-1858*, 2 vols. (St. Petersburg, 1859-61), I:72. Gumilevskij even suggested that Skovoroda may have translated some of Böhme's works into Russian.
16. P. Miljukov, *Očerki po istorii russkoj kultury*, 2 vols. (Paris, 1931), II: part 1, p. 123.
17. A.S. Lebedev, "G.S. Skovoroda kak bogoslov," *Voprosy filosofii i psixologii*, no. 2 (1895):175-6.
18. V. Èrn, *Grigorij Savvič Skovoroda* (Moscow, 1912), 336.
19. Ibid., 332, 336.

secularization" of his thought.[20] In opposition to Ėrn and Zen'kovskij, Soviet critics with too few exceptions have characterized Skovoroda as 1) "a writer and philosopher-enlightener who condemned the exploitative structure of society, addressed himself to the common people, and strained to arouse them to knowledge, enlightenment and action";[21] 2) "A Ukrainian thinker, humanist, democrat and enlightener who brought his anger down against the feudal system, and who, in his world-view, reflected the hatred of both the peasants and rank-and-file Cossacks for their oppressors, and their yearning for a better society."[22]

These divergent, though representative, opinions doubtless bear witness to the ethnic identifications, religious inclinations, and ideological attachments of their respective authors. But even more, they testify to the scope and nature of Skovoroda's thought, as well as to the range and variety of his sources. Despite the difficulties that Skovoroda's thought and sources have presented to his critics, it is possible to fashion a balanced evaluation of the character, Orthodoxy and significance of his work.

The central fact of Skovoroda's thought was his Platonic contention that reality lay beyond the realm of appearances.[23] He found this to be so for man, nature, and the Bible, and as a result he rejected empirical knowledge as something to be pursued for its own sake.[24] Though Skovoroda emphasized the reality of the unseen nature, or divinity, which sustained appearances, he did not conclude that physical matter was illusory or unreal.[25] Instead, basing his argument on the existence of an immanent-transcendent God who was both within and without matter, he contended that matter was a necessary attribute of God and therefore, like God, unlimited in time and space.[26] Skovoroda's argument concerning the eternity and infinity of matter, though it may have been influenced in part by Western scientific accomplishments, originated in his religious conception of divine immanence. Therefore, it does not demonstrate Skovoroda's

20. V.V. Zen'kovskij, op. cit., 80-81.
21. O.V. Traxtenberg, "Filosofskaja mysl' na Ukraine vtoroj poloviny XVIII v.: G.S. Skovoroda," Akademija Nauk SSSR, *Istorija filosofii*, 6 vols. (Moscow, 1957-65), I:653.
22. V.E. Evdokimenko and I.A. Tabačnikov, "Filosofskaja i sociologičeskaja mysl' narodov SSSR s konca XVI do poslednej treti XVIII v.: Ukraina," Akademija Nauk SSSR, *Istorija filosofii v SSSR*, 5 vols. (Moscow, 1968), I:411. More recent Soviet authors have challenged this view. See A.M. Niženec' and N.H. Korž, "Narodnyj myslytel'," *Prapor*, no. 3 (1970):103.
23. Skovoroda, "Dialog. Imja emu: Potop zmiin," *Sobranie sočinenij*, 498.
24. Skovoroda, "Kol'co," *Sobranie sočinenij*, 252; "Razgovor družeskij o duševnom mire," *Sobranie sočinenij*, 225.
25. Skovoroda, "Dialog ili razglagol o drevnem mire," *Sobranie sočinenij*, 309; "Da lobžet mja ot lobzanij ust svoix," *Sobranie sočinenij*, 59; "Razgovor družeskij o duševnom mire," *Sobranie sočinenij*, 226.
26. Skovoroda, "Izrailskij zmij," *Sobranie sočinenij*, 368; "Dialog. Imja emu: Potop zmiin," *Sobranie sočinenij*, 507.

"materialistic" inclinations so much as it illuminates both the religiosity of his thought and his capacity for integrating religious and scientific insights.

Skovoroda's insistence on the immanence of God in man, nature and the Bible, an insistence which manifested itself in his statements that "the true man and God are the same,"[27] "it is impossible to find a more suitable name for God than Nature,"[28] and "understand that the Bible has itself become God,"[29] reflected his familiarity with both German mysticism and Russian and Ukrainian sectarianism. This familiarity, as well as Skovoroda's extraordinary emphasis on divine immanence, gave cause to consider some elements of his thought as contrary to Orthodox dogma. But his effort to demonstrate that the Divinity is at once fused with and separated from matter, i.e., simultaneously immanent and transcendent, mitigated his apparent deviation from Orthodoxy, if it did not entirely dispel it. Beyond this, his firm belief in the essential Christian dogmas of the Trinitarian God and the divinity of Christ evinced his close ties to Orthodox thought.[30]

Skovoroda's stress upon the divine in man and nature produced as a consequence a moral philosophy that rested on the ability of man to put his will in harmony with the divine will, i.e., the divine law or nature.[31] While this may appear quite abstract, Skovoroda, by his teaching on practical morality and his own living example, demonstrated that living moderately and in accord with nature was the way for man to remain simultaneously detached from and happy in the world.[32] Although this practical morality was primarily the consequence of his speculation concerning the immanence of God, one cannot disregard the influence on it of Skovoroda's critical attitudes toward his society and his church, nor his allied contention that if men lived in accord with nature social harmony would result.[33]

The following, then, are the crucial features of Skovoroda's thought: 1) his emphasis on the divine reality that sustained man, nature and the Bible; 2) his contention, based upon both religious and scientific insights, that matter was eternal and infinite; and 3) his morality, dependent jointly upon Orthodox speculation and social criticism, which aimed at the creation of a harmonious society. If one keeps these elements in mind while he considers the sources of

---

27. Skovoroda, "Narkiss," *Sobranie sočinenij*, 92.
28. Skovoroda, "Razgovor družeskij o duševnom mire," *Sobranie sočinenij*, 216.
29. Skovoroda, "Dialog. Imja emu: Potop zmiin," *Sobranie sočinenij*, 506.
30. Skovoroda, "Beseda narečennaja Dvoe," *Sobranie sočinenij*, 202; "Dialog ili razglagol o drevnem mire," *Sobranie sočinenij*, 312; "Dialog. Imja emu: Potop zmiin," *Sobranie sočinenij*, 512.
31. Skovoroda, "Razgovor družeskij o duševnom mire," *Sobranie sočinenij*, 232.
32. Skovoroda, "Sad božestvennyx pěsnej: Pesn' 12-ja," *TDT* II:23-4.
33. Skovoroda, "De libertate," *TDT* II:80; "Razgovor družeskij o duševnom mire," *Sobranie sočinenij*, 220; "Načal'naja dver' ko xristianskomu dobronraviju," *Sobranie sočinenij*, 71-2.

Skovoroda's thought, then he can begin to appreciate Skovoroda's intellectual significance. Skovoroda saw himself as surrounded by those who were living, in the words of Socrates, "the unexamined life,"[34] by people who were thoughtlessly in pursuit of their individual power, wealth and pleasure. He reacted strongly against this aimless concern with worldly affairs and began to question, by both his life and thought, the values of the institutional church and the "official" society, which approved and encouraged such mundane cares. In the process of this questioning, Skovoroda created a powerful religious philosophy, one in which he sought to integrate divinity and matter, faith and reason, theory and practice, man and nature, and the individual and society. Further, in the process of moulding this holistic philosophy, he synthesized a wide range of religious and secular sources, including ancient thought, the Bible, Orthodoxy, German mysticism, Russian and Ukrainian sectarianism and Western science. It is fair to argue that this holistic and synthetic philosophy stood in his own time and stands today as a reproach to the one-sided materialism and science that have become the political and intellectual fashion. In this inheres the continuing significance of Skovoroda's thought.

---

34. Skovoroda did not quote this famous Socratic dictum, but in the same spirit of criticism he noted that, "Some men live to eat, but I eat to live." Skovoroda, "Pis'mo k S.I. Tevjašovu," *Sobranie sočinenij*, 359.

Part Four

A Bibliography of Skovorodiana

A Bibliography of Skovorodiana

Richard Hantula

The number of works dealing with Skovoroda either at length or in passing is very large. Should we add fleeting references to the man, the number would become greater still. It is well known, for example, that Tolstoj was interested in Skovoroda, but does everyone remember that a certain Skovorodnikov is one of the senators in *Resurrection*? The relatively thorough—within certain limits—Soviet bibliography of Skovorodiana[1] lists, in some cases, mere mentions of Skovoroda's name. The present bibliography, though extensive, is not all-inclusive. It is meant to supplement the Soviet bibliography. That is, except for purposes of identification in listing book reviews, the present bibliography lists solely works not to be found in the Soviet one. Moreover, certain categories of works are excluded here: belletristic works about Skovoroda, publications about Skovoroda exhibits and museums, announcements of conferences, bibliographies, memorabilia or souvenirs. The bibliography includes not only works that have or purport to have a scholarly character, but also interpretative works and popularizations. Shorter pieces of a very general or trivial nature, however, are not listed. Newspapers, aside from literary newspapers such as *Literaturna Ukrajina*, were not checked, and the presence of material from them here is

---

1. E.S. Berkovyč et al., compilers. *Hryhorij Skovoroda: Biobibliohrafija*, 2nd ed. (Xarkiv: Xarkiv University, 1972).

exceptional. Lengthy publications of Skovoroda's works, including translations, are listed. This is a bibliography of dissertations and published works. Unpublished reports and works such as Hlobenko's translations and glossary of Skovoroda's philosophical terminology that almost saw the light of day in published form[2] are not included here.

The bibliography is divided into the following parts: Texts; General (works on Skovoroda's biography, works discussing more than one facet of Skovoroda at length, works not falling into the other groups); Philosophy (works on Skovoroda's philosophy or religious beliefs, works on his views on society, history, etc.); Literary Problems; Linguistic Problems; Pedagogy; Music; Studies on Skovoroda in Belletristic Literature; Reviews. These categories should not be viewed as rigid or exclusive. Works do not always permit of easy classification, and the categories used here should be viewed simply as aids to the digestion of the bibliography. A strong believer in the worth and interest of reviews, the compiler has attempted to locate representatives of that genre. "Review" here is taken to include long review articles, shorter reviews, informative articles about books, and interviews with authors. Reviews are listed for works wholly or in large part devoted to Skovoroda. Thus, no reviews are to be found here for Treadgold, for Billington, or for Čyževs'kyj's *History of Ukrainian Literature*, although such reviews exist. Reviews here are listed under the work they concern. The last portion of the bibliography contains solely review-surveys of more than one book and reviews of books listed in the Soviet bibliography.

Within each part "authors" (or titles, if there is no author, editor, or compiler) are arrayed alphabetically, using an alphabet in which š, for example, follows s. Each author's works are in chronological order by year. Works published in one year are in alphabetical order by title, with books following articles. For works that deal only in part with Skovoroda, page numbers are sometimes offered, but these usually identify merely the chief material on him—other mentions of Skovoroda may occur. Titles not in a Latin or Cyrillic alphabet are translated into English. Annotation is offered in a very few cases for the purposes of identification or of supplying information about publication.

It unfortunately was not possible to verify every entry *de visu*; some entries are based on published listings or references. The literature on Skovoroda is quite elusively dispersed in place and time of origin, and the present bibliography cannot pretend to contain everything worthy of being mentioned in it. No works are listed that appeared after 1986.

---

2. See M. Hlobenko, *Z literaturoznavčoji spadščyny* (Paris: Nacionalistyčne vyd-tvo v Evropi, 1961), 247.

Abbreviations

AN SSSR — Akademija nauk SSSR (Academy of Sciences of the USSR)
AN URSR — Akademija nauk URSR (Academy of Sciences of the Ukrainian Soviet Socialist Republic)
UAN — Ukrajins'ka akademija nauk (Ukrainian Academy of Sciences)
ZfsPh — *Zeitschrift für slavische Philologie*

Published Texts

This list does not include publications of individual poems, aphorisms, fables, etc. The now standard academy edition is listed first.

Collections of Works

1. Skovoroda, Hryhorij S. *Povne zibrannja tvoriv u dvox tomax*. Editorial board: V.I. Šynkaruk et al. Introductory article by V. Šynkaruk and I. Ivan'o. Kyiv: Naukova dumka, 1973.

    Reviews: P.B.T. Bilaniuk, *Slavic Review* 33 (1974):559-60. E.W. Federenko, *Ukrainian Quarterly* 31 (1975):196-7.

2. Edie, James M., James P. Scanlan, and Mary Barbara Zeldin, editors. *Russian Philosophy: An Historical Anthology*. Vol. 1, *The Beginnings of Russian Philosophy: The Slavophiles, the Westerners*. Chicago: Quadrangle, 1965. 11-62.

    Contains an introduction by George L. Kline and selected English translations by Kline (a pseudo-Skovoroda piece by Hasdeu, portions of Kovalins'kyj's biography and of "Razgovor pjati putnikov") and by Edie (letters). Reviews: N.S. Care, *New Republic*, 25 September 1965, 30-31. R.T. DeGeorge, *Slavic Review* 25 (1966):361-3. S.M. Eames, *Journal of the History of Philosophy* 4 (1966):340-41. F.P.V.D.P., *Personalist* 47 (1966):429. A. Field, *New York Times Book Review*, 28 November 1965, 6. E. Kamenka, *Soviet Studies* 20 (1969):401-2. G. Florovsky, *Russian Review* 25 (1966):409-11. R.W. Simmons, *Slavic and East European Journal* 11 (1967):490. A. Vachet, *Dialogue* 9 (1970):470-73.

3. Skovoroda, Hryhorij S. *Literaturni tvory*. Compiled and annotated with an introductory article by B.A. Derkač. Kyiv: Naukova dumka, 1972.

4. ——— . *Sčastlivyj sled*. Tbilisi: Tbilisi University, 1972.
    Parallel Russian and Georgian text.

5. ——. *Selected Works*. Translated by L. Miridžanjan, introductory article by G. Tatosjan. Erevan: Ajastan, 1972.
   Review: A. Arjaruni, *Literaturna Ukrajina*, 27 February 1973, 4.
6. ——. *Vybrani tvory v dvox tomax*. Compiled and annotated by B.A. Derkač. Kyiv: Dnipro, 1972.
   Review: O. Kaharlyc'ka, *Literaturna Ukrajina*, 6 October 1972, 3.
7. ——. *Sočinenija v dvux tomax*. Editorial board: V.I. Šynkaruk et al. Compiled and translated by I.V. Ivan'o and M.V. Kašuba. Introductory article by I.V. Ivan'o and V.I. Šynkaruk. Moscow: Mysl', 1973.
   A Russian translation. Noteworthy for the presence of a subject index.
8. ——. *Sad pisen': vybrani tvory*. Compiled and annotated, with introductory article, by Vasyl' Jaremenko. Kyiv: Veselka, 1980.
9. ——. *Virši, pisni, bajky, dialohy, traktaty, prytči, prozovi pereklady, lysty*. Compiled and annotated, with introductory article, by I.V. Ivan'o. Kyiv: Naukova dumka, 1983.

Cycles

Garden of Divine Songs

10. Skovoroda, Hryhorij. *Sad božestvennyx pesnej*. Edited by D. Čyževs'kyj. Prague: Ukrajins'ke ist.-filol. tovarystvo, 1941.
11. ——. *Garden of Divine Songs*. Foreword and notes by Dž. Asatiani. Tbilisi: Merani, 1972.
    In Georgian.

Xarkiv Fables

12. Skovoroda, Hryhorij. *Xarkivs'ki bajky*. New York: Howerla, 1955.
    In Ukrainian.
13. ——. *Bajky xarkivs'ki, aforyzmy*. Foreword by N.O. Batjuk. Xarkiv: Prapor, 1972.
    In Ukrainian.
14. ——. *Xarkiv Fables*. Translated with an afterword by R. Čilačava. Tbilisi: Nakaduli, 1972.
    In Georgian.
    Review: V. Hresa, *Literaturna Ukrajina*, 16 February 1973, 4.
15. ——. *Xarkivs'ki bajky (Z nahody 250-rokiv vid dnja narodžennja H. Skovorody) 3.12.1722—3.12.1972*. New York: Vyd-tvo Čartoryjs'kyx, 1972.
    In Ukrainian.
16. ——. *Fábulas*. Translated with an introduction by Wira Selanski. Rio de Janeiro: Companhia Brasileira de Artes Graficas, 1978.

Newly Found Mss.

17. Raškovskij, E.B., and V.M. Smirnov. "Novoe o Grigorii Skovorode." *Izvestija Akademii nauk SSSR: Serija literatury i jazyka* 43 (1984), no. 2, 168-72.
    Newly found 1785 letter of Skovoroda to M.I. Kovalinskij (Kovalins'kyj).

General Works

18. "Arxyjepyskop Žan Rjup pro Skovorodu." *Homin Ukrajiny*, 21 April 1973, 9.
19. Bagalej [=Bahalij], D.I. *Ukrajinskij stranstvujuščij filosof G.S. Skovoroda.* Xarkiv, 1923.
    Includes Javorskij, M.I., "Skovoroda i ego obščestvo." Review: A. Kovalivs'kyj, *Červonyj šljax*, 1923, no. 6-7:250-52.
20. Bakanidze, Otar. *Hryhorij Skovoroda.* Tbilisi: Merani, 1972.
    In Georgian.
    Review: O. Muškudiani, *Literaturna Ukrajina*, 28 November 1972, 4.
21. Barabaš, Ju. "Sii raznorodnye o nem suždenija: Grigorij Skovoroda v ocenkax i sporax." *Voprosy literatury*, 1985, no. 3, 97-118.
22. Barka, Vasyl'. "Apostoličnyj starčyk." *Sučasnist'* 17, no. 1 (1977):5-13.
23. Bažynov, Ivan. "Spovnenyj hlybokoji povahy: L.M. Tolstoj pro H.S. Skovorodu." *Literaturna Ukrajina*, 1 December 1973, 3.
24. Billington, James. *The Icon and the Axe: An Interpretive History of Russian Culture.* New York: Knopf, 1966. 238-42.
25. Bilodid, I.K. "Vydatnyj ukrajins'kyj filosof-demokrat, prosvytytel', poet H.S. Skovoroda." *Visnyk AN URSR*, 1972, no. 11:76-88.
26. Bobrinskoj, Petr A. *Starčik Grigorij Skovoroda: žizn' i učenie.* Paris: Imp. de Navarre, 1929.
    A second edition was published in Madrid in 1965. Review: D. Čiževskij, *Sovremennye zapiski* 45 (1931):529-31.
27. Bojko, Jurij. "H.S. Skovoroda im Lichte der ukrainischen Geschichte." *Die Welt der Slaven* 11 (1966):306-16.
28. Bučylo, L. "Hryhorij Skovoroda — vyznačnyj ukrajins'kyj filosof XVIII st.: do 250-x rokovyn z dnja narodžennja." *Cerkovnyj kalendar na 1972 r.* Warsaw, 1971. Reprinted in *Vyzvol'nyj šljax* 25 (1972):576-90.
29. Čyževs'kyj, D. "Zu den Einflüssen Skovorodas." *ZfsPh* 13 (1936):66-7.
30. ———. "Zu den ausländischen Wanderungen Skovorodas." *ZfsPh* 18 (1942): 52-3.

31. ———. *Skovoroda: Dichter, Denker, Mystiker*. Munich: Fink, 1974. Harvard Series in Ukrainian Studies, 18.
    Reviews: P. Bilaniuk, *Canadian Slavonic Papers* 18 (1976):91-2. R. Hantula, *Slavic Review* 34 (1975):624-5.

32. Dzjuba, Ivan. "Peršyj rozum naš..." *My i svit* 48 (1963):4-7.
    A reprint from *Literaturna Ukrajina*, 4 December 1962. Also in: Ivan Koševlivec', ed., *Panorama najnovišoji literatury v URSR: Poezija, proza, krytyka* (New York: Prolog, 1963), 317-23; second edition (Munich: Sučasnist', 1974), 637-41. O. Kopač, *Xrestomatija z novoji ukrajins'koji literatury* (Toronto: Ob"jednannja ukrajins'kyx pedahohiv Kanady, 1970), 76-9. *Novi dni*, January 1973, 19-20. *Svoboda*, 9 March 1973.
    In English: *Ukrainian Review*, Autumn 1966, 67-70.
    In French: M. Maslow, ed., *La nouvelle vague littéraire en Ukraine* (Paris: Éds. P.I.U.F., 1967), 233-8.

33. Èrn, V. *Zyttja i osoba Hryhorija Skovorody*. Translated by E. Malanjuk. "Do svitla," 1923.
    Reviews: *Knyžka*, 1923, part 1-5, 26. V. Zajikin, *Trybuna Ukrajiny*, 1923, nos. 2-4, 80-81; *Naš svit*, 1924, nos. 10-12.

34. Fedenko, Panas. "Pro Skovorodu bez kadyla." *Novi dni*, June 1973, 13-18.

35. Floryns'kyj, I. *Hryhorij Skovoroda — predteča ukrajins'koho evanhelizmu*. Winnipeg: National Publ. Ltd., 1956.

36. Fuhrmann, Joseph T. "The First Russian Philosopher's Search for the Kingdom of God." In *Essays on Russian Intellectual History*, edited by Leon Borden Blair. Austin: University of Texas Press, 1971. 33-72.
    Reviews: J. Cracraft, *Historian* 34 (1972):508. J.M. Edie, *Journal of the History of Philosophy* 11 (1973):563-4. M. Nicholson, *Soviet Studies* 24 (1973):452-5. M. Raeff, *American Historical Review* 78 (1973):464-5. L.J. Shein, *Canadian Slavonic Papers* 15 (1973):579-80.

37. Galuzinskaja, Viktorija. "Strannik na doroge dobra." *Nauka i žizn'*, 1973, no. 5:60-64.

38. Himka, John-Paul. "H.S. Skovoroda: His Place in Intellectual Tradition." *Minutes of the Seminar in Ukrainian Studies Held at Harvard University*, no. 2 (1971-1972):83-4.

39. ———. "Skovoroda — poet i myslytel'." *Novi dni*, December 1973:14-18.
    Includes translations from Skovoroda by A. Humec'ka.

40. Holovaxa, I.P., and I.P. Stohnij. *Filosof-humanist H.S. Skovoroda*. Kyiv: Politvydav Ukrajiny, 1972.

41. Hrycaj, M.S. "Vydatnyj filosof i poet." *Ukrajins'ka mova i literatura v školi*, 1972, no. 12: 74-81.

42. Ivan'o, I.V. "Skavarada, Ryhor Savyč." *Belaruskaja saveckaja encyklapedyja*. Vol. 9. Minsk, 1973, 542-3.
43. Janiv, V. "Skovorodyns'kyj juvilej v Evropi." *Literatura i mystectvo*, literary supplement to *Homin Ukrajiny*, April 1973, 1.
44. ———. "Skovoroda – vysliv ukrajins'koji duxovnosty." *Literatura i mystectvo*, literary supplement to *Homin Ukrajiny*, March 1973, 1.
45. Jastrzębiec-Kozłowski, Cz. "Grzegorz Skoworoda, myśliciel ukraiński." *Problemy Europy wschodniej*, nos. 2, 3. Warsaw, 1939.
46. Jefremov, Serhij. "Skovoroda na tli sučasnosty." *Zapysky Naukovoho tovarystva im. Ševčenka* 141-3 (1925).
47. Kirchner, P. "Studenten aus der Linksufrigen Ukraine an deutschen Universitäten in der zweiten Hälfte des 18. Jahrhunderts." In *Ost und West in der Geschichte des Denkens und der kulturellen Beziehungen: Festschrift für Eduard Winter zum 70. Geburtstag*. Berlin: Akademie-Verlag, 1966. 367-75.
    On Vasyl' Skovoroda.
48. Konstantinov, F.V. "Filosof, gumanist, prosvetitel'." *Literaturnaja gazeta*, 3 December 1972, 6.
49. ———. "G.S. Skovoroda — vydajuščijsja gumanist." *Voprosy filosofii*, no. 2 (1973):142-9.
50. Kotovyč, A. *Hryhorij Savyč Skovoroda, ukrajins'kyj filosof XVIII st.* New York: Ukrajins'ka pravoslavna cerkva v Z.D.A., Naukovo-bohoslovs'kyj instytut, 1955.
51. Kovalyns'kyj, M. *Hryhorij Savyč Skovoroda: žyttja i dejaki dumky ukrajins'koho filosofa-spirytualista*. London: Ukrajins'ka vydavnyča spilka, 1956.
52. Kratochvil, Josef, et al. *H.S. Skovoroda, J.A. Komenský, T. G. Masaryk*. Stuttgart: Omnipress, 1974.
53. Kubijovyč, V., ed. *Ukraine: A Concise Encyclopaedia*. 2 volumes. Toronto: University of Toronto Press, 1963, 1971.
    "A revised and substantially augmented version of the three-volume work published in Ukrainian in 1949 by the Ševčenko Scientific Society."
    Chiefly to be noted are the articles on philosophy by Mirčuk and on literature by Čyževs'kyj in volume one.
54. László, Magdalena. "Cîteva din scrierile lui Skovoroda aflate în manuscris în bibliotecile din România." *Romanoslavica* 12 (1965):243-8.
55. Lavrinenko, Jurij. "Na počatkax ukrajins'koho vidrodžennja, 3: Do 200-riččja narodžennja Vasylja Karazyna 10 ljutoho 1773-1973: 5. Karazyn i Skovoroda." *Sučasnist'*, 1974, no. 4:55-64.

56. Levyc'kyj, V. "Hryhorij Savyč Skovoroda." *Ukrajins'kyj samostijnyk*, 1973, no. 11-12:61-5.
57. Loščic, Jurij. *Skovoroda*. Moscow: Molodaja gvardija, 1972. A volume from the series Žizn' zamečatel'nyx ljudej. Review: B. Petrov, *V mire knig*, 1973, no. 5:70.
58. ———. "Skovoroda, Grigorij Savvič." *Bol'šaja Sovetskaja Ènciklopedija*. Third edition. Vol. 23, 514-15.
59. Luciv, Luka. "Hryhorij Skovoroda i joho filosofija." *Al'manax Ukrajins'koho Narodnoho Sojuzu na rik 1972*. Jersey City: Svoboda. 26-58.
60. Lysak, M. "Hlašataj rozumu: do 250-riččja vid dnja narodžennja H.S. Skovorody." *Donbas*, 1972, no. 6:99-104.
61. Lysenko, O. "Hryhorij Skovoroda i sučasnist'." *Duklja*, no. 1 (1972):43-8. Also, *Švetlosc* 10 (1972):327-32.
62. Martus', Volodymyr. "Poltavs'ka tema." *Vitčyzna*, 1972, no. 12:217-18. Tolstoj's views on Skovoroda.
63. Maxnovec', Leonid, introduction and commentary. "Epistoljarnyj dokument 1824 roku pro Skovorodu: lyst I.F. Martosa do V.Ja. Lomykovs'koho." *Narodna tvorčist' ta etnohrafija*, 1972, no. 5:37-44.
64. ———. "Pro atrybuciju i xronolohiju lystiv Skovorody." *Radjans'ke literaturoznavstvo*, 1972, no. 10:34-47.
65. ———. "Rukoju Skovorody." *Literaturna Ukrajina*, 28 July 1972, 2.
66. ———. "Tut vin žyv: do 250-riččja z dnja narodžennja H.S. Skovorody." *Nauka i suspil'stvo*, 1972, no. 12:55-7.
67. ———. *Hryhorij Skovoroda: biohrafija*. Kyiv: Naukova dumka, 1972. Reviews: Z. Genyk-Berezovská, *Slavia* 43 (1974):435-36. R. Hantula, *Recenzija* 4, no. 1 (1973): 34-48. O.I. Hončar and M.L. Hončaruk, *Radjans'ke literaturoznavstvo*, 1973, no. 6:79-80. R. Łużny, *Slavia Orientalis* 23 (1974):382-4. P.P. Oxrimenko, *Prapor*, 1973, no. 4:94-7. Je. Šabliovs'kyj, *Literaturna Ukrajina*, 27 February 1973, 4.
68. Mazurkevyč, Oleksandr. "Žyvym slovom i pysannjam…" *Prapor*, 1972, no. 11:63-6.
69. *Metodyčni rekomendaciji po pidhotovci i provedennju juvileju H.S. Skovorody*. Xerson, 1972.
70. Mirčuk, J. "Tolstoj und Skovoroda, zwei nationale Typen." *Abhandlungen des Ukrainischen Wissenschaftlichen Institutes in Berlin* 2 (1929):24-51.
71. Mytrovyč, Kyrylo. "Portret Skovorody u 250-riččja joho narodžennja." *Sučasnist'*, no. 11 (1972):44-5.
72. *Na slidax žyttja Hryhorija Skovorody*. Buffalo, N.Y.: Oseredok SUMA im.

L. Ukrajinky, 1972.
Contributors: P. Čujko, D. Doncov, P. Mozoljuk, J. Rusov, M. Sloboz̆anyn, V. Šajan, M. Šerer, V. Ševčuk, P. Trač, O. Voronin, L. Žabko-Potapovyč.
Review: D.V. Čopyk, *Ukrajins'ka knyha* 3 (1973):89-90.

73. Niženec', A.M. "Nad lystamy Bonč-Brujevyča: z arxivnyx džerel." *Prapor*, 1972, no. 11:56-9.
74. ———. "'Meni xočet'sja napysaty pro n'oho...'" *Radjans'ke literaturoznavstvo*, 1973, no. 1:78-9.
    Tolstoj's attitude to Skovoroda.
75. ———. "Pro otočennja H.S. Skovorody u Lypcjax i Valkax: 70-80-i roky XVIII st." *Radjans'ke literaturoznavstvo*, 1983, no. 2:28-35.
76. Niženec', A.M., and I. Stohnij. *Hryhorij Skovoroda: pam"jatni miscja na Ukrajini*. Kyiv: Naukova dumka, 1984.
77. Pascal, Pierre. "Skovoroda, philosophe ukrainien." *Mitteilungen* 14 (1977):215-17.
78. Pascal, Pierre, Arkady Joukovsky, Kyrylo Mytrowytch, Alexandre Koultchytskyi, Wolodymyr Janiw. *Skovoroda, philosophe ukrainien: colloque tenu le 18 janvier 1973 à l'Institut d'Etudes Slaves de Paris à l'occasion du 250e anniversaire de la naissance de Skovoroda, 1722-1972*. Paris: Institut d'études slaves, 1976.
79. Pečars'kyj, Ja. "Slavetnyj syn Ukrajiny: do 250-riččja H.S. Skovorody." *Ljudyna i svit*, 1972, no. 11:31-4.
80. Poliščuk, F.M. *Hryhorij Skovoroda: seminarij*. Kyiv: Vyšča škola, 1972.
    Review: T. Poljek, *Ukrajins'ka mova i literatura v školi*, 1973, no. 11:90-91.
81. ———. *Hryhorij Skovoroda: žyttja i tvorčist'*. Kyiv: Dnipro, 1978.
82. Red'ko, M.P. "Vydatnyj ukrajins'kyj myslytel'-humanist." *Komunist Ukrajiny*, 1972, no. 11:53-62.
83. ———. *Vydatnyj filosof-humanist*. Kyiv: Tovarystvo "Znannja" URSR, 1972.
84. Rudnyckyj, J.B. "A Tribute to Skovoroda on the Occasion of the 250th Anniversary of His Birth." *Ukrainian Review* 20, no. 2 (1973):15-18.
85. Sarbej, V. "Nad tvoramy velykoho prosvitnyka: do 250-riččja vid dnja narodžennja H.S. Skovorody." *Vitčyzna*, 1972, no. 12:201-4.
86. Scherer, Stephen P. "The Life and Thought of Russia's First Lay Theologian, Grigorij Savvič Skovoroda (1722-94)." Ph.D. dissertation, Ohio State, 1969.
    Abstract listed in *Dissertation Abstracts* 30, no. 10, 4384-A-4385-A.

87. ——. "Skovoroda, Hryhorii Savvich." *The Modern Encyclopedia of Russian and Soviet History*. Edited by Joseph L. Wieczynski. Vol. 35. Gulf Breeze, Fla.: Academic International Press, 1983. 185-9.
88. Stefurovszky, I. *Szkovoroda Hrihorij Szávics*. Ungvár, 1943.
89. Stepanyšyn, Borys. "Pobornyk pravdy i svobody." *Vesnjani obriji* 5 (1972):148-61.
90. Stepovyk, D. "Hryhorij Skovoroda j obrazotvorče mystectvo." *Obrazotvorče mystectvo*, 1972, no. 6:26-7.
91. ——. "Xto iljustruvav 'Alfavit'." *Žovten'*, 1973, no. 4:113-15.
92. Šajan, V. *Hryhorij Skovoroda — lycar svjatoji borni*. London: Instytut V. Šajana, 1973.
93. Šynkaruk, V.I. et al., editorial board. *Hryhorij Skovoroda 250: Materialy pro vidznačennja 250-riččja z dnja narodžennja*. Compiled by I.P. Stohnij and P.Ju. Šabatyn. Kyiv: Naukova dumka, 1975.
    Contains information on the Skovoroda anniversary celebration in the USSR — decrees, press notices, commemorative events, speeches, etc. Papers of a scholarly nature include: I.P. Holovaxa, "Ocinka zahal'nosvitohljadnoji pozyciji H.S. Skovorody v istoryko-filosofs'kyx doslidžennjax"; V.M. Konon, "Dejaki humanistyčni džerela svitohljadu H.S. Skovorody"; I.P. Stohnij, "Etyka praci u tvorčosti H.S. Skovorody"; N.F. Utkina, "Filosofija H.S. Skovorody ta nauka Novoho času"; V.M. Ničyk, "H. Skovoroda i etyko-humanistyčnyj naprjam u vitčyznjanij filosofiji"; A.I. Pašuk, "Polemisty i H. Skovoroda"; M.D. Rohovyč, "M. Kozačyns'kyj i H. Skovoroda"; R.T. Hrom"jak, "Jednist' poetyčnoji i filosofs'koji tvorčosti H.S. Skovorody"; I.V. Ivan'o, "Pro styl' filosofs'kyx tvoriv H. Skovorody"; I.D. Bažynov, "Etyčna koncepcija H.S. Skovorody v ocinci L.M. Tolstoho"; V.H. Sarbej, "V.D. Bonč-Brujevyč — doslidnyk i popularyzator spadščyny H.S. Skovorody"; N.V. Komarenko, "D.I. Bahalij — doslidnyk žyttja j tvorčosti H.S. Skovorody"; N.H. Korž, "Latyns'ki viršovani tvory H.S. Skovorody"; F.J. Luc'ka, "Žanr epihramy v tvorčosti Skovorody"; M.K. Borovyk, "Hryhorij Skovoroda i muzyka"; D.V. Stepovyk, "Pohljady H. Skovorody na obrazotvorče mystectvo"; Ja.M. Pohrebennyk, "H. Skovoroda v nimec'kyx vydannjax"; F.P. Medvedjev, "H.S. Skovoroda v istoriji ukrajins'koji literaturnoji movy"; P.Ju. Šabatyn, "H.S. Skovoroda i sučasna ukrajins'ka radjans'ka bajka"; O.R. Mazurkevyč, "Problemy slovesnosti u tvorčij spadščyni H.S. Skovorody"; V.S. Kalašnyk, "Hryhorij Skovoroda v poetyčnij tvorčosti Pavla Tyčyny"; P.A. Sotnyčenko, "Osvitni šljaxy Hryhorija Skovorody"; A. Niženec', "Z lystuvannja V.D. Bonč-Brujevyča z K.O. Skovorodoju"; A. Niženec' and H. Štejn, "Pro poxodžennja psevdonimu H.S.

Skovorody"; "Nevidomi pereklady i nasliduvannja viršiv H. Skovorody" (Submitted by I. Ivan'o); "Novi pereklady latyns'kyx viršiv H. Skovorody" (translated by M. Rohovyč). There is also a short bibliography of jubilee literature compiled by V.D. Prokopenko, R.A. Stavyns'ka, and Ju.H. Ševčenko.

94. Tardy, Lajos. *A tokaji Orosz Borvásárló Bizottság története (1733-1798).* Sárospatak: Rákóczi múzeum, 1963.

95. Tkač, R. "Dokumenty CDAŽR URSR pro všanuvannja pam"jati H.S. Skovorody v 1922 r." *Arxivy Ukrajiny*, 1972, no. 5:34-40.

96. Treadgold, Donald W. *The West in Russia and China.* Vol. 1, *Russia, 1472-1917.* Cambridge: Cambridge, 1973. 112-13.

Tschižewskij, D. See Čyževs'kyj, D.

97. Varlamov, A.P., and V.O. Lysenko, compilers. *Všanovujemo slavetnyx: repertuarnyj zbirnyk.* Kyiv: Mystectvo, 1972.

Contains mainly selections from literary works about Skovoroda and Ukrainian translations of individual poems, fables, and aphorisms.

98. Winter, Eduard. *Byzanz und Rom in Kampf um die Ukraine 955-1939.* Leipzig: Otto Harrassowitz, 1942. 116-20.

99. ———. *Frühaufklärung: Der Kampf gegen den Konfessionalismus in Mittel- und Osteuropa und die deutsch-slawische Begegnung.* Berlin: Akademie Verlag, 1966. 220-21, 340-47.

100. Z.K. "Tolstoj i Skovoroda: psyxolohična paralelja." *Dilo*, 8 September 1928.

101. Zahrebel'nyj, P. "Um vseosjažnyj i buntlivlyvyj." *Nauka i kul'tura: Ukrajina.* Kyiv, 1972. 361-9.

102. Zavadovyč, Roman. "Toj, ščo joho svit ne spijmav." *Ovyd*, 1972, no. 4:7-15.

Philosophy and Religion, Skovoroda's Views

103. Andrusyshen, Constantine. "Skovoroda, the Seeker of the Genuine Man." *Ukrainian Quarterly* 2 (1946):317-30. Also, *Ukrainian Review* 28 (1980):86-97.

104. Arseniew, Nikolaus von. "Bilder aus dem russischen Geistesleben: 1. Die mystische Philosophie Skovorodas." *Kyrios* 1 (1936):3-28.

105. Bilanjuk, Petro. "Hryhorij Skovoroda: filosof čy bohoslov?" In *Zbirnyk naukovyx prac' na pošanu Jevhena Vertyporoxa*, edited by Bohdan Stebel's'kyj. Zapysky Naukovoho tovarystva im. Ševčenka, Literature Series, 12 (1972). 55-65.

An English adaptation is in the *New Review* 13, nos. 1-2 (1973):50-61.

106. Buyniak, Victor O. "Doukhobors, Molokans, and Skovoroda's Teachings." *Roots and Realities Among Eastern and Central Europeans*. Edited by Martin L. Kovacs. Edmonton, 1983. 13-23.
107. Čelak, M. "Svitohljad Skovorody i sučasnist'." *Prapor*, 1972, no. 11:50-54.
108. ———. "Vojovnyčyj antyklerykalizm H.S. Skovorody." *Problemy filosofiji*, no. 30 (1973):52-9.
109. Čub, Dmytro. "Hryhorij Skovoroda ta joho filosofs'ki pohljady." *Novi dni*, 1972, no. 11:2-8.
110. Čyževs'kyj, D. *Filosofija na Ukrajini: sproba istoriohrafiji pytannja*. Prague, 1926.
    Review: S. Hessen, *Der Russische Gedanke* 1 (1929):105-6.
111. ———. *Fil'osofija na Ukraini: sproba istoriohrafiji*. Second edition. Part 1. Prague: Sijač, 1928.
    Reviews: G.V. Florovskij, *Put'*, no. 19 (1929):118-19. J. Mirčuk, *Abhandlungen des Ukrainischen Wissenschaftlichen Institutes in Berlin* 2 (1929):191-2.
112. ———. "Filosofija G.S. Skovorody." *Put'*, no. 19 (1929):23-56.
113. ———. "G.S. Skovoroda i nemeckaja mistika." *Naučnye trudy Russkogo narodnogo universiteta v Prage* 2 (1929):283-301.
114. ———. "Skoworoda, ein ukrainischer Philosoph (1722-1794) (Zur Geschichte der 'dialektischen Methode')." *Der Russische Gedanke* 1 (1929):163-76.
115. ———. "Skovoroda-Studien: 1. Skovoroda und Angelus Silesius." *ZfsPh* 7 (1930): 1-33.
116. ———. *Narysy z istoriji filosofiji na Ukrajini*. Prague: Ukrajins'kyj hromads'kyj vydavnyčyj fond, 1931.
    Review: N. Lossky, *Archiv für Geschichte der Philosophie*, n.s. 41 (1932):317-20.
117. ———. "Aus Skovorodas mystischen Schriften." *Orient und Occident*, no. 14 (1933):1-7.
118. ———. "Skovoroda-Studien: 2. Skovorodas Erkenntnislehre und Philo." *ZfsPh* 10 (1933):47-60.
119. ———. "Zu 'Skovoroda-Studien 1'." *ZfsPh* 10 (1933):399-400.
120. ———. "Pro dejaki džerela symvoliky Hr. Skovorody." *Praci Ukrajins'koho pedahohičnoho instytutu v Prazi* 2 (1934):405-23.
    Also published separately.
121. ———. *Fil'osofija H.S. Skovorody*. Praci Ukrajins'koho naukovoho instytutu 24. Warsaw, 1934.

122. ———. "Skovoroda-Studien: 3. Skovorodas Bibel-Interpretation im Lichte der kirchenväterlichen und mystischen Tradition." *ZfsPh* 12 (1935):53-78.
123. ———. "Skovoroda-Studien: 4. Skovoroda und Valentin Weigel." *ZfsPh* 12 (1935):308-32.
124. Dvojčenko-Markova, E. "G. Skovoroda v tvorčestve A. Xaždeu." *Kodry*, 1972, no. 12:135-40.
125. Florovskij, G. *Puti russkogo bogoslovija*. Paris: YMCA Press, 1937. 119-21.
    Reprinted — Ann Arbor: University Microfilms, 1971.
126. Gančikov, L. "Skovoroda, Grigorij Savič." *Enciclopedia Filosofica*. Vol. 4. Venice and Rome, 1957. 669-70.
    In volume 5 of the second edition (1967), 1423-4.
127. Grindell, David C. "Monism in a Ukrainian Philosopher: Gregory Skovoroda." *Vedanta Quarterly: Message of the East*, 1951, 15-19, 84-90.
128. Haase, Felix. "Die kulturgeschichtliche Bedeutung des ukrainischen Philosophen Grigorij Skovoroda." *Jahrbücher für Kultur und Geschichte der Slaven*, n.s. 4 (1928):21-42.
129. Hasdeu, A. "Un filozof mistic." *Convorbiri literare* 63 (1930):568-88.
    A Romanian translation.
130. Hors'kyj, V.S. "Filosofija Skovorody u vitčyznjanyx doslidžennjax." *Filosofs'ka dumka*, 1972, no. 5:44-54.
131. Hruševs'kyj, Myxajlo. *Z istoriji relihijnoji dumky na Ukrajini*. Second, corrected edition, edited by D. Kulykovs'kyj. Winnipeg: Ukrainian Evangelical Alliance of North America, 1962. 106-17.
132. Iakovenko, Boris. *Filosofi russi: saggio di storia della filosofia russa*. Florence: La Voce, 1925. 7-12.
133. Ioann, Episkop. *Filosof cerkvi*. Los Angeles: Za cerkov', 1946.
134. ———. *Cerkov' i mir*. Bela Crkva: Pravoslavno-Missionerskoe Knigoizdatel'stvo, 1929.
135. Ionescu-Nişcov, Tr. "Grigorij Skovoroda i filosofskie raboty Aleksandra Xiždeu." *Romanoslavica* 2 (1958):149-62.
136. ———. "Scrierile filozofice ale lui Alexandru Hasdeu şi gînditorul ucrainean Grigorie Savici Skovoroda." *Romanoslavica* 12 (1965):191-207.
137. Ivan'o, I.V. "Moldavsko-russko-ukrainskie filosofskie svjazi v pervoj polovine XIX v." *Očerki po istorii ukrainskix filosofskix svjazej XVII-XX st.* Kishinev, 1977. 59-72.
138. ———. *Filosofija i styl' myslennja H. Skovorody*. Kyiv: Naukova dumka, 1983.

139. Ivanjo, I., and V. Šinkaruk [=Ivan'o and Šynkaruk], "Velký ukrajinský humanista a osvicenec (k 250 výroči narozeni H. Skovorody)." *Filosofický Časopis* 20 (1972):883-95. Also, a Polish version: "Wielki ukraiński humanista i filozof: w 250 rocznicę urodzin Grigoryja Skoworody." *Studia Filozoficzne*, nos. 11-12 (1972):41-53.

140. Jevdokymenko, V.Ju. "H.S. Skovoroda i ukrajins'ka suspil'no-polityčna dumka." *Filosofs'ka dumka*, 1972, no. 5:35-43.

141. Kaluzny, A. *La Philosophie du coeur de Grigori Skovoroda*. Montréal: Fides, 1983.

142. Kašuba, M. "V poiskax sčast'ja čelovečeskogo: 250 let so dnja roždenija G. Skovorody." *Nauka i religija*, no. 12 (1972):86-8.

143. Kozij, D. "Narcis u duxovnomu sviti Skovorody." *Lysty do pryjateliv*, nos. 11-12 (1964):6-9.

144. ———. "Try aspekty samopiznannja u Skovorody: do 250-riččja narodžennja (1722-3 hrudnja-1972)." *Sučasnist'*, 1972, no. 12:66-78.

145. ———. "Skovoroda — Platon — Epikur." *Slovo*, no. 5. Edmonton: Ukrainian Canadian Writers' Association, 1973. 157-66.

146. Krasyc'kyj, D. "Z odnoho džerela." *Ljudyna i svit*, 1972, no. 10:26-8.

147. Kultschytzkyj, A. "Der universalistische Humanismus Komenskys und der personalistiche Humanismus Skovorodas als Ausdrucksform zweier nationaler Geistigkeiten." *Mitteilungen* in the series Arbeits- und Förderungsgemeinschaft der Ukrainischen Wissenschaften e.V. Nos. 8-9 (1972):11-23.

148. ———. [Kul'čyc'kyj]. "Hryhorij Skovoroda — providnyk personalizmu." *Literatura i mystectvo*, literary supplement to *Homin Ukrajiny*, April 1973, 4.

149. Kyryk, D.P. "Učennja H.S. Skovorody pro mikrokosm." *Filosofs'ka dumka*, 1972, no. 5:67-75.

150. Ladyžens'kyj, O. "Z pryvodu statti: 'Osnovni problemy sučasnoji teoriji piznannja j filosofija H.S. Skovorody' v *Jubilejnomu Zbirnyku na pošanu... Bahalija*, č. 2." *Zapysky ist.-filol. viddilu UAN* 16 (1928):324-5.

151. Lo Gatto, E. "L'idea filosofico-religiosa russa da Skovoroda a Solovjov." *Bilychnis: Rivista Mensile Illustrata di Studi Religiosi*, nos. 8-9 (1927):77-90.

152. Luciv, Jurij A. "Vplyv davnix filosofiv i otciv cerkvy na tvorčist' Hryhorija Skovorody." *Ameryka*, April 1982, 14-21.

153. Łużny, Ryszard. "Teodycea Hryhorija Skoworody na tle słowiańskiej myśli religijnej okresu oświecenia." *Studia Slavica in Honorem Viri Doctissimi*

Olexa Horbatsch: Festgabe zum 65. Geburtstag. Edited by Gerd Friedhof, Peter Kosta, and M. Schütrumpf. Vol. I. Munich: Otto Sagner, 1983. 98-108.

154. Lysenko, A.A. "Problema ličnosti v filosofii Grigorija Skovorody." *Naučnye doklady vysšej školy: filosofskie nauki*, 1972, no. 6:88-96.

155. Miljukov, P. *Očerki po istorii russkoj kul'tury.* Jubilee edition. Paris: Sovremennye zapiski, 1931. Vol. 2, part 1, 123-4.
 Many other editions available. Also an English version: *Outlines of Russian Culture. Part 1, Religion and the Church*, edited by Michael Karpovich (Philadelphia: Pennsylvania, 1942), 94-6; and later editions.

156. Mirčuk, I. "H.S. Skovoroda (Zamitky do istoriji ukrajins'koji kul'tury)." *Praci Ukrajins'koho ist.-filol. tovarystva v Prazi* 1 (1926):19-37.
 Note too comments on 207-8.

157. ———. "H.S. Skovoroda, ein ukrainischer Philosoph des XVIII. Jahrhunderts." *ZfsPh* 5 (1928):36-62.

158. Ničyk, V.M., editor. *Vid Vyšens'koho do Skovorody (Z istoriji filosofs'koji dumky na Ukrajini XVI-XVIII st.).* Kyiv: Naukova dumka, 1972.
 Includes: I.V. Ivan'o, "Etyka Skovorody i filosofija Epikura"; D.P. Kyryk, "Svit symvoliv H.S. Skovorody"; A.P. Markov, "Spivvidnošennja duxovnoho i material'noho u filosofiji H.S. Skovorody"; I.A. Tabačnikov, "Skovoroda i Sokrat."
 Reviews: I.Ja. Matkovskaja, *Voprosy filosofii*, 1974, no. 2:177-8. D. Sijak, *Ukrajins'kyj istoryk*, 1972, no. 3-4:147-8.

159. Ohorodnyk, J. "Skovoroda und Spinoza." *Naukovyj zbirnyk Ukrajins'koho pedahohičnoho instytutu v Prazi* 2 (1934):204-30.

160. Oljančyn, D. *Hryhorij Skoworoda 1722-1794: der ukrainische Philosoph des XVIII. Jahrhunderts und seine geistigkulturelle Umwelt.* Osteuropäische Forschungen, n.s. 2. Berlin: Ost-Europa, 1928.
 Also, Tilsit: O.v. Mauderode, 1928.
 Reviews: D. Čyževs'kyj, *ZfsPh* 6 (1929):279-84; and *Ruch filosofický*, 1931, no. 3-4:176. H. Kiessler, *Philosophisches Jahrbuch des Görres-Gesellschaft* 44 (1931):123-4.

161. Ostrjanyn, D.X. "H.S. Skovoroda — vydatnyj ukrajins'kyj myslytel' XVIII st." *Problemy filosofiji*, no. 30 (1973):33-43.

162. Partolin, M.F. "Velikij ukrainskij myslitel'-demokrat XVIII stoletija G.S. Skovoroda." *Vestnik Xar'kovskogo universiteta*, no. 112 (1974):77-84.

163. Pašuk, A.I. "I. Vyšens'kyj i H. Skovoroda." *Filosofs'ka dumka*, 1972, no. 5:76-83.

164. ———. "Myslytel'-humanist." *Žovten'*, 1972, no. 11:110-16.

165. ——. "Problema ščastja u filosofs'komu včenni H.S. Skovorody." *Ukrajins'ke literaturoznavstvo*, no. 18 (1973):96-102.
166. Pohorilyj, S. "Symvoly u Skovorody." *Sučasnist'*, 1973, no. 3:18-24.
167. Popovyč, M.V. "Antynomija 'prostoty istyny' u filosofiji Hryhorija Skovorody." *Filosofs'ka dumka*, 1972, no. 5:55-66.
168. Rudnyckyj, J.B. "Tribute to Skovoroda on the Occasion of the 250th Anniversary of His Birth." *The Ukrainian Review*, 1973, no. 2:15-18.
169. Sarbej, V.H. "Istoryčni pohljady H.S. Skovorody." *Ukrajins'kyj istoryčnyj žurnal*, 1972, no. 11:54-62.
170. Scherer, Stephen P. "Skovoroda and Society." *Ukrajins'kyj istoryk*, 1971, no. 3-4:12-22.
171. ——. "The Concept of an Unlimited Natural World in the Thought of H.S. Skovoroda (1722-94)." *The New Review* 12, no. 3 (1972):33-42.
172. ——. "Beyond Morality: The Moral Teaching and Practice of H.S. Skovoroda (1722-1794)." *Ukrajins'kyj istoryk*, 1981, no. 1-4:60-73.
173. ——. "Knowledge in an Eighteenth-Century Philosopher: The Views of H.S. Skovoroda." *East European Quarterly* 17, no. 3 (1983):371-81.
174. ——. "Symbol and Bible in the Work of Hryhorii Skovoroda." *Michigan Academician*, Winter 1983, 221-8.
175. Schultze, Bernhard. "Pensatori russi di fronte a Cristo." *Civiltà Cattolica* 2 (1944):273-84.
    One of a series of articles under this title, which was also used for the publication of, apparently, the whole series: Florence, 1947.
176. ——. *Russische Denker: ihre Stellung zu Christus, Kirche und Papsttum*. Vienna: Thomas-Moraus-Presse im Verlag Herder, 1950. 17-27.
177. Shein, Louis J. "An Examination of Hryhory Skovoroda's Philosophical System." *Ukrainian Quarterly* 39 (1983):171-8.
178. Skripilev, E.A. "Social'no-političeskie vzgljady G.S. Skovorody." *Sovetskoe gosudarstvo i pravo*, 1972, no. 11:124-6.
179. Sokurenko, V.H. "Pryrodnopravova teorija H.S. Skovorody." *Visnyk L'vivs'koho universitetu: serija jurydyčna*, 1973, 3-9.
180. Svitlyčna, L.A. "H.S. Skovoroda i L.M. Tolstoj." *Filosofs'ka dumka*, 1972, no. 5:93-8.
181. Šajan, V. *Etyčni, sociolohični i pedahohični pohljady Skovorody*. London: Orden, 1959.
    Apparently the same work reprinted: *Etyčni, sociolohični i pedahohični pohljady Hryhorija Skovorody* (London: Instytut V. Šajana, 1972).

182. Šynkaruk, V.I. "Filosofskoe učenie G.S. Skovorody: k 250-letiju so dnja roždenija." *Voprosy filosofii*, 1972, no. 12:112-18.
183. ──── . "Velykyj seljans'kyj prosvitytel': 250 rokiv vid dnja narodžennja H.S. Skovorody." *Filosofs'ka dumka*, 1972, no. 5:24-34.
184. ──── and I.Ivan'o. "Velikij ukrainskij prosvetitel'." *Izvestija Akademii nauk Kazaxskoj SSR: serija obščestv.*, 1972, no. 4:14-21.
185. ──── , editor. *Filosofija Hryhorija Skovorody*. Kyiv: Naukova dumka, 1972. Contains the following: V.I. Šynkaruk, "Vstup"; I.V. Ivan'o, "Žyttjevyj šljax i formuvannja svitohljadu"; V.M. Ničyk, "H. Skovoroda ta filosofs'ki tradyciji Kyjevo-Mohyljans'koji akademiji"; D.P. Kyryk, "Včennja pro dvi natury ta try svity"; I.V. Ivan'o, "Filosofs'ko-etyčne včennja Skovorody"; I.V. Ivan'o, "Pisljamova."
    Reviews: J.P. Himka, *Recenzija* 4, no. 2 (1974):3-13. P.P. Hrebenna and I.Ja. Matkovs'ka, *Filosofs'ka dumka*, 1974, no. 1:132-3.
186. Tabačnikov, I.A. *Grigorij Skovoroda*. Moscow: Mysl', 1972.

Tschižewskij, D. See Čyževs'kyj, D.

187. Vlasovs'kyj, Ivan. *Narys istoriji Ukrajins'koji pravoslavnoji cerkvy*. Volume 3. New York: Ukrajins'ka pravoslavna cerkva v Z.D.A., 1957. 96-9.
188. Zakydalsky, Taras. "The Theory of Man in the Philosophy of Skovoroda." M.A. dissertation, Bryn Mawr, 1965.
189. ──── . "Skovoroda's Philosophy of Man." *Minutes of the Seminar in Ukrainian Studies Held at Harvard* University, no. 2 (1971-1972):84-5.
190. Zen'kovskij, V.V. *Istorija russkoj filosofii*. Paris: YMCA Press, 1948. Volume 1, 64-81.
    Review: S. Frank, *Novyj žurnal* 22 (1949):294-8.
    There appeared a French translation by C. Andronikov: *Histoire de la philosophie russe* (Paris: Gallimard, 1953-4); on Skovoroda see volume 1, 64-82. George L. Kline produced an English translation: *A History of Russian Philosophy* (New York: Columbia, 1953; London: Routledge and Kegan Paul, 1953); on Skovoroda see volume 1, 53-69.
    Reviews of the English version: C.E. Black, *Annals of the American Academy of Political and Social Science* 293 (1954):201. L.H. Haimson, *American Historical Review* 59 (1954):931-3. C. Hartshorne, *Review of Metaphysics* 8 (1954):61-78. H. Kohn, *Russian Review* 13 (1954): 296-7. *Times Literary Supplement*, 1 January 1954, 13.

Literary Problems — Skovoroda as Writer

191. Angyal, A. *Die slawische Barockwelt*. Leipzig: Seeman, 1961. 303-5.

192. Bahlaj, J.O. "H.S. Skovoroda — teoretyk perekladu." *Ukrajins'ke literaturoznavstvo*, no. 19 (1973):87-92.

193. Barabaš, Ju. "'Vem čeloveka...' O poèzii Grigorija Skovorody i nemnogo o nem samom." *Moskva*, 1972, no. 11:193-209.

194. Busch, W. *Horaz in Russland: Studien und Materialien*. Munich: Eidos, 1964. 66-70.

195. Čyževs'kyj, D. "Džerela symvoliky Skovorody." *Naukovyj zbirnyk Ukrajins'koho pedahohičnoho instytutu v Prazi* 2 (1933):405-23.
Also published separately: Prague, 1934.

196. ———. "Ein Zitat aus Prokopovyč bei Skovoroda." *ZfsPh* 11 (1934):22.

197. ———. "Skovorodas Reime." *ZfsPh* 14 (1937):331-7.

198. ———. "V. Kapnist und Skovoroda." *ZfsPh* 14 (1937):337-46.

199. ———. "Zamitky do tvorčosty Skovorody jak poeta." *Naukovyj zbirnyk v 30 ričnycju naukovoji praci prof. d-ra I. Ohijenka*. Warsaw: Nakl. Juvilejnoho komitetu, 1937. 172-89.

200. ———. "Die 'vermischten Gedichte' Skovorodas." *ZfsPh* 16 (1939):343-6.

201. ———. "Skovorodas Übersetzungen aus Muretus." *ZfsPh* 16 (1939):342-3.

202. ———. "Zu einer Übersetzung von Skovoroda (S. Hosschius)." *ZfsPh* 16 (1939):343.

203. ———. "Zu einer dichterischen Formel Skovorodas." *ZfsPh* 17 (1940):110.

204. ———. *Ukrajins'kyj literaturnyj barok: narysy*. 3 volumes. Prague: Ukrajins'ke ist.-filol. tovarystvo, 1941-4.
Also in *Praci Ukrajins'koho ist.-filol. tovarystva v Prazi* 3 (1941):40-108; 4 (1942):145-210; 5 (1944):78-142. On Skovoroda see *Praci*, vol. 3, pp. 43, 44, 51, 65-6, 83, 100, 101; vol. 4, 145-210 (includes Čyževs'kyj's edition of the *Garden of Divine Songs*); vol. 5, pp. 79-83, 87, 94, 96, 99, 103, 104, 106, 120, 122, 126, 131, 133.

205. ———. "Zu einem Skovoroda zugeschriebenen Gedicht." *ZfsPh* 18 (1942): 370-74.

206. ———. "Ein Zitat aus Theophrast bei Skovoroda." *ZfsPh* 19 (1947):352-3.

207. ———. "Zu einem Skovoroda zugeschriebenen Gedicht." *ZfsPh* 19 (1947):353.

208. ———. *Istorija ukrajins'koji literatury vid počatkiv do doby realizmu*. New York: Ukrajins'ka vil'na akademija nauk u SŠA, 1956.
There is an English translation: *A History of Ukrainian Literature (From the 11th to the End of the 19th Century)*, edited with a foreword by G.S.N. Luckyj (Littleton, Colo.: Ukrainian Academic Press, 1975).

209. ———. "Skovoroda — Gogol'." *Die Welt der Slaven* 18 (1968):317-26.
210. ———. "Hryhorij Savyč Skovoroda (1722-1794) und die ukrainische Versdichtung." *Archiv für das Studium der Neueren Sprachen und Literaturen* 210 (1973):312-17.
211. Dihtjar, S.I. "Obrazy spivbesidnykiv ta jix rol' u babajivs'komu cykli filosofs'kyx dialohiv H.S. Skovorody." *Ukrajins'ke literaturoznavstvo*, no. 18 (1973):103-9.
212. Drač, Ivan. "Duxovnyj meč Grigorija Skovorody." In Skovoroda, *Izbrannoe*. Moscow: Xudožestvennaja literatura, 1972. 5-19.
   An Armenian translation: *Garun*, 1973, no. 3:80-2.
213. ———. "Poètu — čerez veka." *Literaturnaja gazeta*, 3 December 1972, 6.
214. Genyk-Berezovská, Zina. "K pozdně baroknímu ukrajińskému básnictví." *Československá Rusistika* 17 (1972):198-205.
215. Hantula, Richard. "Skovoroda's *Garden of Divine Songs*: Description and Analysis." Ph.D. dissertation, Harvard, 1976.
216. Hromova, Tetjana. "Pravdi torujučy šljax." *Vitčyzna*, 1972, no. 12:205-7.
   Skovoroda's ties with Russian literature and culture.
217. Hrycaj, M.S. "Poetyčna tvorčist' H.S. Skovorody i fol'klor." *Visnyk Kyjivs'koho universytetu: serija filolohiji*, 1972, no. 14:13-8.
218. ———. "Vyvčennja fol'klorystyčnyx interesiv filosofa i poeta." *Narodna tvorčist' ta etnohrafija*, 1972, no. 5:21-4.
219. ———. *Davnja ukrajins'ka poezija*. Kyiv: Kyiv University, 1972. 72-81.
220. ———. "H.S. Skovoroda i narodna poetyčna tvorčist'." *Problemy filosofiji*, no. 30 (1973):44-51.
221. Ivan'o, I. "Hryhorij Skovoroda — perekladač." *Vsesvit*, 1972, no. 12:217-24.
222. ———. "Problemy žanrovoji specyfiky filosofs'kyx tvoriv H.S. Skovorody." *Filosofs'ka dumka*, 1972, no. 5:84-92.
223. Jaremenko, Porfyrij. "Liryka rozdumiv i nastrojiv." *Žovten'*, 1973, no. 2:122-9.
224. Javors'ka-Kopač, Oleksandra. "Z epistoljarnoji spadščyny Hryhorija Skovorody." *Studia Ucrainica*, no. 3 (1986):92-9.
225. Jefremov, Serhij. *Istorija ukrajins'koho pys'menstva*. Fourth ed. Kyiv: Ukrajins'ka nakl., 1919-24. Vol. 1, 254-61.
226. Kopač, O. "'Bran' Arxystratyha Myxajila so Satanoju' H. Skovorody jak literaturnyj tvir." *Juvilejnyj zbirnyk naukovyx prac' z nahody 100-riččja NTŠ u Kanadi*. Compiled by P. Bilanjuk and B. Stebel's'kyj. Toronto: Shevchenko Scientific Society, 1977. 93-103.

227. Kosjačenko, V.T. "'... Jak jablunja v svojim zernjati.'" *Literaturna Ukrajina*, 1 December 1972, 3. On Skovoroda's fables.

228. ——. *"Basni xar'kovskija* H.S. Skovorody i joho tradyciji v ukrajins'komu bajkarstvi." *Ukrajins'ke literaturoznavstvo*, no. 25 (1975):62-7.

229. Kukuškina, O.D., and I.F. Martynov. "Nevidoma rukopysna zbirka XVIII st." *Radjans'ke literaturoznavstvo*, 1975, no. 2:73-81.

230. Laszlo-Kuţiuk, Magdalena. "Fabulele lui Skovoroda şi tradiţia esopică: cu ocazia împlinarii a 250 de ani de la naşterea scriitorului." *Analele Universităţii Bucareşti, Limbi Slave* 21 (1972): 37-51.

231. ——. *Vlijanie tvorčestva G.S. Skovorody na poèziju T.G. Ševčenko.* Bucharest: Associatia Slavistilor, 1973.

232. ——. *Velyka tradycija.* Bucharest: Kryterion, 1979.

233. Lotman, Ju.M. "Ob odnom temnom meste v pis'me Grigorija Skovorody." *Izvestija Akademii nauk SSSR: Serija literatury i jazyka* 44, no. 2 (1985):170-71.

234. Lysenko, O. "Humanistyčni idealy Hryhorija Skovorody: do 250-riččja H. Skovorody." *Radjans'ke literaturoznavstvo*, 1972, no. 11:61-70.

235. Máchal, Jan. *Slovanské literatury.* Vol. 1. Prague: Nákladem matice české, 1922. 276-7.

236. Maljar, Pavlo. "Ševčenko i Skovoroda." *Novi dni*, May 1972, 12-15.

237. Manning, Clarence. *Ukrainian Literature: Studies of the Leading Authors.* Jersey City: Ukrainian National Association, 1944. 17-22.

238. Myšanyč, O.V. *Hryhorij Skovoroda i usna narodna tvorčist'.* Kyiv: Naukova dumka, 1976.
Review: I. Ivan'o, *Narodna tvorčist' ta etnohrafija*, 1978, no. 4:91-3.

239. Odarčenko, Petro. "Taras Ševčenko i joho poperednyky: Skovoroda i Kotljarevs'kyj." *Sučasnist'*, no. 3 (1975):25-36.

240. Pačovs'kyj, T.I. "Žanrovi osoblyvosti viršiv H. Skovorody." *Ukrajins'ke literaturoznavstvo*, no. 18 (1973):110-15.

241. Pil'huk, Ivan. "U suzir'ji myslyteliv." *Dnipro*, 1972, no. 11:122-7.

242. Ponomar'ov, P.P. "Estetyčnyj ideal u liryci H.S. Skovorody." *Ukrajins'ke literaturoznavstvo*, no. 19 (1973):93-7.

243. Pylypčuk, R. "Hryhorij Skovoroda i teatr." *Ukrajins'kyj teatr*, 1972, no. 5:28-30.

244. Slavutyč, Jar. "Trynadcjata pisnja H. Skovorody." *Juvilejnyj zbirnyk UVAN*, 1976, 223-32.

245. Sydorenko, H.K. *Ukrajins'ke viršuvannja vid najdavnišyx časiv do Ševčenka.* Kyiv: Kyiv University, 1972.

246. ———. "Poet vysokoho klasu." *Visnyk Kyjivs'koho universytetu: serija filolohiji*, no. 16 (1974):3-8.

247. Syvačenko, M. "Do istoriji ukrajins'koji paremiohrafiji: H.S. Skovoroda." In the author's *Literaturoznavči ta fol'klorystyčni rozvidky.* Kyiv: Naukova dumka, 1974. 9-69.
Originally published in two parts in *Narodna tvorčist' ta etnohrafija*, 1972, no. 5:25-36, and 1973, no. 1:29-43.

248. ———. "Do komentuvannja 'Alfavita mira' H.S. Skovorody." *Radjans'ke literaturoznavstvo*, 1979, no. 12:54-9.

249. Šabliovs'kyj, Je. *Ukrainian Literature through the Ages.* Kyiv: Mystectvo, 1970. 52-5.

250. ———. "Pobornyk rivnosti i braterstva." *Literaturna Ukrajina*, 1 December 1972, 3.

251. ———. "Vydajuščijsja ukrainskij myslitel', filosof, poet: k 250-letiju so dnja roždenija G.S. Skovorody." *Vestnik AN SSSR*, 1972, no. 11:116-21.

252. ———. *G.S. Skovoroda (K 250-letiju so dnja roždenija ukr. myslitelja i poèta).* Moscow: Znanie, 1972. Also in the author's *Žyttja, literatura, pys'mennyk: vybrani doslidžennja* (Kyiv: Dnipro, 1974), 48-9.

253. Šudrja, K.P. "Tvorča vzajemozumovlenist' filosofiji i mystectva H.S. Skovorody." *Etyka i estetyka*, no. 16 (1974):134-40.

Tschižewskij, D. See Čyževs'kyj, D.

254. Tucker, Thomas. "Rime, Parallelism, and Word Order in Skovoroda's *Garden of Divine Songs.*" *Minutes of the Seminar in Ukrainian Studies Held at Harvard University*, no. 1 (1970-1971):45-6.

255. Vyhodovanec', N.I. "Bajky H.S. Skovorody v ocinci ukrajins'kyx literaturoznavciv ostann'oho desjatylittja (1962-1972)." *Ukrajins'ke literaturoznavstvo*, no. 22 (1974):88-94.

The Language of Skovoroda's Works

256. Beloded [Bilodid], I.K. "G.S. Skovoroda v istorii ukrainskogo literaturnogo jazyka." In *Sovremennye problemy literaturovedenija i jazykoznanija: k 70-letiju so dnja roždenija akademika Mixaila Borisoviča Xrapčenko.* Edited by N.F. Belčikov. Moscow: Nauka, 1974. 368-74.

257. Bilodid, I. *Kyjevo-Mohyljans'ka akademija v istoriji sxidnoslov'jans'kyx literaturnyx mov.* Kyiv: Naukova dumka, 1979.

258. Black, Karen L. "The Sources of the Poetic Vocabulary of Grigorij Skovoroda." Ph.D. dissertation, Bryn Mawr, 1975. Abstract listed in *Dissertation Abstracts* 36, no. 9, 6068-A.
259. Čaplenko, V. "Movna pozycija i mova Hryhorija Skovorody." *Vyzvol'nyj šljax* 16 (1963): 649-71. The final part is reprinted in *Novi dni*, March 1973, 16-18.
260. Čyževs'kyj, D. "Zur sprache Skovorodas." *ZfsPh* 11 (1934):21-2.
261. Medvedjev, F.P. "H.S. Skovoroda v istoriji ukrajins'koji literaturnoji movy." *Ukrajins'ke movoznavstvo*, no. 1 (1973):110-16.
262. Nepokupnyj, A.P. "Formy *Kopernikovy, Kopernikanskii* ta *Kopernikovski* u movi H.S. Skovorody." *Movoznavstvo*, 1972, no. 4:71-3.
263. Peredrijenko, V.A. "Leksyčna spivvidnosnist' novoji i davn'oji ukrajins'koji literaturnoji movy XVIII st." *Movoznavstvo*, 1972, no. 3:63-74.
264. Synjavs'kyj, O. "Mova tvoriv H. Skovorody." *Žyttja i škola*, 1973, no. 3:30-37.
265. Witkowski, Wiesław. "Czy Skoworoda pisał mieszaniną języka starocerkiewnego, rosyjskiego i ukraińskiego?" *Slavia Orientalis* 21 (1972):399-412.
266. Žovtobrjux, M.A. "Vidbyttja procesu stanovlennja fonolohičnoji systemy ukrajins'koji literaturnoji movy u tvorax H.S. Skovorody." *Movoznavstvo*, 1972, no. 4:59-70.

Skovoroda and Pedagogy

267. Docenko, A.M., compiler, *Metodyčni rekomendaciji "Pedahohični ideji H.S. Skovorody i sučasnist'."* Xarkiv: Xark. obl. rada Ped. t-va URSR, Kafedra pedahohiky i psyxolohiji Xark. derž. ped. in-tu im. H.S. Skovorody, 1972.
268. Dzeverin, O.H., et al., editors. *Pedahohični ideji H.S. Skovorody.* Kyiv: Vyšča škola, 1972.
    Contains the following articles: I.A. Tabačnykov, "Svitohljadni osnovy pedahohiky H.S. Skovorody"; H.S. Kostjuk, "Elementy dialektyky v psyxolohičnyx pohljadax H.S. Skovorody"; S.A. Lytvynov, "H.S. Skovoroda pro vyxovannja i rozvytok rozumu"; H.P. Hrebenna, "Etyčni pohljady H.S. Skovorody i problemy moral'noho vyxovannja"; I.V. Ivan'o, "Problemy estetyky ta estetyčnoho vyxovannja v spadščyni Hryhorija Skovorody"; I.V. Puxa, "Dejaki pytannja teoriji navčannja v spadščyni H.S. Skovorody"; O.R. Mazurkevyč, "Literatura jak zasib vyxovannja v učytel's'kij dijal'nosti i tvorčij spadščyni H.S. Skovorody"; F.I. Naumenko and Je.I. Prystupa, "Tradyciji narodnoji pedahohiky v tvorčosti Hryhorija Skovorody"; V.V. Strubyc'kyj, "H.S. Skovoroda pro

osobystist' učytelja"; Z.I. Xyžnjak, "H.S. Skovoroda i Kyjivs'ka akademija"; A.M. Niženec', "Dijal'nist' H.S. Skovorody v Perejaslavs'komu i Xarkivs'komu kolehiumax"; O.H. Dzeverin, "H.S. Skovoroda v radjans'kij istoryko-pedahohičnij literaturi."

269. Grebennaja, P.G., and A.M. Tkačenko. "Pedagogičeskie vzgljady i dejatel'nost' G.S. Skovorody." *Očerki istorii školy i pedagogičeskoj mysli narodov SSSR v XVII-pervoj polovine XIX v.* Moscow, 1973. 393-8.

270. Mac'kiv, T. "Komens'kyj i Skovoroda—pedahohy svoho času." *Svoboda*, 18-19 August 1979.

271. Mazurkevyč, O.R. "H.S. Skovoroda — učytel' poetyky." *Ukrajins'ka mova i literatura v školi*, 1972, no. 10:51-8.

272. ———. "Učytel' slovesnosti." *Literaturna Ukrajina*, 15 September 1972, 2.

273. Sjavavko-Pristupa, E.I. "Tradicii narodnogo vospitanija v pedagogičeskom nasledii Grigorija Skovorody." *Sovetskaja pedagogika*, 1972, no. 12:106-11.

274. Suxorskij, E.A. "Vydajuščijsja ukrainskij myslitel' Grigorij Skovoroda." *Sovetskaja pedagogika*, 1972, no. 12:100-5.

275. Tabačnykov, I.A. "Pedahohični pohljady H.S. Skovorody." *Vyšča i serednja special'na osvita*, no. 6 (1973):133-41.

276. Zakaljužnyj, M.M. "Pedahohična dumka antyčnoho svitu i H.S. Skovoroda." *Inozemna filolohija*, no. 28 (1972):90-94.

Skovoroda and Music

277. Macenko, Pavlo. *Davnja ukrajins'ka muzyka i sučasnist'*. Winnipeg: Kul'tura j osvita, 1952.

278. ———. "Muzyka i H.S. Skovoroda." *Novi dni*, October 1972, 11-12.

279. Šrejer-Tkačenko, O. "Filosof, poet i muzykant: do 250-riččja vid dnja narodžennja H.S. Skovorody." *Muzyka*, 1972, no. 6:28-9.

Skovoroda in Belletristic Literature — Criticism, Commentary

280. Ankudinova, O.V. "Leskov i Skovoroda (k voprosu ob idejnom smysle povesti Leskova 'Zajačij remiz')." *Voprosy russkoj literatury*, no. 21 (1973):71-7.

281. Berezovská, Z. "Tyčynova symfonie o Skovorodovi." *Československá Rusistika* 26 (1981): 158-61.

282. Čyževs'kyj, D. "Skovoroda bei Narižnyj." *ZfsPh* 17 (1940):110-12.

283. Hantula, Richard. "Skovoroda in Subsequent Literature." *Minutes of the Seminar in Ukrainian Studies Held at Harvard University*, no. 2 (1971-1972):85-6.
284. Jacenko, M.T. "Tvorčist' D. Huramišvili v idejno-estetyčnomu konteksti prosvytytel'stva." *Radjans'ke literaturoznavstvo*, 1981, no. 4:42-55.
285. Kolosova-Onkovyč, H. "Narodžennja symfoniji (Obraz H.S. Skovorody v tvorčosti P.H. Tyčyny)." *Literaturna Ukrajina*, 28 January 1975.
286. Kyjivs'kyj, M. "M. Zaboloc'kyj — perekladač ukrajins'koji poeziji." *Radjans'ke literaturoznavstvo*, 1972, no. 12:80-83.
    See p. 80.
287. Lavrinenko, Jurij. *Pavlo Tyčyna i joho poema "Skovoroda" na tli epoxy: (spohady i sposterežennja)*. Munich: Sučasnist', 1980.
288. Lavrov, A. "Andrej Belyj i Grigorij Skovoroda." *Studia Slavica Academiae Scientiarum Hungaricae* 21 (1975):395-404.
289. Pil'huk, I. "Symfonija poetyčnoho myslennja." *Vitčyzna*, 1972, no. 7:175-9.
    On Tyčyna and Skovoroda.
290. Stepanenko, Mykola. "Hryhorij Skovoroda i ukrajins'ke pys'menstvo ostann'oho p"jatdesjatylittja." *Zapysky NTŠ* 187 (1976):138-57.
291. Syrotjuk, M.J. *Ukrajins'kyj radjans'kyj istoryčnyj roman*. Kyiv: Akademija nauk, 1962.
    V. Poliščuk's novel is discussed on pp. 82-6.
292. Valentinov, N. *Dva goda s simvolistami*. Stanford: Hoover Institution, 1969.
    See p. 194 on Belyj's *Peterburg* and Skovoroda.

Reviews

Surveys (more than one work covered)

293. Čyževs'kyj, D. [here spelled Tschižewskij, D.]. "Neue Literatur über Skovoroda." *Die Russische Gedanke* 1 (1929):98-100.
294. Hantula, Richard. "Highlights of the Skovoroda Jubilee." *Harvard Ukrainian Studies* 1 (1977):249-54.
295. Il'nyc'kyj, M. "Nevyčerpna tema." *Žovten'*, 1972, no. 11:144-8.
296. Kirchner, P. "Neue Literatur über das Leben und Schaffen des ukrainischen Aufklärers Hryhorij Skovoroda." *Zeitschrift für Slawistik* 9 (1964):596-9.
    On Skovoroda, *Tvory* (1961), and Popov, *Hryhorij Skovoroda* (1960).

297. Malyc'kyj, F.M. "Hryhorij Skovoroda — 250." *Radjans'ke literaturoznavstvo*, 1977, no. 12:86-97.
298. Mirčuk, I. "Ukrainische philosophische Bibliographie der letzten Jahre (1921-1926)." *Mitteilungen des Ukrainischen Wissenschaftlichen Instituts in Berlin* 1 (1927):60-69.
    See pp. 62-3 on Skovoroda.
299. Mytrovyč, K. "Intérêt et actualité des études sur Skovoroda, premier philosophe en Ukraine." *Mitteilungen* in the series Arbeits- und Förderungsgemeinschaft der Ukrainischen Wissenschaften e.V. Nos. 6-7 (1970):16-25.
300. ———. "Kyjivs'ka *Filosofs'ka dumka* pro juvilej Hryhorija Skovorody." *Ukrajins'kyj samostijnyk*, 1972, no. 9:15-20.
301. ———. "Nevže ž zljakalys' Skovorody? (Do pidsumkiv skovorodyns'koho roku)." *Ukrajins'kyj samostijnyk*, 1973, no. 10:36-40.
    A survey of some anniversary publications on Skovoroda.
302. Poljek, V. "Na svitovyx obšyrax." *Literaturna Ukrajina*, 9 January 1973, 4.
    Work on Skovoroda outside the Soviet Union.
303. Zajikin, V. "Novi praci pro ukrajins'koho relihijnoho myslytelja Hr. Skovorodu." *Elpis* 2 (1927):180-91.
304. Zalozec'kyj, V. "Skovoroda v osvitlennju noviščoji nimec'koji literatury." *Analecta Ordinis s. Basilii Magni* 3 (1930):614-23.

Reviews of Individual Works Listed in the Soviet Bibliography of 1972

305. Bahalij, D.I. *Ukrajins'kyj mandrovanyj filosof Hr. Sav. Skovoroda*, 1926.
    Reviews: D. Čyževs'kyj, *Ruch filosofický* 7 (1928):311-12. J. Mirčuk, *Zeitschrift für slavische Philologie* 5 (1928):238-42. P. Prokof'ev [=D. Čyževs'kyj], *Sovremennye zapiski* 29 (1926): 503-9.
306. Petrov, V. *Do xarakterystyky filosofs'koho svitohljadu Skovorody*, 1929.
    Reviews: D. Čyževs'kyj, *Abhandlungen des Ukrainischen Wissenschaftlichen Institutes in Berlin* 2 (1929):190-91; and *Ruch filosofický* 8 (1929):183.
307. Radlov, E. *Očerk istorii russkoj filosofii*, 1920.
    Review: D. Čyževs'kyj, *Logos* 1 (1924):225-8.
308. Skickij, B.F. *Social'naja filosofija G. Skovorody*, 1930.
    Review: D. Čyževs'kyj, *Orient und Occident*, no. 14 (1933):47.

309. Sumcov, M. "Istorija ukrajins'koji filosofs'koji dumky," 1926.
Review: D. Čyževs'kyj, *Abhandlungen des Ukrainischen Wissenschaftlichen Institutes in Berlin* 2 (1929):189-90.
310. Špet, G.G. *Očerk razvitija russkoj filosofii*, 1922.
Reviews: D. Čyževs'kyj, *Logos* 2 (1924); and *Sovremennye zapiski* 18 (1924):454-7.

Index

Adagia (Erasmus), 41
Aesop, 269
Agrippa von Nettesheim, 17, 18
Albert the Great, 17
Alciatus, Andreas, 46
Alcmaeon, 29
Alexandrine (school), 55, 257-8, 259-60, 261, 262, 263, 265, 266, 267, 268-72, 273
Allen, P.M., 89 n.54
Alstedt, Johann, 18
Ambrose, Saint, 94
Andreä, Johann Valentin, 10, 47
Andrusovo, treaty of: 64
Ankudinova, O.B., 214n.43
Antiochian (school), 258, 259-61
Apollo, Horus, 47
Apophthegmata (Erasmus), 47
Aporetics, The (Aristotle), 21
Aquinas, Thomas, 17, 31, 164
Areopagitica, 23, 28, 30, 40, 56
Arianism, 260
Aristotelianism, 6, 164, 261, 273
Aristotle, 16, 21, 47, 66n.17, 224, 228, 240, 242, 245, 247, 255, 259; *The Aporetics*, 21
Arnd, Johann, 18, 25, 41, 48-9, 58

Arnold, Gottfried, 25, 47, 48
Askočenskij, V., 122
Augustine, Saint, 16, 94, 126, 164, 183
Avksentiev, Ol., 123

Baader, Franz Xaver von, 25, 28, 35, 42, 48, 59-60
Bach, J.S., 116, 117
Bacon, Francis, 17
Bahalij, D.I., 64n.2, 88n.52, 209n.22, 211n.31, 276-7
Balde, Jakob, 47
Baranovyč, Lazar, 49, 106n.21, 206n.11
Barka, Vasyl', 159, 160-2, 163, 166, 167-70, 179-82; and the Bible, 164-5, 182-5; imagery of, 171-3, 175-7
Barskov, Ja., 108n.24
Basil the Great, 94
Baturyn, university of, 80n.15
Baumeister, 18
Bazylevyč, I.I., 79
Beckoj, Ivan, 75, 78, 79, 82-6, 89
Beethoven, Ludwig van, 119
Belinskij, Vissarion, 278

Belyj, Andrej, xv, 203-4, 206-14
Berdjaev, Nikolaj, 39
Berkovyč, E.S., 285n.1
Bernhard, 18, 31
Bernheimer, Charles C., 199n.23, 200n.25
Bernini, Gian Lorenzo, 47
Bezborod'ko (lycée), xiv
Bible, Synodal, 98, 99, 100, 101, 104
Bida, K., 105n.20
Bilec'kyj, O., 122n.35, 216
Bilyč, T.A., 247n.4
Bingen, Hildegard von, 31, 48
Blair, L.B., 77n.8, 264n.37
Blake, William, 117
Bloom, Harold, 162
Blosius, Franciscus, 18, 59
Boccaccio, Giovanni, 17
Bodin, Jean, 17
Boethius, Ancius Manlius, 16, 126
Böhme, Jakob, 8, 18, 24, 25, 28, 31, 32, 42, 48, 58, 67n.20, 77, 81, 88, 172, 261, 264, 278
Bohomo[d]levs'kyj, 17
Bolshakoff, Serge, 67n.22
Bonaventura, Saint, 17, 18, 31, 40, 164
Bonč-Bruevič, V., 215, 217
Boria, Johannes de, 46
Boschius, J., 45, 46, 48
Breslau (gymnasium), 5, 8
Brodsky, Joseph, 235
Browne, Sir Thomas, 160
Bruckner, Anton, 119
Bruno, Giordano, 17, 31
Buddeus, Johann, 18
Buddhism, 268
Bulgakov, Mixail, 39
Burns, Robert, 161n.7
Burton, 160
Buzak, P., 110n.30, 128n.51

Callot, Jacques, 47
Camerarius, Joachim, 45, 46, 49
Cardanus, 17

Cartesians, 6
Catherine II, the Great, xii, xiv, 64, 65, 75, 78, 79, 81, 82, 84, 85, 86, 88; Legislative Commission of, 80
Cellini, Benvenuto, 47
Charter to the Nobility, xiv
Christology, 260, 271, 272
Chrysostom, John, 94
Cicero, 14, 16, 40, 240, 262, 264, 265
Clement of Alexandria, 14, 30, 40, 55, 58, 60, 262, 264, 265
Climacus, John, 271
Comenius, 10, 18, 31-2, 47, 48, 59, 86; pansophism of, 42
Conybeare, Frederick, 67n.22
Cracraft, James, 81n.21
Cynics, 241
Čyževs'kyj, Dmytro, 98, 187-9, 198, 200, 227, 235, 264, 268
Czepko, Daniel, 47, 48

Danilevskij, G.P., 68n.26, 122, 125n.43, 190n.13,
Dante Alighieri, 165
David, Zdenek, 77n.5, 82n.27
De Iside et Osiride (Plutarch), 39-40
De Man, Paul, 185n.33
Dei, Sebastian a Matre, 49
Demetrius, Bishop, 265
Demkov, M.I., 79n.13
Democritus, 16
Derkač, Borys, 256n.17
Deržavin, Gavriil, 142, 157
Descartes, René, 18
Didaskaleion (academy), 265
Diogenes, 240
Diogenes Laërtius, 16
Dionysius the Carthusian, 17
Dionysius the Pseudo-Areopagite, 14, 31, 162, 264, 265-6
Djatliv, S., 124, 215
Dobroljubov, Aleksandr, 211, 212n.34, 213n.39

Donec'-Zaxarževs'kyj, Ja., 120, 123, 124
Dorofeevič, Artem, 84n.39
Dorošenko, D., 80n.15
Dostoevskij, Fedor Mixajlovič, 10, 165n.18, 178
Doukhobors, 67, 209n.24, 278
Dovhans'kyj, Jakov, 118
Drahomanov, Myxajlo, 164
Driessen, F.C., 198n.21, 199n.24
Dukes, Paul, 85n.40
Dürer, Albrecht, 47
Durylin, S.N., 205n.8, 212n.34
Dutoit, 5
Duxnovyč, O.V., 88
Dys'kyj, F., 123, 124

Eckhart, Meister, 18, 23, 31, 48
Edie, James M., 224n.1
Efimenko, A., 122
Elizabeth I (of Russia), 6, 94, 141
Engels, Frederick, 161n.7
Enlightenment, xiii, xiv, 3, 7, 8, 55
Epicurus, 66n.17, 237, 240, 241, 242, 244, 247
Erasmus, 17, 77n.5; *Adagia*, 41; *Apophthegmata*, 47
Erigena, John Scotus, 31
Ėrn, Vladimir, 117n.33,121n.34, 127n.48, 122, 133n.1 204-6, 209-12, 213, 235, 278-9
Eusebius, 40
Evdokimenko, V.E., 63n.4

Felbiger, J.I., 81
Fénelon, François de, 86
Feuerbach, Ludwig, 224
Ficino, Marsilio, 41
Filaret, Archbishop, 215, 218, 261, 278
Filosofov, D.V., 205
First Primer for Youth (Prokopovyč), 81, 86
Fischart, Johann, 47
Florenskij, Pavel, 39, 49

Florovskij, Rev. Georgij, 263
Francis of Assisi, Saint, 212n.34, 257
Franck, Sebastian, 10, 23, 24, 41, 56-7
Francke, August Hermann, 77
Franckenberg, Abraham von, 24-5, 32, 48, 59
Freemasons, xii, 5, 12, 81-2, 84, 88, 89, 108n.24
Frye, Northrop, 182
Fuhrmann, Joseph T., 77n.8, 86n.42, 88n.50,51, 264
Fulda, Robert, 48

Galjatovs'kyj, Ioanikij, 50, 101, 105, 106, 206n.11
Gavriil, Archimandrite, 122, 190
Geoffrin, Madame, 79n.13
Gerhard, Johann, 18
Gess de Kal've, G., 68n.28, 121
Gnosticism, 30, 175, 188-9, 260, 261, 266, 267, 270
Goethe, Johann Wolfgang von, 117
Gogol', Nikolaj Vasiljevič, 6, 187-201, 276n.3
Gorky, Elizabeth, 81n.21
Görres, Johann Joseph von, 42
Gossner, Johannes Evangelista, 49
Goya, Francisco, 117, 119
Gregory the Great, 94
Gregory of Nazianzus, 94
Gregory of Nyssa, 30, 56
Gregory, Saint (Palamas), 189
Grimm, Baron Melchior von, 79
Grimmelshausen, Hans, 48
Grotius, Hugo, 18
Grube, G.M.A., 163n.14
Gumilevskij, D. *See* Filaret, Archbishop
Gusev, N.N., 211n.31,32
Guyon, Madame de, 49

Habsburg Empire, 82
Hahn, Johann Michael, 25, 32, 59
Hahn, Ph. M., 18

Hamalija, S., 8
Hamann, Johann Georg, 42
Harsdörfer, Georg Philipp, 47
Hegel, G.W.F., 25, 28, 35, 43; *Philosophy of History*, 48
Heidegger, Martin, 160, 185, 230n.19
Heraclitus, xi, 21, 29, 234
Herder, Johann Gottfried von, 42
Herzen, Alexander, 69
Hippisley, Anthony, 194
Hlobenko, M., 286n.2
Hobbes, Thomas, 18
Hoffmannswaldau, 25
Homer, 55
Horace, 14, 264, 265
Horban', M., 130n.53
Hruševs'kyj, Myxajlo, 257n.18,19, 262
Hugo, Hermann, 46, 49

Iamblichus, 40, 41
Insulis, Alanus ab, 31
Ivan'o, I., 135n.4, 143n.12, 241n.2, 245n.3, 224, 225
Ivanov, Vjačeslav, 208
Ivanov-Razumnik R.V., 206n.12
Izmajlov, A., 211n.31

Jakovenko, B.V., 205
Jakubovyč, Abbot, 11
Jankovič, Fedor, 75, 81, 82, 84, 85, 88
Jarema, Jakym, 251n.1
Javors'kyj, Stefan, 15, 49, 50
Jerome, Saint, 94
John, Saint, 268
Jonas, Hans, 189n.6
Julian the Apostate, 16
Jurkevyč, Pamfil, 6, 43
Justin, Saint, 39

Kaligraf, Volodymyr, 9, 18
Kant, Immanuel, 204n.6, 207, 208, 224n.6
Kapnist, V., 93

Karamzin, Nikolaj Mixajlovič, 81
Karazyn, V.N., 88
Kašuba, M.V., 225n.9
Keil, Rolf-Dietrich, 201n.26
Kepler, Johannes, 17
Keten, 49
Kierkegaard, Søren, 160, 183n.31, 273
Kilgour, Bayard L., Jr., 216
Kircher, Athanasius, 41, 46
Kjellberg, L., 96n.3, 104-5
Konstantinov, F.V., 277n.13
Konys'kyj, Hryhorij, 7, 77n.5
Korčyns'ka, T.A., 256n.17
Korž, N., 128n.50, 279n.22
Kostomarov, Mykola, 67n.22, 75, 88, 276
Kotljarevs'kyj, Ivan, 88, 159, 160
Kotreleva, N.V., 212n.37
Kovalevs'kyj, A., 13, 123
Kovalins'ka, A.G., 209
Kovalins'kyj, Myxajlo, 64, 68, 76, 80, 81, 83n.29, 87, 123, 124, 125, 209, 236, 239, 249, 258, 264, 265, 266, 278; status as biographer, 5, 7, 9, 11, 12, 275. *See also* Skovoroda, Hryhorij Savyč
Kozačyns'kyj, Myxail, 7
Kraevskij, Andrej, 190
Krasnjuk, M., 263
Krinovskij, Gedeon, 96n.3
Kudrinskij, F., 262
Kuhlmann, Quirinus, 25
Kuliš, Panteleimon, 43, 125, 129-30
Kvitka, F., 123
Kvitka, Hryhorij, 88, 129
Kyiv Academy, xii, 6, 15, 17, 140, 188, 215, 262. *See also* Skovoroda, Hryhorij Savyč

Labzin, A.F., 88
Land Cadet Corps College, 80, 85, 86
Laščevs'kyj, Varlaam, 7, 97, 118, 134

Lauretus, H., 46
Lebedev, A.S., 263, 278
Leibniz, Gottfried Wilhelm von, xii, 18
Lenin, Vladimir Il'ič, 161n.7, 163
Leskov, Nikolaj, 214
Ljubyc'kyj, I., 215
Locke, John, 18, 47, 80, 83, 86, 224
Lohenstein, 47
Lomonosov, Mixail Vasiljevič, 9, 78n.9, 111, 141
Losev, 39
Losskij, 39
Lubjanovskij, Fedor Petrovič, 75, 80
Lubni (dialect), 218
Lucian, 14, 264, 265
Lullus, Raymundus, 17
Luther, Martin, 18
Luyken, 48

Machiavelli, Niccolo, 17
Macijevyč, Bishop Arsenij, 44, 50
Manichaeism, 172, 260
Markovyč, Jakiv, 15, 16, 44, 50, 130-1
Martin, Saint, 5, 18
Marx, Karl, 184, 224
Masenius, J., 46
Maximus the Confessor, Saint, 14, 56, 58, 126, 264, 266
Maxnovec', Leonid, 100, 115
Mazepa, Ivan, 98
Mechtild, 23
Mečnikov, I., 123
Melanchthon, 18
Menestrerius, 49
Merleau-Ponty, Maurice, 160
Miklošič, Fr., 110-11
Miljukov, Pavel, 278
Mohyla Academy. *See* Kyiv Academy
Mohyla, Peter, 15, 17, 49
Molokane, 67
Monthly Compositions, 83

Moscow Academy, 9
Muret, Marc-Antoine, 134
Muscovy, xi, xii, xiii, 99
Myrovyč, P., 130
Myslavs'kyj, Samuil, 77n.5
Mytkevyč, Bishop, 11

Nadeždin, 190
Narbut, Vladimir, 214
Narežnyj, V.T., 214
Neoplatonism, 164, 169, 259, 260, 261, 266-7, 268, 272
Nestorianism, 260
Nicholas of Cusa, 17, 18, 23, 31, 34
Nietzsche, Friedrich, 160
Nikol'skij, B., 210n.26, 261, 277
Nilus, Saint, 14, 264, 265
Niženec, A. M. 279n.22
Novalis, 43, 48
Novickij, Orest, 209n.24
Novikov, Nikolaj, 81

Octavius, Scarlatus, 46
Oetinger, 18, 25, 32, 49, 59
Okenfuss, Max, 81n.21
Oleksjuk, Volodymyr, 256n.16
Onasch, Konrad, 263
Ophites, 30
Opitz, M., 47
Origen, 14, 30, 39, 55, 60, 171, 262, 264, 265, 266
Orlov, Vl., 190n.12
Orphics, 29
Ossian, 121
Ostrih: school of, 15; edition of Bible, 99, 100
Ostrjanyn, D.X., 256n.17
Ostrogožsk (circle), 120, 123
Ovid, 134, 168, 170, 183

Panev, Ivan, 190
Pankov, Panas, 118
Paracelsus, 41
Pascal, Blaise, 160
Pasternak, Boris Leonidovič, 235

Paul I, xii
Paul, Saint, 22, 103, 112, 162n.13, 164, 172, 177n.29, 189, 191, 199, 228, 232-3, 265
Pelagianism, 260
Pelenski, Jaroslaw, xiv n.2
Perejaslav, 9, 78, 99, 120, 134, 146, 151, 152; treaty of, 64
Peter I, the Great, xi, xii, xiv, 15, 44, 50, 76, 104, 105, 262
Petrarch, 17, 166, 169
Petrov, N.I., 66n.15
Petrov, V., 26
Petrova, Z., 109n.25
Petrovyč, Rev. N., 118
Philo Judaeus of Alexandria, 5, 14, 16, 21, 29, 39, 46, 55, 58, 60, 259, 264, 265, 268
Philosophy of History (Hegel), 48
Piccinellus, Philippus, 46
Pico della Mirandola, Giovanni, 17, 31
Pietism, German, 77-8, 81
Pil'huk, Ivan, 256n.17
Pirožkov, M.V., 212n.34
Plato, 21, 41, 47, 48, 55, 66n.17, 160, 164, 178, 209n.25, 228, 232n.21, 234, 235n.25, 240, 244, 245, 247, 255, 262, 266; as poet-philosopher, 163; Christian reading of, 167; cosmology of, 29; images of, 45-6, 170
Platonism, 28, 30, 36, 39, 173, 177, 178, 228, 259, 261, 279
Pletho, Gemistius, 17
Pletnev, Petr, 190
Plotinus, 21, 30, 39, 41, 48, 58, 162n.13, 227
Plutarch, 14, 16, 66, 240, 262, 264, 265; *De Iside et Osiride*, 39-40
Pocco, A.M., 204n.4
Pohorilyj, Semen, 268
Poimander, 41
Polikarpov, F., 109n.26
Poliščuk, F.M., 190n.11

Poltava, 5-6, 159
Poltavcev, 6
Polz, Peter, 83n.28
Ponticos, Euagrios, 265n.45
Popov, P., 125n.44
Pordage, 18
Porphyrius, 40
Potebnja, Oleksander, 43
Potichnyj, Peter J., xiv n.2
Pravyc'kyj, Jakov, 118, 123
Proclus, 21, 30, 34, 40, 162n.13
Prokopovič, Nikolaj, 190
Prokopovyč, Teofan, 7, 18, 44, 76, 77n.5, 97, 98, 118, 134; *First Primer for Youth*, 81, 86; library of, 15-16, 49; quasi-Protestant theology of, 8; style of sermons, 104-5, 106
Pugačev: uprising of, 68n.24
Purchotius (Pourchot), 18
Puškin, Aleksandr Sergeevič, 192
Pythagoras, 14, 16, 56, 66n.17, 240

Quinstädt, 18

Rabbinical exegesis, 259
Rabelais, François, 47
Račinskij, G.A., 204n.4
Radiščev, A., 107
Radov, E. 210n.27
Radyvylovs'kyj, Antonij, 50
Ramus, Peter, 17
Rancour-Laferriere, Daniel, 195n.18, 198n.22, 199n.24
Randall, John Herman, 163n.14
Raphael, 47
Realism, 160
Red'ko, M., 241n.2, 247n.4, 256n.17
Renaissance, 17, 31, 40, 41, 46, 152, 184
Reusner, N., 47
Rilke, Rainer Maria, 35, 47, 49, 170
Robinson, Geroid T., 65n.14

Romanticism, xiv, 4, 35, 42, 43, 48, 121, 123, 131, 160, 163, 169, 173, 178, 188, 235
Rosicrucian, xii, 48, 59
Rottenhagen, 47
Rousseau, Jean-Jacques, 87, 160
Roždestvenskij, S.V., 82n.28
Rozumovskij, Count K., 123
Rudnytzky, Leo D., 252n.3
Runge, P.O., 47
Rupp, Jean, 256n.15
Rusova, S., 122
Ryl's'kyj, Tadej, 164

Saavedra, Faxardo, 45, 46, 47, 48, 49
Šabaeva, M.F., 88n.53
Saint-Martin, Claude, 67n.20
Saint-Victor, Hugo de, 17, 40
Sandaeus, Maximilianus, 18, 46, 49
Sapogonov, V.A., 211n.32
Sartre, Jean-Paul, 170
Saunders, David, xii n.1
Scepticism, 89, 241, 242
Ščerbinin, E.A., 11, 83n.29
Ščerbinin, P., 123
Schelling, 25, 35, 43, 48, 59
Scherer, Stephen, 263
Schlegel, Friedrich, 42
Schleiermacher, Friedrich, 42
Scholasticism, 16-17, 18, 47
Schopenhauer, Arthur, 42
Scleus, Bartholomaeus, 59
Scotus, Duns, 17
Seeberg, E., 49
Semenov, Leonid, 211
Semevskij, V.I., 65n.10
Seneca, 16, 66n.17, 126
Serman, I.Z., 78n.9.,199n.23
Ševčenko, Taras, 121, 160-1, 162, 165, 251
Shakespeare, William, 47, 164n.17
Shapiro, G., 192n.14
Sich, Zaporozhian, 99, 112
Sikorski, I.A., 209n.24

Silesius, Angelus, 14, 18, 23, 24, 28, 32, 46, 47, 48, 58, 59, 264
Silver Age, xiv
Simovyč, Vasyl', 101
Skickij, B.V., 63n.3
Skovoroda, Hryhorij Savyč: alleged foreign travels of, 7-8, 19; Baroque style of, 4, 107, 129, 134, 142, 152-4, 156, 167, 185, 227, 232; and the Bible, 8, 50-5, 77, 94-104, 164-5, 182-5, 240, 253-4; and the Freemasons, 81-2; and Kovalins'kyj, 11-12, 78, 79, 102, 232; and the Kyiv Academy, 7, 71n.39, 76, 94, 100, 128, 143, 262-3; and the Orthodox church, 66-8, 262, 278, 282; polylinguality of, 6, 7, 126n.47, 127-9, 141; symbolism of, 34-8, 119, 174-5, 195-6, 209, 230, 234-6, 268; and the Xarkiv Collegium, 11, 66n.15, 78, 134
Slavophilisim, 165, 204, 207, 208
Slavynec'kyj, Epifanij, 49
Snegirev, I., 121, 141n.9
Socrates, 14, 16, 36, 66n.17, 89, 121, 122, 163, 204, 209n.25, 240, 247, 252, 255, 269, 281
Solger, 43
Solov'ev, Vladimir, xiv, 6, 89, 204, 208-9
Sorokin, Ju. S., 140
Sošal's'kyj, H., 123
Sošal's'kyj, O., 120, 123
Spee, F., 47
Špet, Gustav G., 122-3, 187n.1., 206, 212n.35
Spinoza, Benedict de, 18
Sreznevskij, Izmail, 69n.29, 83n.31, 89, 121, 189-90, 214
Stalin, Joseph, 163
Steiner, Rudolph, 207
Stobaeus, Johannes, 16
Stoicism, 240, 241-2, 245, 254, 276
Stus, Vasyl', 159

Suárez, Francisco, 18
Sudermann, Daniel, 48
Sumcov, Mykola F., 206n.11
Suso, Heinrich, 23, 31, 48
Symbola et emblemata selecta, 44-5; Amsterdam edition of, 48, 50; as genre, 49
Symbolism, xv, 47, 204n.4, 208, 210n.26, 211-12, 236
Šynkaruk, V., 134n.2, 135n.4, 143n.12, 216, 224, 241n.2, 256n.17, 275n.1
Synod, Holy, xii

Tabačnikov, I.A., 63n.4, 224, 225
Table of Ranks, xiv
Tacitus, 5
Tamara, Stepan, 78; son of (student of Skovoroda), 87
Tasso, 17
Tauler, 18, 23, 48, 56
Tertullian, 39
Tevjašov, S., 120, 123, 124
Thales, 14, 217, 240
Tieck, 35, 42-3
Tinjakov, A.I., 214
Titian, 47
Titov, An., 106n.21
Tixij, T., 88n.52
Todors'kyj, Symon, 77
Tokay (Hungary), 7, 94
Tolstoj, Lev Nikolaevič, 107, 210-12
Trediakovskij, 141
Trnava, 7, 8
Troščyns'kyj, 192n.14
Tsiv'jan, Ju.G., 199n.23
Tuptalo, Dmytro, 105n.21
Turgenev, Ivan Sergeevič, 44
Turgeneva, A.A., 204n.4
Turgeneva, N.A., 204n.4
Tyčyna, Pavlo, 160-1, 256n.17
Tyn'janov, Jurij N., 199n.23

Ukraine: Baroque in, 101, 105, 105n, 107; Cossack officer class of, 65, 73; Hetman region of, 63n.5; Slobids'ka region of, 63n.5
Unbegaun, B.O., 140n.7

Vaenus, O. (Veen), 46, 49
Valentinov, N., 212
Valla, Lorenzo, 17
Varčenko, I., 218n.5
Vasil'evič, Ivan, 84n.38
Velyčkovs'kyj, Paisij, 12, 165
Vernet, Ivan, 68n.28
Vinci, Leonardo da, 47
Vives, I.L., 17
Vladimirov, V.V., 204n.4
Völkl, Ekkehard, 263
Voltaireanism, 88
Vyšens'kyj, Ivan, 99n.9
Vyšnevs'kyj, Havrylo, 77

Warne, Frank J., 152n.17
Weigel, Valentin, 14, 18, 24, 28, 31, 41, 57, 58, 98n.7, 264
Winkler, Johann, 18
Wolff, Christian, 7
Wolffians, 6, 18
Wujek, 101

Xarkiv Collegium, xiv, 3, 4-5, 11, 49, 89; founding of, 88. *See also* Skovoroda, Hryhorij Savyč
Xenophon, 5
Xir'jakov, A., 89n.55
Xiždeu, Aleksandr, 75, 121, 189-90
Xmel'nyc'kyj, Bohdan, 64, 64n, 65

Zabarella, 17
Zamkova, V., 108n.23, 109n.28, 110n.29
Žekulin, Gleb, xiv n.2
Zembors'kyj, V., 123
Zen'kovskij, V.V., 80n.19, 235, 236, 277, 278-80
Zeno the Stoic, 16, 66n.17
Zernikow, Adam von, 6
Zvirjaka, Jevstafij Fedorovyč, 216

Zvirjaka, Justyn, 216
Žukovskij, Vasilij, 124
Žytec'kyj, P., 127n.49